European Union Agencies as Global Actors

This book examines a largely unexplored dimension of the European agencies, namely their role in EU external relations and on the international plane. International co-operation has become a salient feature of EU agencies triggering important legal questions regarding the scope and limits of their international dimension, the nature and effects of their international cooperation instruments, their status within the EU and on the global level, and leading potentially to tensions between EU law and international law.

This book fills the existing knowledge gap by scrutinizing the international cooperation legal framework and practice of EU agencies, including their mandate, tasks and instruments, together with their legal status as actors with a global dimension. It sets out a general legal-analytical framework which combines legal parameters from EU and international law to assess EU agencies as global actors, and examines in detail three case studies on carefully selected agencies to shed light on the complexities of EU agencies' daily international cooperation.

Florin Coman-Kund is Assistant Professor in European Union Law at the Erasmus School of Law (ESL) of the Erasmus University Rotterdam, the Netherlands; he is also Associate Researcher in the Academic Research Network on Agencification of EU Executive Governance (TARN).

Routledge Research in EU Law

Available titles in this series include:

The Right to Family Life in the European Union
Maribel González Pascual and Aida Torres Pérez

The European Union as an Area of Freedom, Security and Justice
Maria Fletcher, Ester Herlin-Karnell and Claudio Matera

EU Criminal Law and Policy
Values, Principles and Methods
Joanna Beata Banach-Gutierrez and Christopher Harding

EU Health Systems and Distributive Justice
Towards New Paradigms for the Provision of Health Care Services?
Danielle Da Costa Leite Borges

European Agencies and Risk Governance in EU Financial Market Law
Paul Weismann

Global Data Protection in the Field of Law Enforcement
An EU Perspective
Cristina Blasi Casagran

The Judge and the Proportionate Use of Discretion
A Comparative Administrative Law Study
Sofia Ranchordás and Boudewijn de Waard

The Greening of European Business under EU Law
Taking Article 11 TFEU Seriously
Beate Sjåfjell and Anja Wiesbrock

https://www.routledge.com/Routledge-Research-in-EU-Law/book-series/ROUTEULAW

European Union Agencies as Global Actors

A Legal Study of the European Aviation Safety Agency, Frontex and Europol

Florin Coman-Kund

Routledge
Taylor & Francis Group
LONDON AND NEW YORK

First published 2018 by Routledge

2 Park Square, Milton Park, Abingdon, Oxfordshire OX14 4RN
52 Vanderbilt Avenue, New York, NY 10017

Routledge is an imprint of the Taylor & Francis Group, an informa business

First issued in paperback 2020

British Library Cataloguing in Publication Data
A catalogue record for this book is available from the British Library

Library of Congress Cataloging in Publication Data
Names: Coman-Kund, Florin, author.
Title: European Union agencies as global actors : a legal study of the European Aviation Safety Agency, FRONTEX, and EUROPOL / Florin Coman-Kund.
Description: Abingdon, Oxon [UK] ; New York, NY : Routledge, 2018. | Series: Routledge research in eu law
Identifiers: LCCN 2017052866 | ISBN 9781138293045 (hbk)
Subjects: LCSH: Administrative agencies—European Union countries. | International and municipal law—European Union countries. | European Aviation Safety Agency. | European Agency for the Management of Operational Cooperation at the External Borders of the Member States of the European Union. | Europol. | Aeronautics—Law and legislation—European Union countries. | Aeronautics—European Union countries—Safety measures. | Border security—European Union countries. | Law enforcement—European Union countries—International cooperation.
Classification: LC

ISBN: 978-1-138-29304-5 (hbk)
ISBN: 978-0-367-59090-1 (pbk)

Typeset in Galliard
by Keystroke, Neville Lodge, Tettenhall, Wolverhampton

Contents

Abbreviations

ACER	Agency for the Cooperation of Energy Regulators
AFSJ	Area of Freedom, Security and Justice
ANS	Air Navigation Services
ATM	Air Traffic Management
BASA	Bilateral aviation safety agreement
BEREC	Body of European Regulators for Electronic Communications
CAA	Civil Aviation Authority
CAA	Common Aviation Area
CAMM	Common Agenda for Migration and Mobility
CATS	Comité Article Trente- Six
CdT	Translation Centre for Bodies of the European Union
Cedefop	European Centre for the Development of Vocational Training
CEPOL	European Police College
CFCA	Community Fisheries Control Agency
CFSP	Common Foreign and Security Policy
CIS	Commonwealth of Independent States (Migration, Asylum, Refugees
CISA	Convention Implementing the Schengen Agreement
CJEU	Court of Justice of the European Union
CMA	(ICAO USOAP) Continuous Monitoring Approach
COREPER	Committee of Permanent Representatives of the Governments of the Member States to the European Union
COSI	Standing Committee on Internal Security
CPVO	Community Plant Variety Office
CTC	Counter-Terrorism Coordinator
DAPIX	Working Party on Information Exchange and Data Protection
DCAF	Democratic Control of Armed Forces
DG	Directorate General (European Commission)
EAR	European Agency for Reconstruction
EASA	European Aviation Safety Agency
EASO	European Asylum Support Office
EBA	European Banking Authority
EBRD	European Bank for Reconstruction and Development
EC	European Community
ECAA	European Common Aviation Area
ECAC	European Civil Aviation Conference
ECB	European Central Bank
ECDC	European Centre for Disease Prevention and Control

ECHA	European Chemicals Agency
ECSC	European Coal and Steel Community
EDA	European Defence Agency
EDPS	European Data Protection Supervisor
EDU	Europol Drugs Unit
EEA	European Economic Area
EEA	European Environment Agency
EEAS	European External Action Service
EFCA	European Fisheries Control Agency
EFSA	European Food Safety Authority
EFTA	European Free Trade Association
EIB	European Investment Bank
EIGE	European Institute for Gender Equality
EIOPA	European Insurance and Occupational Pensions Authority
EMA	European Medicines Agency
EMCDDA	European Monitoring Centre for Drugs and Drug Addiction
EMSA	European Maritime Safety Agency
ENFOPOL	Enforcement Working Party
ENISA	European Network and Information Security Agency
ENP	European Neighbourhood Policy
EP	European Parliament
EPSO	European Personnel Selection Office
ERA	European Railway Agency
ESA	Euratom Supply Agency
ESAs	European financial supervisory authorities
ESMA	European Securities and Markets Authority
ETF	European Training Foundation
EU Satcen	European Union Satellite Centre
EU	European Union
EUISS	European Union Institute for Security Studies
eu-LISA	Agency for the operational management of large-scale IT systems in the area of freedom, security and justice
EUMC	European Monitoring Centre on Racism and Xenophobia
EU-OSHA	European Agency for Safety and Health at Work
EURATOM	European Atomic Energy Community Treaty
EUROFUND	European Foundation for the Improvement of Living and Working Conditions
Eurojust	The European Union's Judicial Cooperation Unit
Europol	European Police Office
FAA	(US) Federal Aviation Administration
FRA	European Union Agency for Fundamental Rights
Frontex	European Agency for the Management of Operational Cooperation at the External Borders
FYROM	Former Yugoslav Republic of Macedonia
GAL	Global Administrative Law
GAMM	Global Approach to Migration and Mobility
GSA	European GNSS Supervisory Authority
HR	High Representative for Foreign Affairs and Security Policy
IAC	Interstate Aviation Committee

IBM	Integrated Border Management System of the External Borders
ICAO	International Civil Aviation Organisation
ICJ	International Court of Justice
ICMPDF	International Center for Migration Policy Development
ILC	International Law Commission
INTERPOL	International Criminal Police Organization
IOM	International Organisation for Migration
JAA	Joint Aviation Authorities
JAIEX	JAI-RELEX Working Party
JHA	Justice and Home Affairs
JIT	Joint Investigation Team
JSB	Joint Supervisory Body
LO	Liaison Officer
MAG	Maintenance Annex Guidance
MARRI	Migration, Asylum, Refugees Regional Initiative
MASC	Mediterranean Aviation Safety Cell
MEP	Member of the European Parliament
MLA	Mutual Legal Assistance (treaties)
MOC	Memorandum of cooperation
MOU	Memorandum of understanding
MP	Mobility Partnership
NAA	National Aviation Authority
OCTA	EU Organised Crime Threat Assessment
OECD	Organisation for Economic Co-operation and Development
OHIM	Office for Harmonisation in the Internal Market (Trade Marks and Designs)
OIE	World Organisation for Animal Health
OLAF	European Anti-Fraud Office
PANEP	Pan-European (partner country)
PJCCM	Police and Judicial Cooperation in Criminal Matters
PUC	Practitioners' Common Unit
SAFA	Safety Assessment of Foreign Aircraft
SAP	Stability and Association Process
SARPs	ICAO Standards and Recommended Practices
SCIFA	Strategic Committee on Immigration, Frontiers and Asylum
SES	Single European Sky
SIS	Schengen Information System
SOCTA	EU Serious and Organised Crime Threat Assessment
SRB	Single Resolution Board
STC	Supplemental Type Certificate
TEC	Treaty establishing the European Community
TEU	Treaty on European Union
TFEU	Treaty on the Functioning of the European Union
TIP	Technical Implementation Procedures for Airworthiness and Environmental Certification
UAE	United Arab Emirates
UK	United Kingdom
UN	United Nations
UNHCR	United Nations Commissioner of Refugees

UNICEF	United Nations Children's Fund
UNODC	United Nations Office on Drugs and Crime
US	United States
USA	United States of America
USOAP	ICAO Universal Safety Oversight Audit Programme
WCO	World Customs Organisation
WHO	World Health Organisation
WTO	World Trade Organisation

Boxes

Preface

This book is based on the author's PhD dissertation entitled *European Union Agencies as Global Actors. A Legal Study of the European Aviation Safety Agency, Frontex and Europol*, supervised at Maastricht University by Prof. Dr. Ellen Vos and Dr. Andrea Ott.

The author would like to thank the anonymous reviewers for their valuable comments and suggestions. The author is solely responsible for all remaining errors.

The paper is based on official legal sources available until 1 January 2018. All websites were last accessed on 15 March 2018.

Introduction

1 Going global: the EU agencies on the international arena

For more than a decade, extensive attention has been paid to the European Union agencies in scholarly literature. The emergence and expansion of European Union agencies[1] has been considered by some as one of the most significant developments in the institutional structure of the EU.[2] Whereas the role and powers fulfilled by these agencies are still subject of study, this view certainly holds true from a quantitative perspective.[3] A recent trend reflected both in the practice of most EU agencies and in their legal framework concerns the involvement of these bodies in international cooperation.

Finding an overarching and meaningful definition covering and explaining the essential features of all the bodies within the Union assigned with the label 'agency' is a difficult task. However, one might say at least that European agencies are specific components of the EU bureaucracy entrusted with various administrative and technical functions and tasks.[4] The origins of the 'agency model' are not very recent, the first two EC agencies having already been established in the 1970s.[5] Nevertheless, the true

1 Within this book the terms European Union agency, EU agency and European agency are used interchangeably.

2 See for instance Martijn Groenleer, 'The European Commission and Agencies' in David Spence, *The European Commission* (John Harper Publishing 2006) 156; Ellen Vos, 'European Agencies and the Composite EU Executive' in Michelle Everson, Cosimo Monda and Ellen Vos (eds), *European Agencies in between Institutions and Member States* (Kluwer Law International 2014) 13–17.

3 According to the EU official website, there are more than forty European agencies at present (including the so-called 'decentralised agencies', the agencies under the Common Security and Defence Policy, the executive agencies based on Council Regulation 58/2003, and the EURATOM agencies ‹https://europa.eu/european-union/about-eu/agencies_en›. In a recent contribution, Vos provides a full list of the existing EU agencies and devises several taxonomies of these bodies: see Vos (n 2) 17–23.

4 See for the concept of 'agency' in the EU context Edoardo Chiti, 'An Important Part of the EU's Institutional Machinery: Features, Problems and Perspectives of European Agencies' (2009) 46 CML Rev 1395; Stefan Griller and Andreas Orator, 'Everything under Control? The "Way Forward" for European Agencies in the Footsteps of the Meroni Doctrine' (2010) 35 EL Rev 3, 6–9; Vos (n 2) 17–24; Merijn Chamon, *EU Agencies: Legal and Political Limits to the Transformation of the EU Administration* (OUP 2016) 5–15.

5 The European Centre for the Development of Vocational Training (Cedefop) and the European Foundation for the Improvement of Living and Working Conditions (EUROFUND).

proliferation of agencies within the EU occurred only in the 1990s and continued after 2000. This phenomenon has been linked to the continuous extension of the Union's competences and to the increased degree of complexity in the decision-making and the implementation process of EU policies.[6] Arguably, it has also been boosted by the crisis of the European public administration which culminated with the fall of the Santer Commission in 1999. In this context, European agencies have been perceived as some sort of panacea serving multiple purposes.[7] Thus, delegating administrative tasks to technical and relatively independent bodies would arguably (1) contribute to the efficient implementation of EU policies;[8] (2) remove the criticism concerning the centralisation and the 'politicisation' of the EU administration;[9] (3) lighten the administrative burden of the Commission, allowing it to focus on its core executive functions;[10] (4) foster administrative integration.[11]

Against this background, it is not surprising that European agencies have been examined comprehensively by legal scholars, political scientists and specialists in public administration.[12] In spite of the great number of studies existing on EU agencies, one

6 Ellen Vos, 'Reforming the European Commission: What Role to Play for EU Agencies?' (2000) 37 CML Rev 1113, 1113–14.

7 See Commission, 'European Governance. A White Paper' COM (2001) 428 final 23–24; Commission, 'The operating framework for the European Regulatory Agencies' (Communication) COM (2002) 718 final 5–6.

8 COM (2002) 718 (n 7) 5.

9 Philippe Manin, *Droit Constitutionnel de l'Union Européenne* (Pedone 2004) 315–16.

10 COM (2002) 718 (n 7) 2. See also Vos (n 6) 1119.

11 See Alexander Kreher, 'Agencies in the European Community: A Step towards Administrative Integration in the European Union' (1997) 4 JEPP 225; Vos (n 6) 1119; Herwig C H Hofmann and Alessandro Morini, 'Constitutional Aspects of the Pluralisation of the EU Executive through 'Agencification' (2012) 37 EL Rev 419, 421–23; Vos (n 2) 15–16.

12 See for instance Michelle Everson, 'Independent Agencies: Hierarchy Beaters?' (1995) 1 ELJ 180; Renaud Dehousse, 'Regulation by Networks in the European Community: The Role of European Agencies' (1997) 4 JEPP 246; Giandomenico Majone, 'The New European Agencies: Regulation by Information'(1997) 4 JEPP 262; Martin Shapiro, 'The Problems of Independent Agencies in the United States and the European Union' (1997) 4 JEPP 276; Ellen Vos, 'Agencies and the European Union' in Luc Verhey and Tom Zwart (eds), *Agencies in European and Comparative Perspective* (Intersentia 2003) 113–47; Edoardo Chiti, 'Decentralisation and Integration into the Community Administrations: a New Perspective on European Agencies' (2004) 10 EL Rev 402; Damien Geradin and Nicolas Petit, 'The Development of Agencies at EU and National Levels: Conceptual Analysis and Proposals for Reform' (2004) 1/04 Jean Monnet Working Paper ‹http://www.jeanmonnetprogram.org/archive/papers/04/040101.pdf›; Ellen Vos, 'Independence, Accountability and Transparency of European Regulatory Agencies' in Damien Geradin, Rodolphe Muñoz and Nicolas Petit (eds), *Regulation through Agencies: A New Paradigm of European Governance* (Edward Elgar Publishing 2005) 1–20; Ronald van Ooik, 'The Growing Importance of Agencies in the EU: Shifting Governance and the Institutional Balance' in Deirdre M Curtin and Ramses A Wessel (eds), *Good Governance and the European Union. Reflections on Concepts, Institutions and Substance* (Intersentia 2005) 125–52; Paul Craig, 'EU Administrative Law' in Grainne de Búrca, Bruno de Witte and Francesco Francioni (eds), *The Collected Courses of the Academy of European Law, Vol XVI/1* (OUP 2006) 164–82; Deirdre M Curtin, 'Holding (quasi)autonomous EU Administrative Actors to Public Account' (2007) 13 ELJ 523; Sami Andoura and Peter Timmerman, 'Governance of the EU: The Reform Debate on European Agencies Reignited' (2008) 19 EPIN Working Paper ‹http://aei.pitt.edu/11474/1/1736.pdf›; Martijn Groenleer, *The Autonomy of European Union Agencies. A Comparative Study of Institutional Development* (D Phil thesis, Leiden University 2009); Madalina Busuioc, 'Accountability, Control and Independence: The Case of

aspect of their activity has remained underexplored, namely their performance in the international arena. The European agencies are increasingly interacting in various ways with actors outside the EU and they are becoming increasingly visible actors on the international arena.[13] The agencies' potential to engage in some sort of international relations seems to be supported by their own legal framework,[14] as well as by their current practice.[15] Arguably, the international dimension of European agencies is threefold.[16] First, they provide assistance and support to the Commission, the Council and the Member States with regard to the management of various EU external relations issues related to their field of action (eg EU wider policy initiatives and projects like mobility partnerships, the negotiation of bilateral aviation safety agreements, sector-specific aspects related to the Union's enlargement and neighbourhood policies). Secondly, they establish more or less autonomously formal and informal relations with international organisations and third-countries. Finally, third countries and sometimes international organisations participate in various ways in the work of EU agencies.[17]

This dimension of the profile of EU agencies can be explained by the progressive extension of the globalisation phenomenon leading to an increase of trans-boundary issues and triggering a focus on external aspects in various EU policy fields, such as

European Agencies' (2009) 15 ELJ 599; Morten Egeberg, Maria Martens and Jarle Trondal, 'Building Executive Power at the European Level: On the Role of EU-level Agencies' (2009) 10 ARENA Working Paper ‹http://www.sv.uio.no/arena/english/research/publications/arena-working-papers/2001-2010/2009/WP10_09.pdf›; Chamon (n 4) 1055; Madalina Busuioc, Martijn Groenleer and Jarle Trondal (eds), *The Agency Phenomenon in the European Union: Emergence, Institutionalisation and Everyday Decision-making* (Manchester University Press 2012); Edoardo Chiti, 'European Agencies' Rulemaking Powers, Procedures and Assessment' (2013) 19 ELJ 93; Madalina Busuioc, *European Agencies: Law and Practices of Accountability* (OUP 2013); Mira Scholten, *The Political Accountability of EU Agencies: Learning from the US Experience* (D Phil thesis, Maastricht University 2014); Mira Scholten and Marloes van Rijsbergen, 'The Limits of Agencification in the European Union' (2014) 15 German Law Journal 1223.

13 This dimension of EU agencies has recently raised awareness in academia, an increasing number of studies dealing with various international cooperation issues concerning EU agencies in general or specific EU agencies. See Andrea Ott, 'EU Regulatory Agencies in EU External Relations: Trapped in a Legal Minefield between European and International Law' (2008) 13 EFAR 515; Florin Coman-Kund, 'Assessing the Role of EU Agencies in the Enlargement Process: the Case of the European Aviation Safety Agency' (2012) 8 CYELP 335; Martijn Groenleer, 'Linking up Levels of Governance: Agencies of the European Union and their Interaction with International Organisations' in Oriol Costa and Knud Erik Jørgensen (eds), *The Influence of International Institutions on the European Union* (Palgrave Macmillan 2012) 135–54; Hofmann and Morini (n 11) 440–41; Martijn Groenleer and Simone Gabbi, 'Regulatory Agencies of the European Union as International Actors. Legal Framework, Development over Time and Strategic Motives in the Case of the European Food Safety Authority' (2013) 4 EJRR 479; Andrea Ott, Ellen Vos and Florin Coman-Kund, 'EU Agencies on the Global Scene: EU and International Law Perspectives' in Michelle Everson, Cosimo Monda and Ellen Vos (eds), *European Agencies in between Institutions and Member States* (n 2) 87–122; Juan Santos Vara, 'The External Activities of AFSJ Agencies: The Weakness of Democratic and Judicial Controls' (2015) 20 EFAR 115; Chamon (n 4) 86–93.

14 See Steven Peers, 'Governance and the Third Pillar: The Accountability of Europol' in Deirdre M Curtin and Ramses A Wessel (eds), *Good Governance and the European Union* (n 13) 262–69.

15 Ott (n 13) 518.

16 See Coman-Kund (n 13) 339–40; Ott, Vos and Coman-Kund (n 13) 88–89. Cf Groenleer and Gabbi (n 13) 482.

17 See Coman-Kund (n 13) 339–40.

environment, food safety, border control, police cooperation, transport, health protection, etc.[18] Another reason for their participation at the international level is the high degree of complexity which characterises external aspects of various policy areas of the Union. Thus, as regards very detailed and technical issues requiring a high level of expertise, the Council and the Commission may be inclined to allow the relevant specialised agency to play a role. The need for the EU agencies to increase their autonomy and legitimacy are yet other reasons advanced for the increasing international cooperation activities pursued by these bodies.[19]

This study explores the role of the European agencies in EU external relations and on the international plane. More specifically, it scrutinises the international cooperation mandate, the tasks and instruments entrusted to EU agencies, together with their legal status as actors with an international dimension. This topic is worth in-depth research for several reasons. First, this endeavour has as a starting point a phenomenon occurring in daily practice to which until recently hardly any attention has been paid in the legal and political science literature.[20] Secondly, the international dimension of the European agencies' activities raises important legal questions in terms of institutional balance and delegation of powers, as well as with regard to the division of competences and tasks in the field of EU external relations. Addressing these issues is of utmost importance as this may lead to a reappraisal of the position of agencies within the EU institutional system. Thirdly, the external actions of European agencies arguably trigger legal effects also from an international law perspective. This makes it necessary to examine European agencies through the lens of international law in order to assess better the legal nature

18 See Chiti (n 4) 1415; Groenleer and Gabbi (n 13) 482.

19 Groenleer and Gabbi (n 13) 482–83.

20 See, however, for recent studies on various aspects of EU agencies' international cooperation Ott (n 13); Groenleer and Gabbi (n 13); Ott, Vos and Coman-Kund (n 13). For a study focusing on the international legal personality of the EU agencies see Gregor Schusterschitz, 'European Agencies as Subjects of International Law' (2004) 1 IOLR 163. For studies dealing with the international cooperation carried out by particular EU agencies see Conny Rijken, 'Legal and Technical Aspects of Co-operation between Europol, Third States, and Interpol' in Vincent Kronenberger (ed), *The European Union and the International Legal Order: Discord or Harmony?* (Asser Press 2001) 577–603; Dick Heimans, 'The External Relations of Europol – Political, Legal and Operational Considerations' in Berndt Martenczuk and Servaas van Thiel (eds), *Justice, Liberty and Security: New Challenges for EU External Relations* (VUBPRESS 2008) 367–89; Florin Coman-Kund, 'EU Agencies as Global Actors: A Legal Assessment of Europol's International Dimension' (2014) 6 *Maastricht Faculty of Law Working Paper* ‹http://dx.doi.org/10.2139/ssrn.2506568›; Florin Coman-Kund, 'Europol's International Cooperation between "Past Present" and "Present Future": Reshaping the External Dimension of EU Police Cooperation' (2018) 1 *Europe and the World* (forthcoming), on Europol; Laura Surano, 'L'Action Extérieure d'Eurojust' in Marianne Dony (ed), *La Dimension Externe de l'Espace de Liberté, Sécurité et de Justice au Lendemain de Lisbonne et de Stockholm: un Bilan à mi-Parcours* (Éditions de l'Université de Bruxelles 2012) 211–19, on Eurojust; Melanie Fink, 'Frontex Working Arrangements: Legitimacy and Human Rights Concerns regarding Technical Relationships' (2012) 28 *Utrecht Journal for International and European Law* 20, on Frontex; Coman-Kund (n 13), on EASA; Groenleer and Gabbi (n 13), on EFSA; Vara (n 13), on the EU agencies active in the Area of Freedom, Security and Justice (AFSJ). Whereas these contributions deal with 'bits and pieces' of the international dimension of EU agencies, this study proposes a comprehensive legal-analytical framework supported by fresh empirical insights from multiple case studies, thereby contributing significantly to advancing the scholarly debate on this topic; for a concise overview of these aspects and of some of the main findings of this study, see Florin Coman-Kund, 'The International Dimension of the EU Agencies: Framing a Growing Legal–Institutional Phenomenon' (2018) 23 EFAR 97.

and implications of their actions as well as their legal position as global actors. Taking this step enables us to determine whether the international law perspective regarding the status of EU agencies as global actors, their powers and the nature of their instruments fit well with their status as EU bodies. In particular, those instances in which the international dimension of EU agencies would materialise in legally binding agreements or could result in these bodies acquiring their own legal status on the international plane deserve careful examination.

2 Focus of the research

In dealing with the international cooperation of EU agencies, the study does not address all EU bodies included in the category of 'Agencies', because there are important differences between various types of EU agencies,[21] in particular as concerns the relevant legal framework applicable to these bodies. This heterogeneity makes it virtually impossible to analyse comprehensively the complex legal aspects pertaining to the international dimension of all bodies labelled as an 'EU agency'. This research leaves out the following sub-categories of EU agencies: (1) the EU agencies in the Common Security and Defence Policy area,[22] because they operate under a different (more intergovernmental) legal framework; (2) the executive agencies set up under Regulation 58/2003, because they have quite a specific legal status compared to the 'regular' EU agencies;[23] (3) the EURATOM agencies,[24] because, quite obviously, they are part of a different legal and institutional landscape.

Accordingly, the main focus of this research is on what is now called, according to the Common Approach on EU agencies, 'decentralised agencies',[25] which, for the purpose of this research, encompasses both the 'regulatory' or former 'Community' agencies and the former 'third pillar' agencies.[26] This choice is motivated by several reasons. First, the 'decentralised agencies' constitute the most numerous group of such bodies, but at the same time they are sufficiently homogenous from a legal perspective, which allows them to be examined within a single analytical framework.[27] Within this

21 See COM (2002) 718 (n 7) 3.

22 The European Defence Agency (EDA); the European Union Institute for Security Studies (EUISS) and the European Union Satellite Centre (SatCen).

23 Council Regulation (EC) 58/2003 of 19 December 2002 laying down the statute for executive agencies to be entrusted with certain tasks in the management of Community programmes [2003] OJ L11/1. All the executive agencies have in common the fact that they are established and wound up by the Commission, and strictly subordinated to the latter.

24 The Euratom Supply Agency (ESA) and the European Joint Undertaking for ITER and the Development of Fusion Energy (Fusion for Energy).

25 See Joint Statement of the European Parliament, the Council of the EU and the European Commission on decentralised agencies of 19 July 2012 (referred to thereafter as the 'Common Approach on EU agencies') ‹http://europa.eu/about-eu/agencies/overhaul/index_en.htm›. This terminology is also used in the previous Commission communications on EU agencies (see Chapter 1), subsequent documents related to Common Approach, and on the EU official website ‹http://europa.eu/about-eu/agencies/index_en.htm›.

26 Namely Europol, Eurojust and Cepol. These bodies have been included within the scope of this study, because in spite of maintaining some idiosyncrasies, they have been formally included by the Lisbon Treaty within the common EU legal framework.

27 See in this regard, COM (2002) 718 (n 7); Commission, 'European agencies – The way forward' (Communication) COM (2008) 135 final; Common Approach on EU agencies (n 25).

group, there are differences between individual agencies or sub-groups of agencies as regards their mandate and design, but there are also commonalities in terms of their legal status, the nature of their functions and tasks, their internal organisation, as well as the relevant legal rules and the principles applicable to them. The latter aspect allows horizontal issues and problems concerning the international cooperation pursued by these bodies to be identified, to apply common standards and parameters, and to draw findings pertinent to the whole category. In this way, the impact of this research is amplified by covering a wider range of EU bodies labelled as 'agencies'. In so doing, this study also lays the groundwork for in-depth studies on individual agencies or sub-groups of agencies within this category. Secondly, the category of agencies at issue has been selected as it appears to be the most significant group of EU agencies, at least in view of the extensive attention paid to these bodies, both in academia and in practice.[28] Last but not least, it is arguably this group of agencies which displays the most visible and spectacular developments in the field of international cooperation, both in terms of their formal legal framework and in terms of their practice.

The evolving international dimension of EU agencies raises pressing legal problems regarding the conditions and scope for international cooperation by these bodies, the nature and consequences of their actions, and the status of these bodies as global actors. Along these lines, this study aims to provide an account and a critical assessment of the legal standing and the current practice of the European agencies in EU external relations and on the international plane. Therefore, the *main research question* to be answered is: How can the international dimension of the EU agencies be legally diagnosed and what are the ensuing legal consequences and problems?

To this end, two issues deserve particular attention. First, the nature and extent of the 'international dimension' of the European agencies is investigated by focusing on those aspects which, in the view of the author, are the most relevant from a legal perspective. Whereas international cooperation by EU agencies consists of multifarious aspects, the centre of gravity of this analysis are those elements that can be best assessed against the relevant legal framework enabling and prescribing international cooperation by these bodies. Accordingly, the analysis focuses on the mandate of the EU agencies for international cooperation, including their tasks and in particular their formal international cooperation instruments.[29] The latter bear particular importance from a legal point of view as to what these bodies are doing on the international plane and what the consequences of their actions are. In addition to that, the mandate for international cooperation and the related instruments enacted by EU agencies beg the question of the legal status of these bodies as global actors within the EU and on the international plane. This requires a scrutiny of the interplay between the EU agencies and the relevant EU actors, as well as of the interactions with their international partners. Importantly, this enables us to clarify whether EU agencies may acquire international legal personality *in abstracto* and, if so, whether they have already acquired such a status in practice.

Secondly, it is important to delineate accurately the legal framework against which the international dimension of the EU agencies is to be assessed, as this provides the

28 Regarding the literature on EU agencies, see n 13. As concerns institutional practice, it should be noted that the relevant EU policy documents routinely focus on this category: see, for instance, COM (2002) 718 (n 7); COM (2008) 135 (n 27); Common Approach on EU agencies (n 25).

29 eg agreements, arrangements, memoranda of understanding.

necessary legal standards and parameters for analysis. This helps to identify the main legal issues, problems and consequences and supports the main findings regarding the international dimension of the EU agencies. Accordingly, the legal framework relevant for examining the selected elements of EU agencies' international dimension encompasses both EU and public international law.

As far as the EU law component of the overall legal framework is concerned, it consists of the founding acts of the EU agencies, together with all relevant implementing acts. It also includes all relevant EU law provisions and principles concerning the EU agencies in general, EU external action area and the policy sectors of the EU agencies. For the purpose of this study, the term 'legal framework' is given a broad meaning, also including policy documents bearing significance for the legal assessment of the international dimension of EU agencies. The analysis of these elements sheds light on the relevant Union legal-institutional background, the scope of the mandate for international cooperation of the EU agencies, the nature of their tasks and instruments, the limits and requirements that must be observed by these bodies. This allows potential internal inconsistencies and legal problems related to EU agencies' international dimension to be detected. It furthermore provides a system of reference for appraising the legality of EU agencies' international cooperation practice.

As regards the international law element of the legal framework devised for this study, it enables an assessment in particular of the legal status of the EU agencies as global actors, as well as the legal nature of their international cooperation instruments. Moreover, these findings based on international law have an impact on the assessment of international cooperation by EU agencies within the EU legal system. For this purpose, relevant provisions, case law and doctrine regarding international agreements, legal personality, and delegation are considered.

Bearing this in mind, the following sub-questions are addressed in this study:

(1) How is the international dimension of the EU agencies designed and what are the legal implications of this design?
(2) What is the legal nature of the main international cooperation instruments concluded by the EU agencies?
(3) What is the legal status of the EU agencies on the international level and, in particular, can EU agencies acquire international legal personality?
(4) How does the international dimension of the EU agencies fit within the Union's legal-institutional system?

3 Research design and structure of the study

The methodology used for answering the main research question and the related sub-questions of this study consists of three main components. First, a general legal-analytical framework is set up in order to frame the investigation of the international dimension of the EU agencies along the most relevant issues for answering the research questions. This is based on a careful overview of the international cooperation legal framework and practice of the EU agencies. It results in identifying the main legally problematic aspects of international cooperation by EU agencies, providing the relevant legal parameters for an assessment, and advancing more general conclusions and solutions.

Secondly, the guiding queries of this study along with the main elements and findings of the general legal-analytical framework are examined in practice through case studies on three carefully selected EU agencies. This legal-empirical account sheds light on the complexities of the daily international cooperation practice of the EU agencies and is aimed to 'test on the ground' the main elements and findings of the general legal-analytical framework proposed. The case study selection is intended to cover as large a spectrum as possible, combining both commonalities and idiosyncrasies of the international dimension of EU agencies. It is not contended that the findings from the case studies can be entirely and automatically generalised to the whole population of EU agencies under consideration. Nevertheless, the case studies, using a common format, propose a structured model approach for the investigation of international cooperation by EU agencies in practice. The findings of the case studies are assessed in a comparative fashion, and address issues and concerns regarding the whole category of EU agencies.

Thirdly, the relationship between the general legal-analytical framework and the case studies, with the former providing the structure and the focus for the case studies and with the latter enriching the general part with new empirical insights, allows the final step of this research project to be taken. This entails providing an in-depth examination of the EU agencies as global actors, proposing solutions for existing problems, and revealing new problems and issues for further research.

In setting the scene for the analysis of the international dimension of European agencies, Chapter 1 provides an overall analysis of the legal role and characteristics of these bodies within the EU institutional system. This assessment offers a useful overview of EU agencies' legal profile, which is relevant for the analysis of their international cooperation mandate, tasks, instruments and actions. In so doing, the relevant legal framework governing European agencies is examined in order to sketch the specific role they are designed to play within the EU 'executive branch'. This entails outlining the nature and extent of the tasks and powers that are delegated to them, the legal constraints set on their actions, their organisational set-up, as well as their legal relationships with the main EU institutions and other relevant stakeholders. Next, this chapter offers a panoramic account of the current international practice of EU agencies together with a brief inquiry into the reasons potentially accounting for this phenomenon are. This overview enables selecting and formulating some of the most stringent legal issues and problems posed by the EU agencies' international cooperation. Then, the analysis focuses on the founding acts of the EU agencies and other secondary law measures in order to examine the way in which their international dimension is designed. The mandate, tasks, instruments, as well as the limits and controls regarding EU agencies' international cooperation are scrutinised.

Chapter 2 offers a blueprint for the analysis of EU agencies' international dimension, encompassing relevant EU and public international law. Firstly, it is assumed that the legal parameters applicable to EU agencies' powers and actions in general, namely the principle of institutional balance and the delegation of powers doctrine are relevant also for assessing their international dimension. This requires in turn canvassing the legal setting for the EU external action area in order to specify the actors involved, the division of powers and the interactions between them. The focus lies on the Union's treaty making according to Articles 216–218 TFEU, the Union's international legal personality, and on the management of the Union's external action. In this way, an important background element enabling the legal assessment of the international dimension of EU agencies is provided. Along these lines, it is possible to determine how much room EU law leaves for the involvement of agencies in international relations, and to learn about the role that European agencies actually could or should play in this field.

Secondly, the international dimension of the European agencies raises questions of public international law. This entails assessing the legal nature of the external actions of EU agencies, and also determining the kind of legal status which European agencies can acquire on the international plane. For this purpose, the legal nature and effects of the international practice of European agencies are assessed, focusing on the so-called 'formal international cooperation instruments' enacted with international partners, as they seem to display some sort of embryonic treaty-making ability vested in these EU bodies. The international cooperation instruments concluded by the EU agencies are assessed against international law concepts like 'treaty' and 'agreement'. Accordingly, criteria used in international law for qualifying an international cooperation instrument as legally binding are advanced and applied in general to EU agencies' international cooperation instruments. Furthermore, by drawing on the international law theory and practice, this study examines the issue of the international legal personality of the European agencies.

The main parameters and findings within this wider blueprint enable advancing general conclusions and answers to the legal problems relating to the international cooperation legal framework and practice of the EU agencies. In this context, it is also explored whether the external activities of the European agencies can become a source of tension between EU and international law[30] and how such issues can be addressed.

Chapters 3, 4 and 5 report on the case study research carried out on the European Aviation Safety Agency (EASA), the European Agency for the Management of Operational Cooperation at the External Borders of the Member States of the European Union (Frontex) and the European Police Office (Europol). These agencies have been selected based on a combination of the following factors: a rich potential for international cooperation reflected in their relevant legal framework and documented by their practice; the EU agency's policy area; the features of the (international cooperation) mandate of the agency; the features of the international cooperation instruments of the EU agencies.

The case studies are closely linked to the general legal-analytical framework devised for the study of the international dimension of EU agencies in that the latter informs and guides the selection of the relevant agencies, the focus of the case study investigation, data collection and analysis. The case studies follow a common format designed in accordance with the main directions and parameters of the general analytical framework, with a view to ensure comparability in addressing the aims and research questions of this study. Accordingly, the following main elements are examined in each case study: (1) the general legal-institutional framework governing the policy sector of each agency with a focus on the external dimension of the relevant policy area; (2) the evolution of the agencies and the general features of their design that are relevant for the analysis of their international dimension; (3) the legal framework for international cooperation of the agencies (mandate, tasks, instruments and procedures for international cooperation); (4) the international cooperation practice of the agencies, focusing on setting their priorities and on their formal international cooperation instruments. The final part of each chapter includes an overall evaluation of the international dimension of each EU agency. It does this by addressing the main queries of this

30 eg action performed by a European agency in breach of EU law but still binding under international law, or in breach of EU law precisely because it can be considered as binding under international law.

research – ie the legal nature of the international cooperation instruments of the EU agencies, their legal status on the international plane, including the issue of international legal personality, their legal status within the EU, in particular as far as institutional balance and delegation of powers are concerned.

Chapter 6 takes stock of the analysis in the case study chapters by providing a cross-case overview of the main findings concerning the international dimension of the three selected agencies, linked back to the main elements and legal parameters devised within the general legal-analytical framework of this study.

The Conclusion brings all these threads together, and provides insightful and nuanced answers to the queries of this study. It offers a diagnosis of the relevant legal and practical issues concerning the international dimension of EU agencies, and advances solutions for existing problems. Lastly, some remaining problems and challenges, as well as directions for further research are outlined.

As it can be seen from the previous, this study combines a formalist legal approach through a traditional legal analysis of the relevant EU legal framework and the use of EU and international legal parameters, with legal realism in the form of functionalist analysis and case study investigation.[31] A conscious choice was made to limit the investigation to what were considered as the most relevant formal legal aspects of EU agencies' international dimension (ie the design of their international cooperation mandate, the legal requirements under which EU agencies may pursue international cooperation, the legal nature of their formal international cooperation instruments, their legal status as global actors). The reason for this choice was that these formal issues had not been sufficiently investigated while at the same time raising pressing legal concerns regarding EU agencies' international cooperation. Therefore, this formalistic approach exhibits added value in that it responds to the need for more clarity in a grey legal area by providing a framework for analysis and bringing EU agencies' international dimension within the legal realm. It thus enables determining the legal consequences of EU agencies' international cooperation, whether their international dimension is in accordance with the current EU constitutional framework, revealing clashes between the EU and international legal orders, and enhancing scrutiny and review of the international activities of these bodies.

Whereas informal international cooperation is arguably an important part of EU agencies' international dimension it has not been included within the scope of this study. However, informal aspects of EU agencies' international cooperation are taken into account where appropriate for the analysis of their international dimension. Legal realism also comes into play through an overview of EU agencies' international cooperation practice informing the formal legal analysis, and the inquiry into the reasons, added value and implications of EU agencies' international cooperation. What is more, the case studies offer the opportunity to examine closely the international dimension of particular EU agencies in practice, and to confront the legal-analytical framework developed against the present-day reality of international cooperation.

31 See on legal realism and the functional approach Felix S Cohen, 'Transcendental Nonsense and the Functional Approach' (1935) 6 Columbia Law Review 809.

Part I

Setting the general framework

1 The legal profile of EU agencies and their international dimension according to law and practice

1.1 Introduction

This chapter sets the scene for the analysis of the external dimension of European agencies. It does so by providing an account of the relevant features and problems of European agencies and by placing these bodies within the EU institutional context. Moreover, EU agencies as global actors are introduced by means of an account of their international cooperation practice and relevant legal framework.

First, the institutional background within which European agencies are operating is depicted, focusing on the so-called EU 'executive branch' (section 1.2). Secondly, an overview of the evolution of the EU 'agencification' process and of some relevant legal aspects concerning agency creation is provided; furthermore, various reasons behind the proliferation of European agencies are discussed (section 1.3). In spite of the variety of EU bodies in this category, an attempt is made at providing a working definition of the European agencies and identifying their general features (section 1.4). Next, a closer look at the formal or legal design of European agencies is taken by examining the nature and scope of their powers in light of the principle of institutional balance and of the delegation of powers or the so-called *Meroni* doctrine, as well as by looking at their organisational design with a focus on their main leading bodies (section 1.5). Then, the role of European agencies within the EU institutional framework is briefly depicted by taking a more dynamic perspective based on the constellation of relationships which these bodies establish, not only with the main EU institutions but also with other relevant European, national and international actors (section 1.6). The chapter ends with a panoramic overview of the international dimension of the EU agencies, combining a formal legal perspective with insights from practice in order to provide a more accurate account of the state of art in this field (section 1.7).

1.2 Institutional context: European agencies and the EU 'executive branch'

European agencies could be situated arguably within the so-called 'executive branch' of the EU, where they seem to perform tasks of an administrative or technical nature. This requires some conceptual clarifications with a view to reveal the wider picture relevant to assessing these bodies.

First, the European Union is characterised by a functional separation of powers,[1] combined with an institutional design based on the principle of the representation of interests.[2] Although the European Union is *atypical*,[3] in that it is more than a classical international organisation, but less than a federal state, it is possible, however, to identify within the EU a judicial function, a legislative process and an executive activity.[4] Instead of having separate organs performing distinct functions of the government, the EU has institutions representing different interests,[5] which are involved in various ways and to different degrees in the exercise of the same prerogative or the performance of the same type of activity.[6] Such a design requires the preservation of a fair balance between the powers of the EU institutions. This is guaranteed by the principle of institutional balance, which is intended to maintain a system of checks and balances between the institutions involved and the interests they represent.[7] The principle of institutional balance is dynamic in that it can evolve over time and, moreover, the balance of powers can vary depending on the distribution of powers reflected in the relevant Treaty provision for the policy field or issue at stake.[8] It has also been maintained that the institutional balance of powers could be construed in such a way as to include not only a horizontal dimension (the balance between the EU institutions) but also a vertical dimension (the balance between the EU and the Member States).[9] According to this view, the principle of institutional balance would also cover the division of powers between the EU and Member States, and also the proportionality and subsidiarity issues related to the exercise of EU powers.

Secondly, it is relevant to inquire into the meaning and the functions of the executive branch or power within the EU. Traditionally, the executive power is responsible for the implementation of the legislation, the management of policies, the exercise of

1 Koen Lenaerts, 'Some Reflections on the Separation of Powers in the European Community' (1991) 28 CML Rev 11, 13–14.

2 See in this respect Giandomenico Majone, *Dilemmas of European Integration. The Ambiguities and Pitfalls of Integration by Stealth* (OUP 2005) 46–48; Paul Craig, 'European Governance: Executive and Administrative Powers under the New Constitutional Settlement' (2005) 3 I CON 407, 434–35.

3 The EU is often labelled a *sui generis* system. However, Majone, while recognising the uniqueness of the EU institutional system among the present forms of social organisation, argues that there are some striking similarities between the EU and the system of mixed government, which was dominant from the late Middle Ages in Europe; see Giandomenico Majone, 'Delegation of Regulatory Powers in a Mixed Polity' (2002) 8 ELJ 319–20.

4 Thus, one can identify an 'EU judicial function' – personified mainly by the CJEU – and a legislative process involving the Council and the European Parliament – the 'EU legislature', but also the Commission. As will be seen, there is also an executive power in the EU, although its exercise is shared rather between the relevant EU institutions and bodies and the Member States; see also Lenaerts (n 1) 14–18.

5 The Commission represents the interests of the Union (art 17(1) TEU), the Member States are represented by the Council and, to a great extent, also by the European Council (art 10 TEU), while the European Parliament represents the citizens of the Member States (art 10 TEU).

6 Majone (n 2).

7 See for an elaborated analysis of the principle of institutional balance Merijn Chamon, *EU Agencies: Legal and Political Limits to the Transformation of the EU Administration* (OUP 2016) 249–96.

8 Ellen Vos, *Institutional Frameworks of Community Health and Safety Legislation. Committees, Agencies and Private Bodies* (Hart Publishing 1999) 84.

9 ibid 86 and 88.

supervisory and enforcement tasks. But the executive is also involved in the adoption of the most important political decisions. Thus, it determines the essential political directions of the community, initiates policies and sets the legislative agenda.[10] Based on this reality, a distinction is generally made with respect to the executive branch, between the political or core executive – the government – vested with the leading role within the community and the administrative or subordinate executive – the administration or the bureaucracy – which fulfils technical and implementing tasks.[11]

There are some difficulties in defining and identifying the executive branch of the EU.[12] First, as concerns the implementation of EU law, it should be noted that, traditionally, preference has been given to the indirect or shared administration model (through the authorities of the Member States) rather than to the direct administration model (through EU institutions).[13] Although the former European Community (EC) retained limited implementing tasks (assumed mainly by the Commission), the focus was on the instruments necessary to ensure the implementation of EC law by the Member States (eg coordination and monitoring) and not on the creation at Community level of a coherent system of executive or administrative organs.[14] Secondly, in view of the founding principles of the EU institutional system, the functions usually performed by the executive are not vested in one single institution, but they are shared in a rather complex manner among several institutions.[15] Thus, the Commission represents *par excellence* the executive branch of the EU,[16] but the Council of Ministers also exercises executive functions.[17] Moreover, the rise of the European Council as the most influential political organ of the Union makes the picture even more intricate.

As EU stands today one may argue that there is an 'executive branch' within the Union. This EU executive power does not match the executive power at the national level[18] just as the Union is not the same as a federal state. Thus, the Union still relies heavily on the national authorities of the Member States for the implementation and

10 Craig (n 2) 410.

11 See Jürgen Schwarze, *European Administrative Law* (1st edn, Sweet & Maxwell, Revised, 2006) 12–13.

12 See Alberto J Gil Ibáñez, *The Administrative Supervision and Enforcement of EC Law: Powers, Procedures and Limits* (Hart Publishing 1999) 18–19 and Craig (n 2) 410.

13 See Schwarze (n 11) 25–37. For examples of direct administration/management/implementation by the Commission see Paul Craig, 'EU Administrative Law' in Grainne de Búrca, Bruno de Witte and Francesco Francioni (eds), *The Collected Courses of the Academy of European Law*, Volume XVI/1 (OUP 2006) 32.

14 In this regard, Ibáñez ((n 12) 18) argues that the EC administration was not conceived '(. . .) a classical administration (. . .)', but '(. . .) as a non-executive administration'. This situation does not seem to have changed so much after Lisbon (see art 291(1) TFEU), although in the meantime more complex implementation models based on intense interactions between the European institutions and national actors entered the scene (eg networks).

15 Cf George A Bermann, 'Executive Power in the New European Constitution' (2005) 3 I CON 440.

16 See Ibáñez (n 12) 25–26.

17 Art 291(2)–(3) TFEU.

18 Ibáñez ((n 12) 26) points out that the '(. . .) national concept of executive power cannot be simply transferred to the Community level'.

enforcement of EU law.[19] At the same time, the gradual expansion of Union's competences seems to have led to a steady increase of the executive and administrative tasks at the EU level.[20] This substantive advancement was soon matched by institutional adjustments and enrichment, such as the creation of various EU agencies and other bodies. This intermingling between the Union's own institutional framework and the administrations of the Member States in the process of the implementation of EU decisions and carrying out of policies has been described by some as a 'system of integrated administration' or as a 'composite EU executive power'.[21]

Accordingly, one may attempt, although cautiously, to identify a core executive (setting the main political directions and priorities and taking the most essential decisions) and an administrative executive (in charge of the implementation of legislation and policies) at the EU level. As regards the core or political executive of the Union, at present it includes mainly the European Council, the Council and the Commission interacting with each other in a complex manner.[22] As for the EU administration, if one takes a broad view, all European institutions and bodies performing tasks in the process of the implementation of EU law, the management of Union policies and programmes or fulfilling various administrative technical functions could be included here.[23] The list should start with the Commission which is the main administrative organ of the EU. It is the 'manager' of the EU policies[24] and ensures the implementation of EU law in the context of direct administration;[25] furthermore, the Commission, acting as a 'guardian of the Treaties',[26] supervises the implementation of EU law and policies by the Member States.[27] The Council also has implementing powers, but, as a rule,[28] these powers have been delegated to the

19 This also seems to be the case after the Treaty of Lisbon entered into force, since art 291(1) TFEU clearly specifies that 'Member States shall adopt all measures of national law necessary to implement legally binding Union acts'.

20 It should be noted that in some policy fields, such as education, vocational training or health protection, the EU had recourse more and more to direct actions, instead of relying on the Member States (eg implementation of EU programmes); see Craig (n 13) 32.

21 See for the use of this term, Deirdre M Curtin, *Executive Power of the European Union. Law, Practices, and the Living Constitution* (OUP 2009) 65–66; see also Ellen Vos, 'European Agencies and the Composite EU Executive' in Michelle Everson, Cosimo Monda and Ellen Vos (eds), *European Agencies in between Institutions and Member States* (Kluwer Law International 2014) 11–12.

22 Craig (n 2) 407–39. Within the Common Foreign and Security Policy (CFSP), however, where the prerogatives of the Commission are quite diminished, the Council has an enhanced political role (see art 291(2) TFEU in combination with arts 24 and 26 TEU).

23 Schwarze (n 11) 21–34; Ibáñez (n 12) 19–25.

24 Cf John Peterson, 'The College of Commissioners' in John Peterson and Michael Shackleton (eds), *The Institutions of the European Union* (OUP 2006) 97.

25 According to art 17(1) TEU it is the task of the Commission to '(. . .) ensure the application of the Treaties, and of measures taken by the institutions pursuant to them' whilst art 291(2) TFEU stipulates that 'Where uniform conditions for implementing legally binding Union acts are needed, those acts shall confer implementing powers on the Commission (. . .)'.

26 The Commission '(. . .) shall oversee the application of Union law under the control of the Court of Justice of the European Union', art 17(1) TEU.

27 The enforcement powers exercised by the Commission with respect to Member States are to be found in arts 258 and 260 TFEU.

28 See in this regard ex art 202 TEC and ex art 211 TEC. According to ex art 202 TEC, as interpreted by the CJEU '(. . .) the Council may reserve the right to exercise implementing powers directly

Commission, which in turn is subject to the so-called 'Comitology procedure'.[29] The Lisbon Treaty makes explicit that the Commission is the main repository of most of the implementing powers,[30] whereas the Council retains implementing powers in the field of Common Foreign and Security Policy (CFSP) and also in 'duly justified specific cases'.[31] Finally, the EU public administration comprises many *other bodies* which perform technical and administrative tasks in various policy areas.[32]

1.3 The European agencies

1.3.1 The rise of EU agencies

The European agencies were not all created at once and not even at a constant pace, but rather they were developed in waves.[33] The first wave was rather symbolic consisting of two discrete agencies set-up in 1975. The European Centre for the Development of Vocational Training (Cedefop)[34] and the European Foundation for the Improvement of Living and Working Conditions (EUROFUND)[35] were the first EU agencies and their creation was closely related to the implementation of a social policy action programme adopted in 1974.[36]

The second wave of 'agencification'[37] began in 1990 with the creation of the European Environment Agency (EEA)[38] and the European Training Foundation

only in specific cases, and it must state in detail the grounds for such a decision'; in this respect, the Council is bound to explain '(. . .) why exception is being made to the rule that, under the system established by the Treaty, when measures implementing a basic instrument need to be taken at Community level, it is the Commission which, in the normal course of events, is responsible for exercising that power' (see Case C-257/01 *Commission v Council* EU:C:2005:25, paras 50–51).

29 Council Decision 1999/468/EC of 28 June 1999 laying down the procedures for the exercise of implementing powers conferred on the Commission [1999] OJ L184/23. Following the entry into force of the Lisbon Treaty, Council Decision 1999/468 has been repealed and replaced by Regulation (EU) 182/2011 laying down the rules and general principles concerning mechanisms for control by Member States of the Commission's exercise of implementing powers [2011] OJ L55/13.

30 Art 291 TFEU.

31 eg the implementing measures that the Council enacts within the framework of the Common Agricultural Policy (CAP) on the basis of art 42 TFEU (ex art 36 TEC), but this time it does not seem very clear whether these powers can be delegated to the Commission, see art 291(2) TFEU.

32 Herwig C.H. Hofmann and Alexander H. Türk, 'The Development of Integrated Administration in the EU and Its Consequences' (2007) 13 ELJ 253, 255.

33 See Vos (n 21) 13–17; Martijn Groenleer, *The Autonomy of European Union Agencies. A Comparative Study of Institutional Development* (D Phil thesis, Leiden University 2009) 96–100.

34 Regulation (EEC) 337/75 of the Council of 10 February 1975 establishing a European Centre for the Development of Vocational Training [1975] OJ L39/1.

35 Regulation (EEC) 1365/75 of the Council of 26 May 1975 on the creation of a European Foundation for the improvement of living and working conditions [1975] OJ L139/1.

36 Council Resolution of 21 January 1974 concerning a social action programme [1974] OJ C13/1. See also Vos (n 8) 189–90.

37 See for an early use of the term 'agencification', Edoardo Chiti, 'The Emergence of a Community Administration: The Case of European Agencies' (2000) 37 CML Rev 309, 341.

38 Council Regulation (EEC) 1210/90 of 7 May 1990 on the establishment of the European Environment Agency and the European Environment Information and Observation Network

(ETF),[39] and it reached its apex in 1993 and 1994 when six more agencies were established: the European Centre for Drugs and Drug Addiction (EMCDDA);[40] the European Medicines Agency (EMA);[41] the Office for Harmonisation in the Internal Market (OHIM);[42] the European Agency for Health and Safety at Work (EU-OSHA);[43] the Community Plant Variety Office (CPVO);[44] the Translation Centre for Bodies of the European Union (CdT).[45] This second wave came to an end in the late 1990s with the setting-up of the European Monitoring Centre on Racism and Xenophobia (EUMC) in 1997[46] and the European Agency for Reconstruction (EAR) in 1999.[47] This period also witnessed the birth of the first non-Community 'agency' (Europol), which was established in 1995 within the third EU pillar by way of an international agreement (more precisely, via a specific instrument provided for in Article K3(2)(c) TEU called 'convention') concluded and ratified by the Member States.[48]

[1990] OJ L120/1; the initial founding regulation has been replaced by Regulation (EC) 401/2009 of the European Parliament and of the Council of 23 April 2009 on the European Environment Agency and the European Environment Information and Observation Network [2009] L126/13.

39 Council Regulation (EEC) 1360/90 of 7 May 1990 establishing a European Training Foundation [1990] OJ L131/1; the initial founding regulation has been replaced by Regulation (EC) No 1339/2008 of the European Parliament and of the Council of 16 December 2008 establishing a European Training Foundation (recast) [2008] OJ L354/82.

40 Council Regulation (EEC) 302/93 of 8 February 1993 on the establishment of a European Monitoring Centre for Drugs and Drug Addiction [1993] OJ L36/1; the initial founding regulation has been replaced by Regulation (EC) No 1920/2006 of the European Parliament and of the Council of 12 December 2006 on the European Monitoring Centre for Drugs and Drug Addiction (recast) [2006] OJ L376/1.

41 Council Regulation (EEC) 2309/93 of 22 July 1993 laying down Community procedures for the authorisation and supervision of medicinal products for human and veterinary use and establishing a European Agency for the Evaluation of Medicinal Products [1993] OJ L214/1; the initial founding regulation has been replaced by Regulation (EC) 726/2004 of the European Parliament and of the Council of 31 March 2004 laying down Community procedures for the authorisation and supervision of medicinal products for human and veterinary use and establishing a European Medicines Agency [2004] OJ L136/1.

42 Council Regulation (EC) 40/94 of 20 December 1993 on the Community trademark (OJ 1994 L11/1). The initial founding regulation has been replaced by Council Regulation (EC) 207/2009 of 26 February 2009 on the European Union trade mark [2009] OJ L78/1; as a result of an amendment of this regulation in 2015 OHIM has been rebranded as the European Union Intellectual Property Office (EUIPO).

43 Council Regulation (EC) 2062/94 of 18 July 1994 establishing a European Agency for Safety and Health at Work [1994] OJ L216/1.

44 Council Regulation (EC) 2100/94 of 27 July 1994 on Community plant variety rights [1994] OJ L227/1.

45 Council Regulation (EC) 2965/94 of 28 November 1994 setting up a Translation Centre for bodies of the European Union [1994] OJ L314/1.

46 Council Regulation (EC) 1035/97 of 2 June 1997 establishing a European Monitoring Centre on Racism and Xenophobia of [1997] OJ L151/1.

47 Council Regulation (EC) 2454/99 of 15 November 1999 amending Regulation (EC) No 1628/96 relating to aid for Bosnia and Herzegovina, Croatia, the Federal Republic of Yugoslavia and the former Yugoslav Republic of Macedonia, in particular by the setting up of a European Agency for Reconstruction [1999] OJ L299/1.

48 Convention based on art K.3 of the Treaty on European Union, on the establishment of a European Police Office (Europol Convention) [1995] OJ C316/2.

The fall of the Santer Commission in 1999 demonstrated that there was a need to reform the executive branch of the EU, with one of the leading directions being to enable the Commission to concentrate more on its core executive functions by removing some of its administrative burdens.[49] Accordingly, a new 'agencification' wave commenced after 2000 with the creation of the European Food Safety Authority (EFSA),[50] followed by the European Maritime Safety Agency (EMSA)[51] and the European Aviation Safety Agency (EASA).[52] During the next few years the number of agencies continued to grow at a steady pace. In 2004 five more agencies were officially created: the European Network and Information Security Agency (ENISA),[53] the European Centre for Disease Prevention and Control (ECDC),[54] the European Railway Agency (ERA),[55] the European GNSS Supervisory Authority (GSA)[56] and, finally, the European Agency for the Management of Operational Cooperation at the External Borders (FRONTEX).[57] The Community Fisheries Control Agency (CFCA) followed in 2005,[58] while the year

49 Commission, 'Reforming the Commission – A White Paper' COM(2000) 200 final 2–3.

50 Regulation (EC) 178/2002 of the European Parliament and of the Council of 28 January 2002 laying down the general principles and requirements of food law, establishing the European Food Safety Authority and laying down procedures in matters of food safety [2002] OJ L31/1.

51 Regulation (EC) 1406/2002 of the European Parliament and of the Council of 27 June 2002 establishing a European Maritime Safety Agency [2002] OJ L208/1.

52 Regulation (EC) 1592/2002 of the European Parliament and of the Council of 15 July 2002 on common rules in the field of civil aviation and establishing a European Aviation Safety Agency [2002] OJ L240/1.

53 Regulation (EC) 460/2004 of the European Parliament and of the Council of 10 March 2004 establishing the European Network and Information Security Agency [2004] OJ L77/1; the initial founding regulation has been replaced by Regulation (EU) 526/2013 of the European Parliament and of the Council of 21 May 2013 concerning the European Union Agency for Network and Information Security (ENISA) and repealing Regulation (EC) No 460/2004 [2013] OJ L165/41.

54 Regulation (EC) 851/2004 of the European Parliament and of the Council of 21 April 2004 establishing a European centre for disease prevention and control [2004] OJ L142/1.

55 Regulation (EC) 881/2004 of the European Parliament and of the Council of 29 April 2004 establishing a European Railway Agency (Agency Regulation) (OJ 2004 L164/1); the initial founding regulation has been replaced by Regulation (EU) 2016/796 of the European Parliament and of the Council of 11 May 2016 on the European Union Agency for Railways and repealing Regulation (EC) No 881/2004 [2016] OJ L138/1.

56 Council Regulation (EC) 1321/2004 of 12 July 2004 on the establishment of structures for the management of the European satellite radio-navigation programmes [2004] OJ L246/1; the initial founding regulation has been replaced by Regulation (EU) 912/2010 of the European Parliament and of the Council of 22 September 2010 setting up the European GNSS Agency, repealing Council Regulation (EC) No 1321/2004 on the establishment of structures for the management of the European satellite radio navigation programmes and amending Regulation (EC) No 683/2008 of the European Parliament and of the Council [2010] OJ L276/11.

57 Council Regulation (EC) 2007/2004 of 26 October 2004 establishing a European Agency for the Management of Operational Cooperation at the External Borders of the Member States of the European Union [2004] OJ L349/1.

58 Council Regulation (EC) 768/2005 of 26 April 2005 establishing a Community Fisheries Control Agency and amending Regulation (EEC) No 2847/93 establishing a control system applicable to the common fisheries policy [2005] OJ L128/1. Since 2016, CFCA has been renamed as the European Fisheries Control Agency (EFCA), see Regulation (EU) 2016/1626 of the European Parliament and of the Council of 14 September 2016 amending Council Regulation (EC) No 768/2005 establishing a Community Fisheries Control Agency [2016] OJ L 251/80.

2006 witnessed the birth of the European Chemicals Agency (ECHA)[59] and the European Institute for Gender Equality (EIGE).[60] The Fundamental Rights Agency (FRA) was established in 2007,[61] but this body must be seen as a successor of the former European Monitoring Centre on Racism and Xenophobia (EUMC).[62] Next, in 2009, two agencies featuring a marked network model approach[63] were set up: the Agency for the Cooperation of Energy Regulators (ACER)[64] and the Office supporting the Body of European Regulators for Electronic Communications (BEREC).[65]

The European Asylum Support Office (EASO)[66] was the first EU agency established post-Lisbon, followed shortly by the European Banking Authority (EBA),[67] the European Insurance and Occupational Pensions Authority (EIOPA)[68] and the European Securities and Markets Authority (ESMA).[69] In 2011, the European Agency for the operational management of large-scale IT systems in the area of freedom, security and justice (eu-LISA) has been set up[70] whilst 2014 witnessed the creation of the Single Resolution Board (SRB) intended to ensure the resolution of failing banks within the

59 Regulation (EC) 1907/2006 of the European Parliament and of the Council of 18 December 2006 concerning the Registration, Evaluation, Authorisation and Restriction of Chemicals (REACH), establishing a European Chemicals Agency, amending Directive 1999/45/EC and repealing Council Regulation (EEC) No 793/93 and Commission Regulation (EC) No 1488/94 as well as Council Directive 76/769/EEC and Commission Directives 91/155/EEC, 93/67/EEC, 93/105/EC and 2000/21/EC [2006] OJ L396/1.

60 Regulation (EC) 1922/2006 of the European Parliament and of the Council of 20 December 2006 on establishing a European Institute for Gender Equality [2006] OJ L403/1.

61 Council Regulation (EC) 168/2007 of 15 February 2007 establishing a European Union Agency for Fundamental Rights [2007] OJ L53/1.

62 See Recitals (5), (7) and (10) of the preamble as well as art 23(4) of Council Regulation 168/2007.

63 See Marco Zinzani, *Market Integration through 'Network Governance': The Role of European Agencies and Networks of Regulators* (Intersentia 2012).

64 Regulation (EC) 713/2009 of the European Parliament and of the Council of 13 July 2009 establishing an Agency for the Cooperation of Energy Regulators [2009] OJ L211/1.

65 Regulation (EC) 1211/2009 of the European Parliament and of the Council of 25 November 2009 establishing the Body of European Regulators for Electronic Communications (BEREC) and the Office [2009] OJ L337/1.

66 Regulation (EU) 439/2010 of the European Parliament and of the Council of 19 May 2010 establishing a European Asylum Support Office [2010] OJ L132/11.

67 Regulation (EU) 1093/2010 of the European Parliament and of the Council of 24 November 2010 establishing a European Supervisory Authority (European Banking Authority), amending Decision No 716/2009/EC and repealing Commission Decision No 2009/78/EC [2010] OJ L331/12 (EBA's Founding Regulation).

68 Regulation (EU) 1094/2010 of the European Parliament and of the Council of 24 November 2010 establishing a European Supervisory Authority (European Insurance and Occupational Pensions Authority), amending Decision No 716/2009/EC and repealing Commission Decision 2009/79/EC [2010] OJ L331/48 (EIOPA's Founding Regulation).

69 Regulation (EU) 1095/2010 of the European Parliament and of the Council of 24 November 2010 establishing a European Supervisory Authority (European Securities and Markets Authority), amending Decision No 716/2009/EC and repealing Commission Decision No 2009/77/EC of the European Parliament and of the Council of 24 November 2010 establishing a European Securities and Markets Authority [2010] OJ L331/84 (ESMA's Founding Regulation).

70 Regulation (EU) 1077/2011 of the European Parliament and of the Council of 25 October 2011 establishing a European Agency for the operational management of large-scale IT systems in the area of freedom, security and justice [2011] OJ L286/1.

Banking Union.[71] Last but not least, a European Public Prosecutor's Office (EPPO) has been set up based on Article 86 TFEU,[72] although it remains to be seen whether this structure matches the profile of an EU agency or rather that of a *sui generis* EU body.

The agency phenomenon was not confined to the former 'Community pillar'. Agencies have also been established within the two intergovernmental 'pillars' of the EU, although in a context slightly different than the one pertaining to the creation of agencies within the Community.[73] In the Common Foreign and Security Policy (CFSP) area the European Union Institute for Security Studies (EUISS)[74] and the European Union Satellite Centre (EU Satcen)[75] were set up in 2001, while the European Defence Agency (EDA) was established in 2004.[76] In the field of Justice and Home Affairs (JHA), later reduced to Police and Judicial Cooperation in Criminal Matters (PJCCM), in addition to Europol, the European Police College (CEPOL) (in 2000)[77] and Eurojust (in 2002)[78] were established by Council decisions.

With more than thirty agencies established in a bit more than two decades, one can convincingly argue that there is a phenomenon of agency proliferation within the EU.[79]

71 Regulation (EU) 806/2014 of the European Parliament and of the Council of 15 July 2014 establishing uniform rules and a uniform procedure for the resolution of credit institutions and certain investment firms in the framework of a Single Resolution Mechanism and a Single Resolution Fund and amending Regulation (EU) No 1093/2010 [2014] OJ L225/1.

72 Council Regulation (EU) 2017/1939 of 12 October 2017 implementing enhanced cooperation on the establishment of the European Public Prosecutor's Office ('the EPPO') [2017] OJ L283/1. Since the EPPO has been officially established after this research had been finalised, it is not examined further in this book.

73 Groenleer (n 33) 99–100.

74 Council Joint Action 2001/554/CFSP of 20 July 2001 on the establishment of a European Union Institute for Security Studies (OJ 2001 L200/1); the initial founding act has been replaced by Council Decision 2014/75/CFSP of 10 February 2014 on the European Union Institute for Security Studies [2014] OJ L41/13.

75 Council Joint Action 2001/555/CFSP of 20 July 2001 on the establishment of a European Union Satellite Centre (OJ 2001 L200/5); the initial founding act has been replaced by Council Decision 2014/401/CFSP of 26 June 2014 on the European Union Satellite Centre and repealing Joint Action 2001/555/CFSP on the establishment of a European Union Satellite Centre [2014] OJ L188/73.

76 Council Joint Action 2004/551/CFSP of 12 July 2004 on the establishment of the European Defence Agency (OJ 2004 L245/17); the initial founding act has been replaced by Council Decision 2011/411/CFSP of 12 July 2011 defining the statute, seat and operational rules of the European Defence Agency and repealing Joint Action 2004/551/CFSP [2011] OJ L183/16.

77 CEPOL was initially established by Council Decision 2000/820/JHA of 22 December 2000 establishing a European Police College [2000] OJ L336/1. In 2005 the initial founding act was replaced by Council Decision 2005/681/JHA of 20 September 2005 establishing the European Police College (CEPOL) and repealing Decision 2000/820/JHA [2005] OJ L256/63. The current CEPOL founding act is Regulation (EU) 2015/2219 of the European Parliament and of the Council of 25 November 2015 on the European Union Agency for Law Enforcement Training (CEPOL) and replacing and repealing Council Decision 2005/681/JHA [2015] OJ L319/1.

78 Council Decision 2002/187/JHA of 28 February 2002 setting up Eurojust with a view to reinforcing the fight against serious crime [2002] OJ L63/1.

79 See also Vos (n 21) 13–17; Stefan Griller and Andreas Orator, 'Everything under Control? The "Way Forward" for European Agencies in the Footsteps of the Meroni Doctrine' (2010) 35 EL Rev 3, 4–5.

Along with other reasons and factors behind agency creation,[80] it appears that the establishment of a new agency is one of Union's preferred options in response to novel, urgent, current, or even potential problems and crises.[81] An illustrative example is the recent global financial crisis that affected both the EU and the Member States. Since the Union was apparently neither prepared to prevent the crisis nor to react effectively after it outburst, it was felt that the EU financial framework should be improved. One of the solutions proposed by the Commission with a view to improve the EU system of financial supervision was the creation of three new agencies. What is interesting about this initiative is that it came shortly after the Commission had withdrawn its 2005 Draft institutional agreement[82] and announced a period of reflection during which the agency system would be evaluated and no new agencies would be proposed.[83] In the end, three European supervisory authorities (ie EBA, EIOPA and ESMA) were established and delegated significant supervisory and regulatory powers.

1.3.2 The legal basis of EU agencies

The legal basis is important because it indicates the compromise reached on the role that EU agencies are expected to fulfil by their creators. It is also a paradox since, although at present more than thirty EU agencies have been established, there is still no explicit general legal basis for creating agencies in the Founding Treaties. This gap, combined with a long-standing strict understanding of the principles of conferred powers and institutional balance, might account for the initial widespread use of Article 352 TFEU (ex Article 308 TEC) as a legal basis for creating agencies within the former 'Community pillar'.[84] Thus, all first and second wave agencies, except for the European Environmental Agency (EEA), as well as some of the third wave agencies have been established on the basis of this Treaty provision. From the frequent use of Article 352 TFEU (ex Article 308 TEC), one could infer that agency creation was mostly a 'game' between two main players – the Member States, represented in the Council, and the Commission. Since the outcome of this 'game' was the creation of additional bodies within the EU institutional structure, through ex Article 308 TEC the Member States secured the power to say 'no' to such a development and they kept a large discretion regarding the scope of the mandate and powers of such bodies.[85] Moreover, since ex Article 308 TEC envisaged a situation in which the '(. . .) Treaty has not provided the necessary powers (. . .)' one could infer that the creation of agencies under this legal

80 For a detailed analysis of the reasons behind agency creation within the EU, see Groenleer (n 33) 100–11.

81 See Ellen Vos, 'Reforming the European Commission: What Role to Play for EU Agencies?' (2000) 37 CML Rev 1113, 1117–20 and 1130–33; Groenleer (n 33) 103.

82 Commission, 'Draft Interinstitutional Agreement on the operating framework for the European regulatory agencies' COM (2005) 59 final.

83 See Commission, 'European agencies – The way forward' (Communication) COM (2008) 135 final 10.

84 See Koen Lenaerts, 'Regulating the Regulatory Process: "Delegation of Powers" in the European Community' (1993) 18 EL Rev 23–24 and 42–43; Sami Andoura and Peter Timmerman 'Governance of the EU: The Reform Debate on European Agencies Reignited' (2008) 19 *EPIN Working Paper* 7 ‹http://aei.pitt.edu/11474/1/1736.pdf›.

85 See Lenaerts (n 84) 43.

basis entailed a transfer of powers from the Member States to the European Agencies rather than a mere delegation of executive powers from the Commission.[86]

The situation began to change gradually mainly under the impetus of the Commission, supported by the CJEU.[87] After the breakthrough made with the EEA, most of the third wave agencies have as a legal basis the sectoral Treaty provisions defining the subject-matter competence granted to the EU in the fields where these bodies are operating.[88] Moreover, the new founding acts of some of the old 'Article 308 TEC' agencies replaced their legal basis in accordance with the new trend. The main argument advanced by the Commission was that agencies are mere implementing instruments of particular EU policies and, therefore, the founding acts of each agency should '(. . .) be based on the provision of the Treaty which constitutes the specific legal basis for that policy'.[89] A similar reasoning has been used in support of the EU agencies created on the basis of Article 114 TFEU (former Article 95 TEC), such as ENISA, ESMA, EBA, and EIOPA.[90] However, in addition to this rather logical and apparently neutral argument, the Commission could have had other (more political) aims in mind as well. The fact that most of the specific Treaty provisions used as a legal basis for establishing agencies require majority voting in the Council could, at least formally, lessen the opposition the Commission might face from the Member States with regard to the set-up and design of the EU agencies.[91] Moreover, since it entails the use of the ordinary legislative procedure, the new 'legal basis approach' could be seen as an attempt to limit the influence of the Council by including a new player (the European Parliament) in the agency creation process.[92]

As regards the legal basis for the agencies from the former intergovernmental pillars, the picture is quite different. All of the 'second pillar' agencies have been established by the Council on the basis of Article 28 TEU (ex Article 14) without the Commission being officially involved. As for the 'police and judicial cooperation' agencies, the Commission seems to have been involved to a certain extent in the creation process,[93] albeit the predominant role had been allegedly retained by the Member States.

86 Damien Geradin and Nicolas Petit, 'The Development of Agencies at EU and National Levels: Conceptual Analysis and Proposals for Reform' (2004) 1/04 Jean Monnet Working Paper 15 ‹http://www.jeanmonnetprogram.org/archive/papers/04/040101.pdf›. This line of reasoning is likely to undermine the rigid version of the *Meroni* doctrine advocated by the Commission.

87 See Case C-217/04 *United Kingdom v Parliament and Council* EU:C:2006:279 (the *ENISA* Judgment).

88 The exceptions were the European GNSS Supervisory Authority (GSA) and the Fundamental Rights Agency (FRA), which were established in accordance with the 'art 308 TEC' practice.

89 Commission, 'The operating framework for the European Regulatory Agencies' (Communication) COM (2002) 718 final 7.

90 This type of logic has been confirmed by the Court in the *ENISA* Judgment and in Case C-270/2012 *United Kingdom v Parliament and Council* EU:C:2014:18 (the *ESMA* Judgment).

91 Geradin and Petit (n 86) 43.

92 Craig (n 2) 149–50.

93 Regarding Europol, the Commission was not formally involved in the initial creation process, but when Europol turned into an EU agency the new founding act had been based on a proposal from the Commission. In the case of Eurojust, again the Commission does not appear to have had an input in the original founding act, but Council Decision 2003/659/JHA amending the initial founding act had been based on a Commission proposal. The same holds true for CEPOL in particular as regards Council Decision 2005/681/JHA rebranding this body as a real European agency.

In concreto, the former 'third pillar' agencies (except for the initial establishment of Europol) were formally created by the Council using as a legal basis specific provisions from the former Title VI of the TEU.[94]

If one looks at the formal instruments used and at the practices occurring in the process of agency creation, the picture varies depending on whether the agencies under consideration come within the former Community pillar or under the former EU intergovernmental pillars. Within the former Community pillar, the blueprint used in the creation process consisted of an instrument of secondary legislation (regulation) adopted by the Council (for ex Article 308 TEC agencies) or by the Council together with the European Parliament (for 'specific treaty basis' agencies) always on the basis of a proposal from the Commission. The more intergovernmental agencies seem to originate primarily in initiatives taken by the Member States within the Council or sometimes also within the European Council (eg EDA). Formally, these bodies were created by the Council through specific legal instruments available within the former intergovernmental pillars,[95] without any involvement from the European Parliament or the Commission. However, as already noted, the situation began to change with respect to the 'third pillar' agencies, since the new founding acts of these bodies (Europol and CEPOL) or, sometimes, the amending acts (Eurojust) drew on Commission proposals.[96] After Lisbon, the new founding acts of the former 'third pillar' agencies follow the ordinary legislative procedure.[97]

1.3.3 The rationale for EU agencies

In view of the steady proliferation of EU agencies, one may inquire into their added value and the reasons behind their creation. The official reasons for their creation advanced mainly by the Commission in several white papers,[98] and in a meta-evaluation performed in 2003,[99] seem to reflect to a large extent a functional logic based on effectiveness and efficiency. Agencies are to be preferred because they should master a high level of expertise in their sector, and also because their actions should result in cost-savings for the actors involved.[100] Especially when provided with a certain degree of independence, European agencies are said to increase the credibility and visibility of the EU in their respective area of operation.[101] In the same vein, agencies

94 ie for Europol, ex art 30(1)(b) and (2) TEU combined with ex art 34(2)(c) TEU; for Eurojust, ex art 31 TEU combined with ex art 34(2)(c) TEU; for CEPOL, ex art 30(1)(c) TEU combined with ex art 34(2)(c) TEU.

95 That is, joint actions for the 'second pillar' agencies and decisions for the 'third pillar' agencies; again, Europol should be mentioned here as a special case since this body was initially created by a convention adopted and ratified by the Member States.

96 See Groenleer (n 33) 99–100.

97 This is foreseen in art 85(1) TFEU (for Eurojust) and art 88(2) TFEU (for Europol). This is also confirmed by the existing legislative acts and proposals repealing and replacing the existing founding acts of Cepol, Europol, and Eurojust.

98 See Commission, 'European Governance. A White Paper' COM (2001) 428 final 24; COM (2002) 718 (n 89); COM (2008) 135 (n 83) 2.

99 Commission, Budget Directorate General – Evaluation Unit 'Meta-Evaluation on the Community Agency System' Final Report, 15 September 2003 (referred to hereafter as the 'Meta-Evaluation 2003').

100 COM (2001) 428 (n 98) 24.

101 ibid.

are expected to ensure better involvement for stakeholders in Union's policy fields and to develop networks, thereby stimulating the pooling of relevant information and best practices.[102] By taking over technical and scientific tasks, the European agencies are expected to increase the effectiveness and efficiency of the EU executive and also lighten the administrative burden of the Commission, allowing it to focus on its core executive functions.[103]

It is not always clear, however, whether all the existing agencies actually fulfil these functional standards enshrined in the EU official rhetoric and, more generally, whether, in all the instances in which agencies were established, their creation represented the most appropriate option available to solve Union's problems (proportionality test). As the European Court of Auditors[104] and the Commission itself[105] acknowledged, determining the added value of agencies is problematic because of the frequent absence of clearly specified objectives and performance indicators allowing for the measurement of the results attained by these bodies. Moreover, the creation of agencies is closely linked to the nature and intensity of EU competences. Thus, in the field of non-exclusive competences of the Union, the creation of agencies is subject to a subsidiarity test,[106] in addition to the usual proportionality test.[107] In order to meet these requirements sound and comprehensive reasons should be provided for each agency, but it appears that this is not always the case. For instance, in light of the nature and intensity of the EU competences, one could justify agencies like OHIM or EFSA, whereas in the case of the FRA, EIGE or EMCDDA the justification would be less clear.[108]

Apparently, there is no universal recipe providing for a standard combination of these types of reasons for all EU agencies.[109] It is rather a variable combination of different reasons and factors for each individual agency or group of agencies. As Dehousse argues '(. . .) each agency has a story of its own (. . .)',[110] due to the specific features of the policy fields in which it is operating and also due to the fact that its creation was sometimes influenced by particular circumstances.[111] This case-by-case approach reveals quite clearly the difficulty of identifying a 'universal rationale' for the creation of European agencies.[112] It also accounts for the existing variety in the design and powers of the European agencies, which creates difficulties in understanding these bodies both conceptually and analytically.

102 Meta-Evaluation 2003 (n 99) 30.
103 See COM (2002) 718 (n 89); COM (2008) 135 (n 83) and Meta-Evaluation 2003 (n 99). See also Vos (n 21) 15–16.
104 See European Court of Auditors, Special Report No 5/2008 'The European Union's Agencies: Getting Results' 5 ‹https://www.eca.europa.eu/en/pages/NewsItem.aspx?nid=217›.
105 Meta-Evaluation 2003 (n 99) 77.
106 Even if the EU has already acquired substantive competence in a certain policy field, it is not exempted from a subsidiarity test when establishing an agency as an implementing instrument in that field. This is because a shared administration model is still at issue in such a case (see art 291 TFEU); cf Meta-Evaluation 2003 (n 99) 32.
107 Geradin and Petit (n 86) 39–40.
108 ibid.
109 Groenleer (n 33) 100.
110 Renaud Dehousse, 'Regulation by Networks in the European Community: The Role of European Agencies' (1997) 4 JEPP 246, 255.
111 Groenleer (n 33) 100.
112 ibid.

1.4 The EU agencies as an overarching construct: conceptual clarifications and features

Given the proliferation of European agencies, it is somehow puzzling that there are still problems in defining these bodies. The Commission acknowledged that, in fact, '(. . .) there is no single model for a European agency (. . .)' but rather several models.[113] Accordingly, there is no single definition covering all European agencies but rather several definitions.

Currently, the Common Approach on EU agencies[114] seems to include all the former Community agencies, the former PJCCM agencies and the CFSP agencies under the category of 'decentralised agencies'.[115] Whether the agencies from the former EU pillars can be included in the same category could still be questioned, and is illustrative of the difficulty of finding an overarching concept of agency at the EU level. This conundrum is further confirmed by the Common Approach on EU agencies, which, in spite of creating the expectation of defining the term 'agency', is confined in the end to aligning terminology and to offering a 'checklist' with the general features of EU agencies.[116]

Nevertheless, it is reasonable to strive for a working definition of European agencies including the former first, second and third pillar agencies which, in spite of the differences, they all seem to enjoy a certain degree of formal autonomy and to perform tasks of a similar nature. Therefore, EU agencies could be defined as second layer bodies of the EU institutional system having the following characteristics: (1) separate legal personality; (2) they are mentioned or not in the Founding Treaties, but always fleshed out by the main institutions (Commission, Council and European Parliament); (3) they are provided with a certain degree of formal autonomy; and (4) they generally fulfil tasks of an administrative or technical nature supporting the EU decision-making process and the implementation of EU policies.[117] This definition is largely in line with the EU agencies 'checklist' elaborated by the Commission for the purpose of the Common Approach.[118] It allows for formally distinguishing the EU agencies from other analogous administrative structures which do not have their own legal personality, such as EPSO, the European Administrative School, Eurostat, and OLAF, or which have legal personality but do not enjoy formal autonomy, such as the executive agencies set

113 COM (2002) 718 (n 89) 3.

114 See Analytical Fiche 1, *Definition and classification of "European Regulatory Agency"* 2, accompanying the Joint Statement of the European Parliament, the Council of the EU and the European Commission on decentralised agencies of 19 July 2012 (Common Approach on EU agencies) ‹http://europa.eu/about-eu/agencies/overhaul/index_en.htm›.

115 For various classifications of EU agencies, see Chamon (n 7) 18–44.

116 Common Approach on EU agencies, para 1, and Analytical Fiche 1 (n 114) 1–2.

117 See Edoardo Chiti, 'Decentralisation and Integration into the Community Administrations: A New Perspective on European Agencies' (2004) 10 EL Rev 402, 420–21; Vos (n 21) 19–20. For various definitions of EU agencies, see Chamon (n 7) 5–15.

118 See Analytical Fiche 1 (n 114) 1–2. This 'checklist' includes the following general features: (1) a body governed by European law; (2) set up by an act of secondary legislation (regulation/joint action/decision); (3) own legal personality; (4) sometimes takes legally binding individual decisions for third parties; (5) most often receives financial contributions from the Community budget; (6) most often a permanent body which has its seat in one of the Member States of the European Union; (7) has financial and administrative autonomy and is independent in the execution of the assigned mission/tasks.

up under Regulation 58/2003. Moreover, it is possible to delineate between EU agencies and other 'agency like' bodies provided with legal personality which the Founding Treaties include in the first EU institutional layer (ECB)[119] or provide with genuine independence and powers (EIB).[120]

1.5 The formal design of EU agencies

1.5.1 Powers

A feature common to most EU agencies is that they are entrusted with quite limited formal powers.[121] Thus, usually EU agencies have merely administrative tasks and powers ancillary to (legislative, regulatory or administrative) decision-making.[122] There are a few exceptions,[123] but even these agencies may commonly adopt individual decisions in situations which do not seem to involve a (significant) margin of discretion (applying detailed and technical rules to individual cases).[124] Recent examples of EU agencies entrusted with individual decision-making powers are the European financial supervisory authorities (ESAs),[125] among which ESMA distinguishes itself in that it has been also equipped with the power to impose financial sanctions on undertakings.[126]

119 Majone argues that the ECB is quite close to the regulatory agency model from the United States, Majone (n 2) 100–101. In a similar vein, the ECB is also considered to be '[a]nother form of agency'; see Geradin and Petit (n 86) 40.

120 See arts 309–310 TFEU.

121 Geradin and Petit (n 86) 41 and Vos (n 21) 23–24.

122 See Xénophon A Yataganas, 'Delegation of Regulatory Authority in the European Union: The Relevance of the American Model of Independent Agencies' (2001) 3/01 Jean Monnet Working Paper 32 ‹http://www.jeanmonnetprogram.org/archive/papers/01/010301.html›, and COM (2002) 718 (n 89) 7–8. The ***ancillary administrative powers*** entrusted to EU agencies are construed here as including all kinds of instruments that do not involve formally binding individual or regulatory measures. Consequently, this category encompasses powers regarding information management (gathering, analysis, exchange, comparison, supply), technical and scientific assistance (adopting opinions, recommendations, inspection reports), articulating and managing cooperation with relevant actors (use of soft law instruments, coordination of joint activities), delivery of various services or specific products (eg trainings, seminars, translations, other products), detailed management and operational activities (concluding and monitoring contracts, supply of logistic support, planning relevant activities). For an elaborated examination of EU agencies' powers, see Chamon (n 7) 29–44.

123 ie OHIM/EUIPO (registers trademarks and designs), CPVO (grants plant variety rights) EASA (issues type certificates for aeronautical products), ECHA, EMA; see Edoardo Chiti, 'European Agencies' Rulemaking Powers, Procedures and Assessment' (2013) 19 ELJ 93, 95–96; Herwig C.H. Hofmann and Alessandro Morini, 'Constitutional Aspects of the Pluralisation of the EU Executive through 'Agencification' (2012) 37 EL. Rev. 419, 430–31; see also the *ESMA* Judgment (n 90), para 81. Also Frontex could be included in this category, at least with regard to some of its powers concerning the deployment of European border and coast guard teams, rapid border interventions and joint operations; see Jorrit J. Rijpma, 'Hybrid Agencification in the Area of Freedom, Security and Justice and its Inherent Tensions: The Case of Frontex' in Madalina Busuioc, Martijn Groenleer and Jarle Trondal (eds), *The Agency Phenomenon in the European Union: Emergence, Institutionalisation and Everyday Decision-making* (Manchester University Press 2012) 92–94.

124 See Craig (n 13) 155.

125 See Arts 17–19 of the ESAs Founding Regulations.

126 Arts 65–66 of Regulation (EU) 648/2012 of the European Parliament and of the Council of 4 July 2012 on OTC derivatives, central counterparties and trade repositories [2012] OJ L201/1

What is more, the *Short-selling* Regulation[127] marks a significant deviation from the 'standard' EU agencies' powers toolkit by granting ESMA the responsibility to exercise genuine regulatory powers and to adopt acts of general application.[128] Most notably, this sort of power has been accepted by the CJEU,[129] thereby opening the path for entrusting more substantial powers to EU agencies in the future.[130]

The often referred-to legal obstacles precluding the EU agencies from enjoying more significant formal powers are the principle of institutional balance and the delegation of powers established by CJEU in the *Meroni* cases.[131] The so-called '*Meroni* doctrine' essentially stipulated that the EU institutions could delegate to external bodies executive powers that they themselves possess according to the Treaties, but only if such powers are 'clearly defined' and subject to their supervision.[132] The delegation of other kinds of powers – ie discretionary powers – would bring about '(. . .) an actual transfer of responsibility (. . .)' from the delegator to the delegate thereby disturbing 'the balance of powers',[133] which is a fundamental characteristic of the EU institutional system.[134] The Commission in particular relied on this line of reasoning over time (although without expressly mentioning *Meroni* in its white papers) to advocate for strict limits on EU agencies' formal powers. Thus, in the Commission's view, EU agencies can exercise neither general regulatory powers, nor powers '(. . .) which may affect the responsibilities which the treaty explicitly conferred on the Commission'.[135] The only concession made by the Commission is that EU agencies can adopt individual decisions '(. . .) in specific areas where a defined technical expertise is required, under clearly and precisely defined conditions and without genuine discretionary powers'.[136] This conveys that, overall, while the Council and the Commission stress the importance of agencies, they do not seem to be prepared to accept them as being more than administrative auxiliary bodies.[137] However, as noted before, the recent creation of the ESAs indicates a trend towards entrusting EU agencies with more powers.

and arts 36a–36b of Regulation (EC) 1060/2009 of the European Parliament and of the Council of 16 September 2009 on credit rating agencies [2009] OJ L302/1; see also Chamon (n 7) 38.

127 Regulation (EU) 236/2012 of the European Parliament and of the Council of 14 March 2012 on short selling and certain aspects of credit default swaps [2012] OJ L86/1.

128 Chamon (n 7) 39. It should be also added that the type-certificates issued by EASA in spite of being concerned with specific types of aeronautical products, they are nevertheless of general application in that that they are binding for all the competent authorities of the Member States, for the aviation industry and for the companies operating aircraft of that type.

129 *ESMA* Judgment (n 90).

130 See Merijn Chamon, 'The Empowerment of Agencies under the Meroni Doctrine and art 114 TFEU: Comment on United Kingdom v Parliament and Council (Short-selling) and the Proposed Single Resolution Mechanism' (2014) 39 EL Rev 381, 402–03.

131 Case 9/56 *Meroni & Co, Industrie Metallurgiche, SpA v High Authority of the European Coal and Steel Community* EU:C:1958:7, and Case 10/56 *Meroni & Co, Industrie Metallurgiche, società in accomandita semplice v High Authority of the European Coal and Steel Community* EU:C:1958:8.

132 See Case 9/56 *Meroni* (n 131) 152 and Case 10/56 *Meroni* (n 131) 173.

133 ibid.

134 ibid.

135 COM (2008) 135 (n 83) 5.

136 ibid.

137 Yataganas (n 122) 32; Chiti (n 117) 420–21.

1.5.1.1 The principle of institutional balance as a legal standard shaping the powers of EU agencies[138]

In the Treaties, institutional balance is enshrined in general terms in Article 13(2) TEU providing that 'Each institution shall act within the limits of the powers conferred on it in the Treaties, and in conformity with the procedures, conditions and objectives set out in them'. The reading of this provision in combination with Article 13(1) TEU prompts several remarks.

First, Article 13(2) TEU seems to reflect, on an institutional level, the principle of attributed powers laid down in Article 5 TEU for the Union's competences. Furthermore, this provision enhances the *intra vires* requirement placed on the EU institutions with further instrumental (procedures and conditions) and goal-oriented limits which need to be observed in the exercise of their powers. Secondly, this provision is addressed to the 'institutions' of the Union, which according to Article 13(1) TEU only account for the European Parliament, the European Council, the Council, the Commission, the CJEU, the ECB, and the Court of Auditors. These are the main elements of Union's institutional structure, but the latter also includes other bodies established by the Treaties[139] or mentioned in the Treaties and set-up by secondary law measures.[140] In this respect, Article 13(1) TEU stipulates that, for the exercise of its powers and the attainment of its aims, the Union is equipped with an 'institutional framework', which may very well be interpreted extensively as including all EU bodies and agencies. This implies that these EU bodies could also be concerned with the requirements laid down by Article 13(1) TEU. In any case, when the EU institutions are establishing such bodies and entrust them with certain powers, they must ensure that the institutional balance is not disturbed. In this context, the institutional balance becomes relevant for the EU agencies in that their legal design must not affect it. That is why it is important what powers are or may be entrusted to EU agencies and under which conditions. Thirdly, Article 13 TEU only provides the parameters for ensuring the institutional balance *in abstracto*. Assessing *in concreto* whether the principle of institutional balance is followed requires a thorough analysis of the relevant Treaty provisions regarding the powers of the institutions, the task division in a certain policy area, or with regard to the respective issue under consideration.[141]

Turning to case law, it appears that the first reference to the principle of institutional balance is to be found in the *Meroni* cases,[142] in which the Court used the terms 'balance of powers which is characteristic of the institutional structure of the Community'.[143] Over the years, the principle of institutional balance has been given

138 For an extensive analysis of the institutional balance within the EU more generally, as well as with regard specifically to EU agencies, see Chamon (n 7) 258–96.

139 eg the European Investment Bank (EIB), arts 308–309 TFEU.

140 eg EU agencies (arts 15, 16, 85 [Eurojust], 88 [Europol], 263, 298 TFEU).

141 For instance, in order to determine the institutional balance in the external action area, one has to analyse the relevant Treaty provisions setting the general framework in that field, the prerogatives of the actors involved and the interactions between them, the procedure for concluding international agreements.

142 See Jean-Paul Jacqué, 'The Principle of Institutional Balance' (2004) 41 CML Rev 383, 384.

143 Case 9/56 *Meroni* (n 131) 153.

further substance and developed in landmark cases such as *Köster*,[144] *Isoglucose*[145] and *Chernobyl*.[146] In particular, the *Chernobyl* judgment is relevant for this discussion because, in that case, the Court attempted to specify more clearly what this principle entails. First, the Court linked institutional balance to the '(. . .) system for distributing powers among the different Community institutions, assigning to each institution its own role in the institutional structure of the Community and the accomplishment of the tasks entrusted to the Community'.[147] Secondly, the Court established that '[o]bservance of the institutional balance means that each of the institutions must exercise its powers with due regard for the powers of the other institutions'.[148] Thirdly, the Court affirmed its own prerogative to ensure that institutional balance is maintained.[149]

Accordingly, the principle of institutional balance has been portrayed by scholars as a tool performing a similar function at EU level to the principle of separation of powers in state constitutional systems[150] (ie to preserve the positions of the EU institutions as agreed upon in the Treaties).[151] Institutional balance is thus aimed at a system of checks and balances in which the prerogatives of the EU institutions are guaranteed.[152] The balance of powers does not imply an equal allocation of powers between the institutions; on the contrary, it may vary significantly across policy areas and it changes over time.[153] The ultimate standard against which the balance of powers between institutions is to be assessed are the Founding Treaties. Based on this understanding, institutional balance requires '(. . .) that each institution: (1) has the necessary independence in exercising its powers; (2) must respect the powers of the other institutions; and (3) may not unconditionally assign its powers to other institutions and bodies'.[154] In particular the second and the third requirements illustrate the relevance of the principle of institutional balance as concerns the issue of delegation of powers to other bodies like EU agencies.[155] More specifically, institutional balance requires that EU

144 Case 25/70 *Einfuhr- und Vorratsstelle für Getreide und Futtermittel v Köster and Berodt & Co* EU:C:1970:115.

145 Case 138/79 *SA Roquette Frères v Council (Isoglucose)* EU:C:1980:249 and Case 139/79 *Maizena GmbH v Council (Isoglucose)* EU:C:1980:250.

146 Case C-70/88 *Parliament v Council. Radioactive contamination of foodstuffs (Chernobyl)* EU:C:1991:373, paras 21–22.

147 ibid para 21.

148 ibid para 22.

149 ibid para 23.

150 Sacha Prechal, 'Institutional Balance: A Fragile Principle with Uncertain Contents' in Ton Heukel, Niels Blokker and Marcel Brus (eds), *The European Union after Amsterdam. A Legal Analysis* (Kluwer Law International 1998) 280; Jacqué (n 142) 384.

151 Majone (n 3) 326.

152 Prechal (n 150) 280.

153 ibid 276.

154 The list of 'institutional balance' requirements has been advanced initially by Lenaerts and Van Nuffel mentioning, however, requirements (2) and (3) in a reversed order, Koen Lenaerts and Piet Van Nuffel, *Constitutional Law of the European Union* (Sweet & Maxwell 1999) 414. This list has been taken over and adapted by Majone, and adopted in this study as in author's view the current sequence of requirements reflects more logically the essentials of institutional balance, see Majone (n 3) 327.

155 See Florin Coman-Kund, 'Assessing the Role of EU Agencies in the Enlargement Process: The Case of the European Aviation Safety Agency' (2012) 8 CYELP 335, 350.

agencies do not encroach upon the powers conferred by the Treaties on the EU institutions, and entails setting limits and conditions on the powers entrusted to them by the institutions.

1.5.1.2 *The critique of* Meroni

The *Meroni* doctrine, or at least the very restrictive interpretation of it, encountered some opposition from scholars. First, it has been argued that CJEU's findings in *Meroni* came in a specific context – ie more than 50 years ago, within the ECSC framework and dealing with a different issue (the delegation of powers to private bodies, not European agencies).[156] Therefore, extracting that reasoning out of its specific context and applying it *mutatis mutandis* as a standard for the scope of the powers conferred on EU agencies would be exaggerated.[157]

Secondly, it has been maintained that the 'strict delegation of powers' doctrine is based on a very static understanding of the balance of powers within the EU, precluding the adjustment of the institutional system to day-to-day changes and challenges.[158] On the contrary, the institutional balance is evolving over time and sometimes new actors and mechanisms are put in place namely to preserve it while ensuring the effectiveness of EU action.[159] In this context, the repeated failures of the Commission may be indicative of the fact that EU agencies taking over regulatory tasks of a highly technical nature may actually be beneficial for and reinforce the balance of powers.[160]

Thirdly, one of the basic premises of *Meroni* – ie delegation of powers by an institution possessing those powers to another body – is not entirely valid in the case of EU agencies,[161] as most of these bodies did not derive their powers directly from the Commission. This conclusion is supported by the fact that all former 'Community' agencies have been 'delegated' powers by secondary legislation[162] and, additionally, by the fact that the legal basis for most of them was ex Article 308 TEC referring to powers not conferred by the Treaty.[163] Therefore, technically speaking, it seems that there is no delegation of powers from the Commission in such cases, but a different model is used for empowering EU agencies. This delegation model consists of two steps: (1) a conferral of powers from the Member States to the European Union; (2) a delegation of powers to EU agencies by the EU legislator in the exercise of these powers.[164] This does not mean that the principle of institutional balance is not relevant when setting

156 Yataganas (n 122) 29; Renaud Dehousse, 'Misfits: EU Law and the Transformation of European Governance' (2002) 2/02 Jean Monnet Working Papers 12-13 ‹https://jeanmonnetprogram.org/archive/papers/02/020201.html›.

157 Michelle Everson, 'Independent Agencies: Hierarchy Beaters?' (1995) 1 ELJ 180, 197.

158 ibid 197–98.

159 See Yataganas (n 122) 39–41.

160 Everson (n 157) 197–98; Yataganas (n 122) 31 and 42.

161 See Everson (n 157) 198; Yataganas (n 122) 31; Edoardo Chiti, 'An Important Part of the EU's Institutional Machinery: Features, Problems and Perspectives of European Agencies' (2009) 46 CML Rev 1395, 1422–23.

162 Yataganas (n 122) 31.

163 Chiti (n 161) 1422–23.

164 See Yataganas (n 122) 31; Hofmann and Morini (n 123) 423–31.

up EU agencies, but that the application of this principle does not impose the strict constraints on EU agencies' powers advocated by the Commission.

To sum up, the underlying idea of the criticism directed at *Meroni* is that the delegation of powers doctrine (more precisely the strict version of it) is not an insurmountable legal obstacle in granting more significant decision-making powers to EU agencies.[165] In this context, it is maintained that this doctrine is either not applicable to EU agencies (at least to some of them) or, in the alternative, that it can be viewed in a more lenient and dynamic fashion. Thus, the principle of institutional balance would not necessarily exclude more 'powerful' agencies as long as they enhance the effectiveness and efficiency of EU action and their powers are subject to adequate safeguards and controls.[166] Therefore, it could be the case that the real justification for the rather modest formal powers of most EU agencies lies beyond purely legal considerations.[167]

1.5.1.3 The continuous relevance of the principle of institutional balance and the 'revival' of Meroni

The above discussion reveals the relevance of the principle of institutional balance as a valid standard for evaluating EU agencies from a legal point of view, in particular with regard to the powers delegated to them.[168]

Delegation of powers generally involves a transfer of authority from an institution or branch of government in which such authority is vested to another branch or agency.[169] The Treaties do not define 'delegation of powers', which leaves room for various interpretations of this concept,[170] leading to several 'delegation of power' scenarios within the EU.[171] In a first scenario, an institution vested with certain powers by the Treaties transfers some of its powers to another EU institution.[172] In a

165 Chiti (n 161) 1422–24.

166 See Vos (n 81) 1123–24.

167 See on this issue Chiti (n 161) 1405 and Groenleer (n 33) 104–05.

168 Regarding the relevance of institutional balance as a standard for assessing the lawfulness of EU agencies' powers, see Griller and Orator (n 79) 31. However, according to Chamon, the *ESMA* case represents a confirmation of the irrelevance of the principle of institutional balance, based on the fact that CJEU has not referred explicitly to institutional balance in its judgment, Chamon (n 130) 396–97.

169 Lenaerts (n 84) 24; see also Trevor C Hartley, *The Foundations of European Union Law* (7th edn, OUP 2010) 127.

170 Lenaerts (n 84) 23; Vos (n 21) 40–41.

171 See for a comprehensive analysis Lenaerts (n 84) 23. See for a similar discussion identifying several delegation models as regards specifically EU agencies, Hofmann and Morini (n 123) 423–32.

172 See Lenaerts (n 84) 25–36. The most obvious example was the delegation of implementing powers from the Council to the Commission, subject to conditions and supervision embedded in the 'comitology' system – former arts 202 EC (ex 145 EEC) and 211 EC (ex 155 EEC). It should be pointed out that the delegation in this context was not only about clearly defined executive powers but also about broad discretionary powers. However, under art 291 TFEU, according to which implementing powers are to be conferred on the Commission by legally binding EU acts (not by the Council), to the extent the formulation 'EU legally binding acts' means mostly legislative acts, this delegation resembles rather the third scenario discussed here. Still, the delegation to the Commission of the power to amend non-essential elements of EU legislative acts

second scenario, powers are delegated by an institution to third parties.[173] This latter scenario was at the origin of the *Meroni* doctrine established by the Court back in the 1950s. In a third scenario, 'delegation' may be understood in a broad sense whereby certain powers and tasks are entrusted to or conferred on other bodies by an institution (ie the legislator) which normally does not exercise such powers itself. In the EU context, this is illustrated in particular by the instances in which the legislator sets up administrative bodies and entrusts them with certain powers and tasks.[174] Such a scenario evokes more the idea of a conferment of powers than a 'mere' delegation of tasks as in the previous two scenarios.[175] This situation has been dealt with by the Court starting with *Romano*[176] and continuing with *ENISA*,[177] and most significantly with *ESMA*.[178]

The second and third 'delegation of powers' scenarios are relevant for the EU agencies. The second scenario, entailing a typical delegation of powers, is appropriate for EU agencies within the legal framework laid down by their founding acts. In this context, the Commission, in particular, may delegate certain implementing tasks within its own authority to EU agencies, for instance in the application of the EU Financial Regulation.[179] Such delegation must abide by the standard *Meroni* requirements, as established in the CJEU case law. The third scenario is particularly applicable to the EU 'decentralised' agencies, since they are set up by legislative acts conferring certain (executive) powers on them.[180]

Under the latter scenario, one may wonder under which conditions such bodies may be established and what kind of tasks may be assigned to them. More precisely, the debate around the powers of the EU agencies boils down to two inter-related questions: (1) does the EU legislator have the competence to create new bodies and entrust them with certain tasks and powers? (2) what kind of powers can be entrusted to such bodies and to which conditions should the exercise of such powers be subjected so that the institutional balance is maintained?

Several arguments support a positive answer to the first question. Thus, post-Lisbon, the EU agencies have received recognition in the Founding Treaties as components of the EU institutional framework. It is noteworthy here that Article 263 TFEU refers explicitly to '*acts* (emphasis added) setting up (. . .) agencies', thereby confirming that such bodies are established *via* secondary law measures. This is also confirmed by Treaty provisions dealing with specific agencies (ie Europol and Eurojust) which

under art 290 TFEU amounts arguably to a 'first scenario' delegation as the EU legislator could also exercise this power.

173 Part or not of the Union's institutional framework.

174 Lenaerts (n 84) 26.

175 See Merijn Chamon, 'EU Agencies between Meroni and Romano or the Devil and the Deep Blue Sea' (2011) 48 CML Rev 1055, 1061; Coman-Kund (n 155) 351.

176 Case 98/80 *Giuseppe Romano v Institut national d'assurance maladie-invalidité* EU:C: 1981:104.

177 *ENISA* Judgment (n 87).

178 *ESMA* Judgment (n 90).

179 For example, tasks are delegated to EU agencies in the context of the implementation of the EU budget and various EU programmes in line with the EU Financial Regulation, see for instance, arts 56, 58, 62 and 208–209 of Regulation (EU, Euratom) 966/2012 of the European Parliament and of the Council of 25 October 2012 on the financial rules applicable to the general budget of the Union and repealing Council Regulation (EC, Euratom) No 1605/2002 [2012] OJ L298/1.

180 See Griller and Orator (n 79) 15–21.

mention '(. . .) regulations adopted in accordance with the ordinary legislative procedure' as the founding acts of these bodies.[181] Even before Lisbon, the competence of the legislator to create novel bodies has been supported by scholars and the CJEU. Lenaerts for instance posited the view according to which the EU legislature has the competence to create an EU 'internal body', not solely on the basis of the 'flexibility clause' but also based on the standard legal basis provisions granting legislative powers in the area of EU policies.[182] This view has been confirmed in *ENISA*, where the Court accepted that the EU legislator may establish EU bodies under Article 114 TFEU (ex Article 95 TEC) in order to contribute to the implementation of harmonising measures.[183]

As regards the second question just raised, the answer is less straightforward. In *Romano* and *ENISA*, it appears that the institutional balance test was essential, in particular whether such tasks and powers would encroach on the powers of the EU institutions.[184] However, in these judgments, the Court did not readily provide a list of requirements against which the powers 'conferred' on third bodies (agencies) can be assessed, as it did in *Meroni*.[185] Moreover, in both judgments, the Court did not even refer to the *Meroni* cases.[186] ENISA has been accepted by the CJEU, because this agency was created for adopting non-binding supporting and framework measures under the condition that its tasks are closely related to the subject-matter of the relevant harmonising measures.[187] In *Romano*, the Court denied the competence of the Council to empower a body like the Administrative Commission of the European Communities on Social Security for Migrant Workers to adopt 'acts having the force of law' binding on national courts.[188] Considering the absence of a clear set of standards for evaluating the powers of EU agencies and the degree of vagueness and variation of the principle of institutional balance, the potential outcome was a legally ambiguous area shaped by institutional practices and interpretations of the institutional balance given by the Court on a case-by-case basis.[189]

In spite of the uncertainty surrounding the nature and limits of the powers delegated to EU agencies, a few observations are put forward in an attempt to bring more clarity on this issue. First, it appears that it is not possible for the legislature to delegate its own prerogatives to other bodies, except to the Commission under Article 290 TFEU. Secondly, when the EU legislator entrusts powers to other bodies, it must be ensured that this does not encroach upon the powers conferred by the Treaties on other institutions. In particular, EU agencies may not be entrusted with powers

181 Art 85(1) TFEU (Eurojust) and art 88(2) TFEU (Europol).
182 Lenaerts (n 84) 42.
183 *ENISA* Judgment (n 87) para 44. See also Hofmann and Morini (n 123) 427–28.
184 See for this argument with regard to *Romano*, Griller and Orator (n 79) 18–19. Chamon ((n 130) 386) suggests a similar approach with regard to ENISA.
185 See Chamon (n 175) 1062–63.
186 It may be speculated that one of the main reasons for this might be that neither case involved a situation of the 'proper' delegation of powers; see also Griller and Orator (n 79) 19.
187 *ENISA* Judgment (n 87) paras 44–45.
188 *Romano* Judgment (n 176) para 20; one may speculate that, in this particular case, the Court feared that a body with such a design and provided with such powers would encroach not only upon the powers of the executive, but also on those of the judiciary.
189 See Chamon (n 175) 1062–65.

that belong to the judiciary or that are explicitly reserved by the Treaties for other institutions. Post-Lisbon, this also seemed to be the case with the implementing powers conferred on the Commission in order to ensure uniform conditions for implementing legally binding acts.[190] Thirdly, from the *Romano* and *ENISA* cases, one could infer that only the delegation of powers which do not materialise in legally binding decisions may be assigned by the legislator to bodies like EU agencies. However, post-Lisbon, the relevant provisions in the Founding Treaties, in particular Article 263 TFEU providing for judicial review of the acts of agencies 'intended to produce legal effects vis-à-vis third parties',[191] as well as the founding acts of some EU agencies,[192] indicate that these bodies may enact legally binding decisions. Fourthly, it is essential that the powers of the EU agencies stay within the boundaries of the subject matter of their legal framework.[193] Fifthly, based on the *Meroni* judgment, it has been maintained that bodies like EU agencies cannot be entrusted with powers entailing the autonomous exercise of political discretion.[194] Whilst conferring political discretion on EU agencies created *via* secondary legislation is likely to disturb the institutional balance, one may wonder whether some degree of administrative discretion is acceptable. This seems to be the case in view of the stance taken by the Court in *Schräder*, where deference has been shown towards CPVO's discretion regarding complex technical assessments in the exercise of its tasks.[195]

On this line of argument, Vos points out that discretionary powers could be entrusted to agencies provided that this is '[a]ccompanied by a strengthening or re-balancing of the existing institutions and functions' with an emphasis on the setting up of 'controlling mechanisms in relation to agencies'.[196] Such a view is inspired by a dynamic reading of the principle of institutional balance fuelled by the idea that the powers and tasks of agencies and other bodies would be designed according to functional needs resulting in the consolidation of the EU institutional architecture, not in the disturbance of institutional balance.[197] Accordingly, what seems to be an essential test for the legal acceptability of the EU agencies' powers is whether there is sufficient oversight by the main EU institutions involved in the respective policy area. As pointed out by Lenaerts with regard to the delegated powers of EU agencies, '[t]he bottom line of institutional inventiveness is probably that the margin of political discretion which might be left to a newly-established body may not

190 See art 291 TFEU.

191 Beside art 263 TFEU, references to EU agencies' acts are included in art 267 TFEU, '(. . .) validity and interpretation of acts of (. . .) agencies of the Union', and in art 277 TFEU, '(. . .) an act of general application adopted by an (. . .) agency of the Union'.

192 eg EASA, OHIM, CPVO, EMA, ECHA, ESMA, EIOPA, EBA, Frontex.

193 *ENISA* Judgment (n 87) paras 44–45.

194 Lenaerts (n 84) 42–43.

195 Case T-187/06 *Schräder v Community Plant Variety Office (CPVO)* EU:T:2008:511, confirmed on appeal in Case C-38/09P *Schräder v Community Plant Variety Office (CPVO)* EU:C:2010:196; see also Chamon (n 175) 1059.

196 Ellen Vos, 'Agencies and the European Union' in Luc Verhey and Tom Zwart (eds), *Agencies in European and Comparative Perspective* (Intersentia 2003) 132. This may include a wide range of control mechanisms including judicial review, various administrative, financial and political controls.

197 See Majone (n 3) 331.

remain unchecked (. . .) which is in the end what "balance of powers" and representative democracy are about'.[198]

The Court dealt lately with the issue of the delegation of powers to EU agencies in the *ESMA* case.[199] In so doing, the CJEU largely confirmed the main points of the discussion above. First, the Court finally made it clear that the *Meroni* doctrine is applicable to the EU agencies created by the legislator.[200] Accordingly, only 'clearly defined executive powers' may be delegated, the exercise of which is subject to 'strict review in the light of objective criteria'.[201] Secondly, when applying this requirement to ESMA's powers, CJEU put forward two rather relaxed standards for review: (1) ESMA may not be conferred autonomous powers that go 'beyond the bounds' of its regulatory framework established by its founding act; and (2) the exercise of the powers 'is circumscribed by various conditions and criteria which limit ESMA's discretion'.[202] In applying these requirements, the Court does not seem to deny the agency any discretion in the exercise of its powers, but only a 'very large measure of discretion' that is incompatible with the Treaties.[203] Thirdly, the Court remarkably gives an extensive interpretation of the 'acts of agencies' mentioned by the Treaty provisions.[204] Accordingly, subject to the *Meroni* requirements, the EU agencies are allowed to adopt not only individual acts, but also acts of general application.[205] Fourthly, the Court takes a revolutionary step by recognising the possibility for the EU legislator to delegate powers to EU agencies under other systems of delegation, outside Articles 290-291 TFEU regarding Commission's delegated and implementing acts. Such a possibility flows implicitly from the Treaties and is appropriate in instances where the legislator builds specific legal frameworks in various policy areas with a view to attaining specific EU objectives and, in particular, on issues requiring specific technical and professional expertise.[206]

In short, the main novelty of the *ESMA* decision, is the revival and, at the same time, the relaxation of the *Meroni* doctrine. According to the *Meroni* logic as reinterpreted by CJEU in *ESMA*,[207] and in light of the principle of institutional balance,[208] EU agencies' powers seem to be acceptable as long as these:

198 Lenaerts (n 84) 49.

199 *ESMA* Judgment (n 90).

200 ibid paras 41–43, 53 and 66.

201 ibid para 41.

202 ibid paras 44–45. According to Chamon ((n 130) 393), the *Meroni* doctrine has been reduced by the Court in *ESMA* to a single criterion: 'the single prohibition of delegating discretionary powers'.

203 *ESMA* Judgment (n 90) para 54. In this respect, Chamon ((n 130) 393) argues that the Court introduced a *Meroni*-light doctrine.

204 ie arts 263 and 277 TFEU.

205 *ESMA* Judgment (n 90) paras 65–66. *In casu*, it was about ESMA's power to impose restrictions or a prohibition on short sales under art 28 of Regulation 236/2012, affecting '(. . .) any natural or legal person who has a specific financial instrument or specific class of financial instruments or who enter into certain financial transactions', *ESMA* Judgment (n 90) para 64.

206 ibid paras 79–86.

207 There is no general consensus on the detailed list of requirements which make up the *Meroni* doctrine, the only common aspect so far being that 'discretionary powers cannot be delegated', see Chamon (n 130) 382.

208 Whereas, conceptually, the principle of institutional balance being concerned with preserving the prerogatives of the EU institutions is different from the *Meroni* doctrine, and, moreover, there

(1) are of executive nature[209]
(2) are clearly defined, which, however, has been construed broadly by the Court as meaning that they stay within the boundaries of the agency's broad regulatory framework[210]
(3) there are criteria and conditions limiting the discretion of the agency, which calls for mechanisms ensuring sufficient oversight and control by the main EU institutions[211]
(4) do not encroach upon the powers conferred by the Treaties on the EU institutions.[212]

In the aftermath of *ESMA*, EU agencies may arguably be entrusted with wide-ranging powers provided that the revamped *Meroni* conditions are met. Moreover, alternative routes for the delegation of executive powers by the EU legislator to agencies, outside the Commission's powers under the Treaties, do not necessarily breach the principle of institutional balance. What seems to matter in terms of institutional balance and in light of the revived *Meroni* doctrine is the system of controlling mechanisms set-up under the Treaty framework concerning the exercise of EU agencies' powers in order to preserve the system of checks and balances.

1.5.2 Organisational design

The organisational design of the EU agencies gives an indication of how these bodies work and of the manner in which the interests of various relevant actors are represented in their decision-making and overall activities. In particular, the way in which the leading organs of the EU agencies are designed can illustrate quite accurately the relationship between these bodies and their principals. This constitutes an important parameter for assessing the real degree of autonomy that EU agencies enjoy. Despite the variations between EU agencies, these bodies share some commonalities with regard to the main elements of their organisational structure.[213]

might be instances where *Meroni* is relevant though institutional balance is not affected *per se*, it is maintained that in practice these two parameters are tightly connected. Thus, it can be argued that the *Meroni* doctrine has been initially created to safeguard institutional balance by precluding EU institutions from unconditional and uncontrolled transfer of powers to other actors, whereas the *Meroni* conditions are meant to ensure that EU agencies exercise limited powers and stay within their mandate, and that, as a result, institutional balance is not affected. Based on this 'checks and balances' reasoning, for the purpose of the present analytical framework, conditions regarding delegation of powers to EU agencies *stricto sensu* (1)–(3) have been integrated with requirements dictated by the principle of institutional balance (4).

209 *ESMA* Judgment (n 90) para 67. Here the Court states that the condition that 'only clearly defined *executive* powers may be delegated' is still a valid standard for assessing ESMA's powers.

210 ibid para 44.

211 ibid paras 45–54.

212 ibid, in particular paras 84–86. In this respect, it has been maintained that in ESMA the Court seems to imply that the institutional balance considerations in *Romano* are subsumed under the renewed *Meroni*, see Chamon (n 7) 257.

213 See Groenleer (n 33) 120; Craig (n 13) 170. See also Rambøll-Euréval-Matrix, Evaluation of the EU De-centralised Agencies in 2009, Final Report, Volume I, 'Synthesis and prospects'

Thus, all EU agencies feature as top level structures a collegiate body usually called 'administrative board', 'management board' or 'steering board', and a unipersonal body typically designated as the 'director' or 'executive director'. The collegiate body (the board) formulates the EU agency's strategy, formally adopts its work programme, budget and annual report, and also exercises oversight over the unipersonal organ. The unipersonal organ (the director) is the executive head of the EU agency, being in charge of the daily administration of the agency and ensuring the implementation of its work programme and budget.[214] Based on this two-headed leadership of EU agencies, a standard model of an EU agency has been advanced in the Common Approach on EU agencies.[215] This typical EU agency features a board in which all Member States are represented plus two representatives of the Commission, and a director appointed following a procedure involving the Commission and the management board.[216]

It is accepted, however, that not all EU agencies can completely fit within this mould. Thus, as regards the collegiate body, there are EU agencies in which: (1) not all Member States are represented in the board; (2) the Commission has no representatives or voting rights; (3) the European Parliament is also represented in the board; and (4) the stakeholders are also represented in the board.[217] As regards the director, in some EU agencies s/he is nominated by the Council or by the board without the formal involvement of the Commission.[218] Moreover, there are EU agencies whose main structure is more complex than the standard model. For some EU agencies,[219] in particular those with large boards, both the legal framework and the institutional practice confirm the existence of an executive board comprising a limited number of the members of the board.[220] This is meant to be a flexible working formula ensuring a more effective oversight over the daily activities of the agency and preparing the meetings and agenda of the board.[221] Furthermore, some EU agencies, depending on their functions and the features of their policy field, comprise specific structures intended to provide assistance to the decision-making bodies or to fulfil specific functions within the agency.[222]

(December 2009) 1–3 (the 2009 Evaluation of EU agencies) ‹https://europa.eu/european-union/sites/europaeu/files/docs/body/synthesis_and_prospects_en.pdf›.

214 See Groenleer (n 33) 120; Craig (n 13) 170; Geradin and Petit (n 86) 41.

215 See the Common Approach on EU agencies (n 114) paras 10–19.

216 See the 2009 Evaluation of EU agencies (n 213) 1.

217 ibid. See also the Common Approach on EU agencies (n 114) para 10.

218 See the 2009 Evaluation of EU agencies (n 213) 2.

219 eg CEDEFOP, EEA, EMCDDA, EU-OSHA, EUROFOUND, FRA and Frontex. This internal structure is designated as 'executive board, bureau or committee', see Analytical Fiche 6, ***Role and Functioning of the Management Board*** 4, accompanying the Common Approach on EU agencies (n 114).

220 Groenleer (n 33) 121.

221 The Common Approach on EU agencies confirms the general functions of the executive board and foresees its operation for all EU agencies (para 10).

222 eg scientific committees or panels and advisory forums, see Groenleer (n 33) 124, and Vos (n 21) 25–31.

1.6 Positioning European agencies in the EU institutional constellation

European agencies operate within a rather complex policy-institutional environment, which involves formal and informal interactions with the EU institutions and bodies, the Member States, actors outside the EU, private natural and legal persons.[223] To gain a better understanding of the role EU agencies play, not only formally but also in practice, it is important to examine the relationships between these bodies and the actors which are part of their external environment. These are key aspects for evaluating EU agencies' international cooperation tasks and instruments in light of *Meroni* and the principle of institutional balance, as well as for establishing their legal status as global actors.

In examining the interactions with EU institutions, the analysis is limited to the relationships between the EU agencies and the Commission, the Council and the European Parliament, because these are the institutions upon which the creation and operation of the agencies depends. Out of the three main institutions, EU agencies are involved mostly with the Commission and the Council, although lately the European Parliament appears to be more involved in the agency business.

The nature and extent of the formal relationships between the Commission and the EU agencies varies to a certain extent, depending on factors like the policy field of the EU agencies, whether the agency is self-financed or not, etc. For instance, one may assume that the Commission has more intensive formal relations with the former 'first pillar' EU agencies because in that area the Commission enjoys the most extensive executive powers.[224] Likewise, one would expect the Commission to have less grip on the former 'third pillar' agencies, as police and judicial cooperation are still largely within the realm of Member States' competence.[225] Despite these differences, the formal relationship between the Commission and the EU agencies might be generally characterised as 'influential'. For most EU agencies, the Commission is represented in the board and has a say with regard to the appointment of the director. Along with these prerogatives, the Commission has other instruments available to it through which it can obtain a comprehensive insight into what the EU agencies are doing and to keep them under control. Thus, in most cases the Commission is involved in the preparation of the agency's multiannual planning and annual work programme,[226] provides input concerning the agency's rules of procedure and exerts significant influence with regard to the EU agencies' budget (in particular when it consists of an EU subsidy) and staffing.[227] Finally, during EU agencies' life cycle, it is the Commission which is generally in charge of the external evaluation of the agency; although harmless at the first sight, such evaluations could form the basis of substantial changes in the legal framework of the EU agencies.[228] These prerogatives and mechanisms available

223 See Groenleer (n 33) 130–34 and 346–47.
224 eg EASA, EFSA, EMA, ERA.
225 Similarly, one may expect less Commission influence in relation to the EU agencies created in policy areas perceived as sensitive by the Member States, such as the AFSJ area (eg Frontex, eu-LISA).
226 Common Approach on EU agencies (n 114) paras 28–31.
227 ibid paras 33–35 and 36–45.
228 Groenleer (n 33) 130; see also the Common Approach on EU agencies (n 114) paras 60–63.

to the Commission in relation to the EU agencies indicate a rather prominent position occupied by the Commission. Also, with regard to the international activities of the EU agencies, it seems that the Commission has reserved an important role for itself.[229]

The relationships between the Council and the EU agencies are also subject to variations, but in a rather opposite direction compared to the Commission. Hence, it appears that the formal links with the former 'first pillar' EU agencies are rather weak, whilst the relationships with the PJCCM and CFSP agencies are more intense. Overall, the Council and the Member States can exercise some influence through their representatives in the board and also through their involvement in the appointment of the director. The Council is also able to influence EU agencies in its legislative capacity, as the acts setting up the agencies are instruments of secondary legislation. Other formal controls over EU agencies are exercised by the Council acting as a budgetary authority. More informally, the Council exerts a steering role in relation to the EU agencies through its role in policy-making, such as setting the agenda and laying down action-plans in various policy areas.[230] Concerning the relations with the former 'second pillar', agencies, and to some extent also the PJCCM agencies, the Council has an enhanced role. In this respect, the Council also assumed the formal oversight over the 'external' relations of the CFSP and PJCCM agencies. Good examples in this respect are the agreements concluded by Europol and Eurojust with third states and international organisations, or the administrative arrangements in which EDA might enter, but in all the cases after formal approval by the Council.[231]

The relationships between the European Parliament and the EU agencies are less developed, although during the last years the European Parliament has taken a more active stance towards agencies. At present, this relationship is materialised by the European Parliament having representatives in the boards of some EU agencies,[232] the duty most EU agencies have to send their annual reports to the European Parliament, the possibility for the European Parliament to invite executive directors of EU agencies for hearings, or the possibility for MEPs to visit EU agencies.[233] Additionally, just like the Council, the European Parliament officially has an important say in the creation of EU agencies, their design and powers as a co-legislator. However, the most important formal instrument at the disposal of the European Parliament relates to EU agencies' budgets. More precisely, as the main budgetary authority, the European Parliament approves the EU agencies' budgets and gives discharge to EU agencies receiving subsidies from the EU budget, thereby potentially allowing the European Parliament to exercise some influence over these bodies.[234] It should be noted that the relationships (and influence) between the European Parliament and EU

229 Thus, in practice the working arrangements concluded by (former 'first pillar') EU agencies should be based on a prior opinion from the Commission which, in this institution's view, must be taken into account by the agency to the greatest extent possible, see COM (2005) 59 (n 82) 20–21 and 23, and Common Approach on EU agencies (n 114) para 25.

230 These commandments and directions usually take the form of Council Conclusions.

231 Art 26a of Eurojust Council Decision, art 23 of Europol Council Decision 2009 and art 24 of EDA Council Decision 2011.

232 Such examples are ACER, EMCDDA, ECDC, ECHA, EEA and EMA where the European Parliament designates two members of the management board, see Analytical Fiche 32, *Parliament Role* 3–4, accompanying the Common Approach on EU agencies (n 114).

233 Groenleer (n 33) 132.

234 ibid.

agencies are also subject to variations. They are most intensive with the former 'first pillar' EU agencies, increasingly intensive with PJCCM agencies, and practically lacking with regard to the CFSP agencies.

For an accurate appraisal of the EU agencies within the EU legal-governance framework, one should also take into account the relationships mainly of a cooperative and operational nature established with other relevant actors in their field. To that effect, EU agencies either establish, coordinate or manage various networks or become a component of existing networks.[235] First, it is very important for EU agencies to maintain close relations with the appropriate authorities and structures from the Member States,[236] as they usually must rely on the information and expertise provided by the latter. Furthermore, in the context of the indirect administration model, national authorities actually play an active role in the implementation of the EU legal framework and policies. Secondly, EU agencies establish complex relationships with key actors outside the EU, thereby potentially becoming components of global networks with a specific role to fulfil.

To sum up, the EU agencies, as elements of the EU 'composite' executive,[237] are situated at a crossroads in the present EU legal-governance framework, somewhere in the 'grey area' between implementation and decision-making, between information, technical or scientific expertise and policy-making, connecting the EU to the national and international levels, and sometimes linking public actors and processes to private interests and stakeholders. While enjoying formal or legal autonomy,[238] the organisation and functioning of these bodies, as well as the ways in which they interact with the Council, the Commission, the European Parliament and the Member States suggest a complex principal-agent relationship. In this relationship, the EU agencies appear to depend on the main EU institutions and also on the Member States, to act in furtherance of their interests, and under their supervision and control.

1.7 The international dimension of EU agencies: practice and legal design

1.7.1 EU agencies' practice of international cooperation

1.7.1.1 Main forms and underlying reasons

EU agencies are increasingly interacting in various ways with actors outside the EU and they are becoming arguably visible actors on the international arena.[239] Interactions take place routinely between the EU agencies and various international organisations

235 See Craig (n 13) 176–79, and Vos (n 21) 23–24.
236 eg EFSA, EASA, EMSA, ECDC, Eurojust, Europol and Frontex.
237 See Curtin (n 21) 65–66.
238 See Groenleer (n 33) 15–16, distinguishing between formal or legal autonomy of the EU agencies and *de facto* or actual autonomy.
239 On the international dimension of EU agencies, see Andrea Ott, 'EU Regulatory Agencies in EU External Relations: Trapped in a Legal Minefield between European and International Law' (2008) 13 *EFAR* 515; Andrea Ott, Ellen Vos and Florin Coman-Kund, 'EU Agencies on the Global Scene: EU and International Law Perspectives' in Michelle Everson, Cosimo Monda and Ellen Vos (eds), *European Agencies in between Institutions and Member States* (Kluwer Law International 2014) 87–122.

and (competent authorities of) third countries. Such cooperation ranges from light and informal forms of collaboration (eg common events, exchanges of best practices) to more structured and substantial cooperation formalised through international agreements or treaty-like instruments concluded between the EU agencies and their partners.[240] Sometimes, the international cooperation carried out by the EU agencies takes place within the framework of treaties between the EU and third countries or international organisations.[241] In other instances, the EU agencies formalise relations with partners outside the EU in the absence of such treaties or, quite interestingly, within the framework of agreements between the Member States and the relevant third country or international organisation.[242]

One may discern several closely inter-linked ways in which the international dimension of the EU agencies materialises in practice.[243] First, EU agencies become involved in the management of the external dimension of their respective policy area by assisting the EU institutions and the Member States in their relations with third countries and international organisations. In this context, the EU agencies become involved as sectoral actors, for example, by implementing various projects or providing technical assistance to third countries often in the framework of wider EU programmes and initiatives. Secondly, third countries and international organisations may participate in the internal structures of some EU agencies.[244] Thirdly, the EU agencies establish direct cooperation with third countries or third country authorities and international organisations. Such direct cooperation is often formalised through arrangements and agreements concluded between the agencies and their partners.

Several reasons could be advanced to explain this development.[245] In the context of an ever more globalised and interconnected world, regulatory and administrative processes have inevitably acquired a transboundary dimension. Issues like environmental protection, aviation safety, border management, or tackling criminality can no longer be solved exclusively on a domestic level but are increasingly embedded in various formal and informal international frameworks bringing together various international entities, states and their authorities and bodies. Within the Union, this phenomenon is reflected not only in the way its external policies are designed, but also by the explicit recognition[246] and the quick development of an external dimension to its 'internal' policies. The external dimension of the EU policies triggers interactions with international organisations and third countries both on a political level and on a technical-operational level.

240 Coman-Kund (n 155) 338–40.

241 eg EASA within the framework of the EU bilateral aviation safety agreements (BASAs) with third countries, FRA pursuing cooperation with the Council of Europe on the basis of an international agreement concluded between the EU and the said international organisation, or Europol within the framework of the so-called 'TFTP Agreement' between the EU and the USA (Agreement between the European Union and the United States of America on the processing and transfer of Financial Messaging Data from the European Union to the United States for the purposes of the Terrorist Finance Tracking Program [2010] OJ L195/5).

242 eg Frontex.

243 See Coman-Kund (n 155) 338–40.

244 ibid 340 and 360–61 (with regard to EASA).

245 See Martijn Groenleer, 'Linking up Levels of Governance: Agencies of the European Union and their Interaction with International Organisations' in Oriol Costa and Knud Erik Jørgensen (eds), *The Influence of International Institutions on the European Union* (Palgrave Macmillan 2012) 142–46.

246 Art 21 TEU.

The EU agencies become part of this picture as technical-administrative bodies entrusted with tasks supporting policy formulation and implementation. As such, these bodies assist with technical expertise the main EU political actors in their dealings with relevant international actors, and provide support on sectoral aspects in the context of the Union's wider external policies and initiatives (eg Enlargement, European Neighbourhood Policy, Development cooperation). Moreover, the EU agencies increasingly need to establish direct relationships on a technical operational level with relevant international bodies and third-country counterparts in order to fulfil effectively the core tasks entrusted by their founding acts.[247] An additional reason for the international cooperation pursued increasingly by the EU agencies points to the institutional gains these bodies might pursue in terms of demonstrating their added value and also in terms of gaining more autonomy in relation to their principals.[248]

1.7.1.2 A brief survey of EU agencies' practice of international cooperation

Without going into the diversity of formal and informal interactions between the EU agencies and their partners, in what follows a selective overview of the international cooperation practice of some agencies is provided (see also Annex 1: EU agencies' international dimension – founding acts and international cooperation practice). The focus is on the formal international cooperation instruments enacted between the EU agencies and their partners, as these are the easiest to identify, quantify and analyse from a legal point of view, and they arguably trigger significant legal consequences and problems. The survey of the international cooperation of the EU agencies is based on sources such as the EU agencies' websites, activity reports, annual work programmes, evaluation reports, and policy documents.

Not all EU agencies have developed a rich international dimension (see Annex 1). There are also EU agencies that have a scarce or at least scarcely documented international cooperation practice, at any rate for the time being. This appears to be the case for Cedefop, ENISA, EU-OSHA, GSA. In the case of EU agencies, such as SRB, ESMA, EBA, EIOPA, ACER, eu-LISA, and BEREC, the absence of a significant international cooperation record could at least be partly explained by the fact that they have been established recently. Some of these agencies have begun, however, to engage increasingly in international cooperation, and they have already concluded formal international cooperation instruments.[249]

247 It is difficult to imagine how Frontex could effectively contribute to Union's border management without working in close cooperation with the border guards from the relevant third countries, or how Europol or Eurojust could fight effectively against organised crime without exchanging relevant data with Interpol or third countries, or how EASA could fulfil its tasks related to type certification and design approvals with expedience and minimum costs without entering into arrangements with aviation authorities from third countries with a view to ensuring the mutual acceptance of the type certificates, design approvals and related activities and requirements.

248 Martijn Groenleer and Simone Gabbi, 'Regulatory Agencies of the European Union as International Actors. Legal Framework, Development over Time and Strategic Motives in the Case of the European Food Safety Authority' (2013) 4 EJRR 479, 482–83.

249 eg EBA (see EBA's Annual Activity Report 2015 66–67 ‹http://www.eba.europa.eu/about-us/annual-reports›), ESMA (see ESMA's Annual Activity Report 2015 57 ‹https://www.esma.europa.eu/document/esma-annual-report-2015›), and EIOPA.

Formal international cooperation instruments

In practice, most EU agencies conclude with the competent authorities of third countries and with relevant international organisations cooperation instruments labelled 'working arrangement', 'administrative arrangement' or 'arrangement' (eg Frontex, EMA,[250] EBA[251] and ESMA[252]). EASA is by far the agency with the most impressive international cooperation record, with more than one hundred working arrangements with international partners.[253] Some EU agencies formalised their relationships with external partners also through instruments called 'memorandum of understanding' (MOU) or 'memorandum of cooperation' (MOC) – eg Eurojust,[254] EMCDDA,[255] EFSA,[256] CPVO,[257] ESMA,[258] EIOPA[259] and EBA.[260] Several agencies concluded international cooperation instruments entitled 'agreements', thereby

250 Arrangement for shared non-public information regarding influenza A (H1N1) pandemic concluded by EMA with the Swiss Agency for Therapeutic Products, Swissmedic (12 February 2010) ‹http://www.ema.europa.eu/docs/en_GB/document_library/Other/2010/02/WC500074064.pdf›.

251 EBA's Annual Activity Report 2015 (n 249) 67.

252 ESMA's Annual Activity Report 2015 (n 249) 57.

253 EASA/Partnerships/Working arrangements ‹http://easa.europa.eu/rulemaking/international-cooperation-working-arrangements.php›.

254 Eurojust has concluded memoranda of understanding with the Iberoamerican Network of International Legal Cooperation (Iber–RED), the United Nations Office on Drugs and Crime (UNODC), and with Interpol ‹http://eurojust.europa.eu/doclibrary/Eurojust-framework/Pages/agreements-concluded-by-eurojust.aspx?Page=2›.

255 The agency has concluded Memoranda of Understanding (MOUs) with the United Nations Office on Drugs and Crime (UNODC), the World Health Organisation (WHO), Pompidou Group, the World Customs Organisation (WCO), and the Inter-American Drug Abuse Control Commission (CICAD) established by the General Assembly of the Organization of American States (CICAD–GS/OAS) ‹http://www.emcdda.europa.eu/ about/partners›.

256 EFSA signed MOCs with US Food and Drug Administration (FDA) and the Food Safety Commission of Japan (FCSJ), see EFSA's multi-annual international scientific cooperation 2014–2016 11 ‹http://www.efsa.europa.eu/en/corporate/doc/iscmap1416.pdf›. Another memorandum of cooperation has been concluded with the Food Safety Commission of Japan (JFSC) on 7 December 2009 ‹http://www.efsa.europa.eu/en/networks/international.htm›.

257 CPVO has signed MOUs with the International Union for the Protection of New Varieties of Plants (UPOV) and the African Intellectual Property Organisation (OAPI), see CPVO Annual Report 2010 69–71 ‹http://www.cpvo.europa.eu/documents/Rapportannuel/AR2010_EN.pdf›.

258 Memorandum of Understanding on the Cooperation of Competent Authorities for the Supervision of the Credit Rating Agencies between the European Securities and Markets Authority (ESMA) and the Canadian Authorities (in force from 7 March 2012) ‹https://www.esma.europa.eu/sites/default/files/library/2015/11/mou_esma_uu_canadian_authorities.pdf›.

259 EIOPA has concluded MOUs with the World Bank ‹https://eiopa.europa.eu/Publications/Protocols/MoU_EIOPA_-_World_Bank.pdf#search=world%20bank›, and the Swiss Financial Market Supervisory Authority (FINMA) ‹https://eiopa.europa.eu/Publications/Protocols/MoU-EIOPA-FINMA_21_Sept_2012.pdf#search=Swiss%20Financial%20Market%20Supervisory%20Authority›.

260 In 2015, a MOC was signed between EBA and the supervisory authorities of South East European (SEE) countries, EBA's Annual Activity Report 2015 (n 249) 66.

suggesting heavier forms of cooperation from a legal point of view (eg Europol, Eurojust,[261] Cepol[262] and EMCDDA[263]). A few EU agencies have concluded cooperation instruments with titles less frequently used in the agency international practice, such as 'protocol',[264] 'statement of intent',[265] and 'cooperation'.[266]

The arrangements or agreements concluded by the EU agencies often represent the first step in formalising cooperation on a technical level in a certain policy area (eg Frontex, Europol, Eurojust, EMCDDA). In other instances, the instruments formalising external cooperation are enacted by the EU agencies within the framework of international agreements concluded by the EU. Such is the relationship between EASA and ICAO,[267] the cooperation between FRA and the Council of Europe,[268] or the cooperation arrangements between EMA and some third countries.[269] A quick look at the content of these instruments reveals interesting insights concerning their legal nature, in addition to the title of the cooperation instrument. Thus, some formal international cooperation instruments include explicit provisions stressing their non-binding nature.[270] In other instances, such clauses are lacking[271] or, even more,

261 Eurojust has concluded agreements with Norway, Iceland, Romania, USA, Croatia, Liechtenstein, FYROM, Switzerland, Moldova, Ukraine and Montenegro ‹http://eurojust.europa.eu/doclibrary/Eurojust-framework/Pages/agreements-concluded-by-eurojust.aspx?Page=2›.

262 In addition to the working arrangements in place with some external partners, Cepol has also concluded cooperation agreements with Georgia, Iceland, Interpol, Montenegro, Norway, Switzerland and Turkey ‹https://www.cepol.europa.eu/who-we-are/partners-and-stakeholders/external-partners›.

263 EMCDDA has a cooperation agreement with Interpol ‹http://www.emcdda.europa.eu/about/partners/interpol›.

264 FRA has concluded a Protocol for Cooperation with the United Nations Development Programme (UNDP) ‹http://fra.europa.eu/fraWebsite/networks/partners/international_organisations/international_organisations_en.htm›.

265 ECHA has concluded cooperation instruments called 'Statement of Intent' with the competent authorities from USA and Japan ‹http://echa.europa.eu/about-us/partners-and-networks/international-cooperation/cooperation-with-peer-regulatory-agencies›; see also ECHA Factsheet 'International cooperation' (ECHA-13-FS-02-EN) ‹http://echa.europa.eu/documents/10162/13558/fact sheet_ international_cooperation_en.pdf›.

266 eg Cooperation with the Pharmaceutical Inspection Co-operation Scheme (PIC/S) and the European Medicines Agency ‹http://www.ema.europa.eu/ema/index.jsp?curl=pages/partners_and_networks/general/general_content_000470.jsp&mid=WC0b01ac05801f0a08›

267 Currently, the cooperation between EASA and ICAO takes place within the framework of the Memorandum of Cooperation between the European Union and the International Civil Aviation Organization providing a framework for enhanced cooperation [2011] OJ L232/2.

268 Agreement between the European Community and the Council of Europe on cooperation between the European Union Agency for Fundamental Rights and the Council of Europe [2008] OJ L186/7.

269 eg Japan, Canada, Australia, New Zealand and Switzerland ‹http://www.ema.europa.eu/ema/index.jsp?curl=pages/partners_and_networks/general/general_content_000214.jsp&murl=menus/partners_and_networks/partners_and_networks.jsp&mid=WC0b01ac058 003176d&jsenabled=true›.

270 eg most of the working arrangements concluded by Frontex; the Arrangement for shared non-public information regarding influenza A (H1N1) pandemic concluded by EMA with the Swiss Agency for Therapeutic Products, Swissmedic; the MOUs concluded by EIOPA and ESMA, etc.

271 eg the working arrangements concluded by EASA.

the provisions of the instruments are worded strongly suggesting the intention of the parties to create legally binding commitments.[272] Finally, the various formal cooperation instruments of EU agencies are usually concluded with the competent authorities of the third countries concerned (on ministerial or agency level),[273] not with the state as such. In a few instances, however, the content of the instruments concluded by some EU agencies suggests that their counterpart is the government of the third country concerned.[274]

Informal international cooperation

In addition to the formal cooperation instruments concluded with external partners, the EU agencies also partake in international cooperation in other ways. Before formalising their cooperation with external partners, the EU agencies usually carry out cooperation on an informal basis.[275] Such cooperation usually has a more or less limited scope[276] and may pave the way towards enhanced cooperation formalised through the conclusion of arrangements or agreements. On top of that, the agencies use their sectoral expertise to support the Union's external policies or the external dimension of EU internal policies, where they become involved within the framework of wider EU initiatives and instruments.[277] Most EU agencies participate in different ways in the Union's enlargement and neighbourhood policies, by carrying out projects, providing advice and training, performing inspections etc.[278] EASA, EMCDDA or ECDC are good examples of agencies establishing relationships with candidate, potential candidate and neighbouring countries. Frontex is involved in international cooperation within the framework of EU initiatives and missions, such as Migration and Mobility Partnerships, the Eastern Partnership Initiative, the Building Migration Partnerships.[279] EFSA has increasingly assisted the Commission with scientific and technical advice by participating in meetings of international organisations, such as those organised by the Codex Alimentarius, the World Organisation for Animal Health (OIE), the Organisation for Economic Co-operation and Development (OECD), the World Health Organisation (WHO) and other international bodies.[280] EMA also

272 eg the agreements concluded by Europol and Eurojust, some of the working arrangements concluded by EASA, the MOUs concluded by EMCDDA with Interpol and WCO.

273 eg EASA, ECDC, ECHA, EMA, EFSA, and Frontex.

274 Most obvious examples are Europol and Eurojust.

275 Such is the case of Europol whose legal framework permitted the exchange of personal data in the absence or before the signing of an agreement with a third country or international organisation; the websites and activity reports of EU agencies (eg FRA, ECDC, EEA, EFSA, EMA) also mention various ways of informal cooperation with international partners.

276 It usually consists of informal contacts, working relations, participation in common events, common meetings, informal exchanges of best practices, etc.

277 See Groenleer and Gabbi (n 248) 480–81.

278 On the involvement of EU agencies in the EU enlargement policy, see Coman-Kund (n 155) 342–49.

279 Frontex/Partners/Third countries ‹http://frontex.europa.eu/partners/third-countries›.

280 EFSA/Cooperation/International scientific cooperation ‹http://www.efsa.europa.eu/en/networks/international.htm›.

assists the Commission's cooperation on pharmaceuticals with some third countries and participates in networks involving non-EU actors.[281]

1.7.2 The design of EU agencies' international dimension according to their legal framework

1.7.2.1 General overview

Post-Lisbon the Founding Treaties include several provisions targeting specifically the EU agencies, but they remain silent as to the role, powers, and tasks of these bodies as global actors. However, if one takes a closer look at the detailed legal framework of the EU agencies, and in particular their founding acts, a different picture comes to the fore (see Annex 1: EU agencies' international dimension – founding acts and international cooperation practice). The international dimension of most EU agencies is somehow formalised and sometimes international cooperation is even imposed by their founding acts and other relevant legal instruments. In most cases, the founding acts of the EU agencies include general or more detailed provisions regarding international cooperation. The exceptions are ACER, BEREC, CdT,[282] CPVO, GSA and eu-LISA, whose founding acts do not contain express provisions concerning their international dimension. However, in the case of ACER, Regulation 1227/2011 on wholesale energy market integrity and transparency expands the mandate of this agency and, within this extension, it provides for international cooperation.[283]

Insofar as the EU agencies whose founding documents provide for international cooperation are concerned, in some cases the (task) duty or possibility to establish relations with non-EU actors is mentioned in broad terms with no further indications regarding the detailed powers, instruments and procedures to be used.[284] References to the external dimension of the agencies concerned are to be found usually at the beginning of the founding act where the general roles, objectives and tasks of these bodies are described. For instance, in the case of Cedefop[285] and Eurofund,[286] the founding regulations simply state the general task of these agencies to establish contacts or to cooperate with relevant bodies at international level, with no further details. The tasks of EU-OSHA encompass taking into account the relevant national, EU and international bodies and organisations, as well as collecting and making

281 EMA coordinates, for instance, the European Network of Paediatric Research at the European Medicines Agency (Enpr–EMA) ‹http://www.ema.europa.eu/ema/index.jsp?curl=pages/partners_and_networks/general/general_content_000303.jsp&murl=menus/partners_and_networks/partners_and_networks.jsp&mid=WC0b01ac05801df74a›.

282 CdT is excluded from this discussion, however, as it is not a real EU agency, but rather a horizontal service supporting other EU agencies and bodies.

283 Article 19 of Regulation (EU) 1227/2011 of the European Parliament and of the Council of 25 October 2011 on wholesale energy market integrity and transparency [2011] OJ L326/1.

284 Cedefop, EMSA, ENISA, Eurofund, EU–OSHA.

285 Art 3(2) of Cedefop Regulation.

286 Art 3(2) of Eurofund Regulation.

available information on safety and health matters from and to third countries and international organisations.[287] In the case of OHIM (EUIPO) the founding act contains a general duty for the Office to cooperate with industrial property bodies and offices, and with relevant international organisations.[288] Additionally, OHIM (EUIPO) Regulation comprises very specific provisions regarding the involvement of the Office in the International Registration of Marks procedure, entailing, *inter alia*, interactions with the International Bureau of the World Intellectual Property Organisation.[289]

In other instances, the founding acts and sometimes also other legal instruments contain more detailed provisions as regards the international cooperation mandate of the agency, the instruments used and some relevant procedural aspects.[290] In some cases, the founding acts provide details concerning the powers and scope for international cooperation, although without explicitly naming the instruments that the agencies may use in pursuing such cooperation.[291] ECDC for instance may provide scientific and technical assistance to third countries and international organisations (in particular the WHO)[292] and is required to work in close cooperation with competent bodies with data collection tasks from third countries, the WHO, and other international organisations.[293] EMA's founding act compels this agency to cooperate with international organisations and in particular with the WHO in matters of pharmacovigilance.[294] Additionally, one of the tasks of the agency consists of providing technical and scientific support in order to improve the cooperation between the EU, the Member States, international organisations and third countries.[295] Similarly, EFSA has as a task to provide assistance in order to improve cooperation between the EU and applicant countries, international organisations and third countries in the areas covered by its mandate.[296] By the same token, the agency is committed to cooperating closely with organisations from applicant countries, third countries and international organisations with a view to collecting relevant data.[297] Also EIGE is tasked with establishing cooperation with relevant organisations at the international level and with third countries.[298] However, the founding act stipulates explicitly that any agreements necessary to enable cooperation between the Institute and international partners must be concluded by the EU in accordance with Article 218 TFEU.[299] The Institute is still allowed to pursue *ad hoc* cooperation with international organisations and

287 Art 3(1) of EU-OSHA Regulation.
288 Art 123b(2) of OHIM (EUIPO) Regulation.
289 Arts 145–161 of OHIM (EUIPO) Regulation.
290 Cepol, EASA, EASO, EBA, ECDC, ECHA, EEA, EFCA, EFSA, EIGE, EIOPA, EMA, EMCDDA, ESMA, Eurojust, Europol, ETF, FRA and Frontex.
291 eg ECDC, ECHA, EEA, EMA, EFSA and EIGE.
292 Art 9 of ECDC Regulation.
293 Art 11 of ECDC Regulation.
294 Arts 28c(1) and 52 of EMA Regulation.
295 Art 57(1) of EMA Regulation.
296 Art 23 of EFSA Regulation.
297 Art 33 of EFSA Regulation.
298 Art 8(1) of EIGE Regulation.
299 Art 8(2) of EIGE Regulation. A similar provision is included in the FRA founding act as far as the relationship with the Council of Europe is concerned (art 9 of FRA Regulation).

third countries, but no further details are provided as to the instruments it may use to this effect.[300]

The founding acts of other EU agencies[301] include express provisions regarding the formal instruments these bodies may use in the exercise of their external relations tasks and international activities. For some of these EU agencies, the founding acts mention some important aspects regarding the procedure for the negotiation and conclusion of formal cooperation instruments.[302]

There are several titles in use for EU agencies' international cooperation instruments, such as administrative arrangements,[303] working arrangements,[304] (cooperation) agreements.[305] ETF is an interesting case as both 'co-operation agreements' and 'working arrangements' are mentioned in the founding act. Even more intriguing is that these labels appear to be used interchangeably.[306] Another interesting agency is EFCA, since the founding act mentions both working arrangements as instruments of cooperation with competent authorities of regional international fisheries organisations,[307] and the possibility to conclude administrative agreements in order to contribute to the implementation of the EU Integrated Maritime Policy.[308] This brief overview shows a preference for the term 'arrangement' as a label for EU agencies' international cooperation instruments. However, it also reveals that various terms are used interchangeably in the founding acts of the EU agencies, and that there is no overall consistency as regards the terminology used to designate the formal international cooperation instruments of these bodies.

Finally, it should be noted that in addition to the founding acts, the international dimension of the EU agencies or aspects thereof may be dealt with in other EU legal acts or in international agreements concluded by the EU or sometimes even by the Member States with third countries and international organisations. For instance, ACER's international dimension is not dealt with in its founding act, but in Regulation 1227/2011 on wholesale energy market integrity and transparency. EASA, Europol and FRA are illustrative of instances in which aspects of the agencies' international cooperation are dealt with in agreements concluded by the EU with third countries or international organisations. Frontex can serve as a good example of an agency which can be entrusted with tasks through agreements between a Member State and a third country.[309]

300 Art 8(2) of EIGE Regulation. According to art 4(5), EIGE is empowered to enter into subcontracting arrangements with other organisations; without further specification it is not excluded that such (contractual) arrangements could also be concluded with international actors (third country authorities or international organisations).
301 Cepol, EASA, EASO, EBA, ECDC, EFCA, EIOPA, EMCDDA, ESMA, ETF, Eurojust, Europol, FRA and Frontex.
302 eg Europol, Eurojust, EASA, EFCA, EMCDDA, ETF, FRA and Frontex.
303 ACER, EBA, EIOPA, ESMA and FRA.
304 EASA, EASO, EFCA, EMCDDA and Frontex.
305 Cepol, Eurojust and Europol.
306 Art 3(6) of ETF Regulation
307 Art 4(1) of EFCA Regulation.
308 Art 17g of EFCA Regulation.
309 Since 2011 this possibility has been clearly stated in art 14(7) of the former Frontex Regulation, and it has been maintained in art 54(10) of the New Frontex Regulation.

1.7.2.2 EU agencies' international cooperation mandate: scope and controls

There are several ways in which substantive limits and requirements are set by the founding acts regarding the scope and exercise of EU agencies' mandate for international cooperation (see Annex 2: Substantive and procedural limitations on EU agencies' international cooperation mandate according to their founding acts).

In most instances, the founding acts clearly limit the agencies' capacity to pursue international cooperation to their core mandate. This is done through formulas like 'the agency must fulfil its international cooperation role within the limits of its mandate' (EASO,[310] EFSA,[311] Frontex) or 'to the extent necessary to perform its tasks' (Eurojust,[312] Europol[313]) or 'to achieve its objectives' (ACER[314]). This also becomes obvious when the founding acts link international cooperation aspects to the exercise by the EU agencies of their main tasks.[315] Sometimes the founding acts subordinate explicitly the international cooperation tasks and instruments of the EU agencies to the wider EU legal framework and policies. These are the provisions stipulating that the EU agencies' international cooperation must be performed 'in accordance with EU law' (EASA,[316] EASO,[317] ETF,[318] FRA[319] and Frontex[320]); 'in accordance with agreements concluded by EU' (ECHA,[321] EFCA,[322] EIGE[323] and FRA[324]); or 'in the context of EU external relations policies' (ETF[325] and Frontex[326]).

In some instances, the founding acts specify that the EU agencies' international tasks and instruments must be performed 'without prejudice to the competences of the Member States and EU institutions' (eg ACER,[327] EBA,[328] EIOPA[329] and ESMA[330]). These formulations, together with the instances in which the founding acts provide that the EU agency pursues international cooperation tasks 'in assisting the EU and the Member States' (eg EASA, Frontex) suggest quite a narrow and marginal international cooperation mandate for EU agencies. This conclusion is further supported

310 Art 49 of EASO Regulation.
311 Art 23 of EFSA Regulation.
312 Art 26a(1) of Eurojust Founding Act.
313 Art 23 of old Europol Council Decision and art 23(1) of the new Europol Regulation.
314 Art 19 of Regulation 1227/2011.
315 eg OHIM, EMSA and EMA.
316 Art 27(2) of EASA Regulation.
317 Arts 49 and 52 of EASO Regulation.
318 Art 3(6) of ETF Regulation.
319 Art 8(3) of FRA Regulation.
320 Arts 13–14 of the former Frontex Regulation, and art 54(2) of the new Frontex Regulation.
321 Art 120 of ECHA Regulation.
322 Art 4(2) of EFCA Regulation.
323 Art 8 of EIGE Regulation.
324 Art 9 of FRA Regulation.
325 Art 1(1) of ETF Regulation.
326 Art 14(1) of the former Frontex Regulation, and art 54(2) of the new Frontex Regulation.
327 Art 19 of Regulation 1227/2011.
328 Art 33 of EBA Regulation.
329 Art 33 of EIOPA Regulation.
330 Art 33 of ESMA Regulation.

in other cases (ACER,[331] EBA,[332] EIOPA,[333] ESMA,[334] ERA[335] and Cepol[336]) in which the founding acts anticipate on the nature and breadth of the effects of agencies' international cooperation instruments. The standard formulation used is that the agencies' cooperation instruments 'do not create legal obligations for the EU and the Member States'. In addition to that, it is explicitly stipulated that such instruments cannot preclude Member States from concluding bilateral or multilateral arrangements with other international actors. What is more, in the case of SRB, Article 32(4) of Regulation 806/2014 is quite explicit in providing that the Agency may conclude 'non-binding cooperation arrangements' with third-country competent authorities.

Another way in which the discretion of the EU agencies to pursue international cooperation is confined consists of *ex ante* and *ex post* requirements and conditions concerning specifically the EU agencies' international cooperation powers and instruments. For some agencies, their international cooperation tasks and instruments are subjected to a *prior* Commission request or consultation. In the case of ECHA, EFCA, EFSA and EMA the international cooperation tasks and instruments are triggered by prior requests from the Commission. As regards the arrangements concluded by EMCDDA, ETF, FRA Cepol and ERA a *prior* Commission opinion or consultation is required. Somehow differently, some EU agencies like EASA[337] and EASO[338] feature approval from or agreement with the Commission before concluding working arrangements. The international cooperation instruments (agreements) of former 'third pillar' agencies (Cepol, Eurojust and Europol) were subjected to *prior* Council approval, but this is no longer the case, according to the new founding regulations of these bodies. Finally, there are agencies for which the founding act lacks explicit provisions regarding controls or supervisory mechanisms.[339]

1.7.3 General observations

The previous general overview reveals that, with a few exceptions,[340] the founding acts of the EU agencies at least explicitly circumscribe the international cooperation of these bodies to their core mandate or tasks, suggesting an ancillary and instrumental nature of EU agencies' international dimension. Additionally, in some cases agencies' founding acts explicitly provide that their external relations must be in compliance with EU law, or, more recently, include a standard formula according to which international cooperation by EU agencies may not affect the competences of the EU institutions and of the Member States and/or that such cooperation does not entail legal

331 Art 19 of Regulation 1227/2011.
332 Art 33 of EBA Regulation.
333 Art 33 of EIOPA Regulation.
334 Art 33 of ESMA Regulation.
335 Art 44 of ERA New Regulation.
336 Art 34 of New Cepol Regulation.
337 Art 27(2) of EASA Regulation.
338 Art 49(2) of EASO Regulation.
339 ACER, Cedefop, EBA, ECDC, EEA, EIGE, EIOPA, EMSA, ENISA, ESMA, EU-OSHA, Eurofund, GSA and OHIM.
340 BEREC, CdT, CPVO, eu-LISA, GSA (the founding acts of these agencies do not include explicit provisions on international cooperation by these bodies), and Eurofund.

obligations for the EU and the Member States. This recent trend regarding the drafting of international cooperation provisions for EU agencies seems to indicate an increased awareness on behalf of the main EU institutions as concerns the legal implications the external actions of these bodies might trigger. Moreover, the care shown to preserve the competences of the Member States and to avoid legal obligations being imposed on them by EU agencies' international cooperation activities signals the complex position of these bodies as global actors.

The panoramic survey of EU agencies' international dimension documents a trend to label their formal international cooperation instruments as 'arrangements' in agencies' founding acts, arguably hinting at less legally loaded forms of cooperation. Another observation is that the instruments concluded in practice with third countries and international organisations also feature other names than the one(s) explicitly mentioned in agencies' founding acts, which prompts the question whether such instruments can be equated to the categories formally enshrined in agencies' legal framework. Yet another observation is that EU agencies (eg CPVO) may develop a relatively rich international cooperation record in practice in spite of their founding acts lacking explicit provisions for international cooperation; one may wonder to what extent such practical developments might be problematic in light of the legal standards applicable to EU agencies' powers and activities.

The overview of the EU agencies' international dimension from both a practical and a legal-formal perspective reveals a complex picture with common features, but also idiosyncrasies peculiar to individual agencies or groups of agencies. The existing variety characterising the international cooperation of EU agencies, as well as the multiple aspects of their international dimension make it difficult to provide a strict taxonomy of these bodies as global actors.[341]

1.8 Conclusion

A significant number of agencies are operational at the EU level and there is no reason to believe that the 'agencification' process will stop. European agencies have been created over time in various EU policy areas, using different techniques and on the basis of a variable combination of reasons and circumstances. Furthermore, there are some fluctuations between agencies as concerns their formal tasks and powers, as well as with regard to the relationships between these bodies and other actors.

In spite of this diversity, it is still possible to identify some common threads along which one may sketch some sort of a 'core profile' of the agency system, as confirmed by the Common Approach on EU agencies. All European agencies seem to have been created mainly as technical or administrative components of the EU 'executive branch', most of them enjoying some degree of formal autonomy. Their formal powers seem to be of a rather similar nature. Notwithstanding some exceptions, the European agencies are mostly entrusted with administrative or technical prerogatives ancillary to decision-making. This *status quo* appears to be the result of the unwillingness of

341 See, however, for a working typology of EU agencies according to the criterion of control/supervision over their legal instruments for international cooperation, Ott, Vos and Coman-Kund (n 239) 100.

the agencies' creators to grant more leeway to these bodies, based *inter alia* on a static reading of the principle of institutional balance and the *Meroni* doctrine of delegation of powers. However, the recently created financial supervisory authorities (ESAs) prove that significant decision-making powers can also be entrusted to the EU agencies. This is the more significant as such powers have been validated by CJEU in its *ESMA* Judgment. Importantly, in *ESMA* the Court confirmed the application of the *Meroni* doctrine for assessing the legality of EU agencies' powers, but, at the same time, the judgment displayed the willingness of the Court to read the *Meroni* requirements and the principle of institutional balance in a quite flexible manner.

As regards the interactions between European agencies and their external environment most intensive formal relations are established with the main EU institutions (in particular, the Commission and/or the Council, and increasingly the European Parliament) in such a way that one could question whether the right balance between control, accountability and formal autonomy of these bodies is reached. It is difficult to draw general conclusions about the way in which the relationships with other actors like national and international bodies influences the role and operation of EU agencies. A case-by-case basis approach seems to be most appropriate in this regard.

Overall, the European agencies seem to be placed 'at a crossroads' between implementation and decision-making, between expertise and policy-making, in a complex environment populated with various actors from different levels of governance. While enjoying formal or legal autonomy, the organisation and functioning of these bodies, as well as their interactions with the Council, the Commission and the Member States, suggest a complex 'principal(s)-agent' relationship, entailing that EU agencies are acting mostly in the furtherance of the interests of the main EU institutions and the Member States, and under their supervision and control.

The investigation of the EU agencies' practice reveals that most of these bodies pursue, more or less extensively, various forms of international cooperation. This may consist of informal contacts and exchanges with non-EU partners or it may result in various supporting and assistance activities carried out within the framework of wider EU initiatives and instruments. Importantly, the relationships between the EU agencies and their partners are often formalised through the conclusion of instruments resembling international agreements. There are some variations between EU agencies and sometimes with regard to the same agency as far as the names and the content of their formal international cooperation instruments are concerned. Another apparent source of differentiation relates to the context in which the formal cooperation instrument is concluded (as a milestone in formalising cooperation on a technical level or as an implementing tool within the framework of international agreements concluded by the EU).

With a few exceptions, the international cooperation practice of the EU agencies finds support more or less in their formal legal framework, in particular in their founding acts. Variations range from EU agencies whose international cooperation mandate is depicted in broad terms, to agencies whose founding acts regulate their powers and scope for international cooperation more into detail, but without explicitly naming the international cooperation instruments which they may use, and finally to agencies benefiting from express provisions regarding their formal cooperation instruments. Generally, the legal framework also sets various limitations and conditions on the international cooperation mandate of EU agencies. In most cases, the founding acts clearly circumscribe the agencies' ability to pursue international cooperation to their core mandate. In some instances, the founding acts explicitly subordinate the international cooperation tasks and instruments of the EU agencies to the wider EU legal framework and policies. Yet, for a significant number of EU agencies, the founding acts place specific *ex ante* and *ex post* requirements and controls on their international cooperation powers and instruments. However, only in few cases, the founding acts include some indications as to the legal nature and effects of EU agencies' formal international cooperation instruments.

2 A legal blueprint for assessing EU agencies as global actors

2.1 Introduction

The insights from the practice of the EU agencies' international cooperation together with the overview of the legal design thereof presented in Chapter 1 already provided an overview of the international dimension of these bodies. However, in order to assess the legal nature and consequences of the international cooperation mandate, powers and instruments of EU agencies, as well as their compatibility with the Union's constitutional framework, a wider legal blueprint is needed. This encompasses both EU legal provisions and principles, as well as concepts and criteria from international law. It corresponds to the two facets or angles required for the analysis of the EU agencies as global actors: the internal (EU law) angle and the external (international law) angle.

The EU law angle pertains to the way in which the external tasks and powers of the European agencies, as well as their international practice, fit within their 'domestic' legal system – ie the EU legal-institutional framework (section 2.2). The international law angle is essential for assessing the external relations of EU agencies on the international plane (section 2.3). Some of the elements of this blueprint (institutional balance, delegation of powers, the legal framework in the core policy areas of the EU agencies) concern EU agencies in general and become relevant also for assessing their international dimension. The inclusion of other elements (the EU external action framework, the concepts of 'international treaty' or 'international agreement' and 'international legal personality') is triggered specifically by the international cooperation carried out by the EU agencies. This complex legal blueprint is expected to put the international dimension of the EU agencies in perspective by enabling a legal analysis of what these bodies are doing and what they may do as global actors. In other words, it offers a reference system for assessing: the legal nature and effects of EU agencies' external powers and instruments; the requirements and limits set on their mandate and powers; whether EU agencies' international cooperation framework and practice are in line with the EU constitutional framework; and their legal status as 'global actors'.

2.2 The European Union law dimension

The wider EU legal blueprint for assessing the international cooperation formal design and practice of the EU agencies consists of three main elements. First, there are legal principles and standards, namely institutional balance and 'delegation' of powers, which govern the powers of the EU agencies in general. In the absence of an explicit derogation, it follows that such principles and standards are also relevant parameters for the external powers of the EU agencies. More specifically, the requirements and conditions derived from such principles and standards must be observed in the EU agencies' legal framework and practice regarding international cooperation. In this way, it is possible to assess the relevant legal framework pertaining to the EU agencies' international dimension, and whether the actions and instruments they use in practice match their formal framework. From a broader perspective, EU agencies' legal design and actions must also observe general EU legal principles such as conferral, subsidiarity and proportionality, but the focus has been put deliberately on institutional balance and the *Meroni* doctrine as these are considered as having direct and immediate relevance for assessing EU agencies' international cooperation mandate and practice. Moreover, the *Meroni* requirement that EU agencies' powers stay within the boundaries of their regulatory framework entails arguably that the above-mentioned principles are observed.

Secondly, and linked to the previous point, the wider legal framework corresponding to the policy areas in which the EU agencies are competent is of importance for diagnosing their international dimension. In particular, relevant Treaty provisions, the founding acts and other secondary law sources delimit the role and core mandate of the EU agencies, and establish the relationship between these bodies and other players in the same field. This is something which EU agencies cannot ignore when pursuing international cooperation.

Thirdly, the Union's external action legal framework becomes essential for assessing the compatibility of the international dimension of the EU agencies with the EU constitutional system. Specific Treaty provisions deal with the legal status of the EU as an international actor, define the roles and tasks of the main actors with regard to policy-making and treaty-making, and lay down a particular institutional balance in this area.

The three elements provide standards for determining the legal status which EU agencies may acquire as global actors from an EU law perspective, and the role which may be assigned to these bodies in international relations. They offer a reference system for assessing EU agencies' formal provisions on international cooperation and their practice (instruments) within the Union legal system.

2.2.1 The principle of institutional balance and the doctrine of delegation of powers as legal yardsticks for evaluating the international dimension of EU agencies

The main yardsticks against which the international actions of the EU agencies should be assessed are the principle of institutional balance, as well as the doctrine of delegation of powers.[1] In this context, the specific institutional balance in EU external relations is particularly relevant for assessing EU agencies' international dimension. This entails, in a first step, clarifying who does what and what is the balance of powers established

1 For a detailed analysis of the application of the principle of institutional balance and of the *Meroni* doctrine to EU agencies see ch 1, 1.5.1: Powers. The application of the *Meroni* doctrine to the international cooperation tasks of EU agencies is discussed in more detail later in this chapter, section 2.2.3.5: EU agencies and institutional balance in EU external relations.

by the Treaties between the EU institutions and, then, in a second step, establishing whether the external powers and actions of EU agencies disturb this balance.

The main tool ensuring that the EU agencies do not affect the institutional balance within the EU is the delegation of powers doctrine or the so-called *Meroni* doctrine.[2] The *Meroni* requirements as interpreted by CJEU in *ESMA* are relevant standards for assessing the overall delegated powers of the EU agencies, and, therefore, they are also applicable to their international powers and activities. Moreover, the specific features of EU agencies' international dimension entails in particular that EU agencies must not encroach upon the powers conferred by the Treaties on the EU institutions in Union's external action area.

This requires a close examination of the legal mandate and design of the EU agencies. Additionally, it must be investigated whether the EU agencies' actions and instruments in exercising their powers remain within the realm of their legal mandate.[3] This aspect could become particularly problematic when EU agencies exercise powers that are stipulated in broad terms in their founding acts, or when, in practice, these bodies perform actions and use specific instruments that are not explicitly provided for by their legal framework. Arguably, from a functional perspective, such actions and instruments could remain, in principle, within the mandate of the agency as long as they are instrumental to attaining the agency's mission and objectives.[4] Moreover, the existence of various conditions and supervisory mechanisms limiting the discretion of the agency in the exercise of such powers could result in a 'pass' in relation to the *Meroni* test.

2.2.2 The relevant legal framework governing the EU agencies' policy areas

The general legal framework of the EU agencies provides the system of reference for assessing the powers of these bodies in light of institutional balance and the *Meroni* doctrine. This overall legal framework includes, in addition to the founding act of the agency, the Treaty provisions dealing with the respective policy area, as well as other relevant instruments of secondary legislation.[5]

The relevance of this legal framework for assessing the source, nature and extent of the EU agencies' powers has been confirmed in CJEU case law.[6] In *ENISA*, the Court

2 For a detailed discussion see ch 1, 1.5.1: Powers.

3 Florin Coman-Kund, 'Assessing the Role of EU Agencies in the Enlargement Process: The Case of the European Aviation Safety Agency' (2012) 8 CYELP 335, 352.

4 Such a view seems to find support in Case C-270/2012 *United Kingdom v Parliament and Council* EU:C:2014:18 (the *ESMA* Judgment), para 85. Moreover, this functional view is also embraced with regard specifically to the international cooperation of EU agencies in the Common Approach on EU agencies, Joint Statement of the European Parliament, the Council of the EU and the European Commission on decentralised agencies of 19 July 2012 (Common Approach on EU agencies) para 25 ‹http://europa.eu/about-eu/agencies/overhaul/index_en.htm›.

5 Including other legislative instruments conferring new tasks on the agencies, implementing acts of the founding regulation, general instruments regulating various aspects relevant for the mandate of EU agencies.

6 See eg Case 9/56 *Meroni & Co, Industrie Metallurgiche SpA v High Authority of the European Coal and Steel Community* EU:C:1958:7; and Case 10/56 *Meroni & Co., Industrie Metallurgiche, società*

derived from Article 114 TFEU (ex Article 95 EC) the possibility for the legislator to establish, under certain conditions, an EU body supporting the implementation of the harmonisation process in a certain policy area in the context of the internal market.[7] When assessing the objectives and tasks of the Agency against the subject-matter of the area of electronic communications, the Court pointed out that the founding regulation 'does not constitute an isolated measure, but forms part of a normative context circumscribed by (. . .)' several legislative instruments.[8] Lately, in *ESMA*, the legal framework employed by the CJEU for evaluating the powers delegated to this agency consisted of several Treaty provisions (Articles 114, 263, 265, 267, 277 and 290–291 TFEU)[9] and secondary law instruments (including legislative, delegated and implementing acts).[10] In assessing ESMA's powers against the *Meroni* conditions and the principle of institutional balance, the Court indicated that such powers must be read in conjunction with the relevant regulatory instruments in the field.[11] In this context, the Court adopted a functional-instrumental approach in justifying ESMA's powers by the necessary implications arising from the need to attain the overall objective in the respective area – ie the financial stability within the EU.[12]

A particularly relevant aspect for assessing the international dimension of the EU agencies is the gradual development of an external dimension of most EU policy areas in which the agencies operate. This development is already formalised generally in the Treaties,[13] whilst sectoral Treaty provisions in specific policy areas sometimes also provide for international cooperation.[14] Moreover, general[15] or specific international agreements[16] concluded by the Union with third countries and international organisations may include provisions on tasks of the EU agencies concerning their implementation. On top of that, aspects of the external dimension of EU policies are dealt

in accomandita semplice v High Authority of the European Coal and Steel Community EU:C:1958:8; Case C-217/04 *United Kingdom v Parliament and Council* EU:C:2006:279 (the *ENISA* Judgment), para 60; *ESMA* Judgment (n 4) paras 2–17 and 84–86.

7 *ENISA* Judgment (n 6) paras 44–45 and 47. See also Herwig C H Hofmann and Alessandro Morini, 'Constitutional Aspects of the Pluralisation of the EU Executive through "'Agencification"' (2012) 37 EL Rev 419, 427–28.

8 *ENISA* Judgment (n 6) para 60.

9 ibid paras 65, 78–86, 99–117.

10 *ESMA* Judgment (n 4) paras 2–17.

11 ibid paras 84–86.

12 ibid para 85.

13 Art 21(3) TEU. First, this provision marks a formal distinction between the external aspects of EU (other) policies and the different areas of the Union's external action, as a means to pursue its objectives on the international plane. Secondly, the Union's objectives are to be observed both in the process of development and in the ***implementation*** of the external dimension of its policy areas. Thirdly, a need for consistency between the Union's areas of external action and the external dimension of its internal policies is formally acknowledged. In this respect, the formal duty to ensure such consistency is assigned to the Council and the Commission. The latter aspect is also an important indicator as to the institutional balance relevant for assessing EU agencies' international dimension.

14 eg transports [art 91(1)(a) TFEU], police cooperation [art 88(2)(a) TFEU], area of freedom security and justice [arts 78(2)(g) and 79(3) TFEU], environment [art 191(1) and (4) TFEU].

15 eg Agreement on the European Economic Area (EEA) [1994] OJ L1/3.

16 eg the bilateral aviation safety agreements (BASAs) with the USA, Canada and Brazil.

with in acts of secondary legislation and in various policy papers (eg Commission communications and Council conclusions).

The overall external dimension of the Union policy areas addressed by the core mandate of the EU agencies is an important aspect for assessing their international dimension in light of institutional balance and *Meroni*. It is also a borderline element of the EU wider legal framework for assessing the international dimension of the EU agencies. The external dimension of a certain policy area is developed with a view to attaining the (internal) objectives in that core area and is dependent thereupon, whilst this external dimension is also inextricably linked to the wider EU external action area as regards the means and instruments used.[17]

2.2.3 The EU external action area

2.2.3.1 Conceptual clarifications

In this study, a broad view on the Union's external relations or action is taken,[18] according to which the Union's external relations encompass the international activities performed in all EU policy areas from EU external policies to the external aspects of its internal policies.[19] Such a view also finds support in the Founding Treaties after Lisbon with the introduction of an all-inclusive 'Union's external action' in the TEU (Title V) and in the TFEU (Part Five). It goes without saying that the 'EU's external environment' includes international organisations, third countries and other subjects of international law, except for the Member States and their organs.[20]

The Union's external action system comprises two inextricably linked dimensions: a substantive-instrumental dimension and an institutional dimension. The substantive-instrumental dimension encompasses the whole range of external competences conferred upon the Union, their nature together with the actions and the instruments through which such competences materialise.[21] In line with the broad view taken on the EU's external action area, it includes both formal powers and actions (eg treaty-making) and rather ad hoc and informal instruments and activities (eg various international cooperation arrangements). The institutional view focuses on the

17 See generally Marise Cremona, 'Defining Competence in EU External Relations: Lessons from the Treaty Reform Process' in Alan Dashwood and Marc Maresceau (eds), *Law and Practice of EU External Relations: Salient Features of a Changing Landscape* (CUP 2008) 42 and 46–59. For a similar approach applied to the AFSJ area, see Jörg Monar, 'The External Dimension of the EU's Area of Freedom, Security and Justice. Progress, Potential and Limitations after the Treaty of Lisbon' (2012) 1 *Sieps* 11.

18 After Lisbon, everything pertaining to Union's external dimension seems to be covered by 'EU international relations', Cremona (n 17) 47 and 66.

19 See Andrea Ott and Ramses A Wessel, 'The EU's External Relations Regime: Multilevel Complexity in an Expanding Union' in Steven Blockmans and Adam Lazowski (eds), *The European Union and Its Neighbours* (TMC Asser Instituut 2006) 20–22.

20 This choice is justified by the special nature and characteristics of the EU, although from a formal-legal perspective, the EU and its Member States are separate subjects of international law.

21 Eeckhout also points to the substantive side of Union's external competences (ie the power to pursue a policy in a certain domain) and the instrumental side thereof (ie the capacity to conclude treaties), Piet Eeckhout, *EU External Relations Law* (2nd edn, OUP 2011) 75.

actors and mechanisms enabling the EU to exercise its external competence and to perform its external tasks.

2.2.3.2 The EU external action area after Lisbon

The Union's external action system has been shaped incrementally through case law, EU secondary acts, treaty revisions, and institutional practices. One of the most recent milestones in the EU's evolution was the Lisbon Treaty, which paved the way for new developments in the Union's external relations area.

The Lisbon Treaty had a direct impact on the Union's international legal status by formally suppressing the pillars and by explicitly establishing a single legal personality for the EU.[22] This put an end to the controversy regarding the (international) legal personality of the EU along with that of the former Community.[23] The post-Lisbon international legal personality of the Union is considered to have enabled the introduction of a single procedure for the negotiation and conclusion of the EU international agreements (ie Article 218 TFEU).[24] Furthermore, it has arguably important implications for the possibility of various elements of the EU institutional framework to acquire their own legal status on the international plane.

One cross-cutting innovation post-Lisbon is that the EU external relations area is better systematised. In spite of persisting variations between the EU policy fields, all aspects pertaining to Union's international dimension are brought under one framework called the 'Union's external action' and are made subject to a set of common values and principles.[25] The underlying logic behind this development seems to rely on the increasing need for consistency in the Union's external relations.[26] It is, however, interesting to note, as compared to the pre-Lisbon situation, the formal delineation in Article 21(3) TEU between the areas of the Union's external action and the external aspects of its internal policies. This might also imply that the EU's external action system could gradually become a policy area on its own.[27]

The Lisbon Treaty also attempted to make clearer the delineation between the Union's categories of competences. According to Articles 2–6 TFEU, the EU's competences are exclusive, shared or complementary. This categorisation is also relevant with regard to the nature of the EU's external powers developed mainly through case law and institutional practice.[28] Furthermore, Article 3(2) TFEU specifically provides for several instances in which the Union's power to conclude international treaties has an exclusive character.[29]

22 Art 47 TFEU.

23 See Cremona (n 17) 38; Jean-Claude Piris, *The Lisbon Treaty. A Legal and Political Analysis* (CUP 2010) 86–87.

24 Piris (n 23) 87.

25 Title V, ch 1, arts 21–22 TEU. See also Marise Cremona, 'The Draft Constitutional Treaty: External Relations and External Action' (2003) CML Rev 40 1347, 1348–49 and Piris (n 23) 242–43.

26 See Paul Craig, *The Lisbon Treaty: Law, Politics and Treaty Reform* (OUP 2010) 425.

27 According to Cremona, this framework of general objectives and principles seems to be tailored specifically for the EU's external action, thereby entailing the possibility for loosening the external policy of the Union from its internal objectives and policies, unlike the pre-Lisbon situation, Cremona (n 17) 69.

28 ibid 60–62.

29 According to this provision, the Union's exclusive competence would cover any instance involving the conclusion of an international agreement when: 1. the conclusion of such an international

Two important remarks concern the EU's external instruments and, in particular, the international agreements post-Lisbon. First, the Union's power to conclude international agreements has arguably been extended according to Article 216 TFEU in line with the relevant previous case law of the CJEU.[30] It should be noted that this provision is closely related to Article 3(2) TFEU previously mentioned.[31] Secondly, the provisions regarding the negotiations and conclusion of EU international treaties have been reshaped. Thus, the provisions regarding the negotiation and conclusion of Union's international agreements, including in the CFSP area, have been regrouped in one place (ie Article 218 TFEU).[32] Furthermore, the procedure for negotiating and concluding agreements has been slightly modified.[33]

Not less importantly, the Lisbon Treaty brought some amendments to the institutional framework of the Union's external action. One of the most visible institutional innovations introduced by the Lisbon Treaty are the High Representative for Foreign Affairs and Security Policy (High Representative) together with the supporting European External Action Service (EEAS).[34] Other changes impacting upon the EU's external action system flow from the institutionalisation of the European Council.[35] First, Article 22 TEU formalises the European Council's role to ensure the strategic political leadership over the whole spectrum of the Union's external action area.[36] Secondly, the President of the European Council is given a role in Union's external representation in the CFSP area.[37] Furthermore, the amendments to the procedure for the negotiation and conclusion of EU international agreements entail an increased role for the European Parliament[38] and the inclusion of the High Representative in the process.[39]

Relevant for this study is also the formalisation in Article 17(1) TEU of the general role of the Commission to ensure the external representation of the EU.[40] This provision is said to codify the pre-Lisbon practice of the external representation of the former 'Community',[41] but arguably it has important consequences for the issue of institutional balance in EU external relations. The question arises whether and in how far is the Commission involved with regard to all the issues related to the Union's

agreement is provided in an EU legislative act; 2. the international agreement is necessary to enable the EU to exercise its internal competence; 3. the said international agreement may affect common rules or alter their scope.

30 Craig (n 26) 398–99.

31 ibid 399–400.

32 Piris (n 23) 259.There are derogations, however (discussed later in this chapter).

33 ibid 259–60.

34 The relevant general Treaty provisions are: arts 18, 21–22, 24, 26–27, 30, 34, 36, 38 TEU and arts 218, 220–221 TFEU (for the High Representative) and art 27(3) TEU (for EEAS). See on this Jan Wouters, Dominic Coppens and Bart de Meester, 'The European Union's External Relations after the Lisbon Treaty' in Stefan Griller and Jacques Ziller (eds), *The Lisbon Treaty. EU Constitutionalism without a Constitutional Treaty* (Springer 2008) 150; Piris (n 23) 243–58; Antonio Missiroli, 'Implementing the Lisbon Treaty: The External Policy Dimension' (2010) 14 Bruges Political Research Papers ‹http://aei.pitt.edu/14448/›.

35 Craig (n 26) 383–84.

36 See Wouters, Coppens and de Meester (n 34) 149–50.

37 Art 15(6) TEU.

38 Piris (n 23) 286–87.

39 See art 218(3), (6) and (9) TFEU.

40 Except for the CFSP area.

41 Piris (n 23) 230.

external representation,[42] with the exclusion of other EU institutional actors, such as the European agencies. Whereas in a broad sense, 'external representation' could encompass all forms of expression of the EU position on the international scene, including the negotiation and conclusion of international agreements,[43] the Commission's view was that it ensures the Union's external representation on all different levels.[44] Yet Article 17(1) TEU must be read in conjunction with Articles 16(6) and 21(3) TEU as well as Articles 218[45] and 220–221 TFEU which also grant a role in external representation to other actors, such as the Council and the High Representative. The Commission indeed acknowledged the complexity related to ensuring the EU external representation, which requires the participation of and coordination with various institutional actors.[46]

Recently, the Commission's role in EU external relations has benefited from some clarification from the CJEU in Case C-660/13.[47] In that case the Court decided that the Commission cannot derive an autonomous power to sign 'a non-binding agreement resulting from negotiations conducted with a third country' solely on the basis on its role of external representation under Article 17(1) TEU as this entailed policy-making aspects,[48] which required Council's prior approval.[49]

2.2.3.3 Some relevant aspects regarding the Union's external competences and instruments

2.2.3.3.1 THE UNION'S EXTERNAL COMPETENCES

The Union's external powers are subjected to the principle of conferral, meaning that they are limited to the specific competences transferred by the Member States *via* the Founding Treaties.[50] The development of the Union's external competences was based initially on a set of general objectives and principles explicitly mentioned in or derived from the Treaties, which the CJEU has interpreted in a purposive manner. It has also been based gradually on the express provisions providing for external powers in various policy areas.[51] Hence, there is a distinction between implied and express

42 eg relations on a diplomatic and technical level with third countries and international organisations, participation in international organisations, negotiation of international agreements, EU delegations.

43 Commission, *Vademecum on the External Action of the European Union*, SEC (2011) 881/3 21.

44 Head of state and government, ministerial and expert levels, *Vademecum on the External Action* (n 43) 18.

45 According to the Commission, international agreements are a specific form of EU representation, *Vademecum on the External Action* (n 43) 21.

46 ibid 17–55.

47 Case C-660/13 *Council v Commission* EU:C:2016:616. *In casu*, the Council asked for the annulment of a Commission decision on the signature of an addendum to the 2006 Memorandum of Understanding on a Swiss contribution to the new Member States concluded between the EU and Switzerland.

48 ibid paras 38 and 40.

49 ibid paras 38 and 46.

50 Eeckhout (n 21) 97. See also Opinion 2/94 *Accession by the Community to the European Convention for the Protection of Human Rights and Fundamental Freedoms* EU:C:1996:140.

51 See for instance former arts 131–134 TEC (ex arts 110–114) on the common commercial policy; former art 310 TEC (ex art 238) on association agreements; former art 174 TEC (ex art 130r) on environmental policy; former arts 177–181 TEC (ex arts 130u–130y) on development cooperation.

external powers. Implied external powers were gradually developed by the Court starting with the *ERTA* judgment[52] whereas express external powers were expanded through successive treaty-reforms.[53]

As regards the progressive development of the Union's implied external competences through the *ERTA* line of case law, several points need to be emphasised.[54] In *ERTA*, the Court began by affirming the international legal personality of the former Community[55] in order to derive the Union's general capacity to conclude international agreements in relation to the range of objectives mentioned in the Treaty.[56] The most remarkable element was, however, the recognition by the Court of the Union's power to conclude an international agreement in the absence of an express provision in the Treaty to that effect.[57] The Court came to this result by taking a functional approach, in that it regarded external relations as a necessary corollary of the Union's internal competences.[58] Therefore, there was no need to have explicit provisions on external competence because such powers can be implied from (and also limited to) the necessities of pursuing Union's objectives and internal competences. Another innovative element flowing from this was the recognition of the capacity of the EU institutions to influence the scope and nature of Union's external powers via secondary acts.[59] This influence of the EU institutions has been further clarified in the *WTO Opinion*.[60] More specifically, the Court accepted that the EU legislature may incorporate external relations provisions in secondary acts, and that it can confer on Union institutions powers to negotiate with third countries.[61]

The Union's explicit or express external competence was initially limited to common commercial policy, association agreements, and to establishing cooperation with international organisations,[62] but it was expanded over time through treaty revisions.[63] The Treaty of Lisbon can be regarded as the beginning of a new era in the Union's external action,[64] by inserting *inter alia* a horizontal provision concerning the

52 Case 22/70 *Commission v Council. European Agreement on Road Transport (ERTA Judgment)* EU:C:1971:32.

53 Eeckhout (n 21) 101–02.

54 For an overview of the CJEU case law regarding the doctrine of implied powers see Eeckhout (n 21) 70–119.

55 The international legal capacity of the Community had already been recognised by the Court in Case 6/64 *Flaminio Costa v ENEL* EU:C:1964:66.

56 See Eeckhout (n 21) 114; Ott and Wessel (n 19) 23.

57 Eeckhout (n 21) 75.

58 This has been labelled as the doctrine of parallelism or the complementarity principle, see Ott and Wessel (n 19) 24; Wouters, Coppens and de Meester (n 34) 168, 174 and 178.

59 *ERTA* Judgment (n 52) para 16.

60 Opinion 1/94 *Competence of the Community to conclude international agreements concerning services and the protection of intellectual property* (*WTO*) EU:C:1994:384, para 95; see also Eeckhout (n 21) 92–93.

61 See Eeckhout (n 21) 92–93. Whereas the *WTO Opinion* dealt with a specific situation, the logic according to which the EU legislature has discretion to insert external relations provisions and to delegate external relations powers to elements of the Union's institutional framework within the limits laid down by the Treaties could arguably be extended to the international dimension of EU agencies.

62 Eeckhout (n 21) 70.

63 For an overview, see Ott and Wessel (n 19) 25–26.

64 See Wouters, Coppens and de Meester (n 34) 168–80.

competence of the Union to conclude international agreements. A reading of Article 216(1) TFEU suggests that there will be hardly any areas in which the Union will not be able to enter into international agreements.[65] There are thus four situations in which the Union may conclude agreements: (1) '(. . .) where the Treaties so provide'; (2) where the agreement '(. . .) is necessary in order to achieve, within the framework of the Union's policies, one of the objectives referred to in the Treaties'; (3) where the conclusion of the treaty '(. . .) is provided for in a legally binding Union act'; (4) when the agreement '(. . .) is likely to affect common rules or alter their scope'.[66] In particular the third situation is relevant as concerns the international dimension of EU agencies as it can be seen as a partial codification of the stance taken by the Court in the *WTO Opinion* with regard to the possibility to include external relations provisions in acts of secondary legislation.[67]

2.2.3.3.2 THE UNION'S EXTERNAL ACTION INSTRUMENTS

The external powers of a given international legal entity usually materialise due to the conclusion of (binding) international agreements in the areas covered by the external competences entrusted to that entity. The capacity to conclude treaties, together with the resulting instruments, is also regarded as an important indicator of whether that entity has international legal personality.[68] Although from a legal point of view, formal treaties are probably the most important means for the exercise of external competences, in practice there are also other types of actions and instruments through which competences can be exercised on the global level. These other means are more or less formalised and have various names, such as unilateral actions, resolutions, declarations, memoranda of understanding, administrative arrangements, working arrangements, protocols, exchange of letters/notes, exchange of information, or practices.[69] The use of such external action instruments raises questions as to the legal consequences they might entail, if any.

As far as the EU external action instruments are concerned, the relevant Treaty provisions focus on the Union's treaty-making capacity as illustrated by the horizontal provisions concerned with EU's external competences such as Articles 3(2) and 216 TFEU. The same holds true for Article 218 TFEU laying down the general or 'ordinary'[70] procedure for the conclusion of international agreements by the EU, without mentioning other types of external action instruments. The formal procedure

65 Eeckhout (n 21) 122–23.

66 The first case envisages the explicit power to conclude treaties while the other three rather build upon the CJEU jurisprudence on implied powers, see Eeckhout (n 21) 122–23.

67 However, the formula 'legally binding Union act' included in art 216(1) TFEU may incorporate both legislative and non-legislative acts, and does not mention the word 'institution' thereby surpassing arguably the Court's stance in the *WTO Opinion*.

68 See Nigel D White, *The Law of International Organisations* (Manchester University Press 2005) 42.

69 For an extensive analysis of the terminology and various types of instruments used in the international practice see Anthony Aust, *Modern Treaty Law and Practice* (CUP 2013) 14–25 and 28–50.

70 See for the use of this term Robert Schütze, *Foreign Affairs and the EU Constitution. Selected Essays* (CUP 2014) 383.

assigns specific roles to the three main EU institutions involved in the legislative process (ie the Council, the Commission and the European Parliament) and also to the High Representative for Foreign Affairs and Security Policy, reflecting the institutional balance with regard to the Union's treaty-making.[71] The general distribution of tasks under Article 218 TFEU is as follows:

- the Commission (or the High Representative as far as the agreement in the CFSP area are concerned) has the right to activate the procedure by submitting recommendations to the Council[72]
- the Council decides to open the negotiations and appoints the Union negotiator[73]
- the Commission is normally in charge of the negotiations, in consultation with a special committee designated by the Council[74]
- the Council adopts negotiating directives, oversees the negotiation process through the special committee, authorises the signing of the agreement, and concludes it[75]
- the European Parliament has the right to be immediately and fully informed at all stages of the procedure,[76] and to express its consent or opinion *prior* to Council's decision to conclude the agreement.[77]

So far, the Union has concluded a number of bilateral and multilateral treaties covering a wide spectrum of the EU's competence areas. These agreements, either mixed or exclusively concluded by the EU, further display particular features on the basis of various factors like the area concerned, the issues they pertain to, the institutional settings or particular arrangements with contracting parties.[78] The Union's international practice also features peculiar situations where instruments labelled as 'voluntary partnership agreements' (thereby suggesting non-binding international agreements) nevertheless may turn out to be legally binding treaties based on their content and on the fact that they are concluded according to the 'Article 218 TFEU' procedure.[79]

71 Eeckhout (n 21) 193.
72 Art 218(3) TFEU.
73 ibid.
74 Art 218(3)–(6) does not refer explicitly to the Commission, but uses the term 'negotiator' instead. However, Eeckhout argues that a proper reading of art 218 TFEU leads to the conclusion that the 'the Commission continues to negotiate international agreements, except those which relate exclusively or principally to the CFSP', Eeckhout (n 21) 196.
75 Art 218(2) and (4)–(6) TFEU.
76 Art 218(10) TFEU.
77 Art 218(6) TFEU.
78 For an overview of various types of agreements concluded by the EU, see Ramses A Wessel, 'The EU as a Party to International Agreements: Shared Competences, Mixed Responsibilities' in Alan Dashwood and Marc Maresceau (eds), *Law and Practice of EU External Relations: Salient Features of a Changing Landscape* (CUP 2008) 152–87; an extended and regularly updated overview of the international treaties/agreements concluded by the Union can be found in the Treaties Office Database of the EEAS ‹http://ec.europa.eu/world/agreements/default.home.do›.
79 eg Voluntary Partnership Agreement between the European Union and the Republic of Indonesia on forest law enforcement, governance and trade in timber products to the European Union (FLEGT) [2013] OJ L265/1.

The same applies as regards the memoranda of understanding[80] or memoranda of cooperation[81] concluded by the EU on the basis of Article 218 TFEU.

In addition to international agreements concluded according to Article 218 TFEU, in practice the Union employs other ways and instruments for the exercise of its external competences. Some of these instruments are explicitly provided for in the Treaties, whereas others are not, although they are used in the Union's daily external practice. In the first category, in which the instruments are provided for explicitly, one may include the restrictive measures and other unilateral external actions provided for in Article 215 TFEU. In the second category, in which the instruments are not provided for explicitly, the possibility for such instruments can be inferred from the rather broad and vague wording of some of the Treaty provisions, suggesting that there are other means for taking international action in addition to international agreements. Such examples can be found in Articles 189(3),[82] 191(4), and 212(3) TFEU.[83]

These more or less formalised instruments and actions may be enacted at a political level[84] and/or at a technical, operational and administrative level.[85] Everything ranging from international political statements or declarations by the President of the European Council, the High Representative or the Commission, the conclusion of various administrative agreements or arrangements, to daily administrative and technical activities[86] comes under this umbrella.[87] These instruments constitute the bulk of the Union's external action area. They are enacted sometimes to ensure cooperation in the absence of an 'Article 218 TFEU' agreement, to pave the way to such an agreement, or with a view to ensuring the implementation of 'Article 218 TFEU' agreements.

Whereas it is undisputed that the international agreements concluded by the Union according to Article 218 TFEU result in legally binding effects,[88] there is ambiguity concerning the legal nature and effects of the other international cooperation instruments used in the EU's external relations practice (not mentioned by the Treaties). One may wonder whether these instruments (or at least some of them) also entail some legal consequences or whether they remain exclusively within the

80 eg Memorandum of Understanding between the European Community and the National Tourism Administration of the People's Republic of China, on visa and related issues concerning tourist groups from the People's Republic of China (ADS) [2004] OJ L83/14.

81 eg Memorandum of Cooperation between the European Union and the International Civil Aviation Organization providing a framework for enhanced cooperation [2011] OJ L232/2.

82 According to this provision, the Union establishes '*appropriate relations* (emphasis added) with the European Space Agency'.

83 Both articles include an identically worded provision according to which '(. . .) the arrangements for Union cooperation *may* (emphasis added) be the subject of agreements (. . .)', thereby leaving open the possibility for other ways of cooperation with the third parties concerned.

84 eg general guidelines, declarations, statements.

85 eg memoranda, administrative arrangements, working arrangements, guidelines.

86 For a comprehensive overview of the relations between the Union and international organisations, see Iain Macleod, Ian D Hendry and Stephen Hyett, *The External Relation of the European Communities* (OUP 1996) 165–207.

87 For an overview, see *Vademecum on the External Action* (n 43) 21–36 and 52–55.

88 According to art 216(2) TFEU '[a]greements concluded by the Union are binding upon the institutions of the Union and on its Member States'.

political sphere.[89] Wessel, for instance, seems to consider the exchange of letters between the EU and a third country, the joint declarations and the memoranda of understanding (MOUs) concluded by various EU institutions and bodies with a third country or international organisation[90] as special categories of international agreements.[91] Is there a genuine difference between a MOU and an international agreement concluded by the EU, or could such a MOU be rather an international agreement in disguise?[92] Assessing this in practice is not always straightforward as there are often situations in which the borderline is difficult to draw.[93]

The fact remains that the EU institutions, with the most obvious example being the Commission,[94] have recourse extensively in practice to such *ad hoc* instruments. Arguably, they do so precisely in order to evade the legal problems and constraints related to formal international cooperation instruments.[95] Such a reality can be explained in terms of enhanced effectiveness and efficiency of the EU's external action. Pursuing international cooperation in a wide range of areas and in a very dynamic global world requires flexible and simplified instruments, in addition to the traditional treaties usually requiring long and rigid procedures. This is a salient feature of the present world of international relations, and the use of such simplified or *ad hoc* instruments is widespread in state practice and in the practice of international organisations.[96]

Inevitably, the recourse to international agreements and other formal and *ad hoc* instruments and actions also raises some important legal-institutional questions. First, one may wonder whether it is legally acceptable to use other international cooperation instruments than those explicitly provided for in the Treaties. This is particularly relevant in those instances in which instruments concluded outside the procedure provided for in Article 218 TFEU turn out to be legally binding. Secondly, the question arises which EU institutions are entitled to conclude international agreements and other instruments, and under which conditions. For instance, the Commission could use such instruments in the management of the EU's external relations by virtue of its role in ensuring the Union's external representation according to Article 17(1) TEU, and in establishing cooperation with international organisations in line with Article 220 TFEU. Arguably, the Council and the High Representative

89 Stephan Keukeleire and Jennifer MacNaughtan, *The Foreign Policy of the European Union* (Palgrave Macmillan 2008) 154; for examples, see Ramses A Wessel, 'Revisiting the International Legal Status of the EU' (2000) 5 *EFAR* 507, 532–33.

90 eg Memorandum of Understanding concerning the establishment of a strategic partnership between the European Commission and the United Nations Development Programme (signed on 28 June 2004).

91 See Wessel (n 78) 160 and 173. It is open to debate whether a MOU can only be a soft law instrument or whether it can also entail legal consequences, see Aust (n 69) 46–52.

92 For a view supporting a clear delineation between international treaties and MOUs, see Aust (n 69) 46–49; for an opposite view, see Jan Klabbers, *The Concept of Treaty in International Law* (Kluwer 1996) 108–15.

93 For an overview of various treaty-like instruments with an unclear legal status in international and state practice, see Klabbers (n 92) 15–36.

94 See in this chapter, 2.2.3.4.3: The international cooperation instruments concluded by the Commission and other EU institutions and bodies.

95 Aust (n 69) 54–55.

96 See Klabbers (n 92) 15–36.

could also employ various international cooperation instruments in fulfilling the roles assigned to them by the Treaties in the EU external action area.[97] As shown also by Case C-660/13, this issue has legal and practical relevance because it involves complex issues related to the Union's external representation and institutional balance. Thirdly, it should be investigated whether international cooperation tasks and instruments may be entrusted to other institutions and bodies which are not formally endowed with a role by the Treaties as regards the management of the EU's external action.

2.2.3.4 Institutional balance and delegation of powers in the EU external action area

2.2.3.4.1 THE MANAGEMENT OF THE EU EXTERNAL ACTION AREA

The management of the Union's external relations designates the manner in which the exercise of the Union's external competences and its overall international activities are organised and carried out. It encompasses both a political dimension and a technical-administrative dimension which are closely interlinked, and covers both binding and non-binding, as well as formal and more informal instruments and procedures occurring in Union's international practice.[98] On the one hand, the relevant actors envisaged by the Treaties play various roles in practice and make use of instruments which are not formally listed in the EU legal framework. On the other hand, other actors than those included in the standard institutional model laid down by the Founding Treaties, such as EU agencies, become involved in aspects pertaining to the management of EU's external relations.

Main actors

Whilst Article 22(1) TEU entrusts the European Council with the overall strategic political leadership in external relations matters,[99] this institution is not involved in the daily policy-making and management of the EU's external relations. The more detailed decision-making and implementation processes require the intervention of other actors (ie the Council, the Commission, the newly introduced High Representative of the Union for Foreign Affairs and Security Policy, and the Member States).[100]

It is the overall responsibility of the (Foreign Affairs) Council to '(. . .) elaborate the Union's external action on the basis of strategic guidelines laid down by the European Council and ensure that the Union's action is consistent'.[101] Similar to the *status quo* before Lisbon, Article 21 TFEU entrusts the Council with the formal decision-making powers regarding the use of the most important formal EU external action legal instruments (ie international agreements). Furthermore, according to

97 Arts 21 and 26 TEU, as concerns the Council, and arts 21, 26–27 TEU as well as arts 220–221 TFEU, as concerns the High Representative.

98 In practice, often it is not easy to draw the dividing line between these dimensions and types of instruments, see *Vademecum on the External Action* (n 43) 21–36 and 52–55.

99 See Wouters, Coppens and de Meester (n 34) 149–50.

100 Keukeleire and MacNaughtan (n 89) 69.

101 Art 16(6) TEU.

Article 215 TFEU, the Council formally adopts restrictive measures against third countries, non-Member State entities, natural or legal persons or groups. Last but not least, the Council shares with the Commission the role of ensuring overall consistency in Union's external action area.[102] The Commission initiates the formal decision-making process *via* proposals or recommendations[103] and is heavily involved in the negotiation of international agreements. Furthermore, from Articles 17(1) and 21(3) TEU, as well as from Article 220 TFEU it can be inferred that the Commission is in charge of the Union's external representation, and also of the overall management of its external relations.[104] The role of the European Parliament is slightly enhanced with regard to EU treaty-making by the extension of its assent powers, and by imposing a duty to inform the European Parliament at all stages of the procedure concerning the conclusion of international agreements.[105] However, the position of the European Parliament with regard to the overall management of the Union's external relations remains somewhat marginal.

All this suggests that the management of EU external relations remains largely between the Member States (the Council and the European Council) and the Commission.[106] This appears to be confirmed by Court's judgment in Case C-660/13, explaining that the EU external action is based on an institutional system whereby the European Council defines the strategic interests and objectives of the Union, the Council is in charge of policy-making, and more specifically it further elaborates Union's external action and ensures its consistency, whereas the Commission exercises executive and management functions and ensures Union's external representation.[107] From this judgment, one may also infer that the role of the Council under Article 16 TEU covers all instances where Union's external action involves policy-making aspects. One immediate consequence is that the Commission will need to liaise increasingly with the Council as regards its external relations actions and instruments, otherwise running the risk of being brought before the Court for breaching the principle of institutional balance.

To have a more complete picture of the institutional framework in the Union's external relations, it should be added that the Council and the Commission are assisted and/or complemented by the High Representative. On the basis of the relevant Treaty provisions,[108] it follows that the High Representative is a rather peculiar hybrid formula intended to ensure a tighter connection between CFSP and other policy fields, as well as to ensure better coordination between the main institutions involved in the management of EU external relations.[109] Suffice it to say in this regard that the High Representative participates in the work of the European Council, is a vice-president

102 Art 21(3) TEU.

103 Arts 215 and 218 TFEU.

104 Andrea Ott, 'EU Regulatory Agencies in EU External Relations: Trapped in a Legal Minefield between European and International Law' (2008) 13 EFAR 515, 521; see also *Vademecum on the External Action* (n 43) 18–19.

105 Art 218 (6) and (10) TFEU; see also Eeckhout (n 21) 199 and 202–05.

106 For more details regarding the arrangements and interactions between the main actors as regards the management of EU external relations and Union's external representation, see *Vademecum on the External Action* (n 43) 16.

107 Case C-660/13 *Council v Commission* (n 47) paras 33–34.

108 Arts 18, 21 and 27 TEU and arts 218, 220–221 TFEU.

109 That is, the European Council, but mostly the Council and the Commission, see also Piris (n 23) 245.

(for external relations) of the Commission, and presides over the Foreign Affairs Council. Next to the High Representative, Article 27(3) TEU has introduced the European External Action Service (EEAS) as a supportive structure for the High Representative in the exercise of its powers.[110] The EEAS is yet another *sui generis* hybrid EU body, which acts as a sort of horizontal external action service, whose staffing, tasks and functioning reflect the composite nature of the EU external action.[111]

Other (sectoral) actors in the Union's external action area

In addition to the main EU institutions entrusted with the management of the Union's external relations, other less ordinary actors are involved increasingly in this area, some of them claiming arguably their own international legal status. The most obvious examples are the European Central Bank (ECB), the European Investment Bank (EIB) and the EU agencies.

For some of these EU external actors, the Founding Treaties contain special provisions allowing for their involvement in international cooperation corresponding to their area of competence. The European Central Bank (ECB), for instance, is formally involved in the negotiation and conclusion of agreements regarding the exchange rate system and monetary or foreign exchange regime issues.[112] Moreover, Protocol No 4 (former Protocol No 18) on the Statute of the European System of Central Banks and of the European Central Bank attached to the Founding Treaties specifies in further detail the ECB's external relations tasks and instruments. Article 6(2) of the Protocol mentions explicitly the possibility for the ECB to participate in international monetary institutions. Moreover, the ECB is empowered to establish relations with relevant international institutions and with relevant bodies from third countries, and to perform various external actions pertaining to its mandate.[113] These provisions have been accompanied by a rich international practice developed by the ECB,[114] prompting some to conclude that this institution has acquired international legal personality, and the capacity to conclude international agreements.[115] The ECB's international legal personality has been qualified as derivative and limited to the ECB's specific area of

110 Council Decision 2010/427/EU of 26 July 2010 establishing the organisation and functioning of the European External Action Service [2010] OJ L201/30.

111 See Antonio Missiroli (n 34) 6–7; Piris (n 23) 249–55.

112 Art 219 TFEU.

113 Article 23 of Protocol No 4 on the Statute of the European System of Central Banks and of the European Central Bank [2012] OJ C326/230.

114 ECB has been granted observer status at the IMF, is a full member of the International Bank of Settlements, and participates in the work of the OECD – see ECB Monthly Bulletin, January 2001 60–67 ‹https://www.ecb.europa.eu/pub/pdf/mobu/mb200101en.pdf›. Moreover, the ECB has entered into cooperative arrangements, in particular MOUs, with central banks of third countries – ECB Annual Report 2013 159–60 ‹https://www.ecb.europa. eu/pub/pdf/annrep/ar2013en.pdf›.

115 Chiara Zilioli and Martin Selmayr, 'The External Relations of the Euro Area: Legal Aspects' (1999) 36 CML Rev 273, 282–86. One of the arguments invoked in support of ECB's international legal personality was the explicit reference in ex art 107 TEC (now art 129 TFEU) to ECB's legal personality. Interestingly, post-Lisbon, the legal personality of the ECB is provided for in art 282(3) TFEU in spite of its formal status as an EU institution.

competence.[116] This view has been rejected by other scholars, arguing in essence that the ECB is part of the EU institutional framework and, therefore, it can only act on behalf of the Union.[117] The CJEU took a similar view when qualifying the ECB as being part of the EU institutional framework.[118] The Lisbon Treaty took a step further by explicitly including the ECB in the category of EU institutions, from which one may infer a comparable legal treatment to that accorded to the other EU institutions.[119]

A somewhat similar case of an EU body claiming an autonomous legal status on the international plane is the European Investment Bank (EIB). According to Article 308 TFEU (ex Article 266 TEC), the EIB has its own legal personality, whilst Article 14 of Protocol No 5 (former Protocol No 11) on the Statute of EIB refers to the cooperation between this body and relevant international organisations, as well as institutions from third countries. This provision does not specify how such international cooperation should be implemented, but in practice the EIB managed to build up its international profile *inter alia* by concluding agreements with some states and by becoming one of the founding members of the European Bank for Reconstruction and Development (EBRD).[120] In view of its specific features and international practice, the EIB is said to have acquired the status of an 'international institution'[121] or, even more decisively, its own international legal personality distinct from that of the EU.[122] The Court, without specifically discussing the international legal status of the EIB, accepted that the Bank had its own separate legal personality[123] and full independence in pursuing its tasks, but pointed out at the same time that the EIB is answerable to the EU legal framework.[124] Unlike the case of ECB, the Lisbon Treaty does not list the EIB among the EU institutions, which leaves room for the argument that the EIB might acquire a different status in the international arena, compared to the main elements of the EU institutional framework.[125]

116 Zilioli and Selmayr (n 115) 284.

117 See Ramon Torrent, 'Whom is the European Central Bank the Central Bank of? Reaction to Zilioli and Selmayr' (1999) 36 CML Rev 1229.

118 Case C-11/00 *Commission v European Central Bank (ECB)* EU:C:2003:395, paras 63–65, 92 and 135. For a more nuanced view according to which the ECB as an EU institution did not have the power to conclude agreements on monetary issues, but still could be recognised in the banking sector as an international legal person with limited operational powers, see Eeckhout (n 21) 207–08.

119 For a view suggesting that ECB has kept its separate international legal personality also post Lisbon, see Henry G Schermers and Niels M Blokker, *International Institutional Law. Unity within Diversity* (Revised 5th edn, Martinus Nijhoff Publishers 2011) 994.

120 See D R R Dunnett, 'The European Investment Bank: Autonomous Instrument or Common Policy' (1994) 31 *CML Rev* 721, 732. More precisely, EIB and the EU are mentioned as distinct shareholders of the EBRD, see art 3 of the Agreement establishing the European Bank for Reconstruction and Development [1990] OJ L372/4.

121 Dunnett (n 120).

122 Zilioli and Selmayr (n 115) 282–83.

123 Interestingly, the Court added that the legal personality of the EIB was 'distinct from that of the Community', Case 85/86 *Commission v Board of Governors of the European Investment Bank* EU:C:1988:110, para 28.

124 ibid paras 28–30.

125 Schermers and Blokker (n 119) 994.

The EU agencies resemble, to some extent, the case of EIB, though these bodies developed an external dimension according to a slightly different scenario. In such cases, although the Founding Treaties did not provide for their involvement in EU external relations, it was nevertheless possible for such bodies to develop an external dimension *via* secondary law, in particular on the basis of their founding regulations and other relevant legal instruments. The picture is mixed, as some founding regulations are 'richer' in external relations provisions than others, but the practice of the European agencies reveals that they increasingly perform international cooperation actions within their own field of expertise, sometimes in spite of the rather poor or vague external relations provisions in their founding regulations.[126]

The emergence of these unusual global actors would arguably provide added value to the external dimension of EU policies and would also enhance the effectiveness of the EU as a global actor. These unconventional EU external actors also pose legal problems, particularly with regard to the institutional balance in the EU external relations area, and as regards Union's external representation and treaty-making. Moreover, the legal status such actors may acquire on the global level could arguably entail a fragmentation of the Union's international legal personality and affect the overall consistency of the Union's external action.

The general impression is that the institutional system put in place for the management of the Union's external relations is rather blurry. It is based on multiple and complex interlinks between the main actors involved, whose tasks are not always well defined and clearly delineated, which may at times cause tensions.[127] In spite of this complexity, the previous overview indicates that mostly the Council and the Commission are in charge of Union's external action. The Commission, however, remains a central actor as regards the daily management of EU external relations, including maintaining the Union's relations with international organisations and third countries. The situation is further complicated by the rise of other actors pursuing sector-specific international cooperation and claiming their own status on the international plane. This reality triggers the need for consistency, which was elevated by the Lisbon Treaty to the rank of an all-encompassing commandment for the Union's external action. Achieving this aim requires permanent, close and loyal cooperation between the elements of the EU's institutional external relations framework and, more broadly, also between the Union and the Member States.

2.2.3.4.2 TREATY-MAKING AND NON-LEGALLY BINDING INSTRUMENTS

In addition to the requirement that the balance of powers between institutions is not affected, there seems to be no absolute prohibition established by the Founding Treaties as regards the delegation of powers in the external action area. This entails that the main EU external relations actors may in principle delegate some of their

126 For an overview see ch 1, 1.7: The international dimension of EU agencies – practice and legal design.

127 As illustrated by the recent litigation between the Council and Commission in Case C-660/13 *Council v Commission* (n 47), and in the *ITLOS* case concerning the representation of the Union in proceedings before international courts, Case C-73/14 *Council v Commission (ITLOS)* EU:C:2015:663.

powers, provided that sufficient control over such powers is maintained so that the delegation does not amount to a surrender of powers.

A constant concern over time was the scope of the Commission's powers as regards EU representation, as well as the capacity of this institution to conclude formal cooperation agreements with third countries and international organisations.[128] More recently, the issue of the capacity of other EU institutions and bodies (EIB, ECB, EU agencies) to conclude international agreements has been raised.

Regarding specifically Union's binding international agreements, Article 218 TFEU features a procedure according to which the Council formally decides on the opening of negotiations, the signing and conclusion of the international agreements, while the Commission, in principle, can only propose and negotiate such agreements. On this division of tasks, the CJEU took a rather strict stance relying on the principle of institutional balance. The issue arose most famously in Case C-327/91 *France v Commission*[129] where the Commission invoked a general autonomous power to conclude international agreements as a projection of its internal powers.[130] In support of its claim, the Commission advanced far-reaching arguments, by claiming that, in matters pertaining to its executive powers, it could conclude 'international administrative agreements', requiring that the Council be merely informed.[131] The Court rejected this claim, essentially arguing that there is a particular institutional balance set by the Treaty with regard to the Union's international agreements entailing the conclusion of such agreements by the Council and not the Commission.[132] Furthermore, the Court held that this particular institutional balance laid down in Article 218 TFEU cannot be affected either by the internal powers vested in EU institutions or by the practice of the EU institutions.[133]

Three important issues need to be mentioned in the context of this case. First, in spite of the Commission's arguments that the contested instrument was merely an administrative agreement, which did not affect the domestic law of the parties and which, in case of non-performance, would simply be terminated,[134] the Court had no difficulties in qualifying the instrument as a binding international agreement.[135]

128 See Andrea Ott, Ellen Vos and Florin Coman-Kund, 'EU Agencies on the Global Scene: EU and International Law Perspectives' in Michelle Everson, Cosimo Monda and Ellen Vos (eds), *European Agencies in between Institutions and Member States* (Kluwer Law International 2014) 95–98; Barbara Dutzler, 'Representation of the EU and the Member States in International Organisations – General Aspects' in Stefan Griller and Birgit Weidel (eds), *External Economic Relations and Foreign Policy in the European Union* (Springer 2002) 159.

129 Case C-327/91 *France v Commission* EU:C:1994:305.

130 James Kingston, 'External Relations of the European Community: External Capacity versus Internal Competence' (1995) 44 ICLQ 659. *In casu*, the contested agreement had been concluded between the Commission and the US Government, and concerned the application of the competition law of the signatory parties (Case C-327/91 *France v Commission* (n 129) paras 2–12).

131 Case C-327/91 *France v Commission* (n 129) paras 30–31. The Commission referred specifically to agreements whose implementation did not require action by the Council, and which could be enacted within the limits of the existing budget without creating new financial obligations for the Union.

132 Case C-327/91 *France v Commission* (n 129) para 36.

133 ibid para 41.

134 ibid paras 21–22. See also Kingston (n 130) 662.

135 Case C-327/91 *France v Commission* (n 129) paras 15 and 23.

Secondly, the Court clarified that the Union, not the Commission, had international legal personality causing it to be bound as a result by the contested agreement.[136] Here it is interesting to note that the Court relied on ex Article 281 TEC providing that 'The Community shall have legal personality' in order to reach this conclusion. One may wonder whether such reasoning could be extended by analogy with regard to certain elements of the Union's institutional framework featuring a similar provision on legal personality either in the Founding Treaty or in relevant secondary law (ie ECB, EIB and the EU agencies). Thirdly, the Court admitted that the EU could be bound under international law by an agreement concluded in breach of EU law.[137]

In a second case *France v Commission* of 2004, the Court went even further by stating that the principle of institutional balance also needs to be observed with regard to non-legally binding international cooperation instruments.[138] In this context, the Court looked at the division of powers in the common commercial policy area in order to establish whether the Commission was competent to conclude the non-binding 'Guidelines' with the US competent authority.[139] The Court suggested that regardless of the legal nature of the 'Guidelines' concluded by the Commission with the US Government, the institutional balance would not be affected, since the Council had approved the underlying international cooperation instruments, and the committee set up under Article 207 TFEU (ex Article 133(3) TEC) had been regularly informed.[140]

What can be inferred from this case law is the Court's unwillingness to accept a general power to conclude binding agreements for the Commission, by using Article 218 TFEU as the sole legal standard for assessing the competence of the institutions with regard to the Union's treaty-making. The Court's view seems to hold true as the Lisbon Treaty removed the reference in ex Article 300(2) TEC to 'the powers vested in the Commission in this field'.[141]

This apparently rigid view of the CJEU on the institutional balance in the EU's external relations may be nuanced to some extent. First, the Court was concerned with emphasising the division of powers with regard to the Union's treaty-making in the context in which the Commission claimed a general power to conclude international agreements, based solely on its internal powers, and in the absence of any involvement from the Council. Secondly, the Court did not say explicitly that the Commission could never conclude an international agreement or that the Council could never delegate

136 ibid paras 24–25.

137 ibid para 25. See also Kingston (n 130) 669; Macleod, Hendry and Hyett (n 86) 131; Ott, Vos and Coman-Kund (n 128) 97.

138 Case C-233/02 *France v Commission* EU:C:2004:173, para 40; see also Peter van Elsuwege, *From Soviet Republics to EU Member States* (Martinus Nijhoff 2008) 180.

139 Case C-233/02 *France v Commission* (n 138) paras 40–41.

140 ibid para 41. From this angle, this case can be seen as a precursor of the Court's judgment in Case C-660/13 *Council v Commission* (n 47).

141 Under that provision of ex art 300 TEC, the Commission had concluded agreements on immunities and privileges of its diplomatic missions, as well as in order to enable cooperation with international organisations, but both the Court and the Advocate General Tesauro have considered this to be a derogation from the general rule regarding treaty making and, therefore, subject to strict interpretation: see Advocate General Opinion in Case C-327/91 *France v Commission* EU:C:1993:941, para 24; Kingston (n 130) 667.

such a power to the Commission.[142] As suggested both by Advocate General Tesauro and Advocate General Alber, this would rather mean that the power of the Commission to conclude agreements was specific and must necessarily flow from the powers conferred by the Council.[143] The Court seems to follow the same line when, in the first *France v Commission* case of 1994, it denied a general power for the Commission to make international agreements, analogous to that in Article 101 of the Euratom Treaty.[144] Thirdly, although the principle of institutional balance also needs to be observed with regard to more informal or soft law instruments,[145] the same division of powers as in the case of treaty-making is not necessarily at issue here. Accordingly, the bulk of these more informal international instruments arguably belongs to the Commission by virtue of its role in ensuring the external representation of the EU on the basis of Articles 17(1) TEU and 220 TFEU, and with due respect to the powers of the other EU actors. However, as demonstrated recently by Case C-600/13, the Commission cannot conclude alone, without Council's involvement, non-binding agreements entering the realm of policy-making in Union's external relations.

Whereas the rather strict stance taken by the Court on EU treaty-making seems to be backed up by Article 218(1) TFEU, suggesting a single procedure for Union's international agreements,[146] the delegation of treaty-making powers to the Commission or other actors should not be ruled out, provided that the prerogatives of the main actors involved in the 'Article 218 TFEU' procedure are not affected.[147] This requires not only authorisation and approval mechanisms by the Council but also the involvement of the European Parliament in accordance with its consent/consultation prerogatives, as well as oversight by the Commission over the negotiation process.

In this respect, the Founding Treaties themselves allowed for deviations from the standard institutional balance regarding treaty-making under Article 218 TFEU. To

142 According to one view, the judgment in Case C-327/91 *France v Commission* (n 129) leaves unclear the extent to which the Commission may conclude agreements binding the EU, see Macleod, Hendry and Hyett (n 86) 95. These authors mention three categories of agreements (on privileges and immunities, cooperation with international organisations and administrative arrangements) and express the opinion that in neither case should the Commission have the power to bind the EU (95–96).

143 Advocate General Opinion in Case C-327/91 *France v Commission* (n 141) paras 24 and 34, and Advocate General Opinion in Case C-233/02 *France v Commission* EU:C:2003:503, para 71.

144 Article 101 of the Euratom Treaty delineates between two categories of international agreements: (1) agreements negotiated and concluded by the Commission in accordance with the directives of the Council and subject to Council's approval; (2) agreements negotiated and concluded solely by the Commission (the Council is kept informed) where their '(. . .) implementation does not require action by the Council and can be effected within the limits of the relevant budget'. This provision can be seen as a formalisation of the distinction between legally-politically significant agreements and technical-administrative agreements of an implementing nature.

145 Soft law has been defined as referring to 'rules of conduct which, in principle, have no legally binding force but which nevertheless may have practical effects': Francis Snyder, 'The Effectiveness of European Community Law: Institutions, Processes, Tools and Techniques' (1993) 56 Modern Law Review 19, 32. For a recent analysis of the concept of 'soft law' and of soft law instruments at EU level, see Fabien Terpan, 'Soft Law in the European Union. The Changing Nature of EU Law' (2015) 21 *European Law Journal* 68.

146 See Piris (n 23) 87.

147 Generally on the delegation of treaty-making powers to the Commission and other EU institutions and bodies, see Schütze (n 70) 392–99.

begin with, explicit derogations are provided for by the Treaties in a few instances. Thus, Article 218(1) TFEU acknowledges the special procedure regarding the international agreements concluded in the area of common commercial policy.[148] Furthermore, although not explicitly mentioned in Article 218 TFEU, Article 219 TFEU provides for special procedures with regard to agreements on exchange rate systems for the euro and on monetary and foreign exchange regime matters. These procedures entail the possibility for the Council to delegate tasks regarding the negotiation and conclusion of such agreements. Also, Protocol No 7 on the Privileges and Immunities of the European Union still allows the Commission to conclude agreements for *laissez-passer*.[149]

Moreover, special Treaty provisions explicitly entrust other actors with external relations tasks. In these instances, the relevant Treaty provisions do not mention the conclusion of binding agreements, but they do not explicitly exclude this possibility altogether. In this context, it has been maintained that under Article 220 TFEU the Commission derived the power, by implication, to conclude agreements with international organisations, although this view is not undisputed.[150] In this respect, the statement of the Advocate General Tesauro in Case C-327/91 *France v Commission* is remarkable, according to which the Commission's capacity to conclude agreements was derived by implication from exercising the powers conferred on it by the Treaties in order to ensure the maintenance of appropriate relations with other international

148 A literal interpretation of the wording of art 218(1) TFEU suggests that the only exception allowed from the standard treaty-making procedure is art 207 TFEU. Such a restrictive interpretation is not acceptable as it would conflict with other Treaty provisions deviating from the procedure laid down by art 218 TFEU.

149 According to art 6 of Protocol No 7 'The Commission may conclude agreements for these *laissez-passer* to be recognised as valid travel documents within the territory of third countries.'

150 For a view supporting the Commission's power to conclude international agreements under art 220 TFEU see Dutzler (n 128) 159; for the opposite view see Macleod, Hendry and Hyett (n 86) 96 and 166–68. The Commission revealed that the cooperation established under art 220 TFEU covers political dialogue, thereby suggesting that the conclusion of binding international agreements is excluded under that provision – *Vademecum on the External Action* (n 43) 15. In practice, however, art 220 TFEU has been used in the past as a legal basis for concluding (binding) framework agreements with international organisations (eg the 'Trust Fund and Cofinancing Framework Agreement' with the World Bank on 8 November 2001, and the 'Financial and Administrative Framework Agreement' with the United Nations ('FAFA') on 29 April 2003). Moreover, the framework financing agreements concluded with international organisations also have political value, entailing that the legal basis provided by the financial regulations might not be sufficient and needs, therefore, to be complemented with TFEU art 220 – Explanatory Fiche on the basic procedure to be followed for the signature of Framework Agreements of Financial and Administrative nature with International Organisations (January 2008). Importantly, the Framework Agreement between the European Commission on behalf of the European Union and the International Bank for Reconstruction and Development, the International Development Association, the International Finance Corporation and the Multilateral Investment Guarantee Agency of 2014 has been concluded allegedly on the basis of the EU General Financial Regulation and art 220(1) TFEU, see Commission Decision of 25 July 2014 on the approval of the Framework Agreement between the European Commission on behalf of the European Union and the International Bank for Reconstruction and Development, the International Development Association, the International Finance Corporation and the Multilateral Investment Guarantee Agency C(2014)5432/F1.

organisations.[151] A similar approach could be followed with regard to the ECB and the EIB on the basis of the special Treaty provisions allowing them to establish relations with international organisations and third countries within the scope of their mandate. However, in such cases it is less clear whether agreements concluded by these actors would leave the institutional balance under Article 218 TFEU unaffected.

What is more, a flexible view of the institutional balance in external relations seems to be embraced by the EU legislator, entrusting limited external relations tasks to the Commission and to other actors, in particular the EU agencies. The most obvious examples are the financing agreements concluded by the Commission with third countries and international organisations on the basis of the EU Financial Regulations.[152] As shown in Chapter 1, the founding acts of some EU agencies also enable these bodies to conclude agreements or arrangements with third countries and international organisations. A common thread in all these cases is the fact that the enabled international cooperation is ancillary and instrumental to the implementation of the relevant secondary legislative instrument. One may wonder whether in these cases, and in particular where legally binding agreements are concluded by the Commission and the EU agencies, the EU legislator distorted the institutional balance under Article 218 TFEU, or whether it is still possible to conclude that the relevant secondary law provisions are compatible with the standard EU treaty-making procedure.

2.2.3.4.3 THE INTERNATIONAL COOPERATION INSTRUMENTS CONCLUDED BY THE COMMISSION AND OTHER EU INSTITUTIONS AND BODIES

The non-binding international cooperation instruments of various EU institutions and bodies should not disturb, in principle, the institutional balance in EU external relations, as long as these actors remain within the scope of their competences and observe the relevant requirements and conditions established by their legal framework.[153] What is legally problematic is the question whether the institutional balance specifically addressing the Union's treaty-making procedure leaves any room for other EU actors to conclude binding international agreements. First, one may wonder whether the Commission's international practice consisting of concluding binding agreements respects the balance of powers between the institutions. Secondly, one may

151 Opinion of Advocate General Tesauro in Case C-327/91 *France v Commission* (n 141) para 24.
152 Regulation (EU, Euratom) 966/2012 of the European Parliament and of the Council of 25 October 2012 on the financial rules applicable to the general budget of the Union and repealing Council Regulation (EC, Euratom) No 1605/2002 [2012] OJ L298/1, and Council Regulation (EU) 2015/323 of 2 March 2015 on the financial regulation applicable to the 11th European Development Fund [2015] OJ L58/17 (replacing Council Regulation (EC) 215/2008 of 18 February 2008 on the Financial Regulation applicable to the 10th European Development Fund).
153 For a view that the Commission has the power to conclude non-binding instruments as long as these are in line with the powers of the Commission and with relevant EU law, see Macleod, Hendry and Hyett (n 86) 95–96. In this regard, it is interesting to note the Commission's view post-Lisbon that, except for '(. . .) purely administrative arrangements, the Commission has a duty to keep the Council bodies fully informed about the preparation of non-binding instruments'. Moreover, when the instrument foreseen '(. . .) is not yet covered by an EU position, the Commission can sign it only after Council's approval or endorsement', see *Vademecum on the External Action* (n 43) 54–55.

wonder whether, and if so under which circumstances, other EU institutions and bodies, including EU agencies, may conclude international binding agreements without disturbing the principle of institutional balance.

The Commission

The international practice of the Commission features quite frequently instruments labelled as 'agreements' concluded outside the standard treaty-making framework laid down in Article 218 TFEU.[154] The terminology varies (eg financial administrative framework agreement,[155] framework agreement,[156] administration agreement,[157] contribution agreement[158]), but the common thread is that they pertain to administrative and operational cooperation between the Commission and other international organisations, as well as third countries.[159] Some of these agreements seem to be binding just like any international treaty, while the procedure[160] for concluding such instruments does not seem to involve other EU institutions directly. These agreements normally indicate that they are concluded by the Commission on behalf of the EU, but in some cases the title of the agreement refers only to the Commission as a party to the agreement.[161] In this context, it is interesting to note the Commission's view that its agreements establishing '(. . .) rights and duties on the basis of the Commission's

154 See Ott, Vos and Coman-Kund (n 128) 95–96.

155 eg the Financial Administrative Framework Agreement between the European Community, represented by the Commission of the European Communities and the United Nations (2003) ‹https://ec.europa.eu/europeaid/sites/devco/files/procedures-fafa-un-ec_en.pdf›. A consolidated version Financial and administrative framework agreement between the EU and the United Nations is in force since February 2014, European Commission, International Cooperation and Development, Financial and administrative framework agreement between EU and UN ‹https://ec.europa.eu/europeaid/node/45445›.

156 eg the Framework Agreement between the Commission of the European Communities ('Commission') and the International Monetary Fund ('IMF') of 2009 see also Commission, Directorate General for International Cooperation and Development, DEVCO Companion to financial and contractual procedures applicable to development and cooperation financed from the general budget of the EU and from the 11th EDF 43–44 ‹https://ids.euforneighbourhood.eu/download/companion-to-financial-and-contractual-procedures/›.

157 eg arts 1(b) and 2 of Framework Agreement between the European Commission on behalf of the European Union and the International Bank for Reconstruction and Development, the International Development Association, the International Finance Corporation and the Multilateral Investment Guarantee Agency (World Bank Group) of 2014 ‹http://ec.europa.eu/transparency/regdoc/rep/3/2014/EN/C-2014-5432-F1-EN-ANNEX-1-PART-1.PDF›.

158 See DEVCO Companion to financial and contractual procedures applicable to development and cooperation financed from the general budget of the EU and from the 11th EDF (n 156) 279.

159 The dividing line between operational and technical cooperation and politically sensitive issues is not so easy to draw in the Union's international relations, and may occasionally give rise to disputes on external representation issues between the Council and the Commission, as illustrated by Case C-660/13 *Council v Commission* (n 47).

160 DEVCO Companion to financial and contractual procedures applicable to development and cooperation financed from the general budget of the EU and from the 11th EDF (n 156) 44–45.

161 eg the Framework Agreement between the European Commission (the 'Commission') and the Inter-American Development Bank (the 'IDB') laying down the administrative and financial arrangements for their cooperation of 2011 ‹http://www.iadb.org/en/news/news-releases/2011-07-19/signing-ceremony-of-the-framework-agreement-idb-ec,9466.html›.

administrative powers' are legally binding instruments.[162] This raises the question whether the Commission's practice of concluding binding agreements with third countries and international organisations, as well as the relevant provisions of secondary legislation delegating such powers to the Commission, leave the institutional balance under Article 218 TFEU unaffected.

Moreover, the Commission's international practice features instruments such as 'arrangements', 'exchange of letters', 'letters of intent', or 'MOUs'.[163] These are considered by the Commission, in principle, non-binding, because they express political commitments or administrative arrangements.[164] However, the Commission itself acknowledges that it is the content of the instrument which is decisive for establishing its legal nature.[165]

Regarding the legal basis of the Commission's power to conclude international cooperation instruments, and in particular international agreements, two scenarios are identified on the basis of the previous overview. First, the source of the Commission's power to enact international cooperation instruments with third countries and international organisations may be derived from the Treaty provisions concerning Commission's role and prerogatives in EU external relations.[166] As already noted, Articles 218(7) and 219 TFEU provide for special situations enabling the Council to authorise the Commission to exercise tasks regarding the conclusion of international agreements whereas special Treaty provisions enable the Commission to conclude very specific international agreements (ie Article 6 of Protocol No 7 on Privileges and Immunities). More contentiously, the Commission may derive by implication – and it did so in practice[167] – the power to conclude international agreements with international organisations under Article 220 TFEU.

Secondly, the Commission's power to conclude agreements may be delegated by the EU legislator, but such a 'delegation' should ensure that the balance of powers between the institutions under Article 218 TFEU is not affected in the exercise of these powers. As shown previously, the cases in point are the Commission's financing agreements with third countries and international organisations based on the EU

162 *Vademecum on the External Action* (n 43) 52.

163 ibid. See for an example of MOU concluded by the Commission, Memorandum of Understanding and Administrative Co-operation Arrangements between The European Commission's Directorate General for Health and Consumer Protection (DG SANCO) and The General Administration od Quality Supervision, Inspection and Quarantine of the People's Republic of China (AQSIQ), first signed on 16 January 2006, consolidated on 24 November 2008 ‹http://eeas.europa.eu/delegations/china/eu_china/food_safety_and_consumer_protection/food_safety/index_en.htm›.

164 *Vademecum on the External Action* (n 43) 52.

165 ibid. For instance, the MOUs between the Commission and the SAP countries (member countries of the Stabilization and Association Process) establishing '(. . .) rules governing participation, in particular the administrative capacities required, the planned financial contribution, the mechanisms for taking part in the management (. . .)' of the relevant EU programmes and '(. . .) the financial-control provisions', although administrative in nature, do not seem to be purely non-binding instruments, see Commission, 'Preparing for the participation of the Western Balkan countries in Community programmes and agencies' COM(2003) 748 final 5.

166 Arts 17(1) and 21(3) TEU establish on a general level the Commission's main roles and tasks in the EU external action area.

167 See n 150.

financial regulations.[168] Both the General EU Financial Regulation[169] and the financial regulation regarding the European Development Fund[170] contain explicit references to framework financing agreements and individual and grant agreements between the Commission and international organisations as well as third countries.[171] Interestingly, the Commission associates such financial agreements concluded with third countries and international organisations more with the implementation of the EU budget on the basis of the EU Financial Regulation, and they are considered to depart from the 'Article 218 TFEU' procedure.[172] That is to say that such agreements are seen both as instrumental to the Commission's tasks in the management of EU external relations, including the external dimension of the EU policies, and as an external projection of its role as a budgetary actor.[173] The General EU Financial Regulation also places some requirements on the exercise of these powers by the Commission, such as duties to report and to provide information to the Council and the European Parliament, but these conditions do not seem to match the prerogatives of the Council and the European Parliament under Article 218 TFEU.[174] This scenario arguably comes squarely under one of the possibilities mentioned by Article 216 TFEU, namely where the conclusion of the agreement '(. . .) is provided for in a legally Union binding act' but the legislator deviates from the procedure mentioned in Article 218 TFEU. In this respect, it is still doubtful whether the delegation of such powers to the Commission under the EU Financial Regulation leaves the balance of powers under Article 218 TFEU unaffected.[175]

168 *Vademecum on the External Action* (n 43) 38 and 71; see also Schütze (n 70) 395.

169 See arts 58 and 184–189 of Regulation 966/2012; previously these issues were dealt with in arts 53d, 162 and 166 of Council Regulation (EC, Euratom) 1605/2002 of 25 June 2002 on the Financial Regulation applicable to the general budget of the European Communities [2002] OJ L248/1.

170 See arts 17 and 27 of Council Regulation 2015/323; previously these issues were dealt with in arts 29 and 70 of Council Regulation (EC) 215/2008 of 18 February 2008 on the Financial Regulation applicable to the 10th European Development Fund [2008] OJ L78/1.

171 See for instance DEVCO Companion to financial and contractual procedures applicable to development and cooperation financed from the general budget of the EU and from the 11th EDF (n 156).

172 The Commission sees the (binding) financial agreements concluded according to art 166(1) of Regulation 1605/2002 as an exception from the 'Article 218 TFEU' procedure, *Vademecum on the External Action* (n 43) 38 and 71. The provisions of art 166(1) are replicated, with slight changes, in art 189(1) 'Financing agreements on the implementation of external actions' of Regulation 922/2012.

173 *Vademecum on the External Action* (n 43) 38, 52 and 71.

174 See arts 187(10) and 206 of Regulation 922/2012. No prior authorisation or approval by the Council or consent by the European Parliament is mentioned for the financing agreements concluded by the Commission.

175 The interpretation of the Financial Regulation and of art 218 TFEU in the *ESMA* fashion could perhaps solve this conundrum. It should be remembered that *ESMA* was concerned with the issue of delegation of powers by the EU legislator to EU agencies and the Court reached the conclusion that EU agencies could be entrusted by the legislator with regulatory powers outside the scope of arts 290–291 TFEU, which reserved, as a rule, such powers for the Commission and only exceptionally for the Council. By analogy, it can be argued that the EU legislator could delegate to the Commission the power to conclude specific international agreements, according to a different procedure than that established under art 218 TFEU.

In our view, a more pragmatic option could be to consider the Commission's powers to conclude such instruments under a different scenario than Article 218 TFEU, namely to consider the Commission's tasks and instruments concerning the implementation of EU policies as a form of external administrative action outside the 'monopoly' instituted by Article 218 TFEU. In this regard, it is important to reiterate the Commission's position post-Lisbon, according to which the agreements this institution concludes on the basis of its administrative powers, and which create rights and obligations, are legally binding instruments.[176] This catch-all formula does not seem to be limited solely to the financial agreements explicitly authorised by the EU financial regulations, but it also covers the international cooperation pursued more generally by the Commission (or its services) to the extent necessary for fulfilling its administrative tasks. In these instances, the Commission's power to conclude binding agreements is subsumed to its internal administrative functions in combination with its role in ensuring EU external representation on a technical-administrative level.[177] Whereas such administrative agreements should certainly be in line with Article 218 TFEU and comply with the international agreements concluded pursuant to this provision, the principle of institutional balance would not require maintaining the prerogatives of the Council and the European Parliament in 'Article 218 TFEU' treaty-making procedure. What is essential is that sufficient oversight by the Council and the European Parliament is ensured over the exercise of these powers, ensuring that the balance of powers in the external action area is preserved.[178]

Accordingly, a delineation[179] could be made between the agreements concluded by the EU according to the ordinary procedure laid down in Article 218 TFEU and the agreements concluded by the Commission with third countries and international organisations.[180] The first category embodies the most important legal-political commitments taken by the Union on the international plane corresponding to a sort of 'external legislation-making'.[181] Therefore, the underlying procedure for enacting such instruments requires the involvement of the most important EU institutions, which are also involved in the legislative process.[182] A parallel between the legislative process

176 *Vademecum on the External Action* (n 43) 52.

177 ibid 17.

178 This should include at minimum a duty for the Commission to inform the Council and the European Parliament in advance about its planned 'agreements' with third countries and international organisations. Considering Commission's emphasis on the involvement of the Council even when the Commission concludes non-binding instruments on behalf of the EU (except for purely administrative arrangements), one may assume that, *a fortiori*, this would apply in practice for the binding administrative agreements concluded by the Commission, *Vademecum on the External Action* (n 43) 53–55 and 71.

179 For a similar view, see Schütze (n 70) 392–96.

180 This category includes the agreements concluded by the Commission on the basis of an explicit delegation by the EU legislator, such as the financing agreements based on the EU financial regulations, as well as the agreements concluded by the Commission on the basis of its own administrative powers in combination with its powers to ensure EU external representation on a technical-administrative level see *Vademecum on the External Action* (n 43) 38, 52 and 71.

181 For a parallel between the Union's international law-making and the making of its 'internal' legislation, see Eeckhout (n 21) 193–94.

182 For the observation that '(. . .) within the EU system, the treaty-making is vested '(. . .) in the same bodies as are empowered to exercise (Community) legislative powers internally', see Opinion of Advocate General Tesauro in Case C-327/91 *France v Commission* (n 141) para 37.

and the procedure for international agreements is drawn by Article 218(6) TFEU, specifically with regard to the consent/consultation powers of the European Parliament.[183] The second category is linked rather to technical/administrative aspects and to the daily management of EU external policies or to the external dimension of its internal policies.[184] In addition to explicit delegation by the legislator, the competence of the Commission to act externally could be based on its role in ensuring the external representation of the EU under Articles 17 TEU and 220 TFEU,[185] in combination with its role as the main EU implementing body.[186]

The instruments enacted by the Commission in performing its external administration tasks may be legally binding or non-binding.[187] In order to be legally valid, such instruments need to meet some requirements. They must remain within the scope of the Commission's prerogatives, they must comply with the international agreements concluded in accordance with Article 218 TFEU and with the Union's internal legislation, and they must not affect the powers bestowed on the other actors in EU external relations.[188] In this respect, it is essential that coordination with and oversight by other EU external action actors is ensured (in particular the Council and the European Parliament) in order to ensure that the Commission's administrative agreements are consistent with Article 218 TFEU and with the task division in EU external relations. Such instruments could be adopted in the implementation of treaties adopted pursuant to Article 218 TFEU, could pave the way to 'Article 218 TFEU' agreements by opening and enhancing cooperation with third countries and international organisations on a technical-administrative level, or they could simply be used as pragmatic instruments to further cooperation on specific technical-administrative aspects in detachment from Article 218 TFEU.[189]

183 In this respect, art 218(6) TFEU mirrors the EU internal decision making in that it requires the consent of the European Parliament for those international agreements covering fields '(. . .) to which either the ordinary legislative procedure applies, or the special legislative procedure where consent by the European Parliament is required'. Conversely, for international agreements covering areas for which the special legislative procedure requires only the opinion of the European Parliament, the consultation of the European Parliament is in principle required.

184 The formal distinction between the two categories of agreements would be novel only within the Union, as within Euratom such a delineation is already formalised in art 101 of the Euratom Treaty.

185 *Vademecum on the External Action* (n 43) 18.

186 See arts 290–291 and 317 TFEU.

187 In addition to the label used by the parties, the content of the instrument is of utmost importance for establishing the legal nature of the instrument. However, as a starting point for the analysis, the financial agreements, as well as other agreements which create rights and duties on the basis of Commission's powers are legally binding. On the contrary, instruments labeled as arrangements, exchange of letters, or MOUs usually suggest a non-binding instrument. For a general discussion regarding the delineation between binding and non-binding instruments in international law see Oscar Schachter, 'The Twilight Existence of Non-binding International Agreements' (1977) 71 AJIL 296; Alan E Boyle, 'Some Reflections on the Relationship of Treaties and Soft law' (1999) 48 ICLQ 901.

188 According to one view, Commission's non-binding administrative arrangements should not be unlawful as long as they are consistent with Commission's powers and with existing EU law, Macleod, Hendry and Hyett (n 86) 96.

189 For a view that the Commission could conclude executive agreements only where expressly provided by the Treaties, and on the basis of delegation by secondary law and international agreements, see Schütze (n 70) 394–96.

Although the inclusion in the Founding Treaties of a provision formalising agreements concluded with third countries and international organisations on a technical-administrative level would definitely bring more legal certainty,[190] in our view a functional-purposive interpretation of the existing Treaty provisions also allows enacting such instruments. In this vein, it should be noted that the EU is not a unique example of an organisation whose 'constitution' does not include explicit provisions regarding simplified agreements of an administrative or technical nature.[191] In numerous countries and international organisations, the constitution normally pays little or no attention to technical-administrative agreements without this precluding the enactment of such instruments in practice, and providing for such instruments via secondary legislation.[192]

ECB and EIB

Beside the Commission, the ECB and EIB are explicitly provided with certain international cooperation tasks by the Founding Treaties.[193] These provisions do not specify the instruments the ECB and EIB may use in their international relations, which may allow one to assume that such cooperation could result both binding and non-binding instruments.[194]

The international practice of these two organisations appears to feature legally binding instruments.[195] The EIB, for instance, has concluded numerous framework agreements with third countries covering the lending activities the EIB is authorised to carry out in those countries.[196] The implementation of these framework agreements materialises in more specific contracts being signed and projects being implemented in the relevant country. Such instruments can be seen as a very specific category of sectoral technical agreements enabling the ECB and EIB to fulfil their core tasks. Just like the Commission's agreements, the agreements enacted by the ECB or the EIB should be regarded as remaining outside the scope of Article 218 TFEU. The validation of these agreements would require that they pertain to matters within the competence of the ECB and the EIB, that they are consistent with 'Article 218

190 A provision similar to art 101 of the Euratom Treaty could be inserted in the TFEU.

191 For state practice, see Duncan B Hollis, Merritt R Blakeslee and Benjamin Ederington (eds), *National Treaty Law and Practice* (Martinus Nijhoff Publishers 2005). With regard to international organisations specifically, see further in this chapter, 2.3.1.2.1: Administrative agreements in international and state practice.

192 For examples from the constitutional practice of some Member States and various other states, see Hollis, Blakeslee and Ederington (n 191) 24.

193 Article 23 of Protocol No 4 for ECB and art 14 of Protocol No 5 for EIB.

194 For the view that Treaty provisions concerning international cooperation do not exclude the conclusion of international binding agreements, see Eeckhout (n 21) 122–23.

195 As regards ECB, see Zilioli and Selmayr (n 115). Concerning EIB, see Schermers and Blokker (n 119) 994.

196 Since 2002, the EIB has signed framework agreements with Russia, Ukraine, Moldova, Georgia, Azerbaijan and Armenia ‹http://www.eib.org/projects/regions/eastern-neighbours/framework/index.htm›. In Asia, EIB has Framework Agreements with Myanmar, Bangladesh, Bhutan, Cambodia, China, India, Indonesia, Laos, Maldives, Mongolia, Nepal, Pakistan, the Philippines, Sri Lanka, Thailand, Vietnam and Yemen, Press Release of 11 March 2015 (reference no 2015-051-EN) ‹http://www.eib.org/infocentre/press/releases/all/2015/2015-051-eib-and-myanmar-sign-a-framework-agreement.htm›.

TFEU' agreements and with Union's legislation, that sufficient oversight, in particular by the Council and the Commission, is ensured, so that the balance of powers of the EU institutions under Article 218 TFEU and in EU external relations is preserved.

The international cooperation practice of ECB and EIB are illustrative cases of EU institutions and bodies which derive the power to conclude what seem to be sectoral binding international cooperation instruments on the basis of a more generic mandate for international cooperation. This reveals that under the Treaty framework there may be different scenarios for concluding international binding agreements, outside the standard procedure laid down in Article 218 TFEU.

2.2.3.5 European agencies and institutional balance in EU external relations

Unlike the Commission, EU agencies are not EU institutions. It is true that, post-Lisbon, EU agencies are mentioned in the Treaties as a component of the institutional framework of the EU, but no further details are provided with regard to their role, tasks and legal status. This leaves the EU legislator with some discretion with regard to the set up and design of such entities. Such discretion, however, finds its limits in the general principles flowing from the Treaties, such as conferral, proportionality, subsidiarity, and in particular institutional balance and the *Meroni* doctrine. Nevertheless, this opens the way for some variation regarding the status, composition and powers of the EU agencies, also depending on the specific requirements in one policy area or another.

Whereas the Commission and the EU agencies resemble in that they both pursue, as part of the EU administration, international cooperation on a technical-administrative level, the Treaties are silent as regards the role of agencies in the EU external action area. However, in *ESMA*, the CJEU admitted generally that '(. . .) while the treaties do not contain any provision to the effect that powers may be conferred on (. . .)' EU agencies, such a possibility exists nevertheless.[197] Since there is no distinction between the delegation of internal and external powers, one may assume that the possibility to delegate holds in principle for both categories. Moreover, the Court clarifies that post-Lisbon the Commission's role under the Treaties does not entail a monopoly over the Union's executive and administrative tasks. Thus, the Commission's prerogatives under the Treaties should not be undermined if executive powers delegated to EU agencies are part of the regulatory framework in a policy area which requires specific technical expertise, and they are necessary to attain the objectives of that policy area.[198] Similarly, limited international cooperation tasks and actions performed by the EU agencies within their mandate and with a view to attain the objectives established by the EU legislator, should not be in principle irreconcilable with the powers of the Commission in EU external relations.

The possibility for EU agencies to pursue international cooperation has been acknowledged in the Common Approach on EU agencies[199] through an all-embracing formula covering instances where the mandate or work programme of these bodies '(. . .) foresees cooperation with third countries and/or international organizations'.

197 *ESMA* Judgment (n 4) para 79.
198 ibid paras 82–86.
199 Common Approach on EU agencies (n 4) para 25.

Moreover, the CJEU has for the first time examined the international dimension of an agency with regard specifically to Europol in the recent Case C-363/14 *Parliament v Council*.[200] In its judgment, the Court seems not to question the 'constitutionality' of Europol's international dimension as long as it is ancillary and necessary for the performance of the Agency's core tasks, and provided that it takes place within the framework defined by the EU legislature.[201]

Accordingly, it appears that EU agencies may be entrusted with international cooperation tasks limited to technical issues within their core mandate outside the 'monopoly' of Commission on external representation and the management of EU external relations. Unlike the Commission, EU agencies may get involved in international cooperation as sectoral actors with a role which is restricted to what is necessary to fulfil their core mandate entrusted by the legislator in a certain policy area. By taking such a functionalist approach, one may reason that, even in the absence of express provisions in agencies' founding acts, there is an inherent external dimension attached to the mandate of each EU agency to the extent necessary for an agency to fulfil its core tasks and objectives.[202] This view finds support in the Common Approach on EU agencies in which the main EU institutions acknowledge the international dimension of the EU agencies flowing both explicitly and implicitly from their legal mandate.[203] Moreover, the Commission's Vademecum on External Relations acknowledges that the activities of the EU agencies may '(. . .) imply international action'.[204] Nevertheless, the external powers of the EU agencies must be in line with the Treaties, in particular the provisions governing the EU external action area. Hence, entrusting certain international cooperation tasks explicitly or even implicitly to EU agencies is acceptable, but institutional balance in the EU external action area and the *Meroni* requirements listed previously must be observed.[205]

A resulting question is whether the international cooperation tasks exercised by the EU agencies may culminate in both in legally non-binding and binding instruments. Whereas enacting non-binding instruments does not raise particular questions as regards the fulfilment of the conditions mentioned above, the same conclusion cannot be drawn automatically with regard to the allegedly binding international cooperation

200 Case C-363/14 *Parliament v Council* EU:C:2015:579. The Court examined the overall setting of Europol's international relations, as well as the procedure for the negotiation and conclusion of Europol's agreements with a view to determine whether the Council decision amending the 'list' of Europol's partners pertained to an essential element of the matter regulated by the Europol Council Decision (ECD), which would have required using the legislative procedure established by primary law instead of the more flexible procedure provided for in art 26(1)(a) ECD.

201 ibid paras 49–50.

202 This functionalist logic can be detected also in the *ESMA* case, although in that context the Court did not deal specifically with the external powers of ESMA, *ESMA* Judgment (n 4) para 85.

203 Common Approach on EU agencies (n 4) para 25; this provision refers to the instances in which the 'mandate' or the 'work programme' of the EU agencies *foresees* (emphasis added) international cooperation.

204 *Vademecum on the External Action* (n 43) 18. In this context, the Commission emphasises the need for the EU agencies to '(. . .) operate within the mandate given by the legislator within the existing institutional framework', and to establish working arrangements with the Commission to that effect.

205 For a similar view, see Ott, Vos and Coman-Kund (n 128) 114.

instruments enacted by the EU agencies.[206] The denial of such a power to EU agencies rests on three main arguments. First, it goes against the (strict) stance admittedly taken by the CJEU with regard to the Union's treaty-making in Case C-327/91 *France v Commission*. Secondly, after Lisbon, international agreements can be concluded by the EU only on the basis of Article 218 TFEU. Thirdly, the EU agencies cannot represent the EU and cannot commit the Union to obligations on the international plane, as, according to the Treaties, this power belongs to the Commission and the Council.

It is maintained, however, that EU agencies can be delegated limited powers to conclude binding international agreements inherent to the fulfilment of their mandate by an act of secondary legislation.[207] Similarly to the Commission's administrative agreements, such agreements concluded by the EU agencies may qualify as *a special form of EU external administrative action,* which does not automatically disturb the institutional balance laid down in Article 218 TFEU.[208] In order for such instruments to be validated in light of the principle of institutional balance and the *Meroni* requirements it is essential that: (1) they remain within the core mandate of the agency, and are consistent with 'Article 218 TFEU' agreements and EU legislation; and (2) the agency is subject to sufficient supervision and control, ensuring that the powers of the main actors in the EU external action area are not affected. In particular, the Council and the Commission should be involved in view of their roles under Articles 17(1), 16(6) and 21(3) TEU, as well as Articles 218 and 220 TFEU. The role of the Commission seems notably important in view of the technical-administrative cooperation established by the EU agencies under their international cooperation instruments.

In this respect, the Common Approach on EU agencies lays down important supervisory mechanisms in favour of the Commission. Thus, EU agencies are required to consult in advance and take into account the advice of the Commission regarding their work programme and multiannual strategic programmes.[209] Moreover, the Common Approach foresees an 'Alert/warning system' which may be activated by the Commission with a view to precluding EU agencies from taking decisions violating EU law or contradicting EU policies.[210] Additional generic monitoring and controlling tools covering also EU agencies' international dimension are the general information and reporting duties in relation to the European Parliament inserted in the founding acts of the EU agencies,[211] as well as the possibilities for judicial review of the EU agencies' acts introduced by the Lisbon Treaty.[212]

With regard specifically to the international actions of the EU agencies, the Common Approach requires coordination and oversight by the Commission through the conclusion of detailed working arrangements, as well as through early exchange of information regarding the international initiatives of these bodies.[213] Moreover, the

206 ibid 113–16.
207 See Schütze (n 70) 397–99.
208 See Ott, Vos and Coman-Kund (n 128) 91–93 and 115–16.
209 Common Approach on EU agencies (n 4) para 29.
210 ibid para 59.
211 ibid paras 29 and 59.
212 Arts 263, 267 and 277 TFEU.
213 Common Approach on EU agencies (n 4) para 25.

approval of the management board of the EU agencies is foreseen in relation to the external relations strategy and the specific international cooperation instruments of the agencies. The relevant legal framework of the EU agencies normally provides for more specific requirements and conditions concerning the exercise of their powers in general or specifically as regards their international cooperation tasks and instruments. Such provisions usually require *prior* authorisation, approval or opinions by the Commission or, more rarely, by the Council of their international actions.[214] Furthermore, additional supervisory mechanisms may be present in the daily institutional practice of some EU agencies. Whether such conditions and controls are sufficient, and whether the specific international cooperation instruments of an EU agency meet the required parameters must be assessed on a case-by-case basis, with due regard for the relevant legal framework and international practice of each EU agency.

2.3 The international law dimension

The international cooperation pursued by EU agencies begs two important intertwined legal questions. First, what is the legal nature of international actions by EU agencies, with an emphasis on the formal cooperation instruments concluded with non-EU partners? Secondly, what is the legal status of the EU agencies as global actors from the perspective of international law? Two international law concepts are used in order to address these questions: 'international agreement' and 'international legal personality'.

A conscious choice is made to discuss the concept of 'international agreement' before examining the issue of international legal personality. Whereas an international agreement is always attributed ultimately to a subject of international law, in the case of entities with an unclear legal status, such as EU agencies, an assessment of their powers and instruments used on the international plane is required in order to assess whether they possess international personality. In particular, the finding that some of the international cooperation instruments concluded by EU agencies can be qualified as binding international agreements could be an indicator of their international legal capacity. However, as it will be shown thereafter, the signing of international agreements by bodies of international organisations like EU agencies, does not necessarily indicate that these bodies have a treaty-making power of their own if it turns out that such agreements are concluded on behalf of their respective international organisation.[215] Under such a scenario the treaty-making power belongs ultimately to the international organisation (eg the EU), whilst the exercise of this power is entrusted to bodies of the respective organisation, subject to its internal rules and practice.[216]

214 See Annex 2; see also Ott, Vos and Coman-Kund (n 128) 100–01.

215 Anne Peters, 'Treaty Making Power', *Max Planck Encyclopedia of Public International Law* (Oxford Public International Law, March 2009) paras 55–58 ‹http://opil.ouplaw.com/view/10.1093/law:epil/9780199231690/law-9780199231690-e1494?prd=EPIL#law-9780199231690-e1494-div1-1›.

216 ibid paras 55–57 and 94–100.

2.3.1 The concept of 'international agreement'

2.3.1.1 Definition and criteria

Moving away from the controversies surrounding the concept of 'treaty' or 'international agreement',[217] the most authoritative definition is to be found in the two Vienna Conventions on the Law of Treaties.[218] These instruments define a treaty as 'an international agreement' concluded in a written form and governed by international law, regardless of whether it is embodied in one, two or more instruments and whatever its particular designation.[219] This definition is widely accepted in the international law scholarship[220] and it is also supported by the International Court of Justice (ICJ)[221] as reflecting customary international law.

It should be noted that the international legal personality of the entities becoming parties to an international agreement has relevance for the concept of treaty. However, the link between the two notions has not been fully clarified. Whereas in the case of established subjects of international law like states, international personality is normally a prerequisite for entering into a treaty, it is maintained that the practice of treaty-making may also indicate that an entity possesses international personality.[222] In this case, international personality is not a prerequisite but a consequence of treaty-making.[223] This is particularly the case for those entities whose international legal status is not fully clear or accepted.

Based on this definition, it follows that under international law an essential criterion for assessing the legally binding character of international instruments is the genuine intention of the parties to create binding effects governed by international law, regardless of the name or the form of the instrument.[224] Accordingly, one may identify two essential requirements for an instrument (agreement) to become binding under international law:

(1) there must be an intention to create legally binding effects;
(2) such effects must be governed by international law.[225]

217 For a comprehensive overview see Klabbers (n 92).

218 Vienna Convention on the Law of Treaties between States (the 1969 Vienna Convention) and Vienna Convention on the Law of Treaties between States and International Organisations or between International Organisations (the 1986 Vienna Convention); the 1986 Vienna Convention is not in force yet because of the insufficient number of ratifications by signatory states.

219 Article 2(1)(a) of the 1969 Vienna Convention and art 2(1)(a) of the 1986 Vienna Convention.

220 Duncan B Hollis, 'Defining Treaties' in Duncan B Hollis (ed), *The Oxford Guide to Treaties* (OUP 2012) 12 and Philippe Gautier, 'Article 1' and 'Article 2' in Olivier Corten and Pierre Klein (eds), *The Vienna Conventions of the Law of Treaties. A Commentary* (vol I, OUP 2011) 45 and 60.

221 *Land and Maritime Boundary between Cameroon and Nigeria* (*Cameroon v Nigeria: Equatorial Guinea Intervening*), Judgment [2002] ICJ 303, para 263.

222 See Tom Grant, 'Who Can Make Treaties? Other Subjects of International Law' in Hollis (ed), *The Oxford Guide to Treaties* (n 220) 136 and 148.

223 ibid 136. See also Roland Portmann, *Legal Personality in International Law* (CUP 2010) 173–74.

224 Hollis (n 220) 26, and Schachter (n 187) 296. See also *Maritime Delimitation and Territorial Questions between Qatar and Bahrain*, Jurisdiction and admissibility, Judgment [1994] ICJ 112, paras 23–25.

225 For more elaborated discussions, see Schermers and Blokker (n 119) 1121–23, and Aust (n 69) 17–18.

The first requirement is meant to distinguish treaties from non-binding international agreements which might be enacted by subjects of international law. However, the intentional element becomes problematic in particular with regard to the possibilities for subjects of international law to decide to subject their agreements to international law or not or to determine the legal nature of such instruments. While views vary, it has been observed that certain agreements are to be regarded as treaties under international law on the basis of their subject matter and content, regardless of the manifest intention of the parties.[226] Against this background, it has been maintained that the role of the manifest intention of the parties to an agreement should be limited and complemented with more substantive criteria.[227] According to Klabbers the intention of the parties to create legal rights and obligations should be presumed, be it only because it is hard to imagine that subjects of international law devoted significant time and resources to the process and went through complex procedures simply to conclude something that entails no commitment whatsoever.[228]

The second requirement is intended to distinguish between treaties or international agreements and other similar instruments that may be concluded between subjects of international law. This requirement also raises some difficulties. In particular, it does not seem obvious that the parties to an agreement have complete freedom to evade this condition by simply subjecting their agreement to a domestic law system. In this regard, Lauterpacht maintains that all agreements between states are governed ultimately by international law. Thus, it is the '(. . .) quality as a treaty which causes it (. . .)' to be considered international law, whereas the domestic law agreed by the parties defines the specific rules applicable to their relationship and, as such, it '(. . .) is transformed into conventional international law'.[229] Also the International Law Commission (ILC) supports the view that agreements concluded by states are ultimately subject to international law, in that they must be carried out as a result of the rule of international customary law *pacta sunt servanda*.[230]

It is more difficult to assess whether particular instruments (agreements) fulfil these requirements.[231] This issue occurs because, more often than not, the intention of the parties is not explicitly stated and/or the instruments might also refer to 'domestic' law for the execution of some provisions.[232] Accordingly, one has to use various evidentiary factors in order to assess the legal nature of each particular international instrument. The factors most commonly accepted include the wording and substance, as well as the particular circumstances (context) surrounding the negotiation and conclusion of the instrument.[233]

226 eg agreements regarding boundaries, territorial seas, etc, see Hollis (n 220) 26.
227 ibid 26–27.
228 Klabbers (n 92) 249.
229 Yearbook of the International Law Commission (YILC) 1953, vol II 100. See also Gautier (n 220) 41.
230 Yearbook of the International Law Commission (YILC) 1959, vol II 95.
231 Hollis (n 220) 26–28.
232 See Schachter (n 187) 297.
233 *Maritime Delimitation and Territorial Questions between Qatar and Bahrain* (n 224) paras 23–25; *Aegean Sea Continental Shelf*, Judgment [1978] ICJ 3, para 96. See also Kirsten Schmalenbach, 'Article 2. Use of Terms' in Oliver Dörr and Kirsten Schmalenbach (eds), *Vienna Convention on the Law of Treaties. A Commentary* (Springer 2012) 40–41.

Hence, an instrument with an elaborated structure comprising articles and covering issues such as the purpose of the instrument, rights and obligations of the parties, entry into force, amendment, suspension and termination, liability and dispute settlement is likely to constitute a treaty. Moreover, binding international agreements normally use a certain language featuring 'shall' and 'will' clauses and a certain terminology such as 'parties', 'agree', 'agreement', 'enter into force', etc.[234] In addition to the content, the circumstances *prior*, during or after the negotiation and conclusion of the instrument are relevant for determining its legal nature. Such circumstances may include the wider legal framework within which the instrument has been enacted, the procedure used, as well as decisions taken after the conclusion of the instrument regarding the application of its provisions.[235]

The criteria mentioned above are mere indicators of intent, as '(. . .) there are no magic words to create a treaty or deny an agreement that status'.[236] Even with regard to the explicit provisions stipulating that the relevant instrument is not legally binding it has been maintained that 'the ability of such clauses to definitely deny an agreement treaty status remains unresolved'.[237] As an illustration of the application of these criteria in practice, in the *Maritime Delimitation* case, the ICJ found that the minutes concluded by the foreign ministers of Qatar and Bahrain following a rather simplified procedure constituted nevertheless an international agreement.[238] Therefore, the determination of the legal nature of international cooperation instruments requires a careful analysis combining the above-mentioned factors, by giving consideration to the form, terminology and content of the instrument, as well as to the surrounding circumstances[239] (see Box 2.1 below). This entails looking not only at what the parties state explicitly in the instrument but also considering more objective manifestations of intent for the purpose of qualifying the agreement as binding or non-binding.[240]

Box 2.1 Criteria and indicators for identifying international binding agreements

Criteria	*Indicators*
Wording	– Party – Agree / decide / agreement – Shall / will language – Rights and obligations / commitments – Enter into force – Suspension – Done – Terminate

234 Anthony Aust, 'Alternatives to Treaty-making: MOUs as Political Commitments' in Hollis (ed), *The Oxford Guide to Treaties* (n 220) 48–49.

235 *Maritime Delimitation and Territorial Questions between Qatar and Bahrain* (n 224) para 27.

236 Hollis (n 220) 27.

237 Hollis (ed), *The Oxford Guide to Treaties* (n 220) 655.

238 *Maritime Delimitation and Territorial Questions between Qatar and Bahrain* (n 224) paras 25–27.

239 Hollis (n 220) 27.

240 ibid 27–28.

Criteria	*Indicators*
Structure and content	– Provisions structured in articles – Purpose and scope – Rights and obligations between the parties and as regards third parties – Liability provisions – Provisions on entry into force / duration/ amendment / suspension / termination – Dispute settlement clauses (voluntary or binding dispute settlement) – Clauses repealing previous instruments – Clauses preserving the effects of the instrument
Context	– Procedure for negotiation and conclusion (formalised, complexity, duration) – Publication (website, official journal) – Registration UN

Things are not different within the European Union. The CJEU ruled that the binding character of an agreement should be established, in principle, based on the intention of the parties as results from the wording of the instrument and the history of negotiations.[241] Moreover, the Commission's Vademecum on the External Action of the European Union stresses the decisive character of the content of an instrument for the purpose of determining its legal nature, and warns about a careful drafting in order to avoid an instrument being considered as legally binding.[242]

In particular, the Commission insists on refraining from using terms like 'Party', 'shall/will', 'entry into force/coming into effect', 'articles', 'agree/decide', 'obligations/commitments'.[243] Moreover, the Commission instructs that using a treaty structure (preamble, articles, final provisions) and inserting clauses concerning dispute settlement, entry into force, amendment and termination should be avoided.[244] The use of standard clauses explicitly stating the non-binding nature of instruments is encouraged, but the Commission warns that such a provision is not sufficient '(. . .) to express the real intentions of the signatories, which result from an analysis of the wording, content and purpose of the instrument'.[245]

This indicates that a case-by-case analysis of each instrument or category of international cooperation instruments used by the EU agencies is required in order to determine their legal nature. An assessment of EU agencies' legal framework pertaining to international cooperation, including the procedure for negotiating and concluding international cooperation instruments, together with a more detailed analysis of the international cooperation instruments in place should enable clarifying their legal nature.

241 Case C-327/1991 *France v Commission* (n 129) para 15.
242 *Vademecum on the External Action* (n 43) 52.
243 ibid.
244 ibid.
245 ibid 53.

2.3.1.2 The category of 'international administrative agreements'

Whilst from the perspective of international law, all the instruments fulfilling the criteria of the definitions of the Vienna Conventions qualify simply as treaties or binding international agreements, different meanings and classifications can be given to international agreements within the domestic legal system of states and international organisations.[246] Thus, a distinction is usually made between important agreements which require approval by the legislative body or the main body of the organisation, and less important agreements which may be concluded by the executive branch following different procedures.[247] The latter category is usually designated as 'administrative' or 'executive' agreements.[248] Although EU agencies cannot interfere with the EU treaty-making under Article 218 TFEU, they may arguably enact international administrative agreements which are not necessarily incompatible with the EU constitutional framework.

2.3.1.2.1 ADMINISTRATIVE AGREEMENTS IN INTERNATIONAL AND STATE PRACTICE

Concept and overview

Administrative agreements understood as (binding) international cooperation instruments concluded by executive or administrative organs, usually in accordance with simplified procedures and pertaining to technical, operational, financial and other issues related to policy implementation, have a long history in the international cooperation practice.[249] Such instruments are acknowledged as a matter of law and/or practice in many states and also on the international plane. While generally they lack explicit legal foundation in constitutions, numerous states recognise various types of treaties or agreements concluded on the executive level in their internal legislation and practice, such as: treaties concluded by the government; treaties concluded by government departments or ministries;[250] treaties concluded by various agencies.[251]

246 This is acknowledged in art 2(2) of the 1969 Vienna Convention and in art 2(2) of the 1986 Vienna Convention.

247 Fred L Morrison, 'Executive Agreements', *Max Planck Encyclopedia of Public International Law* (Oxford Public International Law, May 2007) 1052 ‹http://opil.ouplaw.com/view/10.1093/law:epil/9780199231690/law-9780199231690-e1403?rskey=DsV0M0&result=3&prd=OPIL›.

248 For the use of the term 'administrative agreements' in various states, see Gautier (n 220) 55; Hollis (n 220) 15. The term 'executive agreements' is used particularly within the US legal system, see Morrison (n 247).

249 Klabbers (n 92) 20. See also in the US context, Arthur W Rovine, 'Separation of Powers and International Executive Agreements' (1976–1977) 52 *Indiana Law Journal* 397, 398; Elbert M Byrd Jr, *Treaties and Executive Agreements in the United States. Their Separate Roles and Limitations* (Martinus Nijhoff 1960). For a discussion of the concept of 'administrative agreement' in the EU context, see Opinion of Advocate General Tesauro in Case C-327/91 *France v Commission* (n 141) paras 18, 22 and 30–32 (in particular, para 32 refers to 'administrative arrangements' as agreements in simplified form).

250 Duncan B Hollis, 'A Comparative Approach to Treaty Law and Practice' in Hollis, Blakeslee and Ederington (eds), *National Treaty Law and Practice* (n 191) 17–18. Such states are China, India, Russia and Germany.

251 Including Mexico, Switzerland and the USA; see Hollis (n 250). In the US context, 'agency-level executive agreements' are described as 'normally limited in scope and often highly technical and

In this context, it does not come as a surprise that EU Member States have similar international agreements concluded at the ministerial and agency level (eg Austria, France, Germany, the Netherlands, United Kingdom).[252] Sometimes, agreements made by the executive branch are referred to explicitly in the constitution, such as in the case of Germany.[253] Interestingly, it appears that even in states that apparently deny constitutionally administrative agreements, extra-constitutional practices of inter-agency agreements have nevertheless been developed.[254] Also within international organisations, dealings pertaining to detailed administrative and technical issues are exercised routinely by the main executive organ or by subsidiary organs using streamlined procedures.[255]

Quite significantly, the ILC Commentaries on both Vienna Conventions acknowledge the existence of a specific category of (binding) international agreements concluded by states and international organisations. They cover technical, administrative and financial issues, are less formalised than 'formal treaties' and are concluded according to streamlined procedures.[256] In this context, the ILC Commentaries on the 1986 Vienna Convention point to the category of '"interagency" agreements' whose legal nature is not always clear.[257] Remarkably, explicit reference is also made to the possibility for international agreements to be concluded by entities, other than states and international organisations.[258]

complex', illustrating primarily concerns of 'non-diplomatic agencies', David J Kuchenbecker, 'Agency-level Executive Agreements: A New Era in U.S. Treaty Practice' (1979–1980) 18 *Columbia Journal of Transnational Law* 1, 19–21.

252 Hollis (n 250). In France, the category of '*arrangements administratifs*' has been accepted in practice to designate the agreements concluded between the French governmental agencies and similar agencies abroad; whilst it is accepted that such agreements may be binding, it is contended that they commit only the agency concerned, not the state as such, see Pierre M Eisemann and Raphaële Rivier, 'National Treaty Law and Practice: France' in Hollis, Blakeslee and Ederington (eds), *National Treaty Law and Practice* (n 191) 254–55. This view is rebutted, however, by Klabbers who argues that such instruments concluded by agencies are ultimately binding on the state: Klabbers (n 92) 246.

253 Article 59(2) of the German Basic Law.

254 eg Colombia: see Hollis (n 250); Germán Cavelier, 'National Treaty Law and Practice: Colombia' in Hollis, Blakeslee and Ederington (eds), *National Treaty Law and Practice* (n 191) 195. A similar case is Japan, where, in spite of the fact that in principle only the Ministry of Foreign Affairs has the authority to conclude executive agreements, exceptionally other ministries can also conclude similar instruments where they '(. . .) fall within the agency's jurisdiction and are duly authorised by existing treaties or domestic laws', Hollis (n 250) 18.

255 See S. J D Hungdah Chiu, *The Capacity of International Organizations to Conclude Treaties, and the Special Legal Aspects of the Treaties so Concluded* (Martinus Nijhoff 1966) 173–84, referring to various agreements concluded within the UN system by subsidiary organs such as UNICEF, as well as to agreements concluded by the World Bank. See also J W Schneider, *Treaty-making Power of International Organizations* (Librairie E Droz 1959) 21–25, 61–67 and 70–73.

256 See International Law Commission, Draft Articles on the Law of Treaties with Commentaries, Yearbook of the International Law Commission (YILC) 1966, vol II 197, and International Law Commission, Draft Articles on the Law of Treaties between States and International Organizations or between International Organizations with Commentaries, Yearbook of the International Law Commission (YILC) 1982, vol II 18–19.

257 ibid.

258 ibid 22.

In spite of their widespread use in practice,[259] the agreements of an administrative nature continue to be surrounded by ambiguity and neglect.[260] Although this category of instruments is mentioned quite regularly by scholarly[261] and official sources,[262] in-depth research clarifying the concept, the categories, the features, the legal sources and implications of such instruments is rather scarce.[263] Also, the terminology used in practice to designate such instruments is varied: administrative agreements;[264] executive agreements;[265] agency-level executive agreements;[266] inter-agency agreements;[267] agency-level agreements;[268] technical agreements;[269] technical-assistance agreements;[270] operational agreements;[271] administrative arrangements;[272] technical arrangements.[273]

Types of administrative agreements

Attempting to categorise the types of instruments which may qualify as 'executive' or 'administrative' agreements meets with difficulties. For instance, looking at the binding agreements concluded by the executive branch at the state level, Hollis identifies several overlapping categories of what he terms 'executive treaties'. These are: (1) treaties not requiring legislative implementation; (2) treaties the conclusion of which is authorised by a prior law or treaty; (3) treaties falling outside of categories

259 For instance, in the USA, hundreds of executive or administrative agreements are concluded annually 'for the purpose of implementing broad policy decisions already made' for which the constitutional formal treaty-making procedure should not be used because of political and practical considerations, see Byrd (n 249) 132.

260 For a similar observation concerning the lack of attention by EU legal scholars with regard to this issue, see Schütze (n 70) 392.

261 See Klabbers (n 92) 20–22; Schermers and Blokker (n 119) 1136–37; Hollis (n 250) 17–28.

262 See for instance *Vademecum on the External Action* (n 43).

263 See, however, for a broader study covering this issue, Hollis, Blakeslee and Ederington (eds), National Treaty Law and Practice (n 191). The category of the US executive agreements, including the agreements concluded by various US agencies has received, however, more extensive attention: Kuchenbecker (n 251); Byrd (n 249); George A Bermann, 'Regulatory Cooperation with Counterpart Agencies Abroad: The FAA's Aircraft Certification Experience' (1992–1993) 24 *Law and Policy in International Business* 669. For studies concerning executive and administrative agreements within the EU see Ott, Vos and Coman-Kund (n 128); Schütze (n 70) 392–99; Florin Coman-Kund, 'EU Agencies as Global Actors: A Legal Assessment of Europol's International Dimension' (2014) *Maastricht Faculty of Law Working Paper* 6/2014 ‹https://papers.ssrn.com/sol3/papers.cfm?abstract_id=2506568›.

264 See generally Klabbers (n 92) 20–22. See in the EU context, Ott, Vos and Coman-Kund (n 128) 91–93.

265 Especially in the US context, see Byrd (n 249). See in the EU context, Schütze (n 70) 392–99.

266 Kuchenbecker (n 251).

267 See Draft Articles on the Law of Treaties between States and International Organizations (n 256) 18.

268 Hollis (n 250) 18–19.

269 ibid 27.

270 Chiu (n 255) 168–73.

271 Schneider (n 255) 73.

272 Hollis (n 250) 18; Jean-Pierre Plouffe, 'Les Arrangements Internationaux des Agences et Ministerès du Canada' (1983) *Annuaire Canadien de Droit International* XXI 176.

273 Schneider (n 255) 34.

that require the legislature's approval; (4) treaties within the executive's sole authority; (5) minor technical or administrative treaties; and (6) other executive treaties.[274]

As far as international organisations are concerned, the previous categories are not fully applicable because of the lack of a clear delineation between the legislative and the executive branches. Here the distinction is made rather between ***politically significant agreements*** and ***executive agreements***. The former entail the participation of the main organ(s) and the use of the formal treaty-making procedure laid down in the constitution of the organisation. The latter deal with technical, administrative, financial matters and are enacted by the main organ entrusted with the management of the organisation or by subsidiary administrative organs.[275] In this vein, the practice developed for reasons of efficiency in international organisations is to leave implementation of the politically significant treaties,[276] as well as the small, daily, technical matters to the administration or subsidiary organs of the organisation.[277]

Legal status

Regarding the legal status of the agreements concluded on the executive/administrative level, the tendency in state practice is to consider them as agreements of the 'State' within the scope of the concept of treaty as defined in the 1969 Vienna Convention.[278] In some states, however, it appears that in particular the international agreements concluded by agencies are regarded as binding only upon the agency concerned, not upon the state itself.[279] It is not sure whether under international law such a solution is fully acceptable as the agency relationship between the administrative body concluding the agreement and the state could lead to the conclusion that the relevant agency is acting ultimately on behalf of the state.[280] This solution might be tenable when the agency is acting formally and actually independently from the government, but not when it is simply acting under the control of the government.

As regards international organisations, there is more ambiguity surrounding the legal status of their various technical-administrative agreements. Whereas some

274 Hollis (n 250) 24.

275 See Schneider (n 255) 110–15; Schermers and Blokker (n 119) 1137–39. For more details and examples, see Chiu (n 255) 84–99.

276 See T. I. H. Detter, 'The Organs of International Organizations Exercising their Treaty-making Power' (1962) 38 *British Yearbook of International Law* 421.

277 ibid 425–26.

278 Hollis (n 220) 22. According to another view, the international arrangements concluded by ministerial departments and agencies with their counterparts are mere 'gentlemen's agreements' deprived of binding effects in international law, see Plouffe (n 272) 203.

279 eg France and Mexico: see Hollis (n 250) 18; Eisemann and Rivier (n 252) 254–55; Luiz M Diaz, 'National treaty law and practice: Mexico' in Hollis, Blakeslee and Ederington (eds), *National Treaty Law and Practice* (n 191) 443.

280 See Hollis (n 220) 22 and Klabbers (n 92) 246. For the argument that the agreements concluded between administrative agencies are ultimately agreements between states by virtue of the principle of the unity of the state and of Article 46 of the 1969 Vienna Convention see Geneviève Burdeau, 'Les Accords Conclus entre Authorités Administratives ou Organismes Publics de Pays Différents' in Paul Reuter (ed), *Mélanges Offerts à Paul Reuter. Le Droit International: Unité et Diversité* (Pedone 1981) 108–09. For international organisations, see Detter (n 276) 425–26 and 433–34; Schermers and Blokker (n 119) 995.

express doubts regarding their binding nature or their status as international agreements,[281] others propose a more nuanced view advocating a careful assessment based on various factors, such as the form and content of the instruments.[282] Accordingly, to the extent that such agreements are concluded in a similar manner as treaties and create legal norms, they are to be considered international agreements; the mere fact that they are a different kind of treaty is not sufficient to deprive them of their legal character.[283] Such agreements would qualify as treaties concluded by international organisations under the 1986 Vienna Convention or, possibly, provided that they are concluded by organs or agencies of international organisations equipped with a large measure of independence, as interagency agreements concluded by other subjects of international law.[284]

Furthermore, administrative agreements often refer to the application of various internal rules of the parties. However, this feature does not transform these instruments *per se* into some sort of 'domestic agreements' which are no longer governed by international law. This issue needs to be seen as part of the wider discussion regarding the distinction between agreements governed by international law and agreements governed by a system of domestic law.[285] In the absence of clear formal criteria for making a distinction and lacking sound conceptual underpinnings regarding the 'domestic agreements' concluded between subjects of international law,[286] it is difficult to draw the dividing line between the two categories. In this context, it is noteworthy the remark in the ILC commentaries of the 1986 Vienna Convention concerning the considerable increase of the number of agreements regulating administrative and financial matters between subjects of international law and emphasising that, in certain instances, it is not certain which legal system governs them.[287]

Whilst it is acknowledged that the legal qualification of the agreements needs to be done on a case-by-case basis in light of the practice, context and purpose of the instruments,[288] there are sound arguments supporting, as a matter of principle, the qualification of such instruments as international agreements according to international law.[289] In this regard, the view has been expressed that the very nature of the contracting parties would turn an agreement between states into an international agreement.[290] Moreover, it has been pointed out that often agreements concluded by subjects of international law will be governed by international law regardless of the preferences of the contracting parties.[291] Even those strongly supporting the category

281 See Schneider (n 255) 20–34; Chiu (n 255) 65 and 138.
282 Chiu (n 255) 138.
283 ibid.
284 Draft Articles on the Law of Treaties between States and International Organizations (n 256) 18 and 22.
285 For more details, see Klabbers (n 92) 55–63.
286 Draft Articles on the Law of Treaties (n 256) 189 and Draft Articles on the Law of Treaties between States and International Organizations (n 256) 18–19; see also Klabbers (n 92) 55–57.
287 Draft Articles on the Law of Treaties between States and International Organizations (n 256) 18.
288 ibid 18–19; see also Schermers and Blokker (n 119) 1121–22.
289 For an overview of the different arguments referring to the views of Sir Lauterpacht, Sir Gerald and Sir Waldock, see Klabbers (n 92) 55–57.
290 See Draft Articles on the Law of Treaties (n 256) 189 and Klabbers (n 92) 57, quoting Sir Humphrey.
291 See Klabbers (n 92) 57.

of 'domestic' agreements, in particular with regard to purely commercial matters and matters governed entirely by an internal law system, admit that agreements between states are in principle governed by international law, at least as far as the principle *pacta sunt servanda* is concerned.[292] This suggests that the agreements concluded between international organisations or between the former and states would as a rule qualify as international agreements, and only exceptionally as other kinds of agreements. For an illustrative example concerning the European Union, it is worth referring once more to the first *France v Commission* case in which the Court did not have any difficulties qualifying the international cooperation instrument concluded between the Commission and the US government as a 'treaty' within the scope of the 1986 Vienna Convention.

Competent organs and procedural aspects

Since state constitutions and constitutive acts of international organisations do not usually include detailed provisions regarding the category of administrative agreements, there is room for different arrangements concerning the distribution of treaty-making authority among executive agencies and organs, as well as with regard to the coordination and supervision of such authority.[293]

In various states, including EU Member States, as a matter of internal law and/or practice, government departments and agencies are allowed to conclude agreements falling within their subject-matter mandate.[294] Subject to the peculiarities of each domestic system, to the extent that such executive or administrative agreements do not interfere with the competence of the legislative or with politically significant treaty-making, they do not necessarily require *prior* authorisation or approval by the legislature.[295] However, in many states, the administrative agreements concluded by government agencies and departments are subject to various levels of oversight by the ministry of foreign affairs or any other executive authority entrusted with the management of external relations.[296] Moreover, formal and informal controls by the government and/or by the legislature, such as advance notice, consultation and reporting duties, are usually established.[297]

Regarding international organisations, whilst international law does not contain clear rules on the matter, treaty-making is normally vested in one or more of the main organs.[298] Save an explicit prohibition in the constitutive act, the main organs have the possibility to delegate treaty-making powers to other organs of the organisation.[299] In the exercise of such powers, express authorisation by the competent organ is normally

292 See Sir Gerald's view in Yearbook of the International Law Commission (YILC) 1959, vol II 95.
293 For more details, see Hollis (n 250) 20–21.
294 ibid.
295 ibid 24–27.
296 ibid 21–23.
297 ibid 25–27.
298 See Schermers and Blokker (n 119) 1136. For a more detailed analysis concerning the organs of international organisations competent to conclude treaties, see Detter (n 276) 421–44.
299 Chiu (n 255) 89, and 91–92. According to this author, in practice, in most cases the executive organ would not take the initiative to conclude treaties without express authorisation by the competent organ of the international organisation.

required, but this does not usually include agreements dealing with purely administrative matters.[300] However, the agreements concluded by various organs of an international organisation may be subject to various forms of supervision, including, at a minimum, information and reporting duties.[301] According to Detter, while the delegation of some treaty-making powers to subsidiary organs of an international organisation is inevitable, it is important to find ways to keep such powers under control.[302] In this regard, it is possible either '(. . .) to control the scope of the powers delegated to subsidiary organs'[303] or to subject the agreements concluded by such organs to some level of approval.[304] In any case, even in the absence of explicit provisions in the internal law of the organisation regarding treaty-making by administrative organs, it seems to be accepted that, as long as the organ concerned acts within the limits of its mandate, its acts would in principle bind the international organisation.[305]

2.3.1.2.2 INTERNATIONAL ADMINISTRATIVE AGREEMENTS AT THE EU LEVEL

At the EU level, administrative agreements, have been used increasingly in institutional practice. As shown previously, the international cooperation practice of the Commission features numerous agreements, arrangements and MOUs concluded with international organisations and third countries.[306] Sometimes such instruments have been authorised by the Council[307] or they were enacted based on an explicit delegation by the legislator.[308] In other instances, agreements were allowed by specific Treaty provisions[309] or they were concluded on the basis of Commission's role in the management of EU external relations based on Article 220 TFEU.[310] Yet another scenario consists of the possibility for a treaty concluded by the Union under Article 218 TFEU to enable the Commission to enter into specific arrangements or agreements to ensure its implementation.[311] The Commission has enacted various

300 ibid 90.

301 See, particularly for the UN context, Schermers and Blokker (n 119) 1137–38.

302 Detter (n 276) 444.

303 ibid. In this context, Detter refers to some sort of *prior* authorization by the main organs of the organization, which may, however, '(. . .) be couched in the most general terms'.

304 ibid. In this regard, he points out that in the practice of international organisations, *prior* authorisation is rather the rule as compared to the 'approval' requirement.

305 Chiu (n 255) 91–92; Detter (n 276) 434.

306 See in this chapter, 2.2.3.4.3: The international cooperation instruments concluded by the Commission and other EU institutions and bodies.

307 eg monetary agreements concluded according to art 219 TFEU.

308 eg the financing agreements concluded by the Commission on the basis of the EU Financial Regulations.

309 eg the '*laissez-passer*' agreements concluded between the Commission and third countries according to art 6 of Protocol No 7 'On the Privileges and Immunities of the European Union'.

310 eg the Framework Agreement between the European Commission on behalf of the European Union and the International Bank for Reconstruction and Development, the International Development Association, the International Finance Corporation and the Multilateral Investment Guarantee Agency (n 150).

311 Schütze (n 70) 395–96.

arrangements and agreements in the exercise of its own administrative tasks.[312] In addition to the Commission, other EU institutions and bodies (ECB, EIB, agencies) made use of similar instruments with regard to international cooperation aspects within their mandate. The analysis of such instruments in light of the relevant criteria of international law[313] leads to the conclusion that some of them can be qualified as legally binding.[314] This could be the case also with regard to instruments labeled as 'arrangement' or 'memorandum of understanding'.

In spite of the widespread use of technical-administrative agreements in the Union's institutional practice, they are not formally acknowledged in the Treaties. As mentioned above, more often than not international agreements concluded by the Union according to Article 218 TFEU,[315] as well as secondary legislation, include more or less detailed provisions regarding international cooperation on an administrative-technical level. Sometimes, 'Article 218' agreements and secondary legislation include explicit provisions with regard to the international cooperation instruments which may be used by the Commission, agencies and other bodies.[316] In some instances, this is accompanied by explicit provisions regarding conditions, limitations and procedural matters.

Also, EU agencies lacking explicit provisions to that effect in their legal framework concluded formal international cooperation instruments in the performance of their tasks.[317] The concerns voiced both in the Common Approach on EU agencies and in the Commission's Vademecum on External Relations, that the EU agencies cannot commit the Union to international obligations,[318] seem to indicate that the administrative

312 See *Vademecum on the External Action* (n 43) 52.

313 ie the wording, purpose, content and context of the instrument – see in this chapter, 2.3.1: The concept of 'international agreement'.

314 eg the Financial and Administrative Framework Agreement with the United Nations, signed 29 April 2003 (this agreement features treaty-like terminology such as 'parties', 'agree', and 'shall/will' clauses laying down specific rights and obligations for the parties, and it entails financial contributions by the parties for actions of common interest, subject to specific criteria and conditions, includes dispute settlement clauses, as well as clauses regarding the entry into force, amendment and termination of the agreement); Framework Agreement between the Commission and IMF, signed 12 January 2009 (although it is rather concise, this agreement features treaty-like terminology such as 'parties', 'agree', 'shall/will' clauses laying down specific rights and obligations for the parties, and it entails financial contributions by the Commission to IMF in the form of contribution agreements, and includes clauses regarding entry into force, amendment and termination of the agreement). In the case of the EIB, it is beyond doubt that this body participated in a binding multilateral international agreement as far the establishment of EBRD is concerned (the Agreement Establishing the European Bank for Reconstruction and Development was signed in Paris on 29 May 1990 and entered into force on 28 March 1991).

315 eg the Bilateral Aviation Safety Agreements (BASA) concluded between the European Union and USA, Canada and Brazil provide explicitly for specific implementing instruments to be concluded between technical agents (ie EASA and the competent aviation authority from the third country concerned).

316 For more details as regards EU agencies, see ch 1, 1.7: The international dimension of EU agencies – practice and legal design.

317 ibid.

318 Common Approach on EU agencies (n 4) para 25; *Vademecum on the External Action* (n 43) 18. The founding regulations of some of the recently created EU agencies (eg EBA, ESMA, EIOPA, SRB) include provisions on international cooperation reflecting this concern.

agreements entered into by these bodies should always be non-binding or, in the alternative, binding only on the EU agencies themselves.[319]

Whereas in most states and international organisations the absence of explicit provisions in the constitution did not preclude the formalisation of administrative agreements through internal legislation and the acceptance of the practice of concluding such instruments, within the EU, (binding) administrative agreements seem problematic.[320] As discussed, the source of the problem lies particularly in the 1994 *France v Commission* case where the Court denied a general and autonomous competence for the Commission to conclude binding international agreements by pointing to the general principle of institutional balance in combination with the division of tasks between the main EU institutions according to the standard treaty-making procedure laid down by the Treaty. More radically, except for the derogations explicitly allowed by the Treaty,[321] the Court allegedly denied the legal validity of any binding agreement concluded outside Article 218 TFEU by indicating ***inter alia*** that mere practice cannot override Treaty provisions, and by pointing out that the international cooperation pursued on the basis of the internal powers vested on institutions may not affect the division of powers between the EU institutions with regard to the treaty-making procedure laid down by the Treaty.[322]

As could be seen, in spite of the ban arguably imposed by the Court on the conclusion of international agreements outside Article 218 TFEU, the Commission's practice of concluding international cooperation instruments of a technical-administrative nature and also increasingly followed by other EU bodies, such as EU agencies, has continued.[323] Moreover, as emphasised earlier, the existing practice finds support in explicit provisions included in international agreements concluded according to Article 218 TFEU,[324] as well as in secondary legislation, such as the EU financial regulation and the founding acts of the EU agencies.[325]

If one sticks to the strict interpretation of the CJEU in *France v Commission* judgments, it follows that such technical-administrative agreements are legally valid only if they are non-binding. Thus, any international binding agreement, regardless of how minor or technical it is, should be concluded in accordance with the procedure

319 This latter scenario would require, however, that the EU agencies have a status of their own on the international plane. Provided that the EU agencies act as mere Union bodies, their actions may be attributed ultimately to the EU itself: see on the issue of the international legal personality of EU agencies in this chapter, 2.3.2: International legal personality.

320 See in this chapter, 2.2.3.4.3: The international cooperation instruments concluded by the Commission and other EU institutions and bodies.

321 See Schütze (n 70) 394–95.

322 Case C-327/91 *France v Commission* (n 129) paras 36 and 41.

323 For more details regarding the international cooperation practice of the EU agencies see ch 1, 1.7: The international dimension of EU agencies – practice and legal design, and Annexes I and II. For details regarding the international cooperation of the Commission, see in this chapter, 2.2.3.4.3: The international cooperation instruments concluded by the Commission and other EU institutions and bodies.

324 For an example of international agreement between the EU and USA enabling the Commission and the Department of State to conclude 'implementing arrangements' as 'Executive Agents' see Schütze (n 70) 395–96.

325 See ch 1, 1.7: The international dimension of EU agencies – practice and legal design, as well as Annexes I and II.

mentioned under Article 218 TFEU, involving the main EU political actors. Such a solution, regardless of how logical it looks in light of the formal provisions in the Founding Treaties, raises important legal and practical problems. First, going through the whole standard procedure involving political actors for every minor agreement is likely to result in significant delays and unnecessary complications in the negotiation process. Secondly, it may be politically unfeasible to use this procedure in particular in those instances in which, on the other side, the competent authority to conclude the agreement is a state agency or a subsidiary organ of an international organisation competent for the matter within the scope of the agreement.[326] Thirdly, the conclusion of agreements according to Article 218 TFEU does not necessarily alleviate the need for concluding additional international cooperation instruments between the Commission or the competent EU body and the corresponding competent authority from the third country or international organisation concerned. Although they are concluded to implement the 'mother' agreement based on Article 218 TFEU, such instruments may include detailed obligations and procedures enabling concrete co-operation between the parties, which would nevertheless turn them into binding instruments. The only remaining solution to solve this tension would be to force the reality into the legal mould by interpreting such instruments as non-binding.

However, a more flexible perspective has been proposed previously which takes into account the realities of the present-day international cooperation and furthers the legal acceptability of the EU international administrative cooperation.[327] Thus, it is maintained that the stance adopted by the Court in *France v Commission* cases does not *per se* exclude the delegation of treaty-making powers to other actors or international agreements being concluded according to different scenarios, outside the scope of Article 218 TFEU.[328] What is essential is that under such scenarios the institutional balance in the EU external action area, and particularly under Article 218 TFEU, is not upset. This would require at least that the treaty-making powers entrusted to other EU actors are necessarily specific[329] and subject to limitations and conditions ensuring that the prerogatives of the main EU institutions under Article 218 TFEU are preserved.

Against this background, it is proposed to finally acknowledge also the category of 'technical-administrative' agreements within the EU along with the category of 'politically significant' agreements concluded on the basis of Article 218 TFEU.[330] As could be seen, such a distinction reflecting to a certain extent the interplay between legislative and administrative action in the field of foreign affairs is accepted one way

326 See on this point Kingston (n 130) 670.

327 See in this chapter, 2.2.3.4.3: The international cooperation instruments concluded by the Commission and other EU institutions and bodies.

328 For a view accepting the possibility for delegation of treaty-making powers to the Commission and other EU institutions and bodies (including EU agencies), see Schütze (n 70) 395–99. For a view according to which the Commission may conclude agreements with international organisations under the current art 220 TFEU without touching 'upon the realm of political and legal commitment under Article 218 TFEU' see Ott, Vos and Coman-Kund (n 128) 97–98.

329 ie they remain within the boundaries of the core mandate of the respective EU institution or body, and pertain to technical and administrative agreements concerned with the implementation of legislation or 'Article 218 TFEU' agreements.

330 For a view suggesting such a distinction, see Schütze (n 70) 396.

or another within states and international organisations.[331] This is inevitable as the current international practice actually compels the EU to use such instruments in establishing cooperation on a technical-administrative level.[332] The administrative agreements as used currently in the Union's international practice are concluded with a view to implementing specific Treaty provisions[333] or existing agreements under Article 218 TFEU, or to enable external administrative action implementing existing EU legislation. Such agreements are illustrative of the Union's external executive action, and are enacted by EU institutions and bodies entrusted with executive and administrative tasks, in particular the Commission, ECB and EIB, and the EU agencies.

In the absence of an explicit prohibition in the Treaty, such instruments may be concluded in accordance with explicit provisions to that effect.[334] The mandate to conclude administrative agreements may be expressed in very clear terms specifying the instruments to be used. This is the case of the Commission's power to conclude agreements for *laissez-passer* according to Protocol No 7, the Commission's power to conclude agreements according to the EU Financial Regulations or the cooperation agreements mentioned in the (old) founding acts of Europol, Eurojust and Cepol. As already noted, the founding acts of other EU agencies provide for 'arrangements' to be concluded by these bodies in the discharge of their international cooperation tasks. Whereas the use of this term rather than 'agreement' might suggest in the EU jargon a preference for a non-binding instrument, the wording, content and context of the instrument are decisive for determining its legal nature. In this context, Schütze regards the 'implementing arrangements' concluded by the Commission in the application of various agreements concluded by the Union as an illustration of a limited delegation of treaty-making powers to the Commission.[335] Moreover, the careful drafting concerning the 'administrative arrangements' that may be concluded by the EU financial supervisory authorities[336] can be taken as a sign that the use of term 'arrangement' alone is not sufficient for qualifying such instruments as non-binding.

The mandate enabling EU institutions and bodies to conclude administrative agreements may arguably consist of more generally worded provisions. This applies to the Commission's powers under Article 220 TFEU, as well as to the powers of ECB and EIB to conclude administrative agreements according to the relevant provisions of

331 See in this chapter, 2.3.1.2.1: Administrative agreements in international and state practice.

332 Such agreements of a technical-administrative nature concluded by EU institutions, bodies and agencies are to be regarded, in principle, as international agreements, not as agreements of a different kind (see for the general discussion regarding the distinction between international agreements and 'domestic' agreements in this chapter, 2.3.1.2.1: Administrative agreements in international and state practice).

333 eg art 17(1) TEU and art 220 TFEU in the case of the Commission, arts 6 and 23 of Protocol No 4 in the case of ECB, art 14 of Protocol No 5 for EIB.

334 For a view that the Commission could conclude executive agreements only where expressly provided by the Treaties and on the basis of delegation by secondary law and international agreements, see Schütze (n 70) 394–96. However, it should be noted that this author mentions under the 'express delegation' scenarios also those instances where the relevant provisions do not explicitly specify the instruments that the Commission may conclude.

335 ibid 395–96.

336 Art 33 of the EBA, EIOPA and ESMA founding regulations.

their respective statutes.[337] In these instances, such generally worded provisions on international cooperation are said to entail the conclusion of administrative agreements[338] as a necessary means to ensure their full effectiveness. There is no reason that this logic should not apply *mutatis mutandis* to those EU agencies whose founding acts include an explicit mandate for international cooperation, without specifying the concrete instruments to be used by these bodies in fulfilling this role.

Arguably, administrative agreements could also be enacted where the attainment of the core mandate of a certain institution or agency requires instrumental external action. This entails an implied mandate for international cooperation inherent to the main functions and tasks of the respective institution or agency. Such instrumental international cooperation may arguably entail both non-binding and binding actions provided that they remain within the boundaries of the core mandate of the respective institution or agency, and within the EU institutional framework. Particularly for EU agencies, both the Commission's Vademecum on External Relations[339] and the Common Approach on EU agencies[340] acknowledge the possibility for implied international cooperation by these bodies. While accepting this scenario, it is made clear that the international actions of EU agencies should remain within their mandate, and respect the EU institutional framework.[341]

In all instances, such international cooperation instruments as a form of external administrative action must be in line with 'Article 218' agreements, and must not affect the balance of powers laid down in that article and, more generally, in the management of the EU external action area. In this respect, formal and informal limitations and conditions must ensure that these standards are met. These are the provisions in the relevant legal framework limiting the scope of the instruments, formal authorisations and approvals by the Council or the Commission, duties of information, consultation and reporting, etc. Since these administrative agreements are outside the scope of Article 218 TFEU, the control exercised by the main EU institutions does not have to be in line with the requirements of Article 218 TFEU. Instead, the legislator has discretion to provide for specific arrangements ensuring that the principle of institutional balance is observed. This entails coordination with and oversight by the main EU external action actors, in particular the Council, the Commission, the High Representative and the EEAS, and the EU delegations.[342] The principle of legality also requires legal safeguards, including the possibility for judicial review of administrative agreements.[343]

337 See in this regard Schütze (n 70) 392–93 and 396–97.
338 ibid.
339 *Vademecum on the External Action* (n 43) 18.
340 Common Approach on EU agencies (n 4) para 25.
341 ibid.
342 The Common Approach on EU agencies insists on exchange of information between the EU agencies and the Commission, as well as the EU delegations to ensure the consistency of the EU policy (para 25). In line with the Common Approach, the *Vademecum on the External Action of the European Union* re-emphasises the need for coordination by the Commission of the international activities of the EU agencies, *Vademecum on the External Action* (n 43) 18.
343 This could be provided by specific provisions in the relevant legislation or may result from the general system of the Treaties, such as arts 263, 267 or 277 TFEU.

When administrative agreements are concluded by the Commission in implementing the external dimension of EU policies, coordination with the Council and the Member States seems to be essential.[344] As for the EU agencies, their powers to conclude technical-administrative agreements need also to be in line with institutional balance in EU external relations and the present-day *Meroni* requirements. In this respect, the inclusion of the Commission and the Member States in the design of the agencies by their founding acts, together with the formal and informal relationships between these bodies and the Council, as well as the Commission, should guarantee that their administrative agreements remain within the scope of their regulatory framework, and that their discretion is sufficiently limited. Moreover, a channel of communication between the agencies and the EEAS, as well as the EU delegations could provide an additional safeguard for ensuring coordination and consistency between the international cooperation of EU agencies and the Union's overall external action.[345] These and other safeguards (eg duties to inform and report to the European Parliament on international cooperation activities) may be shaped *via* the founding acts of the EU agencies and through various instruments implementing them, such as Commission's implementing decisions and EU agencies' acts. More informal safeguards and controls may be established through institutional practice based on the roles of the main institutions according to the Founding Treaties. This includes, for instance, the need for EU agencies to conclude working arrangements with their parent DGs within the Commission ensuring that the agencies operate within their mandate and in accordance with the EU institutional framework.[346] In this context, one should also mention the demand uttered in the Common Approach for early information exchange on international activities between EU agencies, the Commission and the EU delegations.[347]

2.3.2 International legal personality

2.3.2.1 Concept and criteria

The concept of 'international legal personality' is instrumental to determining whether the EU agencies, when pursuing international cooperation activities, act as distinct entities on the international plane[348] or as mere organs of the Union.[349] This issue has

344 The Commission stresses the need to inform the Council and, in certain circumstances, to obtain the Council's approval or endorsement as regards its non-binding administrative arrangements, *Vademecum on the External Action* (n 43) 54–55; in the Commission's view, should the instrument prove to be binding, then the 'Article 218 TFEU' procedure should apply (52). For a similar view that the Commission's binding administrative arrangements would require authorisation by the Council, see Macleod, Hendry and Hyett (n 86) 96. For a view suggesting that the Commission's administrative agreements are acceptable as long as these '(. . .) concern technical and non-political questions', see Schütze (n 70) 396.

345 Common Approach on EU agencies (n 4) para 25.

346 ibid.

347 ibid.

348 In other words, are EU agencies a distinct category of 'other' subjects of international law?

349 For a preliminary analysis of the EU agencies in the context of the emergence of an 'international agency' phenomenon, see Edoardo Chiti and Ramses A Wessel, 'The Emergence of International

theoretical and practical consequences as it is closely linked to the problem of attribution of the EU agencies' international activities. In this regard, clarifying the legal status of the EU agencies on the international plane is also important in view of the statement in the Common Approach on EU agencies and in the Commission's *Vademecum on External Relations* that EU agencies may not commit officially the Union to international obligations.

International legal personality indicates that an organisation can act as a distinct subject at the international level and is capable of having rights and duties.[350] However, for international organisations and other entities international personality remains a nebulous concept, and is subject to intensive debates in academia.[351] The views range from denying international personality in the absence of an express conferment of such a status,[352] to accepting the international personality even in the absence of the explicit will of the creators of the relevant entity provided that certain conditions are met. According to the prevailing view the international personality is derived from the creators of the organisation, but it can also be implied from the competence or powers of the relevant entity as laid down in its founding act.[353] This approach has been used by the International Court of Justice (ICJ) in its famous 'Reparations for Injuries' Advisory Opinion.[354] Accordingly, the following standard requirements should be fulfilled by an organisation with international legal personality:[355]

(1) it must be 'a permanent association of states' (organisation)
(2) it must be possible to make 'a distinction in terms of legal powers and purposes, between the organisation and its members states' (creators)
(3) the entity must be equipped with 'legal powers exercisable on the international plane and not solely within the national systems of one or more states'.

In short, an entity with international legal personality must have organisational distinctiveness, sufficient autonomy so as to act in detachment from its creators, and

Agencies in the Global Administrative Space. Autonomous Actors or State Servants?' in Richard Collins and Nigel D White (eds), *International Organisations and the Idea of Autonomy. Institutional Independence in the International Legal Order* (Routledge 2011) 142–59.

350 White (n 68) 30–32; Schermers and Blokker (n 119) 993.

351 See White (n 68) 32 and 35–40.

352 That is, a pure subjective approach.

353 See Schermers and Blokker (n 119) 989 and White (n 68) 39.

354 The ICJ established the international legal personality of the UN by combining both objective elements (separate organs and special tasks indicating autonomy from the creators) and subjective elements (intention of the states to entrust the organisation with international legal capacity or, in other words, to confer the respective entity functions and powers on the international plane), *Reparation for injuries suffered in the service of the Unite Nations*, Advisory Opinion [1949] ICJ 174. See also White (n 68) 43–44.

355 Ian Brownlie, *Principles of Public International Law* (7th edn, OUP 2008) 677. The reasons for choosing and adapting Brownlie's criteria are twofold: (1) the list is drawn up on the basis of the predominant functional test used in the ICJ Advisory Opinion in 'Reparations for Injuries', thereby reflecting the mixed objective and subjective approach to international legal personality; (2) the list of criteria seems to be widely accepted by scholars: see eg Rachel Frid, *The Relations Between the EC and International Organizations: Legal Theory and Practice* (Kluwer Law International 1995) 13–16; White (n 68) 44–45.

international capacity. The application of these criteria may prove difficult in practice, and there may be particular entities that cannot be easily accommodated within this theoretical framework.[356] In this respect, beside the design of the entity as provided in its founding act and the relevant legal framework, there are also other factors which might be indicative of international legal personality. Thus, to the extent that the international legal personality of a certain entity is not explicitly denied by its relevant legal framework, the international cooperation practice developed by that entity and the recognition by other subjects of international law could result in establishing the legal personality of the respective organisation.[357]

With regard to the question whether agencies and semi-autonomous organs set up by states and international organisations may acquire their own international legal personality, no definite answer is provided in the international law literature, whilst practice offers different solutions.[358] Regarding specifically the organs or agencies of international organisations, this issue has been called the '(in)divisibility of international legal personality'[359] or 'multiple legal personalities'.[360] In any case, the conferment of legal personality under the rules of the particular state or organisation does not seem to be necessarily conclusive as to the existence of the international personality of the respective entity.[361] Two elements appear to be important for such an entity to claim its own international status: (1) it must have powers which it can exercise on the international plane (the exercise of certain treaty-making powers would be an important indicator in this respect, although not necessarily a *sine qua non* condition);[362] and (2) it must have sufficient organisational and decision-making autonomy, so that it can be perceived as an entity detached from its creators.[363]According to Brownlie, the higher the degree of autonomy and legal powers of an agency increase, the more can it be approximated to an international organisation.[364] In addition, the agency's international cooperation practice and the recognition of that entity by states and international organisations as an independent subject of international law would play a role (see Box 2.2 below).[365] In this context, there is a 'careful tendency'[366] to recognise various agencies of states and international organisations as subjects of international law with a limited legal capacity.[367]

356 Brownlie (n 355) 678.
357 See Frid (n 355) 16–19 and 23; Schermers and Blokker (n 119) 992–93.
358 See Schermers and Blokker (n 119) 994; Brownlie (n 355) 61 and 66–67.
359 Schermers and Blokker (n 119) 994.
360 Ott, Vos and Coman-Kund (n 128) 94.
361 Brownlie (n 355) 66.
362 White (n 68) 41. This author considers that it is unnecessary to attempt to equip international personality with some core features such as treaty-making capacity, privileges and immunities, *locus standi* before international tribunals, capacity to bring claims or international responsibility duties. According to him, for the purpose of international legal personality, it is the separate will of the entity that is important, whilst the exact extent of its legal capacity will depend mainly on the constituent act of the organisation, White (n 68) 34–35.
363 Brownlie (n 355) 66–67.
364 ibid 61.
365 ibid 67.
366 See for the use of this expression in the EU context, Ott, Vos and Coman-Kund (n 128) 94.
367 See Brownlie (n 355) 61 and 67; Schermers and Blokker (n 119) 994; Gregor Schusterschitz, 'European Agencies as Subjects of International Law' (2004) 1 IOLR 163.

Box 2.2 Checklist international legal personality of semi-autonomous organs established by states and international organisations

Criteria	*Indicators*
Own organs, structure, tasks, legal personality (organisational distinctiveness)	Legal design and framework
Sufficient autonomy from creators (separate will)	International cooperation practice
Can exercise powers on the international plane (international capacity)	Recognition by other subjects of international law

2.3.2.2 International legal personality of the EU agencies

Article 47 TEU endows the Union with its own legal personality. Reading this provision in light of the *ERTA* case law and in combination with the Treaty provisions regarding EU external action[368] supports the conclusion that the Union also has international legal personality.[369] This begs the question whether it is still possible for various EU institutions and bodies to claim a separate legal status on the international plane.

Pre-Lisbon, this issue raised academic interest and also proved to have practical relevance. In Case C-327/1991 *France v Commission*, the CJEU made it clear that the EU, not the Commission, had international legal personality. Also, the special functions and features of the ECB and EIB prompted some academics to support a functionally limited international legal personality for such EU bodies.[370] Unlike the case of the Commission, the Court took a midway approach as regards the legal status of these EU bodies. While subsuming these bodies under the EU legal framework, the Court also emphasised their individual features and, in particular, their high degree of independence.[371] Also, in the case of the EU agencies, notwithstanding the majority view denying such bodies the status as subjects under international law, some authors supported a view favouring international legal personality for these bodies.[372] The main arguments supporting a restricted international legal personality for EU agencies are

368 Art 21 TEU, as well as arts 216, 218, 220–221 TFEU.

369 See Piris (n 23) 86–87; Monar (n 26) 21; Juan Santos Vara, 'The External Dimension of the Area of Freedom Security and Justice in the Lisbon Treaty' (2008) 10 *European Journal of Law Reform* 577, 587; Schermers and Blokker (n 119) 992.

370 See in this chapter section, 2.2.3.4.1: The management of the EU external action area. The main arguments supporting the international legal personality of the ECB and EIB are as follows: (1) these EU bodies were endowed by the Treaty with their own legal personality, very much in the same way as the Union; (2) they were equipped with powers which can be exercised independently on the international plane; (3) the international cooperation practice of these bodies confirms their international legal personality.

371 See in this chapter section, 2.2.3.4.1. The management of the EU external action area.

372 Schusterschitz (n 367) 188; Ronald van Ooik, 'The Growing Importance of Agencies in the EU: Shifting Governance and the Institutional Balance' in Deirdre M Curtin and Ramses A Wessel (eds), *Good Governance and the European Union. Reflections on Concepts, Institutions and Substance* (Intersentia 2005) 132.

related to the provisions on legal personality in the founding acts of these bodies,[373] their autonomy and their international cooperation practice.[374]

Post-Lisbon the situation has not changed fundamentally as far as the '(in)divisibility'[375] of the Union's international legal personality is concerned. The main relevance of Article 47 TEU is that it ends the pre-Lisbon ambiguity and complexities caused by the parallel action of the Community and the EU on the international plane.[376] The explicit inclusion of the ECB on the list of EU institutions seems to militate against recognising its international legal personality.[377] However, the fact that the Treaty maintains the explicit provision conferring legal personality on the ECB, in combination with the provisions in Protocol No 4 regarding its international cooperation tasks, still provides arguments for the ECB's functionally limited international legal personality. In this regard, Schermers and Blokker argue that '[e]xcept for the European Central Bank, the institutions of the European Union (. . .) do not have legal personality'.[378] Eeckhout acknowledges that, post-Lisbon, the ECB is 'part of the EU's institutional framework in much the same way as any of the other institutions', but at the same time that 'in the small world of banking operations (. . .) the ECB is recognized as an international legal person with certain powers stemming from the merely operational tasks it is entrusted with'.[379] As for the EIB, its functionally limited international personality seems more plausible, since the Lisbon Treaty did not transform it into an 'institution' and kept untouched the previous Treaty provisions regarding its legal personality and international cooperation tasks. In these circumstances, some continue to support the separate legal status of the EIB on the international plane.[380]

Thus, assuming that post-Lisbon, the EU maintains a degree of "divisibility" of its international legal personality, the EU agencies might qualify for the status of 'subject of international law with a limited functional capacity'. EU agencies are explicitly equipped with legal personality according to their founding regulations, but such provisions have generally been interpreted as conferring only domestic legal personality.[381] Accordingly, EU agencies' international personality and capacity depend essentially on the degree of autonomy and on the tasks and powers exercisable on the international plane they possess. They must be assessed on a case-by-case basis for each EU agency.

Should the case-by-case analysis carried out conclude that the relevant EU agency has a functionally limited international personality, then its international actions in principle should be attributed to the agency itself. Conversely, if it turns out that the

373 In general, the provisions in the EU agencies' founding acts concerning their legal personality are formulated very similarly to the Treaty provisions regarding Union's legal personality.

374 Schusterschitz concludes that EU agencies may acquire, and in fact some of them have acquired, a restricted international legal personality with regard to their headquarters agreements, Schusterschitz (n 367) 188.

375 For the use of this term, see Schermers and Blokker (n 119) 994.

376 Piris (n 23) 86–87.

377 Eeckhout (n 21) 208.

378 Schermers and Blokker (n 119) 994.

379 Eeckhout (n 21) 207–08.

380 See Schermers and Blokker (n 119) 994. The fact that the EU and the EIB participate separately as founding members in the European Bank for Reconstruction and Development (EBRD) provides quite an impressive illustration of the separate legal status of the EIB on the international plane.

381 Schusterschitz (n 367) 163; Ott (n 104) 526–28.

respective EU agency does not fulfil the criteria for international legal personality, its international actions should be attributed ultimately to the EU. In these circumstances, the statement inserted in the Common Approach[382] and reiterated in the Commission's Vademecum on External Relations,[383] according to which EU agencies cannot represent the EU position or commit the EU to binding obligations, is not entirely accurate. While the EU agencies obviously do not have the power to represent the position of the Union on a political and diplomatic level, their international actions pursued within their mandate would nevertheless create limited international obligations for the EU on a technical-administrative level. From the perspective of international law,[384] it is very likely that even international agreements concluded by the EU agencies in breach of EU law would nevertheless bind the Union on the international plane.[385]

The controls and supervisory mechanisms regarding international cooperation by EU agencies may have an impact on their legal status as global actors. The more EU agencies are controlled by the main EU institutions, the more likely it is that these bodies are seen as acting on behalf of the EU from an international law perspective. Conversely, the more independently the EU agencies act on the international plane, the more likely it is for these bodies to claim their own limited legal status under international law, in a similar manner as in the case of the ECB and the EIB. This would require, however, a loose interpretation of the *Meroni* requirements concerning the criteria and conditions limiting the discretion of the EU agencies.

2.4 Conclusion: a general legal-analytical framework for assessing EU agencies as global actors

The legal-analytical framework for assessing the EU agencies as global actors requires using the lens of both EU and international law. From the *EU law angle*, the global dimension of the EU agencies needs to be in line with the principle of institutional balance and the *Meroni* doctrine entailing that EU agencies' powers must meet certain conditions, which can be summarised as follows: (1) powers of executive nature; (2) powers sufficiently defined in that they remain within the boundaries of the relevant regulatory framework of the agency (3) criteria and conditions limiting the discretion of the agency; (4) they do not encroach upon the powers conferred by the Founding Treaties on the EU institutions.

However, in the context of the international dimension of the EU agencies the system of reference relevant for assessing their powers and actions embraces both

382 Common Approach on EU agencies (n 4) para 25.

383 *Vademecum on the External Action* (n 43) 18.

384 See in particular art 46 of the 1969 Vienna Convention and art 46 of the 1982 Vienna Convention stipulating that the violation of internal rules regarding the competence to conclude treaties may be invoked as an invalidating factor only when 'the violation was manifest and concerned a rule (. . .) of fundamental importance'. See also Olufumi Elias, 'Who Can Make Treaties? International Organisations', Hollis (ed), *The Oxford Guide to Treaties* (n 220) 81–83.

385 See in particular with regard to EU agencies, Ott, Vos and Coman-Kund (n 128) 97. Regarding international agreements concluded in violation of EU law, see more generally Macleod, Hendry and Hyett (n 86) 129–32.

the legal framework in the area of agencies' core competences and the constitutional framework governing EU external action.

First, the general EU external action framework laid down in the Founding Treaties does not preclude, in principle, international cooperation tasks being entrusted to EU agencies. To the extent that the international cooperation pursued by the EU agencies remains within the boundaries of their core mandate and is instrumental to fulfilling their objectives within their competence, their international cooperation tasks are limited in principle to the external dimension of the specific EU policy areas of the particular agencies. Whereas for the sake of clarity it is desirable that the legal framework of the EU agencies includes explicit and detailed provisions regarding their international dimension, arguably the absence of such provisions does not necessarily preclude international cooperation. The instrumental function of their international cooperation arguably also allows these bodies to establish relations outside the EU on the basis of vague provisions concerning their external dimension or even solely on the basis of general provisions regarding their core mandate. This seems possible as long as the *Meroni* requirements are met and the principle of institutional balance is not affected.

Secondly, international cooperation pursued by the EU agencies may materialise both in non-binding and in binding instruments. In spite of the CJEU's allegedly strict stance on EU treaty-making in Case C-327/91 France v Commission, it is maintained that, within the mandate entrusted by the legislator, the EU agencies may enact binding international cooperation instruments subject to the *Meroni* requirements and provided that the institutional balance in the EU external action area is not affected. In this respect, it is maintained that EU agencies may conclude administrative agreements, not only on the basis of an express mandate specifying the instruments to be used, but also on the basis of a more generally worded express mandate for international cooperation. As acknowledged by the Common Approach on EU agencies, international cooperation instruments may also be enacted by EU agencies on the basis of an implied mandate for international cooperation inherent to their main functions and tasks, although reluctance is expressed with regard to the possibility for EU agencies to conclude binding agreements in this way.

It is maintained that EU agencies' legally binding instruments should be qualified as 'technical-administrative agreements', which are distinct from the most legally-politically significant agreements concluded by the EU according to Article 218 TFEU. Such a distinction would finally acknowledge a long-standing international cooperation practice by EU institutions and bodies, and is widely accepted in the practice of states and international organisations. As a result, the administrative agreements concluded by the EU agencies illustrate a specific form of EU external administrative action which remains outside the scope of Article 218 TFEU, and which should be consistent with the Union's agreements concluded under this provision, as well as with the EU legislation. It is essential that such agreements remain within the core mandate of the agency and that the design of the agency ensures sufficient supervision and control by the main actors in the EU external action area. In particular, the Council and the Commission should be involved in view of their roles in EU external representation, and in order to ensure consistency in the Union's external action area under Article 21 TEU. In this context, supervision by these actors should also ensure that international cooperation instruments concluded by EU agencies are in line with the Union's agreements under Article 218 TFEU, and that the powers of the Commission under Articles 17 TEU and 220 TFEU are not affected. Additionally, ensuring the involvement of the European Parliament in EU agencies' international dimension, and legal review of their international cooperation instruments can only enhance the system of supervision and controls, thereby guaranteeing that EU agencies' powers remain within the boundaries set by the EU constitutional framework.

The legal nature of the administrative agreements concluded by the EU agencies needs to be determined ultimately according to international law standards. This entails examining the international cooperation instruments of the EU agencies against the criteria for binding international agreements. In other words, it must be determined whether there is a genuine intention to create legally binding effects under international law based on the wording and substance of the instruments and taking into account the context in which the instruments have been negotiated, concluded and implemented.

Moreover, the concept of 'international legal personality' enables a determination of whether the international cooperation carried out by the EU agencies is attributable solely to the agencies themselves or ultimately to the EU. The EU agencies are set up outside the main EU institutional framework and entrusted with their own legal personality, as well as with a variable degree of autonomy. While this does not automatically mean that the EU agencies have international legal personality, they may nevertheless acquire such a status if two essential requirements are met: (1) they are entrusted with powers that they can exercise on the international plane; (2) they have sufficient organisational and decision-making autonomy so that they can be perceived as an entity acting independently from their 'mother' organisation (the European Union). Meeting the latter standard would require, however, a loose interpretation of the *Meroni* requirement concerning the criteria and conditions limiting the discretion of EU agencies.

Whilst the criteria for international agreements and international legal personality for entities such as the EU agencies are established *in abstracto*, a case-by-case analysis of the instruments and of the particular legal status of each particular agency is required for a more precise diagnosis. Such an analysis is undertaken in the next chapters of this study on three EU agencies: EASA, Frontex and Europol.

Part II

Case studies

3 Common methodological aspects

The case study research reported in Chapters 3, 4 and 5 follows a multiple case study design,[1] where the subject of analysis is the EU agency as defined earlier. The case studies provide an in-depth analysis and illustration of the international cooperation framework and practice of specific agencies, and assess this in light of the parameters laid down in the general legal-analytical framework of this study. In line with the queries of this study, all three case studies address the following common aspects: the legal nature of the international cooperation instruments of the selected EU agencies; their legal status on the international plane; and the compatibility of their international dimension with the EU constitutional framework, in particular the principle of institutional balance and the *Meroni* doctrine.

The case studies have been carried out following qualitative research techniques combining triangulation of data with a comparative approach. Triangulation of data through the use of various relevant sources of information was intended to increase the thoroughness and accuracy of analysis as well as the soundness of the conclusions drawn from each case study. The comparative approach taken entailed devising a common structure for the case studies that enabled cross-case study observations accounting for the variations characterising the international dimension of the EU agencies examined, while supposedly increasing the reliability of the general conclusions of this study.

Desk research has been combined with fieldwork, with a view to providing a comprehensive overview of the relevant legal framework and empirical insights into the international cooperation practice of the selected EU agencies. In addition to the analysis of the founding acts and other official legal sources, the desk research covered relevant agency documents and procedures, activity reports, work programmes, strategies, EU policy documents, reports and evaluations of the agencies' activities, and relevant scholarly literature. An important element of the desk research was the comprehensive analysis of the formal international cooperation instruments concluded by the selected EU agencies with their partners.

The fieldwork carried out resulted in direct contacts being established with the selected EU agencies, the Commission and the Council in order to obtain empirical insights and documents regarding important aspects of the international cooperation practice of the agencies. Information has been collected mainly through semi-structured interviews with EU officials, and the participation of the author in various formal and informal events concerning EU agencies. The use of semi-structured interviews with relevant EU officials was an important tool eliciting fresh 'real-life'

1 See Robert K Yin, *Case Study Research: Design and Methods* (Sage Publications 2003) 32–35, 37, 46–55.

insights concerning the elements of the EU agencies' international dimension examined within this study.[2] They proved to be a valuable source of information for a more complete and complex understanding of EU agencies' international cooperation role and mandate, instruments and legal status, by revealing perceptions and data from practice complementing, supporting or questioning data available from other sources.

Three techniques have been used with a view to ensure increased validity, reliability and comparability of interview findings. First, the interviews followed a similar design with a list of topics/questions based on the research questions of this study, the elements and parameters of the general-analytical framework, and the common structure of the case studies. Some flexibility has been adopted by slightly adapting the interview list used for officials from EU agencies when interviewing officials from the Commission and the Council. Secondly, the relatively low number of interviews has been compensated by a careful selection of interviewees ensuring that persons with expertise and closely involved with EU agencies' international co-operation were interviewed. Accordingly, experts from the selected EU agencies directly involved in the agency's international cooperation activities along with officials from the Commission and the Council in charge of the relationship with each EU agency (including international cooperation aspects) have been interviewed. This selection logic was aimed at bringing together different practitioners' perspectives on EU agencies' international dimension while keeping at a minimum the potential bias of some interviewees. A conscious choice has been made to limit interviewing to relevant officials from the Commission and the Council based on the assumption that these institutions are, in view of their role in Union's external action, the main 'principals' and interlocutor of the EU agencies' as far as their international cooperation is concerned. Thirdly, the vast majority of interviews have been recorded and transcribed in order to preserve as much as possible the authenticity and accuracy of the source of information.

The selection of the three EU agencies for the case study research has not been guided primarily by the idea of identifying a representative sample of cases, generating findings with a high degree of generalisability with regard to all EU agencies. A sampling logic would not be feasible for this study because each agency has its own identity, resulting from factors like the policy sector of the EU agencies, their particular evolution, the features of their formal design, or particularities resulting from their practice.[3] Therefore, there is a limited potential for generalising the findings concerning one agency or a few agencies, and applying them to the broader population of EU agencies.

Providing a meaningful and in-depth analysis within the framework of this study allowed the investigation of no more than three agencies. The selection of the three agencies followed a replication logic, in that the three case studies feature similar patterns as concerns international cooperation.[4] This required selecting three EU agencies which have as a common thread a rich potential for international cooperation reflected in their relevant legal framework and documented by their practice. Examining such agencies (rather than agencies with an underdeveloped international cooperation

2 Seventeen targeted interviews with one or more relevant EU officials have been conducted within the framework of this project (the interviews have been conducted via the phone or face to face and, in one instance, the interview questions and the corresponding answers were exchanged via email). In line with the interview protocol used, the identity of the interviewees is not revealed in this study.

3 See Yin (n 1) 47–50.

4 ibid 47–54.

record)[5] was likely to result in substantial evidence and findings for the purposes of this study. In this way, the findings from the three case studies could provide conclusions that could potentially be generalisable beyond the boundaries of each case study, by linking the findings to the overall legal-analytical framework concerning EU agencies as global actors. In this respect, the case study findings reflect the application of parameters which are shared by all EU agencies pursuing international cooperation, and cast light onto common legal problems these bodies are faced with or may be faced with in the future.[6] The ensuing results can provide input for refining the general legal-analytical framework in light of the findings from the case studies, proposing solutions to existing problems, advancing new or more specific queries for research, carrying out new in-depth case studies on other EU agencies.[7]

Against this background several more specific factors have been considered when choosing the case studies. To begin with, an important selection criterion concerned the policy area in which an EU agency is involved. In that sense, the agencies selected are active in EU policy areas with a well-developed external dimension. This is a factor that reveals the legal-policy context in which the EU agencies pursue their international cooperation, and that also potentially impacts upon the legal framework and the practice of international cooperation by these bodies. Other aspects taken into account are: the particular features of the (international cooperation) mandate of the agency as provided by its founding act;[8] the particular features of the international cooperation instruments concluded by the selected agencies;[9] the particular evolution of an agency allowing it to serve as some sort of 'critical' or as a revelatory case study within this project.[10] In view of these criteria and factors, the agencies that have been selected as case studies are the European Aviation Safety Agency (EASA), the European Agency for the Management of Operational Cooperation at the External Borders of the Member States of the European Union, relabelled recently as the European Border and Coast Guard Agency (Frontex) and the European Police Office (Europol).

5 This is the main reason for which, at the time of the selection, recent EU agencies such as ACER, ESMA, EBA, EIOPA, EASO were left out (at that time they had not developed a meaningful international cooperation record). For other new agencies like BEREC and eu-LISA, an additional reason was that the founding acts did not include any provisions with regard to their international dimension.

6 Yin (n 1) 31–33.

7 ibid 48 and 53–54.

8 Agencies with more detailed international cooperation provisions in their founding acts (providing for international cooperation tasks, formal cooperation instruments, procedural aspects, formal limits and restrictions) were preferred, since it was assumed that such bodies are less controversial from an EU legal point of view with regard to the development of their international dimension, and they could best illustrate the legal design of EU agencies as global actors.

9 While all the agencies selected feature explicit provisions with regard to their international cooperation instruments in their founding acts, the selection made sought to cover a broad range of such instruments not only *qua* terminology used (eg agreements, working arrangements, administrative arrangements, memoranda of understanding) but also *qua prima facie* legal nature (apparently binding [Europol]; apparently non-binding [Frontex]; not clear [EASA]).

10 This is the case for Europol, whose intergovernmental past and international cooperation instruments distinguish it from other EU agencies. Even if Europol deviated to some extent from the agency pattern, it nevertheless reflects a development which is particularly relevant from a legal perspective. Accordingly, as a global actor, Europol encounters important legal and practical problems and issues which may display important explanatory value as regards the overall legal-analytical framework employed, and may open paths for further research concerning EU agencies' international dimension.

EASA is an example of a so-called 'internal market' or a former 'Community agency' agency which, nevertheless, developed a significant global dimension, probably because of the inherent external dimension of air transport. There are similar EU agencies fulfilling primarily an internal mandate with an external twist such as EMSA, ERA and EMA. However, EASA has been chosen due to its impressive international practice which is evidenced by its working arrangements with various countries and its enhanced cooperative relations with international organisations such as ICAO. Unlike in the case of Frontex, the working arrangements concluded by EASA do not contain an express clause regarding their legal nature. Since this is also normally the case for other EU agencies concluding similar arrangements, the findings regarding the legal nature and effects of the working arrangements concluded by EASA could also be relevant for other bodies. Furthermore, there is yet another factor which causes this agency to be a suitable candidate for the case study. Namely, in several instances of cooperation, EASA has arguably been referred to as the representative of EU Member States or of the Commission and the EU. This raises complex issues concerning the legal status of this agency on the global level and the conclusions from this case study could arguably be generalised within the analytical framework of this study.

Frontex is similar to Europol in that it is also active in the Area of Freedom, Security and Justice (AFSJ). Frontex has been selected as a case study because it is an agency whose mandate (unlike most agencies) includes an inherent external focus (ie the management of EU external borders). It is thus interesting to see how this agency's international dimension has been accommodated to the EU external relations institutional framework, and whether the status of the agency as a global actor is influenced by its function of assisting Member States in their cooperation with third countries with the aim of strengthening Union's external border security. This agency has also developed quite a rich international practice formalised through working arrangements. One interesting feature of its instruments for international cooperation seems to be their intended soft law nature.

Europol has been chosen as a case study because it is an example of an agency with a strong international profile, rooted in its particular history as an intergovernmental organisation until 2009. Europol is one of the few EU agencies which, at the time this research had been carried out, were still allowed to conclude within the scope of their mandate international cooperation instruments labeled as 'agreements'. While Europol is a rather special agency, it is nevertheless very relevant for this study as it may offer valuable insights with regard to more general issues, such as the nature of the external powers that may be conferred on EU agencies and institutional balance, as well as the international status EU agencies may acquire. Accordingly, Europol has been selected for closer examination precisely because of its 'peculiar international profile', enabling this agency to serve as a case study illustrating the outer limits that international cooperation by EU agencies may reach. Also, Eurojust is an agency which is active in the same policy area and could also conclude international agreements. However, the particular evolution of Europol from an intergovernmental body to an EU agency and the potential impact of this evolution on the present international status of Europol had been decisive in making this choice. Additionally, Europol has undergone a process of transformation which materialised in the adoption of a new founding regulation that substantially redesigned agency's international dimension. A look at Europol's reform enables understanding some of the aspects pertaining to the agency's international practice and previous legal framework, which were perceived as legally problematic over time.

4 The case of the European Aviation Safety Agency

4.1 Introduction

In this chapter, the parameters and conditions devised within the general legal-analytical framework of this project are applied to the international dimension of the European Aviation Safety Agency (EASA). EASA has been chosen for closer examination because of its impressive international cooperation record linked to the inherent global dimension of the aviation sector, and the complex role EASA appears to play as a global actor in between the EU and the Member States.

This chapter focuses on the formal design of EASA's international cooperation without ignoring the legal-policy environment within which the agency is operating. This is complemented by insights from practice regarding mostly the conditions and constraints imposed on EASA's international cooperation as a result of the interactions with other actors (in particular the Commission and the Member States). Special attention is paid to the analysis of EASA's most important formal instruments for international cooperation – ie working arrangements – with a view to determining whether they can qualify as legally binding agreements under international law. Along these lines, a comprehensive evaluation of EASA as a global actor is provided by clarifying its legal status on the international plane (in particular whether EASA has international legal personality) and by assessing its international cooperation tasks and instruments in light of the principle of institutional balance and in light of the *Meroni* doctrine.

The chapter begins with an overview of the legal-policy context relevant for the study of the European Aviation Safety Agency (EASA) as a global actor (section 4.2). This takes into account the relevant legal and institutional framework of the Union, focusing on the external dimension of the EU aviation policy area. Next, EASA's specific features as an EU agency are mapped out (section 4.3). In so doing, the emphasis lies on important design aspects of the Agency (mandate and governance issues) and on its gradual evolution. Next EASA's international dimension is scrutinised (section 4.4). The analysis addresses both the formal legal framework for international cooperation and the international practice of the Agency. The review of EASA's legal framework focuses on the international cooperation mandate, tasks, instruments and procedures of the Agency. From the point of view of international practice, the strategic planning of the Agency and its formal international cooperation instruments are examined. With regard to the latter aspect, the analysis concentrates on the working arrangements concluded by EASA, their content and structure, effects and procedure for their negotiation and conclusion. The last part of the chapter (section 4.5) capitalises on the findings from the previous sections by assessing EASA's international dimension along the cross-cutting inquiries of this study.

4.2 The policy and legal-institutional environment of EASA

4.2.1 The Union's legal and institutional framework in the aviation area

For a long time, the aviation sector has been organised within the International Civil Aviation Organisation (ICAO) framework, with sovereign states as the main actors in the policy-making and regulatory processes, as well as in international relations.[1] However, since 1977 the EU started gradually to develop a policy for air transport, which now covers all aspects of the air transport sector.[2] The regulatory framework developed by the Union in the aviation area has had three important milestones. First, the Internal Market for Air Transport was established as part of the legislative reforms for the completion of the Internal Market in 1991–1993. In this context, the most significant development was the liberalisation of the air transport market through the so-called 'third package' of legislative measures adopted by the Council in 1992.[3] Secondly, between 2002–2004, most notably, the Single European Sky (SES) framework was set up[4] and aviation safety competences were transferred to the EU level. A case in point is the creation of EASA in 2002[5] and the entry into force of the so-called 'SAFA Directive', bringing the Safety Assessment of Foreign Aircraft programme within the realm of EU competences.[6] Thirdly, a second Single European Sky (SES II)[7] package had been adopted in 2008–2009 and the EU's competences in

1 Report of the High-level Group for the Future European Aviation Regulatory Framework (2007) 'European Aviation: A framework for driving performance improvement' 4 ‹https://ec.europa.eu/transport/sites/transport/files/modes/air/doc/hlg_2007_07_03_report.pdf›.

2 Commission, Directorate-General for Energy and Transport: Guide to European Community legislation in the field of civil aviation (June 2007) 1 ‹http://www.ab.gov.tr/files/ardb/evt/1_avrupa_birligi/1_6_raporlar/1_3_diger/transport/guide_to_european_comm_legislation__civil_aviation.pdf›.

3 See Report of the High-level Group for the Future European Aviation Regulatory Framework (n 1); Commission, 'On the consequences of the Court judgments of 5 November 2002 for European air transport policy' (Communication) COM (2002) 649 final 2–3. The 'third package' included the following EU regulations: Regulation 2407/92 on licensing air carriers [1992] OJ L240/1; Regulation 2408/92 on access to air routess [1992] OJ L240/8; and Regulation 2409/92 on fares and rates for air services [1992] OJ L240/15.

4 Regulation (EC) 549/2004 of the European Parliament and of the Council of 10 March 2004 laying down the framework for the creation of the single European sky (the framework Regulation) [2004] OJ L96/1. The 'SES package' also included the following regulations: Regulation (EC) 550/2004 of the European Parliament and of the Council of 10 March 2004 on the provision of air navigation services in the single European sky (the service provision Regulation) [2004] OJ L96/10; Regulation (EC) 551/2004 of the European Parliament and of the Council of 10 March 2004 on the organisation and use of the airspace in the single European sky (the airspace Regulation) [2004] OJ L96/20; and Regulation (EC) 552/2004 of the European Parliament and of the Council of 10 March 2004 on the interoperability of the European Air Traffic Management network (the interoperability Regulation) [2004] OJ L96/26.

5 Regulation 1592/2002 on Common rules in the field of civil aviation and establishing a European Aviation Safety Agency [2002] OJ L240/1.

6 Directive 2004/36/EC on the safety of third-country aircraft using Community airports [2004] OJ L143/76.

7 Regulation (EC) 1070/2009 of 21 October 2009 of the European Parliament and of the Council of 21 October 2009 amending Regulations (EC) No 549/2004, (EC) No 550/2004, (EC)

the area of aviation safety were expanded further.[8] Finally, a SES II + package had been proposed in 2013, further consolidating the reform of the ATM system,[9] together with a corresponding amendment proposal of the EASA's Basic Regulation in the areas of air traffic management and air navigation services.[10]

The actors involved in the regulation of the EU aviation area and the instruments used for this purpose require several general observations. First, air transport is a shared competence between the Union and the Member States,[11] being subject, in addition to the principles of conferral and proportionality, also to the principles of preemption and subsidiarity.[12] Within these boundaries, the regulatory framework of the EU aviation policy area was created following the lines of the 'Community method'.[13] The main legal instruments were adopted in the form of regulations and directives involving the three main legislative players (the European Parliament, the Council and the Commission).

Secondly, the Commission plays an essential role in particular in the aviation policy area, perceiving itself as 'the overall regulator on the EU level'.[14] As such, the Commission informs and guides the strategic design of the aviation policy area, initiates the necessary legislative instruments, adopts the necessary implementing measures, and manages and monitors the overall application of the EU aviation regulatory framework.[15] A good illustration of Commission's role as a strategic planner is provided by its 2015 'Aviation Strategy for Europe'[16] setting forth the main priorities, measures and actions in the aviation sector, including the improvement of EU aviation safety

No 551/2004 and (EC) No 552/2004 in order to improve the performance and sustainability of the European aviation system [2009] OJ L300/34.

8 Regulation (EC) 216/2008 on common rules in the field of civil aviation and establishing a European Aviation Safety Agency, and repealing Council Directive 91/670/EEC, Regulation (EC) No 1592/2002 and Directive 2004/36/EC [2008] OJ L79/1, amended subsequently by Regulation 1108/2009 of the European Parliament and of the Council of 21 October 2009 amending Regulation (EC) No 216/2008 in the field of aerodromes, air traffic management and air navigation services and repealing Directive 2006/23/EC [2009] OJ L309/51.

9 Commission, 'Accelerating the implementation of the Single European Sky' (Communication) COM (2013) 408 final.

10 Commission, 'Proposal for a Regulation of the European Parliament and of the Council amending Regulation (EC) No 216/2008 in the field of aerodromes, air traffic management and air navigation services' COM(2013) 409 final, and Commission, 'Proposal for a Regulation of the European Parliament and of the Council on the implementation of the Single European Sky (recast)' COMe (2013) 410 final.

11 See art 4(2)(g) TFEU juncto art 100(2) TFEU.

12 See art 5 TEU and art 2(2) TFEU.

13 See Report of the High-level Group for the Future European Aviation Regulatory Framework (n 1) ii.

14 Conference on Future of Aviation Regulation 20 September 2006, Results of the conference (presented by vice-president Barot) 1–2 ‹https://ec.europa.eu/transport/sites/transport/files/modes/air/events/doc/2006_09_20_barrot_results_en.pdf›.

15 See Commission, Discussion paper in preparation of the Conference on Future of Aviation Regulation 20 September 2006, 'Follow-up of the Edinburgh Conference: The Organisation of Regulatory Functions in Aviation within Europe' ‹https://ec.europa.eu/transport/sites/transport/files/modes/air/events/doc/2006_09_20_organisation_regulatory_functions_aviation.pdf›.

16 Commission, 'An Aviation Strategy for Europe' (Communication) COM (2015) 598 final.

through the reinforcement of EASA's role via the revision of the Agency's Basic Regulation.

Thirdly, the Commission, whilst fulfilling its role as a main actor in developing the EU aviation regulatory framework and ensuring its application, needs to coordinate with the Member States and the associated European countries within the European Civil Aviation Conference (ECAC) and to rely on the expertise of other specialised bodies, foremost EASA and Eurocontrol.[17] Accordingly, while the legislative competence in the aviation (safety) area is exercised at EU level, the implementation of the EU legal framework is shared between the Union's competent institutions and bodies and the Member States, with the Member States playing an important role in this regard.[18] Moreover, somehow differently from the division of competences within the EU, on the international plane, the Member States are still recognised as the main actors in the aviation (safety) area. The most notable example is ICAO which accepts only the membership of the Member States and not the membership of the EU, in spite of the fact that the EU has acquired competences related, for instance, to the State of Design under the Chicago Convention. It should be noted that in 2011 a Memorandum of Cooperation has been concluded between the EU and ICAO, establishing enhanced cooperation between the parties, including the participation of the EU as an observer in the activities of ICAO.[19]

4.2.2 The international (external) dimension of the EU aviation area

Already in 1993, the Council foresaw the 'operational development of an external aviation policy' based on Article 100 TFEU (former Article 80 TEC).[20] Since 2001, the Commission has stressed the importance of developing an external dimension to the EU aviation policy in view of the fact that this area is '(. . .) particularly dependent on the international context'.[21] In the Commission's view, such a development should match '(. . .) the importance of the internal *acquis*', thereby reflecting an internal-external competence parallelism approach in the aviation area.[22] The external dimension of the EU aviation area started to develop significantly since the *Open Skies* judgments of the Court of Justice (2002),[23] confirming the EU's exclusive external competence in

17 Report of the High-level Group for the Future European Aviation Regulatory Framework (n 1) 7–8.

18 See Martijn Groenleer, Michael Kaeding and Esther Versluis, 'Regulatory Governance through Agencies of the European Union? The Role of the European Agencies for Maritime and Aviation Safety in the Implementation of European Transport Legislation' (2010) 17 JEPP 1212, 1226–27; Florin Coman-Kund, Mikołaj Ratajczyk and Elmar Schmidt, 'Shared Enforcement and Accountability in the EU Aviation Safety Area. The Case of the European Aviation Safety Agency' in Mira Scholten and Michiel Luchtman (eds), *Law Enforcement by EU authorities. Political and Judicial Accountability in Shared Enforcement* (Eduard Elgar Publishing 2017) 115–40.

19 Memorandum of Cooperation between the European Union and the International Civil Aviation Organization providing a framework for enhanced cooperation [2011] OJ L232/2.

20 Council, Conclusions, 1647th Council Meeting, Transport, Brussels (15 March 1993).

21 Commission, 'European transport policy for 2010: time to decide' (White Paper) COM (2001) 370 final 99.

22 ibid.

23 Case C-466/98 *Commission v United Kingdom (Open Skies)* EU:C:2002:624; Case C-467/98 *Commission v Denmark (Open Skies)* EU:C:2002:625; Case C-468/98 *Commission v Sweden*

relation to certain aspects of the area of international air services.[24] Additionally, the *Open Skies* judgments provide an excellent illustration of the Commission's justification for establishing an external policy dimension in the aviation area as a means to ensure the effectiveness of the EU internal *acquis*. In the Commission's view: '[I]n the field of air transport (. . .) purely internal measures would hardly be effective (. . .) given the international nature of the activities carried on and the impossibility of separating the internal and external markets both economically and legally'.[25] In the aftermath of the *Open Skies* judgments, the Commission emphasised the great need for developing an EU external policy for air transport[26] and later on advanced an agenda to that effect.[27]

Accordingly, attempts were made to enhance the EU aviation external policy along several lines:[28] (1) by the so-called 'horizontal agreements' between the EU and third countries pertaining to aspects of air services within the exclusive EU competence and introducing clauses to bring the existing bilateral agreements between the Member States and the relevant third countries in line with EU law;[29] (2) by establishing relationships and concluding agreements with global partners (eg air transport agreements with the USA[30] or Canada[31] and bilateral aviation safety agreements (BASAs) with the USA,[32] Canada[33] and Brazil[34]); (3) by establishing a Common Aviation Area (CAA) with candidates for EU accession and with neighbouring countries; and (4) by

(Open Skies) EU:C:2002:626; Case C-469/98 *Commission v Finland (Open Skies)* EU:C:2002:627; Case C-471/98 *Commission v Belgium (Open Skies)* EU:C:2002:628; Case C-472/98 *Commission v Luxembourg (Open Skies)* EU:C:2002:629; Case C-475/98 *Commission v Austria (Open Skies)* EU:C:2002:630; Case C-476/98 *Commission v Germany (Open Skies)* EU:C:2002:631. See also Christophe Hillion, 'ERTA, ECHR and Open Skies: Laying the Grounds of the EU System of External Relations' in Luis Miguel Poiares Pessoa Maduro and Loic Azoulai (eds), *The Past and Future of EU Law* (Hart Publishing 2010) 224–33.

24 Case C-476/98 *Commission v Germany (Open Skies)* (n 23) paras 122–32. The issues covered by the EU exclusive external competence concerned computerised reservation systems (CRS), intra-Community tariffs and time slots; see also COM (2002) 649 final (n 3) 7.

25 Case C-476/98, *Commission v Germany (Open Skies)*, para 72.

26 COM (2002) 649 final (n 3) 15.

27 See Commission, 'Developing the agenda for the Community's external aviation policy' (Communication) COM (2005) 79 final.

28 ibid; see also Commission, 'The EU's External Aviation Policy: Addressing Future Challenges' (Communication) COM (2012) 556 final 15.

29 See COM (2005) 79 final (n 27) 6–7. Examples are the Agreement between the European Community and the Republic of Chile on certain aspects of air services [2006] OJ L300/46, and the Agreement between the European Community and the Government of the Republic of Azerbaijan on certain aspects of air services [2009] OJ L265/25.

30 Air Transport Agreement between the European Community and its Member States, on the one hand, and the United States of America [2007] OJ L134/4. The agreement has been concluded as a mixed agreement.

31 Agreement on Air Transport between Canada and the European Community and its Member States [2010] OJ L207/32. The agreement has been concluded as a mixed agreement.

32 Agreement between the United States of America and the European Community on cooperation in the regulation of civil aviation safety [2011] OJ L291/3, entered into force on 1 May 2011.

33 Agreement on civil aviation safety between the European Community and Canada [2009] OJ L153/11, entered into force on 26 July 2011.

34 Agreement between the European Union and the Government of the Federative Republic of Brazil on civil aviation safety [2011] OJ L273/3, entered into force on 27 August 2013.

strengthening relations and getting involved in relevant international (in particular ICAO)[35] and regional organisations (eg ECAC and Eurocontrol).[36]

This framework is aimed both at enhancing the international visibility and involvement of the Union in the aviation sector, and at promoting as well as extending Union's (internal) *acquis* in other European countries and worldwide.[37] In particular, the promotion of the Common Aviation Area model, envisaging *inter alia* the exportation of the EU regulatory standards in the fields of safety and security, provided seemingly tangible results.[38] Depending on the degree of involvement of the neighbouring countries in pan-European aviation cooperation, the Commission adopted a flexible approach which resulted in different frameworks for cooperation.[39] First, a comprehensive multilateral agreement establishing a European Common Aviation Area (ECAA) following the 'Single Market Model' was concluded with European countries fully engaged in pan-European cooperation in the aviation area.[40] Secondly, Euro–Mediterranean aviation agreements have been concluded[41] or are being concluded with the countries involved in the Barcelona process[42] with a view to building progressively a Common Euro–Mediterranean Aviation Area.[43] Thirdly, with other neighbouring countries (eg Georgia and Moldova),[44] common aviation area agreements are being concluded as a preliminary step towards full integration into the ECAA model. Looking to the future, Commission's 2015 'Aviation Strategy for Europe' foresees the consolidation of the Union's external aviation policy mainly through the negotiation of comprehensive aviation agreements with third countries and through expanding EU bilateral aviation safety agreements (BASAs).[45]

35 eg Memorandum of Cooperation between EU and ICAO providing a framework for enhanced cooperation (n 19).

36 See COM (2005) 79 final (n 27).

37 ibid 4; see also Report of the High-level Group for the Future European Aviation Regulatory Framework (n 1) 8.

38 COM (2012) 556 final (n 28) 16–17.

39 ibid 3; see also COM (2005) 79 final (n 27) 8–9.

40 Multilateral Agreement between the European Community and its Member States, the Republic of Albania, Bosnia and Herzegovina, the Republic of Bulgaria, the Republic of Croatia, the former Yugoslav Republic of Macedonia, the Republic of Iceland, the Republic of Montenegro, the Kingdom of Norway, Romania, the Republic of Serbia and the United Nations Interim Administration Mission in Kosovo on the establishment of a European Common Aviation Area [2006] OJ L285/3.

41 eg Euro–Mediterranean Aviation Agreement between the European Union and its Member States, of the one part, and the Hashemite Kingdom of Jordan, of the other part [2012] OJ L334/3; Euro–Mediterranean Aviation Agreement between the European Community and its Member States, of the one part, and the Kingdom of Morocco, of the other part [2006] OJ L386/57.

42 The Barcelona process includes the following countries: Morocco, Algeria, Tunisia, Egypt, the Palestine Authority, Israel, Jordan, Lebanon, Syria and Turkey. Since its participation in the April 1999 Stuttgart conference as a special guest of the EU Presidency, Libya took part as an observer in some of the meetings of the Barcelona process. It finds its origins in the Barcelona Declaration adopted at the Euro–Mediterranean Conference of 27–28 November 1995 which laid the foundations for the Euro–Mediterranean Partnership, see Commission, 'A Community aviation policy towards its neighbours' COM (2004) 74 final 3–4.

43 ibid 3–4.

44 eg Common Aviation Area Agreement between the European Union and its Member States and the Republic of Moldova [2012] OJ L292/3; Common Aviation Area Agreement between the European Union and its Member States and Georgia [2012] OJ L321/3.

45 COM (2015) 598 final (n 16) 4.

With regard to strategic decisions and enacting the most important legal instruments, the overall responsibility for the development of the EU aviation external policy rests mostly with the Commission and the Council. Thus, the Commission sets the agenda in consultation with the Council, and is in charge of the negotiation of agreements and other formal cooperation instruments, whereas the Council is kept informed and adopts the instruments at issue. The Commission takes the lead in the process of implementing the main framework for international cooperation, but it needs to coordinate efforts with the Member States.[46] This may at times raise complex issues of representation and delegation in relation to third countries and the international fora where the Member States sometimes represent the EU (eg ICAO)[47] or the EU is acting on behalf of the Member States.[48] Furthermore, at the EU level, specialised bodies, such as EASA, play a role in supporting the Commission and the Member States with regard to specific issues.[49]

4.3 EASA's profile as an EU agency

4.3.1 EASA's design and incremental evolution

The initiatives for setting up an aviation safety body in the EU date back to 1996, but the European Aviation Safety Agency (EASA) was only established as an EU body in 2002 by Regulation 1592/2002. The Agency became operational in 2003 and it was built upon the foundation of the pan-European Joint Aviation Authorities (JAA), an informal network entrusted with standardisation and inspection tasks of the national aviation authorities (NAAs) of most European countries.[50] Within this framework, EASA has been enabled to coordinate the work of the aviation authorities of the Member States, to represent them for matters within the exclusive competence of the EU and to cooperate with JAA authorities not subject to the EASA Regulation.[51] On 30 June 2009, the JAA officially came to an end and was replaced by the EU civil

46 See COM (2005) 79 final (n 27) 11.

47 Under the 2011 Memorandum of Cooperation between EU and ICAO, the Union acquires only a limited 'observer' status in the activities of ICAO. Accordingly, the EU (the Commission, in particular) has to coordinate efforts with the Member States having 'full member' status in order to exercise its competences in the areas covered by the MOC.

48 Such is the case with the competences in the aviation area transferred by the Member States to the Union, where common rules have been adopted at EU level. The most obvious example concerns the State of Design certification tasks under the Chicago Convention, which have been taken over at EU level and are exercised by EASA in relation to third countries on behalf of all EU Member States, see art 20 of Regulation 216/2008.

49 Report of the High-level Group for the Future European Aviation Regulatory Framework (n 1) 5.

50 See Adriaan Schout, 'Inspecting Aviation Safety in the EU: EASA as an Administrative Innovation?' in Ellen Vos (ed), *European Risk Governance. Its Science, its Inclusiveness and its Effectiveness* (Connex Report Series 06/2008) 266–70. The JAA was an associate body of the European Civil Aviation Conference (ECAC), representing the civil aviation regulatory authorities of a number of European States (both EU and non-EU members) that had agreed to cooperate in developing and implementing common safety regulatory standards and procedures.

51 See arts 4–6 of the Protocol to the Cyprus Arrangements on the Participation of the European Aviation Safety Agency, concluded on 25 November 2003 ‹http://www.easa.europa.eu/rulemaking/docs/international/archive/Protocol_Cyprus.pdf›.

aviation safety system. With a view to ensuring the full substitution of the JAA system, EASA has gradually concluded working arrangements with the NAAs of the European countries which are not members of the EU with a view to ensure the pan-European dimension of aviation safety.[52]

EASA has been established as 'the centrepiece of the European Union's aviation safety system',[53] comprising, in addition to the Agency, the Commission and the Member States (National Aviation Authorities).[54] The Agency has been created as a technical implementing tool of the EU regulatory framework pertaining to civil aviation safety. The initial mandate of the Agency, according to Regulation 1592/2002, covered airworthiness and environmental type-certification of aircraft, as well as the certification of aircraft design organisations and of production organisations. This has been gradually extended within a relatively short period of time. First, EASA's mandate was expanded *via* the 'SAFA Directive'[55] and the Commission's implementing regulation[56] entrusting EASA with tasks pertaining to the collection and exchange of information on the air safety of aircraft and on air operators. Secondly, the initial Founding Regulation of EASA was replaced with a new one in 2008, adding pilot certification, air operation certification and third-country operators to EASA's tasks.[57] Thirdly, EASA's second Founding Regulation had already been amended in 2009, further enhancing the mandate of the Agency with ATM/ANS and air traffic controller certification.[58] At present, the mandate of EASA covers a variety of regulatory, certification, as well as monitoring, investigation and standardisation tasks. According to EASA's Founding Regulation,[59] complemented by the Agency's self-perception of its role as highlighted in its annual activity reports,[60] the main tasks of the Agency include:

(1) coordination of safety programmes, data collection, analysis and research to improve aviation safety
(2) regulation: drafting aviation safety legislation and providing technical advice to the European Commission and to the Member States

52 See Council, 'EASA: Transition aspects from JAA to EASA', Report from the Aviation Working Party (9889/01) 4 and 6.
53 See EASA, Annual General Report 2013 9 ‹https://www.easa.europa.eu/newsroom-and-events/general-publications/annual-general-report-2013›.
54 See Commission 'Setting up an Aviation Safety Management System for Europe' (Communication) COM (2011) 670 final 2–4.
55 Directive 2004/36. This directive has been repealed by Regulation 216/2008 (art 69).
56 Commission Regulation (EC) 768/2006 of 19 May 2006 implementing Directive 2004/36/EC of the European Parliament and of the Council as regards the collection and exchange of information on the safety of aircraft using Community airports and the management of the information system [2006] OJ L134/16; following the repeal of the 'SAFA Directive', this legal instrument has been superseded by Commission Regulation (EU) No 965/2012 of 5 October 2012 laying down technical requirements and administrative procedures related to air operations pursuant to Regulation (EC) No 216/2008 of the European Parliament and of the Council [2012] OJ L296/1.
57 See art 18 of Regulation 216/2008.
58 Art 18 of Regulation 216/2008, as amended by Regulation 1108/2009. A new extension of EASA's tasks is foreseen along with the SES II+ Regulation, see Commission, 'Proposal for a Regulation of the European Parliament and of the Council amending Regulation (EC) No 216/2008 in the field of aerodromes, air traffic management and air navigation services' COM (2013) 409 final.
59 Arts 17–27 of Regulation 216/2008.
60 See, for instance, EASA, Annual General Report 2013 (n 53) 9–10.

(3) inspections and training to ensure the uniform implementation of European aviation safety legislation in all Member States
(4) airworthiness and environmental type-certification of aeronautical products, parts and appliances
(5) approval of aircraft design organisations worldwide and of production and maintenance organisations outside the EU
(6) coordination and monitoring of the EU Ramp Inspections Programme, and in particular the management of the centralised SAFA (Safety Assessment of Foreign Aircraft) database
(7) *coordination with international civil aviation bodies and aviation safety authorities in countries outside of the EU* (emphasis added).[61]

In this context, several observations can be made. First, in fulfilling its tasks, EASA sometimes plays a supportive role for the Commission, in other instances it acts on its own, while in some cases it seems to act as an agent for the Member States. The Agency provides expert advice to the Commission in the regulatory process in place for enacting implementing measures of the EU aviation safety legislative framework. The Agency arguably acts on its own in particular when performing standardisation inspections and investigations in the process of monitoring the application of the EU common rules, as well as with regard to certain aspects of the certification process.[62] It may act generally on behalf of the Member States[63] in fulfilling tasks under the Chicago Convention[64] and, in particular, in fulfilling its tasks pertaining to airworthiness and environmental certification,[65] as well as with regard to acceptance of third-country certification.[66] Also, within the ICAO, EASA carries out on behalf of the Member States tasks related to the ICAO audit programmes.[67]

Secondly, it is interesting to note the open-ended texture of EASA's tasks in its Founding Regulation. To that effect, Article 17 of Regulation 216/2008 enables EASA to '(. . .) undertake any tasks and formulate opinions on all matters (. . .)'

61 ibid. EASA's Annual General Report 2013 lists, for the first time, international cooperation as one of the main tasks of the Agency, which appears to indicate the growing importance the Agency attaches to its own international dimension.

62 This seems at least to be the case according to arts 21–22b and 24 of Regulation 216/2008.

63 On the issue of the tasks carried out by EASA on behalf of the Member States as an aspect of a relationship of international agency between the EU and its Member States, see Mikołaj Ratajczyk, *Regional Aviation Safety Organisations. Enhancing Air Safety through Regional Cooperation* (Kluwer Law International 2015) 139–45.

64 Art 17(2)(e) of Regulation 216/2008. See also Andrea Ott, Ellen Vos and Florin Coman-Kund, 'EU Agencies on the Global Scene: EU and International Law Perspectives' in Michelle Everson, Cosimo Monda and Ellen Vos (eds), *European Agencies in between Institutions and Member States* (Kluwer Law International 2014) 103.

65 Art 20(1) of Regulation 216/2008. It should be noted that, according to the EASA Basic Regulation, the Agency has the exclusive competence to issue airworthiness type certificates, whereas the competent aviation authorities of the Member States issue, based on that, individual certificates for each aircraft. However, from an external perspective, and specifically under the umbrella of the Chicago Convention, EASA acts as a regional body exercising tasks on behalf of the Member States, see Ratajczyk (n 63) 147–62.

66 Art 12(2) of Regulation 216/2008.

67 See Memorandum of Cooperation between the EU and ICAO providing a framework for enhanced cooperation (n 19).

covered by it and to '(. . .) take the necessary measures within the powers conferred on it by this Regulation or other Community legislation'. This suggests, at least at first sight, a design providing EASA with a far-reaching potential for powers and responsibilities in the EU aviation safety area.

Thirdly, as regards the instruments and measures enabling EASA to discharge its responsibilities, several categories can be distinguished on the basis of the Agency's Basic Regulation.[68] Most importantly, EASA issues type certificates for aircraft, certificates for parts and appliances and certificates for design organisations, and production and maintenance organisations located outside the territory of the Member States.[69] According to Ratajczyk, in 2014, EASA was competent to issue certificates regarding '(. . .) approval of design of aeronautical products, parts and appliances, third country organisations and operators, and organisations providing pan-European air navigation services'.[70]

In the context of the alleged expansion of EASA's formal mandate, two observations need to be made with regard the nature and discharge of the Agency's tasks. In the first place, the Commission still retains the overall formal regulatory powers in the area of aviation safety, the role of the Agency being to provide expert and technical input in the regulatory process. Although this role is essential, it should be emphasised that EASA does not formally regulate the aviation safety sector. Nevertheless, the Agency issues certificates which are binding for all national aviation authorities in the Member States, as well as for the aviation sector.[71] From this perspective EASA's type certificates can rather be qualified as technical acts of general application. It should be noted that EASA's type certificates also affect third countries in that the latter need to recognise the certificates as being issued by the State of Registry under the Chicago Convention.[72] In the second place, in fulfilling its information exchange, standardisation and certification tasks, EASA is either under a duty to consult or to notify the Commission and/or the Member States in advance[73] or it must rely on the cooperation and resources of the aviation authorities of the Member States.[74] One may conclude, therefore, that EASA has no genuine regulatory powers but rather advisory/recommendatory and implementing tasks (certification/approvals, standardisation and information exchange).[75]

68 According to art 18 of Regulation 216/2008, EASA issues: (1) opinions, in supporting the Commission in the regulatory process; (2) recommendations to the Commission in the context of the flexibility clause; (3) certification specifications; (4) reports, in the context of standardisation inspections; (5) (appropriate) decisions, in the application of the relevant provisions regarding certification (airworthiness, pilots, air operation, ATM/ANS, air traffic controllers), third-country organisations, inspections of Member States and investigation of undertakings.

69 See in particular art 20, and also arts 21–23 of Regulation 216/2008.

70 Ratajczyk (n 63) 154.

71 See Groenleer, Kaeding and Versluis (n 18) 1226–27; Ratajczyk (n 63) 154–55. The latter author has qualified the Agency's certification process as a 'one-stop-shop for the aeronautical industry' (154).

72 Interview 9 with a Commission official (phone) (2 July 2013).

73 See arts 18, 24 and 52 of Regulation 216/2008.

74 See Schout (n 50) 266–89. An indication in this regard is provided by art 52(1)(a) of Regulation 216/2008 specifying that the procedures for EASA's measures must 'draw on expertise available in the aviation regulatory authorities of Member States'.

75 As discussed, the type certificates issued by EASA, though of a technical-implementing nature, entail binding effects in all Member States, and also in third countries.

Moreover, in view of its limited resources, the Agency is dependent on the capacity and resources of the Member States in discharging its implementing tasks.[76] In relation to the certification process under Regulation 216/2008, EASA may and, in practice, does 'delegate' tasks to the aviation authorities of the Member States concerning the investigations associated with products, parts and appliances certification, as well as technical inspections and audits.[77] In the end this results in a cooperative approach which characterises the EU civil aviation safety system as a network of civil aviation authorities at the EU level and in the Member States.

Lastly, in 2015 the Commission launched a proposal for a new framework regulation in the field of civil aviation, which at the time of writing remains subject to negotiations between the European Parliament and the Council.[78] Whilst the final outcome of the negotiations is difficult to predict at this moment, based on the text of the proposal one may foresee that EASA's role and tasks will not change fundamentally.[79] Yet, the proposed regulation includes a number of provisions which will further bolster the Agency's powers and position within the EU civil aviation safety system. Among others, the Member States would have extended possibilities to delegate to EASA responsibilities for certification, oversight and enforcement tasks, and an emergency support mechanism enabling EASA to assist closely a competent authority of a Member State that is experiencing serious difficulties in ensuring effective safety oversight.[80] What is more, the proposed regulation is expected to enable EASA to issue safety directives, and will enhance the Agency's information-related tasks by establishing a repository of information (managed by EASA) for ensuring effective cooperation between the authorities in the exercise of certification, oversight and enforcement tasks.[81]

4.3.2 Governance of EASA

In the same way as other EU agencies, EASA's main organs are the management board and the executive director. The management board comprises one representative from each Member State plus one representative of the Commission.[82] It is chaired by a chairperson and a deputy chairperson elected from the management board members. Currently, the main powers and tasks of the management board include:[83] (1) appointing the executive director and the directors of EASA and exercising

76 See Groenleer, Kaeding and Versluis (n 18) 1226–27.

77 See arts 20–23 and 38(3) of Regulation 216/2008.

78 Proposal for a regulation of the European Parliament and of the Council on common rules in the field of civil aviation and establishing a European Aviation Safety Agency, and repealing Regulation (EC) No 216/2008 of the European Parliament and of the Council, COM (2015) 613 final.

79 Coman-Kund, Ratajczyk and Schmidt (n 18) 129.

80 Art 55 of the draft EASA Regulation, according to Council, 'Proposal for a regulation of the European Parliament and of the Council on common rules in the field of civil aviation and establishing a European Aviation Safety Agency, and repealing Regulation (EC) No 216/2008 of the European Parliament and of the Council. Analysis of the final compromise text with a view to agreement', Brussels, 15 December 2017 (15689/17).

81 Arts 63 and 65(6) of the proposed EASA Regulation (n 78); see also generally Coman-Kund, Ratajczyk and Schmidt (n 18) 129–31.

82 Art 34 of Regulation 216/2008.

83 ibid art 33(2).

disciplinary authority over them; (2) adopting the annual activity report of the agency and the annual work programme; (3) adopting the budget of the agency and other tasks related to the budget; and (4) establishing its own rules of procedure, procedures for decision making by the executive director and establishing the organisational structure of the Agency.

The executive director is the person actually running the Agency on a day-to-day basis.[84] In so doing, he is assisted by the directors heading the main departments of the Agency. The executive director is appointed by the management board on a proposal by the Commission, and the other senior officials are appointed by the management board on a proposal of the executive director.[85] The executive director makes all the important decisions in the Agency and s/he is deemed to act fully independently in the performance of his/her duties.[86] S/he approves the measures of the Agency and takes decisions in the discharge of EASA's functions and tasks. Furthermore, s/he takes the appropriate decisions in order to ensure the functioning of the Agency, exercises powers with regard to the staff of the agency, prepares and implements the budget and the work programme of the Agency. Notably, the executive director is entrusted with '(. . .) *any international functions and technical cooperation with third countries* (. . .)' (emphasis added) on behalf of the Agency.[87] The formalisation in the Basic Regulation of the possibility for the executive director to allocate certain certification tasks to national aviation authorities in conformity with the guidelines decided by the management board is indicative of EASA's reliance on the Member States.[88]

The decision making by EASA is inevitably linked to the main organs of the agency and to their respective functions and tasks. Decisions taken by the management board are usually based on previous proposals or drafts submitted by the executive director or on proposals, opinions, advice, or approval (agreement) by the Commission.[89] All other kinds of decisions remain with the executive director, in line with EASA's legal framework and the guidelines and procedures adopted by the management board.[90] In adopting the Agency's decisions, the executive director needs, at times, to obtain *prior* consent or approval from the management board and to report *post-factum* to the European Parliament and the Council on the decisions taken.[91]

4.4 EASA's international dimension

4.4.1 The legal framework for international cooperation

4.4.1.1 Mandate, tasks and instruments

The international cooperation mandate and tasks of EASA are to be integrated within the overall framework and objectives of its Founding Regulation. Accordingly, EASA's

84 ibid art 38.
85 ibid art 39.
86 ibid art 38.
87 ibid art 38(3)(d).
88 ibid art 38(3)(c).
89 eg adoption of EASA's annual work programme, art 33(2)(b) of Regulation 216/2008; appointment of the executive director, art 39 of Regulation 216/2008.
90 See art 38 of Regulation 216/2008.
91 ibid art 38(2).

international dimension must be linked to the main objective of Regulation 216/2008 (ie '(. . .) establish and maintain a high uniform level of civil aviation safety in Europe') and to one of its additional objectives (ie to promote the Union's '(. . .) views with regard to civil aviation safety standards and rules throughout the world by establishing appropriate cooperation with third countries and international organisations').[92] In this context, the international cooperation performed by EASA is focused on promoting Union's civil aviation safety system[93] to the outside world, assisting the Commission in managing relevant aspects of EU external aviation policy area, and coordinating and providing technical cooperation activities.[94] Not less importantly, EASA is entrusted with the task of supporting the Member States in their international relations, in particular in the discharge of their obligations under the Chicago Convention.[95]

The international dimension of EASA's mandate is primarily defined in Article 27 of Regulation 216/2008. The three paragraphs of this provision, although interlinked, arguably address three different aspects of EASA's international mandate. Article 27(1) covers in general aspects related to the assistance which EASA should lend to the Union and the Member States in their relations with third countries. However, this provision focuses on assistance with regard to specific aspects (ie harmonisation of rules and mutual recognition regarding approvals). Moreover, it is explicitly stated that the assistance provided by EASA must be in accordance with the relevant EU law. In practice, it appears that, according to this provision, EASA assists most commonly in the negotiation and implementation of the BASAs between the EU and third countries.[96] Another way in which this provision is implemented by EASA consists of technical cooperation activities and projects carried out in supporting the Commission to manage and implement EU programmes and projects in third countries.[97]

Article 27(2) pertains to the possibility of establishing direct cooperation with third countries and relevant international organisations. First, the subject matter of such direct international cooperation must remain within the scope of EASA's Founding Regulation. Secondly, as regards EASA's international partners, it is noteworthy that they are not in principle the governments of the third countries, but they are rather the competent aviation authorities of those third countries. Thirdly, EASA's direct international cooperation is in principle based upon and takes place within the framework of working arrangements concluded with third country authorities or international organisations. Accordingly, the working arrangements seem to be the most important formal cooperation instruments concluded by the Agency, and they seem to be required for EASA to establish direct cooperation with bodies outside the EU. As such, these are subject to a double requirement: (1) they must be in accordance with the relevant provisions of the Founding Treaties, and (2) they must obtain *prior* approval

92 ibid arts 2(2)(e) and (3)(c).

93 COM(2011) 670 final (n 54) 2–4.

94 See, for instance, EASA Annual General Report 2010 64–65 ‹https://www.easa.europa.eu/document-library/general-publications/annual-report-2010›.

95 See recitals (3) and (23) of the preamble of Regulation 216/2008.

96 See EASA's work programmes and activity reports (2010–2012). This conclusion has also been confirmed by EASA officials, Interview 25 with EASA officials, Brussels (13 May 2013).

97 See Florin Coman-Kund, 'Assessing the Role of EU Agencies in the Enlargement Process: the Case of the European Aviation Safety Agency' (2012) 8 CYELP 335, 361–62.

from the Commission.[98] The reason for including this formal requirement in EASA's Basic Regulation was to ensure consistency of the Agency's working arrangements with its own mandate and with the Union's external aviation policy.[99]

According to Article 27(3), EASA is to assist the Member States with regard to their compliance with international obligations, in particular those under the Chicago Convention. In practice, it seems that this provision is relevant most prominently in relation to the assistance provided by EASA to the Member States and the Commission with regard to State Letters under the ICAO Universal Safety Oversight Audit Programme (USOAP).[100] In this context, EASA strives to support the Member States to notify, in a uniform manner, the differences between their rules (these are now actually the EU rules in most cases)[101] and the ICAO Standards and Recommended Practices (SARPs).[102]

There are also other provisions in Regulation 216/2008 that are relevant for EASA's international cooperation dimension. Article 12, which provides for a derogation from EASA's Founding Regulation with regard to the acceptance of third-country certification, entitles the Agency to issue certificates on behalf of any Member State in the application of an agreement concluded by one Member State with a third country. This particular issue is linked back to Article 27(1) and may result in formalised cooperation as provided for in Article 27(2).[103] Other provisions relevant for the international cooperation pursued by EASA under Article 27 are Article 17(2)(e) and those pertaining to certification,[104] most notably Article 20. Thus, more generally, Article 17(2)(e) enables the Agency to perform "on behalf of the Member States" functions and tasks assigned to them on the basis international agreements. Article 20(1) entrusts EASA with the functions and tasks of the State of design, manufacture or registry when related to design approval. These functions and tasks are to be performed as specified in the Chicago Convention and on behalf of the Member States. Yet another aspect of the international cooperation mandate of EASA concerns the participation of European third countries in the work of the agency. The participation of European third countries is subjected to several requirements according to Article 66 of EASA's Founding Act: (1) they must be contracting parties to the Chicago Convention; and (2) they must have concluded agreements with the EU whereby they adopted and apply EU law in the area covered by Regulation 216/2008

98 This latter requirement has been formally introduced by the 2008 EASA Basic Regulation, but EASA officials revealed that, even before that, the Agency used to seek the approval of the Commission as a matter of working practice, Interview 21 with EASA officials, Cologne (7 November 2012).

99 See Ratajczyk (n 63) 146.

100 See EASA Annual General Report 2013 (n 53) 43 and 66; EASA Business Plan 2014–2018 23 ‹https://www.easa.europa.eu/system/files/dfu/EASA%20MB%20Decision%2012-2013%20adopting%20the%20BP%202014-2018%20-%20Annex.pdf›.

101 Interview 25 with EASA officials, Brussels (13 May 2013).

102 See Memorandum of Cooperation between EU and ICAO providing a framework for enhanced cooperation (n 19).

103 For instance, EASA is making use of the 'Article 12' derogation under an agreement between Italy and Israel, which had been further implemented via a working arrangement concluded between the Agency and the competent aviation authority of Israel, Interview 25 with EASA officials, Brussels (13 May 2013).

104 Arts 20–23 of Regulation 216/2008.

and its implementing rules.[105] On the basis of such agreements, further arrangements are to be developed by EASA specifying the details of such participation.

Within its mandate, a list of the main tasks and activities currently performed by EASA concerning international cooperation includes:[106]

(1) assistance activities (eg technical advice and recommendations; participation in negotiation meetings, etc.) to the Commission in the negotiation and implementation of BASAs with third countries
(2) conclusion and implementation of working arrangements with aviation authorities from third countries and international organisations pertaining to subject-related matters within its competence
(3) activities to strengthen its involvement in ICAO and to support the EU and the Member States within this organisation (in particular with a view to supporting the coordination of ICAO State Letters by the Commission)
(4) technical cooperation activities (including supporting the Commission in defining assistance projects and managing EU programmes within its area of operation; direct management of assistance programmes; participation in technical missions; organising trainings and workshops).[107]

Overall, the international dimension of EASA, as governed by Regulation 216/2008, indicates a projection on the international plane of EASA's role in the EU aviation safety area. In this context, the international cooperation tasks and activities performed by the Agency appear to be inherent to its core mandate, which defines both the scope and the limits *ratione materiae* of such cooperation. In this vein, Article 27 in combination with other relevant provisions in the EASA's Basic Regulation indicate quite clearly that EASA does not pursue international cooperation completely independently, but within the framework of the EU external aviation policy and in cooperation with the Member States.[108] Furthermore, the international dimension of EASA is explicitly circumscribed by the wider EU Treaty framework. Regulation 216/2008 does not provide details on this, but one may assume that this would include at least provisions regarding the competences of the EU institutions in the aviation area, the principle of institutional balance, and provisions regarding Union's external action.[109] Finally, EASA plays a complex role on the international plane. Whereas one could easily assume

105 This is the case for the time being with EEA/EFTA states and with the candidate and potential candidate countries to EU accession, see Coman-Kund (n 97) 360–61.
106 eg EASA Work Programme 2012 23–24 ‹https://www.easa.europa.eu/the-agency/management-board/decisions/easa-mb-decision-10-2011-adopting-2012-work-programme-written›; EASA, Annual Activity Report 2015 28 ‹https://www.easa.europa.eu/system/files/dfu/EASA%20Annual%20Activity%20Report%202015.pdf›.
107 See, for instance, EASA Annual General Report 2011 56–57 ‹https://www.easa.europa.eu/the-agency/management-board/decisions/easa-mb-decision-09-2010-adopting-2011-work-programme-written›.
108 EASA's 'growing international role' is subjected to the international dimension of the EU safety policy and is subsumed to the overall EU external aviation policy, see COM (2012) 556 final (n 28) 2–3.
109 It has been revealed that mostly the Treaty provisions regarding transport (art 100 TFEU) and those concerning the Union's external action were considered 'relevant' for the international cooperation carried out by the Agency, Interview 25 with EASA officials, Brussels (13 May 2013).

that EASA acts as an EU body, the Agency also acts on behalf of the Member States when performing some of its international tasks.[110] This is particularly obvious with regard to the tasks exercised by EASA in relation to ICAO[111] or as concerns the cooperative arrangements with third countries regarding EASA's certification tasks with regard to design approvals.[112]

Lastly, it should be noted that the coming EASA regulation will likely maintain the basic principles of the current international cooperation framework, but it will further elaborate upon certain aspects of the Agency's international dimension. In this respect, the proposed regulation features more detailed provisions regarding the Agency's role and tasks in supporting Union's and Member States' participation in the activities of ICAO.[113] It also aims to formalise existing practice by inserting a provision enabling the Agency to enter into technical assistance projects with third countries and international organisations provided that this compatible with the Agency's mandate.[114] Yet, Article 77(2) of the future EASA regulation foresees rather significant changes as concerns Agency's working arrangements by replacing Commission's prior approval with prior consultation, and by specifying that these instruments do not create legal obligations for the EU and its Member States.

4.4.1.2 The procedure for EASA's international cooperation instruments

The working procedures put in place in order to enable EASA to carry out its international cooperation tasks include two different internal processes:

- an internal procedure regarding the assistance provided by EASA with regard to bilateral aviation safety agreements (BASAs) concluded by the EU with third countries[115]
- an internal procedure regarding the working arrangements concluded by the Agency.[116]

BASAs

The internal procedure with regard to BASAs covers the concrete steps taken by EASA to assist the Commission during the different stages involved under a bilateral agreement: mandate, assessment, negotiation, and implementation phases. For each particular phase, the document provides in detail the concrete actions to be performed

110 See Ott, Vos and Coman-Kund (n 64) 103–04. This peculiar situation has been also noted by EASA officials, Interview 25 with EASA officials, Brussels (13 May 2013).

111 See Ratajczyk (n 63) 161.

112 See art 20 of Regulation 216/2008. In other instances, such as cooperation on production issues, where the competence is still shared with the Member States, the Agency coordinates closely with the national aviation authorities, Interview 25 with EASA officials, Brussels (13 May 2013).

113 Art 77(4)–(5) of the draft EASA Regulation, according to Council, 'Analysis of the final compromise text with a view to agreement' (n 80).

114 ibid art 77(6).

115 EASA internal procedure regarding BASAs, EASA PR. BASA 00001-001, 'Bilateral agreements', approved 4 October 2012.

116 EASA internal procedure for working arrangements, EASA PR.WARG 00001-001, 'Working arrangements', approved 19 August 2012.

by the Agency, the people and structures involved, as well as the interactions between EASA and the Commission, and third country actors (eg competent regulatory authorities). An important aspect concerning the implementation of BASAs pertains to the technical implementing procedures (TIPs) and maintenance annex guidance (MAG) concluded by EASA with the competent aviation authorities from the relevant third country. The TIPs and MAGs are formal cooperation instruments rather similar to the regular working arrangements concluded by EASA, although they have some specific characteristics, such as the lack of a formal approval by the Commission or the fact that the instrument is signed by the certification director (TIPs) and the standardisation director (MAGs) instead of the executive director.

Working arrangements

The internal procedure with regard to the working arrangements concluded by EASA provides for the Commission's involvement from the initiation phase, throughout the drafting and negotiation phase, up to the stage the working arrangement is concluded.[117] This reveals a much more intensive level of involvement by the Commission than the formal *prior* approval mentioned in Article 27(2) of EASA's Basic Regulation. As a general rule, the working arrangements are formally concluded on behalf of EASA when they are signed by the executive director. Remarkably, neither the procedure regarding EASA's formal cooperation instruments under BASAs nor the procedure for working arrangements provide at any stage for the direct involvement of the Agency's management board.

4.4.2 EASA's international dimension in practice

4.4.2.1 Setting the international cooperation priorities and actions

The main directions and objectives of EASA's international cooperation were laid down in a multiannual programming document known as the 'EASA Business Plan'. This was a framework document providing an overall strategic plan for all of the activities of the Agency for a period of five years. EASA's Business Plan was prepared by the executive director and endorsed by the management board. It was updated every year and it provided the basis for all other planning documents of the Agency.[118] In this document, EASA's needs and priorities in the international cooperation area were explained and backed up by more concrete objectives, key performance indicators, and targets. Accordingly, the main priority areas identified for EASA's international cooperation were: (1) cooperation with ICAO and (2) enhancing external relations.[119] In the latter case, the emphasis was on implementing existing bilateral aviation safety agreements (BASAs), as well as on supporting the Commission in the negotiation of new BASAs or annexes to existing BASAs.[120] Equally important for the Agency's

117 EASA PR.WARC 00001-001 (n 116).
118 See EASA Business Plan 2013–2017 4 ‹https://www.easa.europa.eu/the-agency/management-board/decisions/easa-mb-decision-09-2012-adopting-business-plan-2013-2017›.
119 ibid 22.
120 ibid.

external relations are the working arrangements negotiated and concluded with third countries with a view to supporting the certification exercises and the export of European products, or dealing with specific issues such as ensuring the full effectiveness of the SAFA Programme.[121] Next, the Agency's international cooperation objectives and activities were planned in further detail in the annual work programmes adopted by the management board on the proposal of the executive director. Both the business plan and the work programme were prepared in coordination with the Commission.[122]

Recently, the Agency's multiannual programming document and the annual work programme have been integrated in a single programming document (SPD).[123] The current SPD for the period 2017–2020 lists a number of strategic objectives, including ensuring the worldwide recognition for the European aviation safety system through implementing an 'international strategy', promoting EU aviation standards, and improving global safety and environmental protection.[124] Next, similarly to the previous EASA business plans, the multiannual programming for the period 2017–2020 translates EASA's broad strategic directions regarding international cooperation in more concrete objectives, actions and outputs along the priority areas of the Agency's international cooperation (ie ICAO, BASAs and working arrangements, as well as technical cooperation).[125] Within this framework, the Agency's work programme further specifies short-term objectives and actions.[126]

In addition to the official documents touching upon the Agency's international cooperation, the existence of internal documents setting more detailed priorities and roadmaps with regard to third countries and international organisations has been confirmed during interviews with EASA officials.[127] Also in practice, a look at EASA's external representation in third countries gives an indication who the strategic global partners of the Agency are.[128] These documents are sent to the Commission (DG MOVE), which is expected to provide its view, especially from the wider perspective of Union's aviation and external relation policies. Receiving the Commission's input may take quite some time in practice, but the general line established by the Commission is that EASA's international cooperation strategy needs to fit with the political lines adopted by the Commission.[129] This may hinder sometimes the Agency from fully achieving its international cooperation aims and targets. In particular, the discrepancy between the time needed to plan and carry out international cooperation activities by EASA and the short life of the Union's political goals in the aviation area and external relations has been emphasised as a problematic issue.[130] In

121 EASA Business Plan 2014–2018 (n 100) 22–23.
122 See arts 38(2)(c) and 56 of EASA Basic Regulation.
123 EASA, Single Programming Document 2017–2020 ‹https://www.easa.europa.eu/system/files/dfu/EASA%20MB%20Decision%2011-2016%20Annex%20SPD%202017-2020.pdf›.
124 ibid 14.
125 ibid 30–32.
126 ibid 47–48.
127 Interviews with EASA officials 21, Cologne (7 November 2012) and 25, Brussels (13 May 2013).
128 For the time being, EASA has external representations for China, USA, Canada/ICAO and Singapore ‹https://www.easa.europa.eu/easa-and-you/international-cooperation/international-cooperation-explained›.
129 Interview 9 (phone) with a Commission official (2 July 2013) and Interview 21 with EASA officials, Cologne (7 November 2012).
130 Interview 21 with EASA officials, Cologne (7 November 2012).

this context, EASA has to be flexible and ready to reprioritise and adjust its international cooperation activities and resources depending on the relevant changes on the political level. This may be difficult to achieve in practice and may negatively affect the Agency if account is taken of the resources and time invested in concluding a working arrangement which, in the end, is dropped or postponed following a sudden change in the EU's political position.

One may thus conclude that EASA does not enjoy full independence in setting and pursuing its international cooperation strategy, but it is dependent on other EU actors, in particular on the Commission.

4.4.2.2 EASA's formal international cooperation instruments

With some 150 formal international cooperation instruments concluded with various partners,[131] EASA is by far the EU agency with the most prolific international cooperation record. The typical instrument used by EASA in formalising direct cooperation with third countries and international organisations is the 'working arrangement'. Depending on the particular circumstances of the cooperation with a particular non-EU partner, special instruments labelled as implementing procedures,[132] TIPs, MAGs, memoranda of understanding (MOUs) or memoranda of cooperation (MOCs) are also concluded by the Agency.

4.4.2.2.1 WORKING ARRANGEMENTS

Arguably, the working arrangements are the most important instruments through which EASA formalises its cooperation with third countries and international organisations.[133] These working arrangements are the only category of international cooperation instruments mentioned explicitly in EASA's Basic Regulation. According to the Agency's relevant internal documents, working arrangements can be concluded either as self-standing instruments for cooperation or as implementing tools of BASAs[134] or other international agreements between the Union and third countries and international organisations.[135]

It is important to note that, in practice, almost all working arrangements concluded by EASA are with third countries or, more precisely, with the competent third country authorities (see Annex 3: Examples of EASA's formal international cooperation instruments). This suggests that the international cooperation pursued by EASA

131 EASA/Working arrangements ‹http://easa.europa.eu/rulemaking/international-cooperation-working-arrangements.php›.

132 eg with the Interstate Aviation Commission (IAC) and United Arab Emirates (UAE).

133 More than 100 working arrangements have been concluded so far between EASA and the national aviation authorities (NAAs) from various third countries.

134 For a recent example of a working arrangement concluded between EASA and FAA as technical agents under the BASA between EU and USA, see Working Arrangement between the Federal Aviation Administration of the United States of America and the European Aviation Safety Agency on the Airbus A320 Aircraft Family Final Assembly Line and Delivery Centre in Mobile, Alabama, United States (entered into force on 22 September 2014) ‹http://easa.europa.eu/document-library/working-arrangements/working-arrangement-airbus-a320-aircraft-family-final-assembly›.

135 EASA PR.WARG 00001-001 (n 116) 3.

under such instruments takes place on a low technical level, between authorities competent on aviation safety issues. While EASA may conclude working arrangements with international organisations, to date only a few such instruments have been concluded: with ICAO,[136] and with a regional international body.[137]

'A zoo with different kinds of animals'

According to EASA's official website, work programmes and activity reports, numerous working arrangements have been concluded by the Agency, in particular with aviation authorities from third countries. In a few cases, the instruments concluded are referred to as 'arrangements',[138] 'extended arrangements'[139] or 'technical arrangements'[140] but, according to EASA officials, this difference in the titles of the instruments does not reflect a substantive difference in relation to the instruments called 'working arrangements'. The working arrangements entered into by EASA are characterised by a certain degree of heterogeneity. This is determined, among other things, by the Agency's various tasks related to aviation safety, the special international cooperation needs and priorities of EASA regarding a certain country or group of countries, the peculiarities as well as the demands of EASA's international partners, and the wider EU international cooperation initiatives and framework with certain countries. Moreover, the implementation of some of the working arrangements concluded between EASA and its partner requires other formal cooperation instruments often bearing different names.[141] Hence, the working arrangements currently in place have been portrayed as 'a zoo with different kinds of animals'.[142]

Despite such diversity, one may start by distinguishing between the working arrangements concluded (1) with relevant aviation authorities from non-EU European countries, and (2) those with third countries worldwide.

As far as the non-EU European countries[143] are concerned, EASA has generally sought to conclude two types of working arrangements: (1) on the collection and exchange of information on aircraft safety, for implementing the Safety Assessment of Foreign Aircraft (SAFA) Programme, and (2) on regulatory cooperation and standardisation, in the context of the transition from the JAA system to the EASA system. Within the second sub-category of working arrangements, there are some differences in content depending on whether the respective country is associated with the EU *via*

136 Working Arrangement on Continuous Monitoring Activities between the EASA and ICAO (July 2014) ‹http://easa.europa.eu/document-library/working-arrangements/working-arrangement-continuous-monitoring-activities-between›.

137 ie the Interstate Aviation Committee (IAC). It should be noted that on the EASA website, the arrangement with IAC is included under the cooperation framework between the Agency and Russia ‹http://www.easa.europa.eu/document-library/working-arrangements/russia›.

138 eg Singapore, Australia.

139 United Arab Emirates.

140 China.

141 Implementing procedures, adopted under the umbrella working arrangements concluded with IAC and UAE.

142 This expression has been used by an EASA official during an interview in order to describe, at a glance, the diversity characterising EASA's working arrangements, Interview 21 with EASA officials, Cologne (7 November 2012).

143 Also referred to as PANEP or pan-European partner countries.

an agreement or not. Accordingly, in practice EASA uses two different templates called Type 1 and Type 2 working arrangements.[144] Type 1 working arrangements are used for the Pan-European Partners (PANEP) which have undertaken the commitment to adopt the EU Aviation Safety system as part of an agreement concluded with the EU.[145] Type 2 working arrangements are concluded with competent aviation authorities from the remaining non-EU European countries and they do not reflect a very strong commitment since they do not include an agreement at a high level.[146]

Russia and other former Soviet countries concluded a working arrangement in 2004 between EASA and the Interstate Aviation Committee (IAC), established under the Minsk Agreement[147] signed on 30 December 1991. Referred to by EASA's experts as 'the working arrangement with Russia', it has been admitted that in reality IAC is a regional international body competent in aircraft type and production certification, a kind of 'EASA of those countries'.[148] From this perspective, this working arrangement can also be seen as a sample of formalised direct cooperation with an international body/organisation. The main aim of the working arrangement is to lay down procedures for granting design approvals and airworthiness and environmental certification of aviation products imported from the other contracting party.[149] The umbrella working arrangement has been complemented by numerous implementing instruments dealing generally with detailed aspects regarding the validation and certification procedures of specific European and Russian aviation products, and they are considered to be a special category of working arrangements.[150]

Worldwide, EASA has concluded working arrangements with Canada, United States, Australia, New Zealand, Asian countries (China, Hong Kong, Japan, Vietnam, Singapore and Taipei), countries from the Mediterranean Aviation Safety Cell (Morocco, Israel, Jordan, Lebanon, Tunisia),[151] and other countries in the Middle East (Saudi Arabia and United Arab Emirates).

144 Interview 21 with EASA officials, Cologne (7 November 2012).

145 Such agreements are the Agreement establishing the European Economic Area, the Agreement between the European Community and the Swiss Confederation on Air Transport, and the Multilateral agreement on the establishment of a European Common Aviation Area, or common aviation area agreements (CAAs) such as in the case of Moldova, Georgia or Ukraine ‹https://ec.europa.eu/transport/modes/air/international_aviation/external_aviation_policy/neighbourhood_en›.

146 eg Armenia, Azerbaijan and Turkey.

147 The Intergovernmental Agreement on Civil Aviation and Air Space, concluded between Azerbaijan, Armenia, Belarus, Georgia, Kazakhstan, Kyrgyzstan, Moldova, Russian Federation, Tajikistan, Turkmenistan, Uzbekistan and Ukraine.

148 Interview 21 with EASA officials, Cologne (7 November 2012).

149 Article 2 of the Working Arrangement.

150 Interview 21 with EASA officials, Cologne (7 November 2012).

151 The Mediterranean Aviation Safety Cell (MASC) has been created by EASA as a pragmatic framework for technical cooperation in aviation safety with the competent authorities of the countries involved in Euro–Mediterranean cooperation under the Barcelona process. It builds upon the EU relevant technical projects, in particular the Euromed Aviation Project, as well as on the Euro–Mediterranean Aviation Agreements concluded or currently negotiated with the Mediterranean countries. The main purpose of the MASC cooperation was to reach full harmonisation of the aviation safety rules and procedures in the countries concerned with the rules of the EU as a means to achieving the Euro–Mediterranean Common Aviation Area, see for details about the Euro–Mediterranean cooperation in the aviation area, see COM (2004) 74 (n 42) 2–3 and 7–14 and COM (2011) 670 (n 54) 8.

It should be noted that the SAFA Programme has been extended to third countries outside Europe, with SAFA working arrangements being concluded between EASA and the competent authorities from Canada, Australia, Morocco, Israel and Singapore. Recently, EASA and FAA concluded a very specific working arrangement for the implementation of the BASA between the USA and the EU.[152] EASA also has very specific working arrangements with Australia and Singapore, ensuring enhanced cooperation (exchange of information) pertaining to the airworthiness oversight of the Airbus A380 fleet operated by Qantas Airlines (Australia) and Singapore Airlines, respectively.[153] Additionally, EASA has concluded with the civil aviation authority in Singapore a special working arrangement on cooperation in the domain of wake turbulence separation and aircraft categorisation standards.[154] The working arrangements with New Zealand and Japan cover, in particular, the validation by EASA of the type certificates for aircraft, parts and appliances issued by the competent aviation authority from that respective country.

China is a peculiar case, since almost half of the total number of EASA's working arrangements have been concluded with this country.[155] This is apparently owing to the special requirement from China to conclude a separate working arrangement for the validation of every type of aviation product and, in specific cases, even for supplemental type certificates.[156] Most working arrangements[157] address the validation by the Chinese competent authority of the type certificates and design approvals issued by EASA.[158] The working arrangements with the competent aviation authorities from Taipei, Vietnam and Hong Kong are similar.

Israel is a very interesting case as the working arrangement from 2004 concerning the mutual acceptance of certificates and technical findings regarding design approval and airworthiness certification was concluded in order to implement an agreement between Israel and Italy on airworthiness certification, approval and acceptance of imported civil aeronautical products, and the acceptance of maintenance service from 1990.[159] Saudi Arabia's working arrangement deals with the validation and acceptance by the competent aviation authority of the changes in type designs and of repair designs approved by EASA or by organisations within the EASA system.[160] The United

152 Working Arrangement between The Federal Aviation Administration of the United States of America and The European Aviation Safety Agency on the Airbus A320 Aircraft Family Final Assembly Line and Delivery Centre in Mobile, Alabama, United States (n 134).

153 The arrangement with Singapore and that with Australia appear to follow the same template.

154 EASA/Working arrangements ‹http://www.easa.europa.eu/system/files/dfu/WA%20between%20EASA%20and%20CAAS%20on%20cooperation%20in%20the%20domain%20of%20Wake%20Turbulence%20Separation%20and%20Aircraft%20Categorisation%20Standards..pdf›.

155 EASA/Working arrangements ‹https://www.easa.europa.eu/document-library/working-arrangements/working-arrangement-china›.

156 Interview 21 with EASA officials, Cologne (7 November 2012).

157 More than 60 working arrangements have been concluded until now between EASA and the Civil Aviation Authority in China.

158 Interview 21 with EASA officials, Cologne (7 November 2012).

159 The working arrangement was concluded under the derogation provided currently in art 12(2) of EASA Basic Regulation. Apparently, this happened because, under Regulation 1592/2002, EASA had become the competent airworthiness authority, also *inter alia* substituting the Italian Aviation Authority.

160 EASA/Working arrangements ‹http://easa.europa.eu/document-library/working-arrangements/saudi-arabia›.

Arab Emirates' working arrangement mainly covers the procedure for acceptance by the competent authority of the design approvals and airworthiness certification made by EASA.[161] Furthermore, an implementing procedure was concluded between the two aviation authorities with a view to facilitating and accomplishing the certification tasks of the two aviation authorities under the working arrangement.

Following the 2011 MOC between the European Union and ICAO, in 2014 a 'Working Arrangement on Continuous Monitoring Activities' was concluded between EASA and ICAO. As observed by Ratajczyk, the primary aim of the working arrangement is to '(. . .) implement the provisions of the EU–ICAO MoC and its safety annex related to the coordination of the ICAO USOAP and EU standardisation inspections'.[162]

Wording, content and structure

In spite of the existing diversity, the working arrangements concluded by EASA feature a similar structure consisting of a preamble and the main part or the content of the instrument. Often, the working arrangements are supplemented with one or several Annexes. It should be noted that the provisions of EASA's working arrangements are not structured in articles but are in numbered paragraphs.

The *preamble* of the working arrangements usually provides an overview of the background, the reasons and the objectives of the relationship formalised between EASA and its partners. The preamble can be concise or more detailed depending on the subject matter of the working arrangement, the framework and the aims of the cooperation between the parties. The preambles routinely include the formula according to which 'the Parties' 'have agreed' to the (provisions of) the working arrangement.[163]

The *content (main body)* of the working arrangements is configured along the following structure: an introductory part, an inner part establishing the details of cooperation between the parties, and final provisions. A common feature of the content of the working arrangements is the widespread use of the words 'Party'[164] or 'Contracting Party'[165] to designate EASA and its partner.[166] Another feature of the main body of the EASA working arrangements is the widespread use of 'will/shall' clauses.

The introductory part normally concerns provisions with regard to the objectives and/or purposes of the cooperation, the scope of the cooperation, and definitions, with no regard for a certain sequence. The inner part of the working arrangements includes the more detailed procedures, the activities performed and the responsibilities

161 EASA/Working arrangements ‹http://easa.europa.eu/document-library/working-arrangements/united-arab-emirates›.

162 Ratajczyk (n 63) 161.

163 In few instances, a similar formula that the parties 'have decided to co-operate as follows' is inserted (eg Singapore and Australia). The working arrangement with Saudi Arabia stipulates that the 'Contracting authorities (. . .) Have reached the following understanding', whilst the preamble to the working arrangement with ICAO provides that the parties 'make the following arrangement'.

164 eg the JAA–EASA transition working arrangements, the SAFA working arrangements.

165 eg the working arrangements with IAC.

166 Sometimes terms like 'Contracting authority' (working arrangement with Saudi Arabia) or simply 'Authority' (working arrangements with Australia, China, United Arab Emirates) are used.

undertaken by the parties within the scope of the cooperation thus formalised. Sometimes it also refers to ancillary aspects of the cooperation between the parties, such as costs and communication matters.

Within these general lines, there is some differentiation regarding the set-up of the inner part of the working arrangements, depending on the particular scope and objectives of the cooperation between EASA and its partners. Thus, the working arrangements pertaining to certification issues include routinely provisions regarding design approval, airworthiness certification, continuing airworthiness, communication, and mutual assistance between the parties.[167] Numerous working arrangements include quite detailed provisions regarding the procedure under which one competent authority validates or accepts the type certificates and supplemental type certificates issued by the other competent authority on aircraft models, parts and appliances.[168] These working arrangements also include usually airworthiness support activities determining specific duties of the contracting parties with regard to product deliveries and continued airworthiness. Note that these certification procedures often include specific rights and duties for third parties, labelled as 'the applicant', 'the type certificate applicant', 'the type certificate holder', 'the supplemental type certificate holder', 'the approval holder', 'the manufacturer'.

The working arrangements ensuring the transition from the JAA to the EASA system are mainly concerned with the standardisation of the PANEP countries with regard to the adoption and implementation of the relevant EU rules. In this context, stipulations are made with regard to the procedures and requirements for the certification of products, parts and appliances, persons and organisations, as well as for mutual acceptance of certificates and technical findings. The cooperation between EASA and the competent authorities from the PANEP countries is shaped slightly differently in the Type 1 working arrangement compared to the Type 2 working arrangement.

Type 1 working arrangements reflect the commitment of the third country authority to implement the rules and standards set by the EU as regards the certification of aircraft, as well as for design and production organisations. In this regard, the working arrangements provide for continuous monitoring by EASA of the implementation of relevant EU rules by the competent NAA. Moreover, the working arrangements provide for standardisation inspections by EASA not only of the respective NAA, but also of the undertakings under its oversight.[169] As a result, EASA accepts the certificates issued by the third-country authority according to EU law, whereas for matters within the scope of the arrangement but for which third country authority does not apply EU standards, the acceptance of certificates takes place according to national, EU or international law. Additionally, the most recent Type 1 PANEP working arrangements stipulate that the third country NAA '(. . .) accepts and recognises, without further

167 eg working arrangements with IAC, New Zealand, Japan, the JAA–EASA transition working arrangements.

168 eg most of working arrangements with China, working arrangements with Vietnam, Taipei, Hong Kong. In other instances, the body of the working arrangements only includes basic provisions regarding the mutual acceptance of certificates and refers to the annexes of the instrument, in which the detailed certification procedures are included (eg Japan, the JAA transition arrangements with PANEP countries).

169 The Type 1 PANEP working arrangements.

technical requirements or evaluation' certificates issued within the scope and in accordance with EASA's Basic Regulation.[170]

The Type 2 working arrangement does not create an obligation for the third country authority to automatically adopt and apply the EU rules and standards in the area of certification.[171] Accordingly, the acceptance of the certificates issued by one party is done according to the other party's own standards and usually entails the issuance of another certificate. Additionally, certification procedures which include specific features, in addition to EASA's standard certification procedures, are established in detail in the Annexes to the working arrangement.

The SAFA working arrangements mainly address issues related to the nature and form of the exchange of information between the parties within the SAFA programme, related procedural aspects and responsibilities, regulatory cooperation within the scope of the arrangement, as well as confidentiality duties in handling the information received from the other party. A common feature of the SAFA working arrangements is the extensive use of 'shall' clauses. The latest SAFA working arrangements provide for more detailed procedures and obligations regarding the confidentiality of the information exchanged, such as the duty of the third country authority to reject (and to take legal action to enforce such a rejection) a request for information from a third party when so advised by EASA. Not least importantly, these working arrangements include a detailed procedure regarding standardisation inspections carried out by EASA with a view to examining compliance by the third-country authority with the EU SAFA requirements, after which the SAFA member status of the relevant third-country authority may be suspended by EASA.

Finally, the core provisions of the EASA–ICAO working arrangement focus on information exchange and related confidentiality arrangements within the framework of ICAO's Universal Safety Oversight Audit Programme (USOAP). In this regard, it is interesting to note the provision granting the EU Member States and the non-EU states participating in EASA a right to access ICAO's USOAP CMA activities pertaining to EASA.[172]

The final provisions of EASA's working arrangements cover the entry into force, amendment procedure and termination of the cooperation instrument. Additional aspects usually dealt with in the final provisions are the language of the instrument, the interpretation of its provisions and the procedure for solving disagreements and conflicts regarding the interpretation and the application of the working arrangement. As concerns the latter aspect, most working arrangements simply stipulate that disagreements are to be solved by common accord between the parties,[173] but in a few working arrangements, the conflict resolution procedure and rules are more elaborated.[174]

Some observations are pertinent with regard to the final part of some of EASA's working arrangements. First, the latest SAFA arrangements concluded with the PANEP countries, as well as the SAFA arrangements with Morocco, Singapore,

170 Paragraph 7(3) of the new generation Type 1 PANEP working arrangements.

171 eg Armenia, Azerbaijan, Monaco, San Marino and Turkey.

172 Paragraph 6(7) of the working arrangement.

173 eg the JAA–EASA transition working arrangements, the working arrangements with China, Singapore, Australia and Vietnam.

174 eg working arrangements with New Zealand, Israel (2004), IAC and ICAO.

Canada, and the United Arab Emirates explicitly provide for the possibility to suspend the application of the arrangement in case of persistent failure by one of the parties to comply with its provisions. Secondly, some working arrangements include a sort of a 'limiting clause', stating that the provisions do not affect or limit the rights and obligations of the parties stemming from relevant international agreements.[175] In this context, the working arrangement between EASA and the competent authority of Israel, concluded in 2004 on the basis of a bilateral agreement between Italy and Israel, is particularly interesting. It contains a 'limiting clause' according to which it does not affect the other provisions of the Agreement between Italy and Israel, while the provisions of that Agreement are implemented to the extent that they are not contrary to the working arrangement.[176] It should be added furthermore that in one particular working arrangement, in addition to the 'limiting clause', it is specifically laid down that the cooperation instrument is 'of a practical and technical nature' and that it 'is not legally binding' for the EU and the third country concerned'.[177] Thirdly, in a few working arrangements addressing certification matters, the validity of the certificates and approvals granted by EASA or the partner aviation authority under the working arrangement is safeguarded in case the arrangement is terminated.[178]

Usually, one or more supplementary documents called 'Annex' or 'Appendix' are attached to the main provisions of the working arrangement and constitute an integral part of the working arrangement. Sometimes they simply include contact information of the focal points set-up by the competent authorities for the purpose of the cooperation carried out under the working arrangement[179] while, in some cases, the annexes list applicable regulations and technical standards,[180] various procedures concerning standardisation,[181] certification of aircraft products and organisation approvals.[182]

The procedure for the negotiation and conclusion of working arrangements

According to EASA's internal procedure, concluding a working arrangement with a competent authority from a third country or with an international organisation entails three distinct phases: (1) initiation; (2) drafting and negotiation; (3) conclusion, communication and publication.[183] The initiation phase usually begins with a request

175 This is the case of the working arrangements on the transition from the JAA to the EU aviation system with the competent authorities from PANEP countries, as well as the new generation of Type 1 PANEP working arrangements.

176 Para 1.2 of the working arrangement. The phrasing of this clause suggests a duty of consistent interpretation placed on Italy and Israel in implementing the provisions of their bilateral agreement, indicating that the provisions of the working arrangement are legally binding.

177 Para 10(2) of the working arrangement with Armenia (2009).

178 eg working arrangements with Japan and Hong Kong.

179 eg working arrangements with Australia and Vietnam, as well as some of the working arrangements with China.

180 eg the new generation of Type 1 PANEP working arrangements.

181 eg working arrangements with PANEP countries concerning the transition to the EU aviation system, and also those concluded under the SAFA Programme since 2011.

182 eg working arrangements with Japan, Saudi Arabia and Type 2 PANEP working arrangements.

183 EASA PR.WARG 00001-001 (n 116) 4–11.

from a third country authority, international organisation, the Commission or the industry, but it can also start at the initiative of the Agency itself. The Commission (DG MOVE) is informed from the very beginning about the receipt of such request.[184] After a preliminary assessment of the relevance of the request within the Agency, approval in principle is sought from the Commission to pursue the request further, if the Agency would consider it relevant.[185] In case the Commission approves the request, the Agency will contact the foreign competent authority or the relevant international organisation in order to initiate the drafting and negotiation phase. The Commission is informed regularly about the progress of negotiations.[186] When the negotiation with the foreign competent authority or with the international organisation is successful, then the final formal Commission approval provided for in Article 27(2) of the Basic Regulation is requested, before the working arrangement is signed.

After Commission's approval,[187] the working arrangement enters the conclusion phase.[188] This entails first that the heads of EASA's Directorates give their consent to the working arrangement. Secondly, the working arrangement is signed by the executive director, which officially marks the formal conclusion of the instrument on behalf of EASA. This is followed by the publication of the working arrangement on EASA's webpage and by informing the relevant stakeholders.

Several comments can be made with regard to the procedure for negotiation and conclusion of EASA's working arrangements. First, the Commission appears to be omnipresent throughout the procedure from the beginning, when it approves the request to negotiate a working arrangement, until the conclusion phase, when it approves the final text of the instrument according to Article 27(2) of the Basic Regulation. Within these milestones, the Commission can always interfere and stop or delay the process as it deems appropriate. Secondly, the procedure formally only involves the executive director, the directors of the Agency and the relevant internal administrative structures. There is no role assigned to the management board in the process. Thirdly, the conclusion of the working arrangement does not seem to entail any formal legal act adopted by the Agency. In this respect, it appears that the formality attesting the conclusion of the working arrangement consists of a list of signatures of the directors of the Agency on a routing slip accompanying the working

184 ibid 5.

185 In principle, the Commission receives and approves each request for a working arrangement, but it is possible for the Commission to grant a generic approval for certain types of working arrangements; in the latter case, no approval is needed for each individual request, EASA PR. WARG 00001-001 (n 116) 5–6.

186 EASA PR.WARG 00001-001 (n 116) 8. It has been revealed that there are meetings between EASA and the Commission every few months, where the Agency informs the Commission (DG MOVE) about the progress with the negotiation of working arrangements, while the Commission keeps EASA updated on the relevant policy/political developments, Interview 21 with EASA officials, Cologne (7 November 2012).

187 It has been conveyed that in practice the Commission has blocked or delayed the conclusion of working arrangements several times by refusing to grant approval, and that the Commission's refusal is usually motivated by political rather than technical reasons, Interview 21 with EASA officials, Cologne (7 November 2012).

188 EASA PR.WARG 00001-001 (n 116) 9–10.

arrangement, and, finally, the signature of the executive director on the instrument itself.[189]

4.4.2.2.2 OTHER FORMAL COOPERATION INSTRUMENTS CONCLUDED BY EASA

In addition to the working arrangements, either as self-standing instruments or implementing international agreements and other (umbrella) working arrangements, EASA also employs specific instruments to formalise cooperation with its partners. Two categories of such instruments are worth mentioning in this context: (1) the formal cooperation instruments concluded by EASA with a view to implementing the bilateral aviation safety agreements (BASAs) in force and (2) the memoranda of understanding.

BASA implementing instruments

Under the Bilateral Air Safety Agreements with the USA, Canada and Brazil, two different instruments have been concluded by EASA with the corresponding aviation authority, each being linked to one of the two Annexes of the respective BASA. One is called technical implementation procedures (TIPs) and provides for the detailed certification and validation procedures and activities of the competent authorities for the '(. . .) import, export, and continued support of civil aviation products'.[190] The other is referred to as a maintenance annex guidance (MAG) laying down the detailed procedures and activities for the purpose of the reciprocal acceptance of findings in the field of aircraft maintenance (repair stations and maintenance organisations).[191]

With regard to the content, these instruments look very similar to the 'regular' working arrangements concluded by EASA on certification, such as the detailed procedural provisions establishing rights and duties for third parties, labelled as 'applicants'. This is also the case with the 'safeguard clause' included in all of the TIPs concluded so far covering the validity of the activities conducted *prior* to termination of the cooperation under this instrument. An interesting aspect is that the TIPs stipulate explicitly the possibility to adopt 'further working arrangements' for issues that are not covered by the TIP itself, but which are nevertheless within the scope of the BASA.[192] As mentioned above, such a working arrangement has been concluded between EASA and FAA in 2014. Both TIPs and MAGs include detailed dispute settlement procedures, comprising several steps and contacts on different levels and, in the case of TIPs, it also includes norms for solving conflicting interpretations. Furthermore, TIPs and MAGs have their own formal internal EASA procedure for negotiation and conclusion consisting of similar steps like in the case of the 'regular'

189 Interview 25 with EASA officials, Brussels (13 May 2013).

190 eg Technical implementation procedure for airworthiness and environmental certification under the Agreement on civil aviation safety between the Government of Canada and the European Union, 20 September 2011 ‹https://www.easa.europa.eu/document-library/bilateral-agreements/eu-canada›.

191 See Agreement on civil aviation safety between the Government of Canada and the European Union [2009] OJ L153/11, Annex B, para 1.

192 See, for example, Section VII of the TIP between EASA and FAA ‹https://www.easa.europa.eu/document-library/bilateral-agreements/eu-usa›.

working arrangements, although they also feature a number of specific characteristics.[193] EASA officials explained that the TIPs and the MAGs are very similar tools to the working arrangements.[194] In conclusion, one may qualify TIPs and MAGs as very specific working arrangements implementing the EU BASAs currently in force.

Memoranda of understanding

The memoranda of understanding (MOUs) or memoranda of cooperation (MOCs) are yet another category of instruments that EASA concludes with third countries[195] and international organisations.[196] Unlike the working arrangements and the specific arrangements implementing the BASAs, these instruments are not published on EASA's website. Instead, they may be referred to in the preambles of some working arrangements[197] and in the activity reports of the Agency. The main reason for this difference in treatment appears to be that, in the view of the Agency, the memoranda are not at the same level as the working arrangements. As explained by EASA officials, the memoranda concluded by the Agency resemble more a letter of intention to pursue more enhanced cooperation in the future.[198] Such documents are usually concise and may also include some political aspects.[199] If this is the case, it follows that the Agency may be suspected of transgressing its (technical) mandate; the only way to validate the inclusion of politically sensitive aspects in the MOUs concluded by EASA is by linking this to some sort of authorisation from the Commission.

A closer look at the text of some MOUs concluded by EASA so far seems to support the view that they are lighter forms of cooperation compared to the standard working arrangements. First, the language used in the instrument refers to cooperation in general terms and does not seem to indicate the same degree of commitment between the parties as in a working arrangement. In this regard, the terminology according to which the parties 'acknowledge' a set of principles for cooperation and 'endeavour'

193 eg the conclusion of the instrument within the framework of the joint structures established by the BASAs, such as the Joint Sectorial Committee on Certification (SCC) and the Joint Sectorial Committee on Maintenance (SCM), respectively, or signature by the Certification Director (for TIPs) and the Approvals and Standardisation Director (for MAGs), see EASA PR. BASA 00001-001 (n 115).

194 Interview 21 with EASA officials, Cologne (7 November 2012).

195 eg Memorandum of Understanding on the Airbus A320 Aircraft Family Final Assembly Line and Delivery Centre in China between the General Administration of Civil Aviation of China (CAAC) and the European Aviation Safety Agency (EASA) of 8 November 2006; Memorandum of Understanding on Aviation Safety and airworthiness between UAE General Civil Aviation Authority and European Aviation Safety Agency of 7 February 2006.

196 eg Memorandum of Cooperation between EASA and ICAO regarding safety oversight audit and related matters (signed on 21 March 2006), superseded by the 2014 EASA-ICAO working arrangement.

197 eg working arrangement with UAE (2008); working arrangement with Chinese aviation authority on the Airbus (Tianjin) A320 Aircraft Family Final Assembly Line and Delivery Centre in China (2009).

198 According to one EASA official, the memoranda of understanding concluded by the Agency should not be included within the scope of the term 'working arrangement' mentioned in art 27 of EASA Basic Regulation, Interview 21 with EASA officials, Cologne (7 November 2012).

199 Interview 21 with EASA officials, Cologne (7 November 2012).

to progress towards more enhanced forms of cooperation seems much weaker than the 'will/shall' language from the working arrangements establishing more precise responsibilities.[200] Secondly, the memoranda examined by the author include explicitly the objective to adopt in the future a working arrangement establishing detailed co-operation procedures and the responsibilities of the parties. Thirdly, although these instruments are signed by the executive director, the negotiation and conclusion procedure followed is very much simplified. In conclusion, it appears that MOUs represent only a first basic step in formalising the cooperation between EASA and its partners, whilst the working arrangements lay down enhanced forms of cooperation between the parties.

4.5 EASA on the global scene: a legal assessment

4.5.1 The legal nature of EASA's formal international cooperation instruments

The legal nature of EASA's international cooperation instruments needs to be determined in light of the criteria for international binding agreements followed in this study – ie the wording and substance/content of the instrument, as well as the particular circumstances (context) surrounding the negotiation and conclusion of the instrument – and along the indicators corresponding to each criterion.[201] Closely linked to this issue, some objections concerning the binding or international character of EASA's working arrangements need to be discussed first.

4.5.1.1 Working arrangements

Non-binding or binding (international) agreements?

EASA's working arrangements are described on the Agency's website as instruments limited to technical cooperation, which are '(. . .) typically used to facilitate EASA's certification tasks or the validation by a foreign authority of EASA certificates'.[202] The legal nature of the working arrangements concluded by EASA is a complex issue. First, because they are concluded by an agency of an international organisation whose legal status under international law is not fully clear or accepted yet. Secondly, from an EU perspective, the use of the label 'arrangement' instead of 'agreement' arguably indicates that these instruments were intended to be a separate category from the 'normal' international agreements concluded by the EU.[203] Thirdly, EASA officials tend to regard these instruments as vehicles for technical cooperation, rather than

200 ibid.

201 See ch 2, Box 2.1: Criteria and indicators for identifying international binding agreements.

202 EASA, International cooperation ‹https://www.easa.europa.eu/easa-and-you/international-cooperation/international-cooperation-explained#international-offices›.

203 See Commission, *Vademecum on the External Action of the European Union*, SEC (2011) 881/3 52, and Joint Statement of the European Parliament, the Council of the EU and the European Commission on decentralised agencies of 19 July 2012 (Common Approach on EU agencies), para 25 ‹http://europa.eu/about-eu/agencies/overhaul/index_en.htm›.

fully-fledged international agreements.[204] In this context, it is also maintained that the working arrangements either pave the way for or are concluded within the framework of existing international agreements concluded by the EU. In a similar vein, Ratajczyk points out that the working arrangements are the instrument used by the Agency '(. . .) to exercise the implementing powers which have been given to it as a technical agent'.[205] As a result, EASA's working arrangements cannot bind the EU or the Member States under international law. Additionally, Ratajczyk suggests that the clause included in some working arrangements that '(. . .) they are without prejudice to international agreements' indicates that these instruments are non-binding.[206] Fourthly, doubts are expressed whether such working arrangements, even if binding, are governed by international law in view of the fact that the parties arguably agree to apply their own legal rules and not the rules of international law.[207]

In the view of the author, none of these objections is decisive for qualifying EASA's working arrangements as binding international agreements. First, international law accepts in principle that international agreements can also be concluded by entities other than states and intergovernmental organisations.[208] This does not seem to exclude (semi-)autonomous agencies established by the states or by international organisations. Moreover, if such agencies are organs of the state or of an international organisation and they act internationally on behalf of or under the oversight of their 'mother', then the international agreement will ultimately be deemed to be concluded by the relevant state or international organisation.[209] According to international law, in principle this would not change even when the agency enacted the international agreement in breach of the domestic rules of the relevant state or international organisation.[210]

Secondly, according to international treaty law,[211] the title of the instrument alone is not sufficient for qualifying it as an international agreement. In this regard, the term 'arrangement' instead of 'agreement' does not mean that the instrument cannot be binding under international law. From an internal (EU) perspective, the use of different terms and corresponding procedures may indicate nevertheless different types of international cooperation instruments – ie high-level international agreements concluded by the main political EU institutions directly (covered under Article 218 TFEU), and administrative or technical agreements concluded at lower levels according to simplified procedures by EU institutions and bodies on the basis of the provisions of the Treaties and of the mandate given by the main EU institutions.[212] In spite of

204 Interview 21 with EASA officials, Cologne (7 November 2013).

205 Ratajczyk (n 63) 146.

206 ibid.

207 Interview 21with EASA officials, Cologne (7 November 2012). Also, Ratajczyk points out that EASA's working arrangements '(. . .) cannot derogate from EU law, which is in fact their main limitation', Ratajczyk (n 63) 147.

208 See ch 2, 2.3.1: The concept of 'international agreement'.

209 This was exactly the situation in the 1991, in Case C-327/91 *France v Commission* [1994] ECR I-3641, where the Court found that the agreement concluded by the Commission bound ultimately the former European Community, see ch 2, 2.2.3.4.2: Treaty-making and non-legally binding instruments.

210 See ch 2, 2.2.3.4.2: Treaty-making and non-legally binding instruments.

211 See ch 2, 2.3.1: The concept of 'international agreement'.

212 For a more detailed discussion see ch 2, 2.3.1.2.2: International administrative agreements at the EU level.

this differentiation, nothing precludes instruments from both categories from being qualified as binding agreements according to international law.

Thirdly, the technical nature of the instrument does not necessarily mean that its provisions cannot be legally binding, as this ultimately depends on the precise content and effects of the instrument. The fact that the working arrangements are sometimes adopted in the implementation of existing international agreements concluded by the EU does not change that. It should be noted that, in spite of the reluctance to assimilate EASA's working arrangements to international treaties, EASA officials admitted that such instruments are binding for the Agency, this view being also reflected in the Agency's Rulemaking Programme 2010–2013.[213] Interestingly, a Commission official concurred with this view when pointing out that EASA's working arrangements: '(. . .) are obviously binding to some extent. Maybe not to the extent of a treaty that may be signed by the EU, but nevertheless binding international documents'.[214] In addition, Ratajczyk acknowledges that, in practice, sometimes EASA's counterparts also tend to regard the working arrangements as binding international agreements.[215]

Fourthly, the provision included in some working arrangements that they do not affect or limit the rights and obligations of the parties under other international agreements does not necessarily imply that they cannot produce any legal effects. Such a provision, which can also be found in regular international agreements,[216] is rather a 'limiting clause' delineating the precise scope of the provisions and effects of the instrument in relation to other relevant international cooperation instruments.[217]

Fifthly, the reference to the domestic rules of the parties in the implementation of cooperation under the working arrangement does not turn the agreement into a domestic one. In international law literature and practice, the view is expressed that the mere fact that an agreement is concluded between international actors makes it subject to international law.[218] Furthermore, a trans-boundary element is involved in EASA's working arrangements, where a party applies the rules of the other party or accepts the findings and decisions made by the other party according to its own rules. As a result, principles such as *pacta sunt servanda*, *ius cogens* and international liability become applicable to such cooperation, even if the parties agree to apply domestic rules.

Assessment

The working arrangements are concluded according to quite a detailed and standard[219] formal procedure, finalised with the signature of the instrument by the authorised

213 EASA, Rulemaking Programme 2010–2013 4 ‹https://www.easa.europa.eu/document-library/rulemaking-programmes/2010-2013-rulemaking-programme›.

214 Interview 9 (phone) with a Commission official (2 July 2013).

215 See for a concrete example involving the Turkish competent authority, Ratajczyk (n 63) 146–47.

216 See eg art 13(3) of the BASA between the EU and Canada.

217 See ch 2, 2.3.1: The concept of 'international agreement'.

218 See ch 2, 2.3.1: The concept of 'international agreement'. By using this line of reasoning, the outcome would be that the BASAs concluded by the EU with third countries are also mere 'domestic' agreements since they also cover mutual acceptance by the contracting parties of certification and technical findings made by each party in accordance with their own standards.

219 The exceptions are the TIPs and the MAGs which follow a different procedure originating from the specific features of the BASAs.

representatives of the parties or by an exchange of letters signed by each representative. An important feature of this procedure is the Commission's *prior* approval formalised in Article 27(2) of EASA's Basic Regulation. These aspects seem to indicate the importance attached to such instruments.

Conversely, the internal procedure of the Agency does not include the issuing of a formal decision by the executive director or by the management board with a view to concluding the working arrangement, which suggests that there is a certain degree of informality. EASA's working arrangements are not concluded with the head of state or government of the third country concerned, but they are usually concluded with the competent aviation authority and sometimes with the specialised ministry. It is also true that the working arrangements are not subjected to a ratification procedure, but under international law there is no such mandatory requirement in order to become bound by a treaty. In particular, so-called 'executive' or 'administrative' agreements usually feature simplified procedures, engendering little or no action by the legislative authority.[220]

It should also be noted that EASA's working arrangements are neither registered with the UN nor are they published in the Official Journal of the European Union, but they are published on the Agency's website instead. However, under international law, UN registration and publication in an official journal or gazette only represent complementary indicators as to the binding nature of an international cooperation instrument.[221] Accordingly, the fact that EASA's working arrangements are only available *via* the Agency's website does not mean that these instruments are non-binding. In this respect, it should be noted that, in Case C-327/91, the Court had no difficulties to qualify the agreement between the Commission and the US Government regarding the application of their competition laws as binding, although it had not been published in the Official Journal.

A look at the content of the working arrangements provides evidence supporting their qualification as legally binding instruments under international law. Such indicators are: the treaty-like language used (ie 'the parties have agreed', 'have concluded', widespread use of 'shall/will' clauses), quite clearly worded rights and obligations for the contracting parties and sometimes also for third parties,[222] the inclusion of clauses related to the entry into force, amendment and termination of the agreement, inclusion of dispute settlement procedures (see examples below). The commitments undertaken by the parties are limited to various aspects of regulatory cooperation within their respective mandates, such as procedural rights and obligations related to the certification and continuous airworthiness of aircraft products, parts and appliances, information exchange, including confidentiality duties.[223] However, the fact that EASA's working arrangements pertain to limited regulatory cooperation is

220 See ch 2, 2.3.1.2.1: Administrative agreements in international and state practice.

221 See in this regard Duncan B Hollis, 'Defining Treaties' in Duncan B Hollis (ed), *The Oxford Guide to Treaties* (OUP 2012) 30–31; Kirsten Schmalenbach, 'Article 2. Use of Terms' in Oliver Dörr and Kirsten Schmalenbach (eds), *Vienna Convention on the Law of Treaties. A Commentary* (Springer 2012) 41.

222 In this regard, Ratajczyk maintains that the working arrangements suggesting obligations for third parties should be considered as *ultra vires* and void; nevertheless, he admits that the working arrangements may affect third parties from '(. . .) a practical point of view', Ratajczyk (n 63) 147.

223 See Annex 3: Examples of EASA's formal international cooperation instruments.

not sufficient to limit the commitments undertaken by the competent authorities to non-binding commitments.

As mentioned above, some working arrangements feature specific clauses providing additional evidence in favour of the conclusion that they are intended to produce legal effects (see examples below). The provisions in the SAFA working arrangements regarding the handling of requests for information from third parties, as well as those regarding the suspension of the 'SAFA member' status of the third-country authority or the suspension of the application of the working arrangement in case of a persistent failure to comply with its clauses are good examples in this respect. The same holds true as regards the clauses in some working arrangements on certification, providing that the certificates already issued under that instrument will not be affected by the termination of the respective arrangement.[224] It should be noted further that many of the provisions included in the working arrangements on certification concluded by EASA are very similar to those included in the relevant agreements concluded by the EU with third countries (such as BASAs).[225] All of this appears to suggest that such working arrangements concluded by EASA feature legally binding provisions.

Examples of prescriptive clauses in EASA's working arrangements:

Box 4.1 Working arrangement between the European Aviation Safety Agency and the State Aviation Administration of Ukraine on the participation of the State Aviation Administration of Ukraine in the SAFA programme and on the collection and exchange of information on the safety of aircraft using EU airports and airports of non-EU States that participate in the EU SAFA programme, including airports of Ukraine, 2015

(. . .)

4. Collection of information by the State Aviation Administration of Ukraine

(. . .)

4.2 The State Aviation Administration of Ukraine shall ensure an active participation to the EU SAFA programme by means of its commitment to carry out a minimum annual number of ramp inspections, to be agreed with EASA.

224 Working arrangements with Saudi Arabia, Hong Kong and Japan; TIPS with Brazil, Canada and the USA.

225 eg provisions regarding the responsibilities of the parties, interpretation and dispute settlement, entry into force, amendment and termination. It is interesting to note in this context that art 13(2) of the BASA between the EU and Brazil provides explicitly that it supersedes the previous arrangements between EASA and the corresponding competent aviation; a similar provision is inserted in para 1.2(2) of the TIP concluded between EASA and the competent authority of Canada. This suggests that the previous working arrangements were not merely of a non-binding nature, but, on the contrary, that they produced some legal effects.

6. Confidentiality and Conflict of Interest

(. . .)

6.3 Where the State Aviation Administration of Ukraine receives a request, from a third party, for information in its possession that originates from EASA . . . the State Aviation Administration of Ukraine shall consult with EASA in order to take a decision that does not jeopardise the fulfilment of the objectives of this Working Arrangement (. . .) If EASA advises against disclosure of the requested information, the State Aviation Administration of Ukraine shall, within its powers, reject the request and if necessary take legal action to enforce such rejection.

8. Standardisation inspections

8.1 The State Aviation Administration of Ukraine shall accept standardisation inspections carried out by EASA in order to examine in particular compliance of the State Aviation Administration of Ukraine with the rules and procedures set out in this Working Arrangement and in particular with the relevant EU SAFA technical requirements as set out in Annex 1 to this Working Arrangement.

(. . .)

8.5 Should the actions taken by the State Aviation Administration of Ukraine not satisfy EASA, consultations would be held between the parties. If, within 30 days after the notification by EASA of the supplementary report to the State Aviation Administration of Ukraine, no agreement has been found through such consultations, the granting of the SAFA member status to the State Aviation Administration of Ukraine shall be suspended by EASA.

Box 4.2 Working arrangement between The European Aviation Safety Agency (EASA) and The Civil Aviation Agency of the former Yugoslav Republic of Macedonia (CAA FYROM), 2015

(. . .)

4. Certification of products, parts, appliances, personnel, organisations, aerodromes and related equipment and ATM/ANS and related systems and constituents

The relevant certification activities of CAA FYROM will be carried out in accordance with Annex 1, where the applicable rules of that Annex have been implemented by CAA FYROM.

5. Continuous monitoring and standardisation activities

5.1 CAA FYROM accepts that the following working methods will be used by EASA:

a) Continuous monitoring of the implementation of the applicable rules in Annex 1 to this Working Arrangement;
b) Standardisation inspections of CAA FYROM, including undertakings under the oversights of CAA FYROM, on the basis of the applicable rules set out in Annex 1 to this working arrangement.

7. Acceptance of certificates

(. . .)

7.3 CAA FYROM accepts and recognises, without further technical requirements or evaluation, certificates issued under the scope of and in accordance with Regulation (EU) No 216/2008.

Box 4.3 Working arrangement between The Hong Kong Civil Aviation Department and The European Aviation Safety Agency on validation of certificates for civil aeronautical products, parts and appliances, 2014

(. . .)

4. Type certificate validation process

(. . .)

4.3 Type certificate validation

(. . .)

b) HKCAD will establish a certification basis for the product as including the EASA type certification basis plus any additional technical conditions imposed by HCKAD in order to comply with HKCAD requirements. (. . .) HKCAD will notify in writing both EASA and the applicant of any additional technical conditions necessary for the HKCAD type validation.
c) HKCAD will accept the findings and approvals of EASA, unless notified formally, as subjects to be retained against additional technical conditions defined under b).

5. Supplemental type certificate validation process

5.2 Supplemental Type Certificate Validation

(. . .)

b) HKCAD will establish a validation basis for STC as including the EASA supplemental type certification basis plus any additional technical conditions imposed by HCKAD in order to comply with HKCAD requirements. (. . .) HKCAD will notify in writing both EASA and the applicant of any additional technical conditions necessary for the HKCAD supplemental type validation.

c) HKCAD will accept the findinqs and approvals of EASA, unless notified formally, as subjects to be retained against additional technical conditions defined under 5.2.b).

8. Airworthiness support activities

8.2 Continued airworthiness

(. . .)

b) The HKCAD will promptly notify EASA and the applicant of any unsafe condition associated with the design or manufacturing of the products, parts and appliances which are in service in Hong Kong and for which EASA acts as the State of Design.

Box 4.4 Working arrangement on Continuous Monitoring Activities between The European Aviation Safety Agency and The International Civil Aviation Organization, 2014

(. . .)

5. Exchanging information and data

5.1 ICAO will grant EASA access to the final reports of the USOAP CMA activities as they are published, as well as to subsequent updates on corrective action plans submitted, progress reports received and responses to Mandatory Information requirements (MIRs); the information provided therein will be taken into account for the planning, the preparation and the conduct of EASA Standardisation Inspections.

(. . .)

5.6 The parties will provide access to each other's safety data in accordance with the rules agreed by both Parties. Each Party will take all reasonable precautions necessary to protect the confidentiality of information received in accordance with Paragraph 10.

6. USOAP continuous monitoring of EASA

(. . .)

6.7 ICAO will grant the EU Member States and States participating in EASA in accordance with Article 66 of Regulation (EC) No 216/2008, access to the results of USOAP CMA activities related to EASA.

In view of these considerations, it seems that the working arrangements concluded by EASA with competent authorities from third countries and with international organisations may qualify as binding agreements of a technical-administrative nature, regardless of whether they are concluded within the framework of the existing treaties between the EU and a third country or international organisation, or in the absence of such treaties. Thus, the working arrangements regarding certification and design approvals concluded worldwide, the TIPs and MAGs implementing the BASAs, including the 2014 FAA–EASA working arrangement, as well as the JAA–EASA transition working arrangements, including the new generation of Type 1 PANEP working arrangements can be qualified as international agreements which include legally binding provisions.[226] The same holds for the SAFA working arrangements[227] and the EASA–ICAO working arrangement, in particular with regard to the responsibilities related to the aviation safety information exchanged between the parties. In this respect, EASA's working arrangements establish technical cooperation and working relationships between authorities and organisations competent in the field of aviation safety within the framework of other international agreements or in the implementation of their own domestic legislation, but they also create specific rights and duties between the parties and, sometimes, also with regard to third parties.

4.5.1.2 Memoranda of understanding

As regards the memoranda of understanding or memoranda of cooperation, the evidence available suggests that they are lighter vehicles of cooperation compared to the working arrangements. Their basic structure and vague language indicates that they are rather a statement on behalf of the parties than a genuine commitment to create rights and obligations under international law. This supports the conclusion that EASA's MOUs are not binding international agreements. However, considering the rather permissive view that the International Court of Justice (ICJ) takes at times in qualifying a certain cooperation instrument as an international agreement,[228] it is not completely excluded that limited legally binding obligations could be identified even in such instruments.

226 An additional element supporting the qualification of these working arrangements as legally binding is the fact that these may also directly affect third parties (ie the aviation industry and airlines). Moreover, in the implementation of such working arrangements, EASA issues type certificates which are legally binding within the EU. The same applies *mutatis mutandis* in the partner country as a result of the validation by the competent authority of the type-certificates issued by EASA.

227 The SAFA working arrangement with Moldova (2013) appears to be an exception as the instrument contains a clause specifying that it cannot be considered as an international treaty. However, a comparative assessment reveals no differences with regard to content between this instrument and other SAFA working arrangements. As discussed above, in spite of the inclusion of such clauses, the analysis of the overall content and context of the instrument are decisive for determining its legal nature. Accordingly, the working arrangement with Moldova is not different from the other SAFA working arrangements with respect to its legal nature.

228 See ch 2, 2.3.1: The concept of 'international agreement'.

4.5.2 The status of EASA as a global actor

4.5.2.1 On the international plane

EASA's international dimension, consisting of multifarious cooperation activities as well as the rights and responsibilities stemming most obviously from the working arrangements concluded with third countries and international organisations, begs the question of the status of the Agency on the international plane. More specifically, it needs to be determined whether EASA is a subject of international law on its own account or whether it is an entity always acting on behalf of some other international legal person such as the EU or the Member States.

Assessing whether public entities like EASA are subjects of international law entails establishing their international legal personality. In accordance with the criteria embraced in this study, EASA must have: (1) organisational distinctiveness; (2) separate will, so that it can be perceived as an entity detached from its creators; and (3) powers which can be exercised on the international plane.[229] Relevant indicators in this respect are EASA's legal framework and its international cooperation practice. An additional indicator is the recognition of the Agency as a subject of international law by other subjects of international law (partners and non-partners).

EASA's Basic Regulation designates the Agency as an organisation of its own, equipped with legal personality,[230] powers, leading organs and an elaborated internal structure, and with its own human and financial resources. Moreover, EASA is equipped by its Basic Regulation and other EU instruments with an explicit international cooperation mandate, including the capacity to conclude working arrangements with third countries and international organisations. This is matched by a commensurate international cooperation practice featuring numerous working arrangements concluded by the Agency worldwide. As shown, the preambles to working arrangements concluded by EASA often point to the capacity of the Agency to conclude such instruments according to its legal framework. Moreover, the analysis of EASA's working arrangements revealed that most of them qualify as binding international agreements of a technical-administrative nature. Accordingly, one may conclude that EASA fulfils the first and the third conditions for international legal personality.

It is argued, however, that EASA fails to meet the 'separate will' condition. First, as regards the recognition of EASA as a distinct subject on the international plane, it is difficult to advance a definite conclusion.[231] The impressive number of working arrangements concluded worldwide by the Agency might be an argument in favour of the recognition of the role of EASA on the international plane by its partners. It is not very clear, however, whether EASA's partners regard the Agency as an international entity of its own account[232] or rather as a body acting on behalf of the EU and its Member States. Additional support for the latter option is provided by Ratajczyk, who maintains that the international aviation safety agreements concluded by the EU

229 See ch 2, Box 2.2: Checklist international legal personality of semi-autonomous organs established by states and international organisations.

230 Art 28 of Regulation 216/2008.

231 In this respect, more empirical research is needed.

232 Some sort of a regional organisation in aviation safety matters.

suggest that EASA is considered only as a technical agent of the EU and its Member States and not as a separate international legal person.[233]

Secondly, both the legal framework and the international practice of the Agency indicate a heavy dependence on the Commission and, to a lesser extent, also on the Member States. As discussed previously, the Agency's priorities and planned activities must be endorsed by the management board, bringing together the Commission and the Member States. Moreover, the international cooperation priorities of EASA seem to be established in agreement with the Commission, whose role as a political actor appears to be predominant. In this context, at times EASA has to adapt its international cooperation priorities and activities according to the wishes of the Commission. Last but not least, the procedure regarding the Agency's working arrangements reserves an essential role for the Commission (which actually initiates the process, may decide to stop it at any time, and gives *prior* consent to the final text of the working arrangement). All these circumstances indicate that, in spite of its formal autonomy granted by the Basic Regulation, when pursuing international cooperation, EASA rather acts as a technical agent of the Commission, and ultimately of the EU, than an independent entity on the international plane.[234]

The situation is further complicated when EASA is exercising tasks related to the state of registry for issues related to aircraft design in relation to its partners where the Agency is deemed to exercise such responsibilities internationally on behalf of the Member States.[235] Although EASA received such competences under EU law, on the international plane EASA also appears to be acting as an agent of the Member States.[236] This is the more obvious in the relationship between EASA and ICAO, since the ICAO ultimately considers that the Member States are responsible for the actions performed by the Agency.[237] These situations are foreseen in EASA's Basic Regulation but, nevertheless, this only reinforces the complex agency relationship between EASA and the Union, together with its Member States.[238]

4.5.2.2 Within the European Union: the principle of institutional balance and the Meroni *doctrine*

From an EU law perspective, EASA's international dimension is subject to the requirements of the principle of institutional balance and of the *Meroni* doctrine. This assessment requires that EASA's international cooperation tasks and actions: (1) are of executive nature; (2) remain within the boundaries of its mandate as defined by its

233 Ratajczyk (n 63) 143.

234 See, however, para 25 of the Common Approach on EU agencies, stating that the EU agencies are not to be seen as representing the EU on the international plane nor as committing the EU to international obligations.

235 See Ratajczyk (n 63) 142.

236 This is more noticeable in those instances where EASA concludes working arrangements in the implementation of bilateral agreements concluded by a Member State with a third country.

237 Interview 25 with EASA officials, Brussels (13 May 2013); see also Ratajczyk (n 63) 143.

238 On the possibility for the Member States to 'borrow' the EU institutions for the purpose of implementing international agreements concluded outside the EU legal framework, see Bruno de Witte and Tom Beukers, 'The Court of Justice Approves the Creation of the European Stability Mechanism outside the EU Legal Order: Pringle' (2013) 50 CML Rev 805, 843–47.

regulatory framework; (3) are subject to conditions and supervisory mechanisms limiting the discretion of the Agency; and (4) do not encroach upon the powers vested in the EU institutions by the Founding Treaties, in particular in the Union's external action area.

EASA is embedded in the institutional architecture of the Union as a technical agency entrusted with some implementing tasks in the aviation safety area. EASA's international cooperation mandate is established by its founding act in correspondence with the core competence of the Agency.[239] Thus, EASA's international cooperation tasks can be seen as an expansion outside the EU of its main tasks in the aviation safety area, providing the incentive for cooperation, but also limiting the scope of the Agency's external actions. In this context, EASA's role is explicitly confined to supporting the Commission and the Member States in their international relations and to establishing direct relationships with third-country competent authorities and international organisations within the scope of its founding act and in accordance with the provisions of the TFEU, including Article 218 TFEU.

Additionally, the use of the most important international cooperation instruments – ie working arrangements – by the Agency is subject to the Commission's *prior* approval. Furthermore, in the exercise of its international cooperation tasks, the Agency appears to be under strict oversight by the Commission, which is also one of the main actors in the EU's external action area. In this way, the necessary control over the international cooperation tasks entrusted to the Agency, as well as the coordination between the Agency's actions and the wider priorities and actions of the EU seem to be ensured. The practice also appears to indicate that EASA does not make any important move in the international cooperation area without informing the Commission. Moreover, empirical findings lend support to the view that the Commission often influences EASA's technical cooperation activities in accordance with its political objectives or with Union's priorities in the external action area. From this perspective, EASA's international cooperation dimension appears to remain within the scope of its mandate and subject to sufficient formal and informal supervision, therefore precluding the Agency from enjoying a very large measure of discretion.

A matter of concern in particular from the perspective of the *Meroni* doctrine, is the duty of the Agency to perform tasks resulting from agreements between Member States and international organisations[240] as well as the possibility to accept third country certificates in application of agreements concluded by the Member States with third countries.[241] Arguably, the explicit limitation set on the Agency, in the first case, to carry out such tasks only within its own field of competence, as well as the duty placed on the Member States, in the second case, to notify their agreements with third countries to the Commission, and to amend, suspend or terminate such agreements on Commission's request seem to ensure at first sight that EASA remains within the boundaries of its legal framework. It should also be noted that the current legal framework also deviates from the Common Approach on EU agencies in that there is no formal approval of EASA's working arrangements by the management board, nor is there an explicit duty for the Agency to coordinate with the EU delegations.

239 See art 27 of Regulation 216/2008.
240 ibid art 17(2)(e).
241 ibid art 12(2).

One problematic aspect pertains to EASA's working arrangements, more specifically when they turn out to be binding agreements under international law. As maintained more generally in Chapter 2 of this study, EU agencies' binding agreements as a form of EU external administrative action would not automatically disturb the institutional balance in EU external relations. In this context, it is essential that: (1) EASA's working arrangements remain within the core mandate of the Agency, and are consistent with Article 218 TFEU agreements and EU legislation; and (2) the Agency is subject to sufficient supervision and control, ensuring that the powers of the main actors in the EU external action area are not affected.[242]

The comprehensive analysis of EASA's formal mandate for international cooperation, as well as of its working arrangements, revealed that these instruments establish cooperation on a technical level between the Agency and its counterparts with a view to ensuring the full implementation of EASA's regulatory framework, including the BASAs[243] or aspects of the common aviation area agreements concluded under Article 218 TFEU. The fact that EASA's working arrangements must follow the provisions of EU law has been identified as the main limitation of these instruments.[244] Moreover, the plethora of formal and informal controls enabling the Commission to steer closely the Agency's international cooperation seems to be capable of ensuring the required consistency with the overall priorities in the EU external action area and to preserve the Commission's role under Articles 17(1) TEU and 220 TFEU. In this context, the Commission's *prior* approval of the working arrangements according to Article 27(2) of EASA's Basic Regulation seems an effective means for ensuring consistency between these instruments and EASA's mandate, as well as the EU external aviation policy.[245] In view of the above, one may conclude that EASA's working arrangements, as binding technical-administrative agreements, do not seem to breach the institutional balance in EU external relations.

Regarding the relationship between EASA's binding agreements and 'Article 218 TFEU' agreements, a current trend adopted by the main EU institutions is to conclude international agreements under Article 218 TFEU, which usually provide for further instruments to be adopted by the relevant EU institutions or bodies in their implementation. For aviation safety, this is the case of BASAs with Brazil, Canada and the USA, allowing EASA to conclude various instruments such as technical implementing procedures (TIPs), maintenance annex guidance (MAG) and specific working arrangements. Whereas this indicates that EASA's working arrangements are the implementing tools of these agreements concluded by the EU under Article 218 TFEU, it does not necessarily mean that such arrangements are not legally binding on the parties. On the contrary, the analysis in this study reveals that in such a scenario the working arrangements would still be binding under international law, meaning that they would still qualify as international agreements, although of a very specific nature.[246] What is more, the fact remains that with many countries there are no agreements

242 See ch 2, 2.3.1.2.2: International administrative agreements at the EU level.

243 The instruments used by EASA to implement the BASAs with the USA, Canada and Brazil are the TIPs and MAGs concluded by the Agency as a 'technical agent'.

244 Ratajczyk (n 63) 147.

245 ibid 146. This is not the case for the TIPs and MAGs as they are concluded on the basis of the derogatory provisions of the BASAs.

246 ie implementing agreements of an umbrella international agreement.

concluded by the EU yet in the area of aviation safety, and the only instruments formalising cooperation between the parties are the working arrangements concluded by EASA. In such instances, the working arrangements are often used as a way to advance cooperation between the third country concerned and the Union with a view to concluding an extended agreement under Article 218 TFEU. However, compared to 'Article 218 TFEU' agreements, such working arrangements entail limited cooperation because they need to comply with EU legislation. This does not mean, however, that they cannot qualify as binding agreements under international law. In fact, it is difficult to see how EASA's working arrangements could bring about enhanced cooperation in the field of aviation safety if they would remain at the level of mere declarations of intent between the parties.

4.6 Conclusion

The comprehensive analysis of EASA's international cooperation legal framework and practice in this chapter reveals an EU agency with a global dimension which is inherent to fulfilling its core mandate in the aviation safety area. The added value of EASA's international cooperation, not only for the Agency itself but also for its stakeholders and the EU at large, is acknowledged in its Basic Regulation. Furthermore, it is evidenced by an impressive number of working arrangements concluded with third country authorities from Europe and worldwide.

That being said, it should be emphasised, however, that EASA's international dimension cannot be seen in isolation from the relevant legal-institutional framework in the EU aviation area, but needs to be subsumed to the EU external aviation policy. In this context, the Agency's priorities to pursue cooperation on a technical level are largely shaped by the objectives concerning the international dimension of the EU aviation area, and are also affected by the changing political climate in the EU external action area. Moreover, the design of EASA's mandate and organisation entail possibilities for the Commission in particular, but also for the Member States to oversee and influence the Agency's priorities and actions. This has been confirmed by empirical evidence, revealing an essential role for the Commission in setting EASA's international cooperation priorities and actions. Also, the involvement of the Commission in the procedure for the negotiation and conclusion of EASA's working arrangements, featuring not only *prior* formal approval but also quite influential informal arrangements, further reinforces the qualification of EASA as a 'Commission agency'.

The examination of EASA's formal framework and practice suggests that the Agency's international cooperation tasks and actions remain overall within the scope of its mandate and are subject to sufficient supervision and conditions. Therefore, the international dimension of EASA appears to comply with the present-day *Meroni* requirements.

The analysis of EASA's working arrangements from an international law perspective provides support for the view that they qualify as binding international agreements. This is the case of the working arrangements regarding certification and design approvals concluded worldwide, the JAA–EASA transition working arrangements, the SAFA working arrangements, the TIPs and MAG implementing EU BASAs, and the EASA–ICAO working arrangement. These working arrangements are to be included in the category of international agreements of a technical-administrative nature, as opposed to the high-level (legal-political) agreements covered by Article 218 TFEU.

The comprehensive analysis of EASA's formal mandate for international cooperation, as well as of its working arrangements revealed that these instruments establish cooperation on a technical level between the Agency and its counterparts with a view to ensuring the implementation of EASA's regulatory framework, including BASAs or aspects of the common aviation area agreements concluded under Article 218 TFEU. The fact that EASA's working arrangements must follow the provisions of EU law has been identified as the main limitation of these instruments. Moreover, the plethora of formal and informal controls enabling the Commission to steer closely the Agency's international cooperation seems to be capable of ensuring the required consistency with the overall priorities in the EU external action area and to preserve the Commission's role under Articles 17(1) TEU and 220 TFEU. In view of the above, one may conclude that EASA's working arrangements as binding technical-administrative agreements do not appear to breach the institutional balance in EU external relations.

The plethora of formal and informal conditions and controls limiting EASA's international cooperation also indicates that, in spite of its formal autonomy, the Agency is rather acting as a technical agent of the Commission, and ultimately of the EU, rather than as an independent entity on the international plane. Accordingly, although it is equipped with legal personality and international cooperation tasks and instruments by its Basic Regulation, EASA does not acquire international legal personality. In view of the fact that the legal status of EASA on the international plane is that of an 'EU agent', contrary to the Common Approach on EU agencies, its working arrangements are to be attributed ultimately to the European Union.

5 The case of Frontex

5.1 Introduction

Frontex has been chosen as a case study for several reasons. First, its mandate encompasses an inherent trans-boundary element which may presumably transform this EU agency quite obviously into a global actor. Secondly, in pursuing international cooperation, the Agency operates in a highly sensitive policy area, which raises particular legal and practical problems as far as its international cooperation tasks and instruments are concerned. Thirdly, Frontex has a well-developed international cooperation record consisting of working arrangements with a rather misty legal status.

In view of the strong pressure on the Union's external borders caused by the increasing migration flows in the past years, Frontex has been recently consolidated and rebranded as the European Boarder and Coast Guard Agency by Regulation 2016/1624 (the new Frontex Regulation).[1] Whilst the new Frontex Regulation reinforces the Agency's international profile, it maintains at the same time the basic principles and instruments for international cooperation under the former Frontex Regulation.[2]

Against this background, this chapter puts Frontex's international dimension in perspective by looking comparatively both at the former Frontex Regulation together with the Agency's current international cooperation practice rooted in that legal framework, and at the adjustments brought by the new Frontex Regulation. This approach enables understanding the extent to which Frontex's international cooperation mandate, tasks and instruments have been 'transformed' by the new Frontex Regulation, and the legal or practical problems and circumstances that motivated these adjustments. This approach is furthermore necessary in order to assess the legal nature of Frontex's international cooperation instruments and its legal status as a global actor, and with a view to appraise both retrospectively and prospectively the compatibility of the Agency's international dimension with the Union's relevant constitutional framework and principles.

1 Regulation (EU) 2016/1624 of the European Parliament and of the Council of 14 September 2016 on the European Border and Coast Guard and amending Regulation (EU) 2016/399 of the European Parliament and of the Council and repealing Regulation (EC) No 863/2007 of the European Parliament and of the Council, Council Regulation (EC) No 2007/2004 and Council Decision 2005/267/EC [2016] OJ L251/1.

2 Council Regulation (EC) 2007/2004 of 26 October 2004 establishing a European Agency for the Management of Operational Cooperation at the External Borders of the Member States of the European Union [2004] OJ L349/1.

The chapter begins with an overview of the legal-policy context relevant for the study of Frontex as a global actor encompassing Union's relevant legal and institutional framework as well as the external dimension of the Union's border management area (section 5.2). Apart from that, the specific features of Frontex as an EU agency are mapped out with an emphasis on important design aspects of the Agency (mandate and governance issues) and on its gradual evolution (section 5.3). Next, a two-fold analysis of Frontex's international dimension based on the former Frontex Regulation is undertaken addressing both the formal legal framework for international cooperation and the international practice of the Agency. From the point of view of international practice, the focus of the analysis lies on the working arrangements concluded by Frontex with its international partners. Subsequently, the renewed Frontex's international dimension according to the new Frontex Regulation is mapped out with a view to assess its legal implications and problems (section 5.4). The last part of the chapter provides an assessment of Frontex's international dimension with regard to the legal nature and effects of its international cooperation instruments, the legal status of the Agency as a global actor, and as to the compatibility of its international cooperation with Union's relevant legal-institutional framework (section 5.5).

5.2 The policy and legal-institutional environment of Frontex

5.2.1 The Union's legal and institutional framework in the border management area

The *legal-policy context* relevant for understanding Frontex is the Justice and Home Affairs (JHA) area before Lisbon, and is respectively the Area of Freedom, Security and Justice (AFSJ) after Lisbon. Within this framework, particular importance must be attached to the Union's border management policy, for which Frontex is one of the main actors.[3] While informal cooperation between the Member States has taken place since the 1970s, it was only with the Treaty of Maastricht that JHA cooperation was integrated into the EU legal-institutional structure.[4] In view of the sensitive nature of the areas covered by JHA for the Member States, the transfer of powers to the supranational level came at a price. Thus, for most of it, the JHA area was included under the former third (intergovernmental) pillar and only very limited aspects related to visa policy were part the former 'Community pillar'.[5]

In parallel, outside the EU, some Member States pursued cooperation in the area of border management and control, which resulted in the conclusion of the Schengen

3 See Commission, 'Impact Assessment accompanying the Proposal for a Regulation of the European Parliament and of the Council amending Council Regulation (EC) No 2007/2004 establishing a European Agency for the Management of Operational Cooperation at the External Borders of the Member States of the European Union (FRONTEX)' Impact Assessment of Regulation No 1168/2011, SEC (2010) 149 10.

4 See Jorrit J Rijpma, 'Hybrid Agencification in the Area of Freedom, Security and Justice and Its Inherent Tensions: The Case of Frontex' in Madalina Busuioc, Martijn Groenleer and Jarle Trondal (eds), *The Agency Phenomenon in the European Union: Emergence, Institutionalisation and Everyday Decision-making* (Manchester University Press 2012) 84. See also arts K.1–K.4 TUE.

5 In ex art 100c EEC.

Agreement with a view to abolishing border controls between the contracting parties.[6] The Schengen Agreement was complemented by the Schengen Implementing Convention (CISA), providing for detailed rules on control at the common external borders, on police cooperation, on a common visa regime, and on asylum issues.[7]

The Treaty of Amsterdam transferred visas, asylum and the management of external borders to the former 'Community pillar', leaving only judicial and police cooperation within the 'third pillar'. Furthermore, most of the Schengen *acquis* was brought under Title IV TEC and was, thereby, 'communitarised', whereas the remaining part relating to the Schengen Information System (SIS) was inserted into the 'third pillar'.[8] The Lisbon Treaty brought former Title IV TEC together with the remnants of the former 'third pillar' under Title V TFEU 'Area of freedom, security and justice', governed by a single legal framework. It should be added that, under the TFEU, the competences in the AFSJ area are shared between the Union and the Member States.[9] However, a careful reading of the provisions of Title V TFEU reveals the yet incipient stage of the Union's involvement in the exercise of its competences in this area, as well as a degree of deference to the Member States' traditional role in these fields.[10]

Along with the legal evolution, there is also a significant *policy dimension* to the former JHA area, now AFSJ. One of the most important elements are the programmes setting Union's policy agenda in the AFSJ area for a five-year period.[11] The first was the 'Tampere programme', adopted by the European Council in 1999, once the Amsterdam Treaty entered into force.[12] The 'Hague programme' followed in 2004, and was replaced in 2009 by the 'Stockholm programme', which laid down the priorities in the AFSJ area until 2014.[13] At the end of 2014, the Stockholm programme came

6 The Schengen agreement was concluded on 14 June 1985, see also Estella Baker and Christopher Harding, 'From Past Imperfect to Future Perfect? A Longitudinal Study of the Third Pillar' (2009) 34 EL Rev 25, 29–30.

7 CISA was signed in 1991, entered into force in 1993, and was applied as from 26 March 1995; see also Baker and Harding (n 6) 29–30.

8 Jorrit J Rijpma, *Building Borders: The Regulatory Framework for the Management of the External Borders of the European Union* (D Phil thesis, European University Institute 2009) 41–42.

9 See art 4(2)(j) TFEU.

10 According to art 67(1) TFEU: 'The Union shall constitute an area of freedom, security and justice with respect for (. . .) the different legal systems and traditions of the Member States' and (2) it '(. . .) shall frame a common policy on asylum, immigration and external border control, based on the solidarity between Member States (. . .)'; art 72 TFEU provides that TFEU Title V: '(. . .) does not affect the responsibilities incumbent upon the Member States with regard to the maintenance of law and order and strengthening of internal security'; art 74 TFEU addresses the Council's prerogative to adopt '(. . .) measures to ensure administrative cooperation' between the relevant departments of the Member States, and between the former and the Commission in the AFSJ area'; art 79(5) TFEU stipulates that the common immigration policy developed by the EU, together with the legislative measures and readmission agreements therein '(. . .) shall not affect the right of the Member States to determine volumes of admission of third-country nationals (. . .)'.

11 See Sergio Carrera and Elspeth Guild, 'Does the Stockholm Programme Matter? The Struggles over Ownership of AFSJ Multiannual Programming' (2012) 51 CEPS 2 ‹https://www.ceps.eu/system/files/No%2051%20Carrera%20and%20Guild%20on%20Stockholm% 20Programme.pdf›.

12 European Council, Presidency Conclusions of the Tampere European Council, Brussels 15–16 October 1999 (SN 200.99); see also Carrera and Guild (n 11).

13 Council, 'The Hague Programme: Strengthening Freedom, Security and Justice in the European Union' [2005] OJ C53/1; European Council, 'The Stockholm Programme – An Open and Secure Europe Serving and Protecting Citizens' [2010] OJ C115/01.

to end and was succeeded by the 'Strategic guidelines' for legislative and operational planning within the area of freedom, security and justice.[14]

These multiannual planning documents essentially reflect the results of the negotiations between the Council, the Member States and the Commission as regards the priorities, directions and measures foreseen in the AFSJ area. They usually address all the actors with powers (legislative, executive, operational) in the AFSJ area, but a particularly significant role is assigned to the Council and the Commission as far as their implementation tasks are concerned. In this respect, unlike the former Community policy areas, the Council appears to assume not only the role of the (co-)legislator, but it also assumes most of the implementing powers of legislative acts adopted in the AFSJ area.[15] The Commission adopts action plans proposing more detailed measures and initiatives and then seeks to bring them about through its right of legislative initiative and its (rather marginal) implementing prerogatives in this area.[16] Furthermore, the Commission monitors the way in which the other relevant actors fulfil their obligations, takes the required corrective measures within its competence and delivers reports and evaluations on the implementation of these policy instruments.

If one looks at the *actors* engaged in the AFSJ area, the picture is complex and encompasses several dimensions (policy-making, legislative decision-making, and implementing-operational activities). On the policy level, the main actors involved are the Council, the European Council,[17] and the Commission. On the legislative decision-making level, after Lisbon, the Council and the Commission are the main players, whereas the European Parliament arguably has an enhanced role, which is subject to variations, however, depending on whether the particular measure is adopted according to the ordinary[18] or a special[19] legislative procedure. With regard to implementation, it appears that the Council plays a role in adopting the required hard law instruments,[20] whereas the Commission takes up a planning role in relation to the detailed AFSJ agenda, initiates implementing measures and monitors the way in which the Member States and various EU actors fulfil their obligations, as the 'guardian of the Treaties'.[21] This picture is complemented by various supporting-operational EU agencies (eg Europol, Eurojust, Cepol, Frontex, EASO, eu-LISA, FRA).[22]

Two horizontal observations are relevant in this context. First, it is worth mentioning the standing committees set up within the Council, such as CATS (Comité Article Trente-Six), SCIFA (Strategic Committee on Immigration, Frontiers and Asylum), and, according to Article 71 TFEU, COSI (Standing Committee on Internal

14 European Council, Conclusions, 26/27 June 2014, Brussels, 27 June 2014 (EUCO 79/14); see also Sergio Carrera and Elspeth Guild, 'The European Council's Guidelines for the Area of Freedom, Security and Justice 2020. Subverting the 'Lisbonisation' of Justice and Home Affairs?' (2014) 13/14 CEPS 1 ‹https://www.ceps.eu/system/files/SC%20EG%20AFSJ%20Guidelines%20 2020.pdf›.

15 See TFEU arts 291 and 75–76; see also Rijpma (n 8) 244.

16 Carrera and Guild (n 11) 3–4 and 9–14.

17 See art 68 TFEU.

18 Arts 77(2), 78(2), 79(2), 82(1)–(2), 83(1), 87(2), 88(2) TFEU.

19 Arts 77(3), 86(1), 87(3), 89 TFEU.

20 Arts 74–76 TFEU; see also Steve Peers, *EU Justice and Home Affairs Law* (OUP 2011) 56–60.

21 See Carrera and Guild (n 11) 3–4 and 9–14.

22 See Rijpma (n 4) 84–86.

Security).[23] These committees, which are composed of high-level officials from the Member States, are involved in preparing the Council's legislative agenda in the AFSJ area (CATS), the general strategy for setting up an integrated border management system (SCIFA) or the Union's internal security strategy covering the whole AFSJ area (COSI).[24] Assuming that these committees are quite influential in shaping EU policy and the legal agenda, they can be seen as reinforcing the intergovernmental trend in the AFSJ area.[25] Secondly, regardless of the 'communitarisation' and then 'lisbonisation'[26] of the AFSJ area, the Member States continue to be significant actors involved at all levels (policy-making, legislation and, in particular, the implementation of the Union's policies and measures).[27]

The *management of the external borders* of the European Union has been included as a shared competence within the Community pillar by the Treaty of Amsterdam.[28] Several important measures have been adopted at the EU level in the field of external borders around the so-called 'three pillar' model (encompassing common legislation, common operations and financial solidarity).[29] These include the adoption of the Schengen Borders Code,[30] the Schengen handbook,[31] the establishment of Frontex, the creation of the Rapid Border Intervention teams,[32] replaced in 2011 with the European Border Guard Teams[33] and further in 2016 with the European Border and Coast Guard Teams,[34] and the creation of the External Borders Fund.[35] These

23 ibid 86–88.
24 ibid 86.
25 ibid 86 and 89.
26 In this context, 'lisbonisation' means the further advance made towards supranationalisation of the AFSJ area through the Lisbon Treaty; see for the use of this term Carrera and Guild (n 14) 1.
27 eg arts 67(1)–(2), 69; 71, 76, 80, 82(2)–(3), 83(3), 86(1), 87(3), 88(3), 89 TFEU.
28 ex art 62 TEC, now art 77 TFEU has provided the legal basis for the EU measures adopted in this area.
29 See Commission, 'Impact Assessment' (n 3) 8.
30 Regulation (EC) 562/2006 of the European Parliament and of the Council of 15 March 2006 establishing a Community Code on the rules governing the movement of persons across borders (Schengen Borders Code) [2006] OJ L105/1; this regulation has been replaced by a recast version of the Schengen Borders Code in the form of Regulation (EU) 2016/399 of the European Parliament and of the Council of 9 March 2016 on a Union Code on the rules governing the movement of persons across borders (Schengen Borders Code) (codification) [2016] OJ L77/1.
31 Commission Recommendation establishing a common 'Practical Handbook for Border Guards (Schengen Handbook)' to be used by Member States' competent authorities when carrying out the border control of persons C(2006) 5186 final.
32 Regulation (EC) 863/2007 of the European Parliament and of the Council of 11 July 2007 establishing a mechanism for the creation of Rapid Border Intervention Teams and amending Council Regulation (EC) No 2007/2004 as regards that mechanism and regulating the tasks and powers of guest officers [2007] OJ L199/30 (RABIT Regulation).
33 Regulation (EU) 1168/2011 of the European Parliament and of the Council of 25 October 2011 amending Council Regulation (EC) No 2007/2004 establishing a European Agency for the Management of Operational Cooperation at the External Borders of the Member States of the European Union [2011] OJ L304/1.
34 According to the new Frontex Regulation.
35 Decision 574/2007/EC of the European Parliament and of the Council of 23 May 2007 establishing the External Borders Fund for the period 2007 to 2013 as part of the General programme 'Solidarity and Management of Migration Flows' [2007] OJ L144/22. In the meanwhile, this instrument has been repealed and replaced by Regulation (EU) 515/2014 of the European

developments are to be seen as part of the wider concept of the integrated border management system of the external borders (IBM),[36] first introduced by the Council in 2006[37] and then integrated in Article 77 TFEU by the Treaty of Lisbon. This concept entails gradual actions and measures centred around five main dimensions:

(1) border control as defined in the Schengen Borders Code
(2) detection and investigation of cross-border crime in cooperation with all enforcement authorities
(3) a four-tier access control model entailing measures in third countries, cooperation with neighbouring countries, border control, control measures within the area of free movement, including return
(4) inter-agency cooperation for border management and international cooperation
(5) coordination and coherence of the activities of Member States and institutions and other bodies of the EU.[38]

However, in the border management area the division of tasks entails that the EU assuming mainly a supportive and coordination role in relation to the actions and operational prerogatives of the Member States, which remain responsible for controlling the Union's external borders.[39] The tools used by the EU in supporting and coordinating the Member States' efforts include setting common normative standards (eg on border checks), financial means (eg the External Borders Fund), as well as operational-institutional means (e.g. the establishment of Frontex).[40] With the recent migration crisis affecting the European Union, there seems to be a trend towards consolidation of the Union's role and capacity with a view to ensure a more effective management of the EU external border, as illustrated by the new Frontex Regulation.

5.2.2 *The international (external) dimension of the Union's border management*

The successful management of the Union's external borders, taken alone or in the context of other EU policies, such as migration, inherently entails a cross-border projection/extension which includes relationships with third countries and relevant international organisations. The need to develop gradually an external dimension to the EU border management has to be seen, however, as part of the broader external dimension of the AFSJ area. Whilst the external dimension of the AFSJ area is largely

Parliament and of the Council of 16 April 2014 establishing, as part of the Internal Security Fund, the instrument for financial support for external borders and visa and repealing Decision No 574/2007/EC [2014] OJ L150/143.

36 See Commission, 'Financial statement accompanying Regulation (EU) No 1168/2011' (Communication) COM (2012) 590 final. See also Rijpma (n 8) 47.

37 Council, 'Conclusions on Integrated Border Management', Brussels, 4–5 December 2006 (15801/06) 27.

38 ibid. The content of European integrated border management is further detailed in art 4 of the new Frontex Regulation.

39 Commission, 'Impact Assessment' (n 3) 10–11; see also Rijpma (n 4) 88–89.

40 Commission, 'Impact Assessment' (n 3) 11.

perceived as an 'internally driven external policy',[41] it is important to recall that starting with the Tampere Programme (1999), followed by the Hague Programme (2005) and Stockholm Programme (2009), increased emphasis has been put on the use of the Union's external relations as a way to establish the AFSJ area.[42] It should be added that the 'Strategic guidelines' (2014) restate the need for intensifying international cooperation as a way to tackle the challenges in this policy field in the coming years.[43]

On the political level, a strategy for the external dimension of the JHA was adopted by the Council in 2005, stressing the need for this policy area to pursue both internal and external objectives.[44] Both the strategy and the underlying communication of the Commission on the Strategy insisted on the partnership with third countries as a *sine qua non* element for the successful development of the AFSJ area.[45] Such cooperation was to cover *inter alia*: tackling irregular migration, efforts to improve border controls and travel documents security, and the conclusion and implementation of readmission agreements.[46] The implementation of the Strategy has been regularly assessed and adjusted based on implementation reports prepared by JAIEX, and, as of 2011, further strategic programming is ensured via the 18-month programmes prepared ahead by the three coming Council presidencies.[47]

As regards the border management area specifically, the concept of 'integrated border management' introduced by the Council in 2006 comprises measures in third countries and cooperation with third countries, as well as international cooperation as key elements[48] of the 'four-tier access model'.[49] Within these areas, there are several ways in which the external dimension of the Union's border management policy is tailored.[50]

41 Rijpma (n 8) 309; Jörg Monar, 'The External Dimension of the EU's Area of Freedom, Security and Justice. Progress, Potential and Limitations after the Treaty of Lisbon' (2012) 1 Sieps 13–14 ‹http://www.sieps.se/en/publications/2012/the-external-dimension-of-the-eus-area-of-freedom-security-and-justice-20121/Sieps_2012_1›.

42 Monar (n 41) 50. See generally on the development of the external dimension of AFSJ, Juan S Vara, 'The External Dimension of the Area of Freedom Security and Justice in the Lisbon Treaty' (2008) 10 European Journal of Law Reform 577.

43 European Council, Conclusions, 26/27 June 2014 (n 14) 1–3.

44 Council, 'A Strategy for the External Dimension of JHA: Global Freedom, Security and Justice', 6 December 2005 (15446/05) 5. According to Monar, the 2005 Strategy still remains 'the main framework programming document' in this area, the reason being that it is 'sufficiently general to allow periodic updating and retargeting at the implementation level', Jörg Monar, 'The EU's Growing External Role in the AFSJ Domain: Factors, Framework and Forms of Action' (2014) 27 Cambridge Review of International Affairs 147, 159.

45 Commission, 'A Strategy on the External Dimension of the Area of Freedom, Security and Justice' (Communication) COM (2005) 491 final 5.

46 Council, 'A Strategy for the External Dimension of JHA' (n 44) 3–4.

47 Jörg Monar (n 44) 159. Such an example is the 18 month programme of the Council (1 January 2013–30 June 2014) prepared by the Irish, Lithuanian and Greek Presidencies, Council, '18 month programme of the Council (1 January 2013–30 June 2014)' 7 December 2012 (17426/12).

48 See Sergio Carrera, 'The EU Border Management Strategy. Frontex and the Challenges of Irregular Migration in the Canary Islands' (2007) 261CEPS Working Document 25 ‹http://www.ceps.eu/publications/eu-border-management-strategy-frontex-and-challenges-irregular-immigration-canary›.

49 Council, 'Conclusions on Integrated Border Management' (n 37) 27.

50 Rijpma (n 8) 312–13.

First, the EU may conclude international agreements concerning the AFSJ area specifically, covering border management issues with relevant third countries and international organisations. Examples are the Schengen association agreements concluded with Norway, Iceland and Switzerland,[51] the agreements concluded with the Schengen associate countries regarding participation in Frontex or in the EU external border funds,[52] visa facilitation and visa exemption agreements,[53] readmission agreements entered into by the EU with third countries as provided in Article 79(3) TFEU, or agreements which may be concluded on asylum according to Article 78(2)(g) TFEU.[54] It should be borne in mind, however, that the deference that Title V TFEU displays to the role of the Member States in the AFSJ area is also reflected in the international cooperation aspects.[55] On the one hand, Member States are still allowed to have their own international agreements on external border issues,[56] readmission or asylum,[57] provided that such agreements are compatible with EU law, including the relevant international agreements concluded by the Union.[58] On the other hand, even the agreements concluded by the EU ensure an important role for the Member States. For instance, the readmission agreements concluded by the Union provide the possibility for the Member States to conclude individual protocols with the third country concerned within the framework of the main agreement.[59]

Secondly, the external dimension of the EU border management policy is also pursued through various instruments within wider EU external policies and initiatives, such as enlargement, neighbourhood policy (ENP), development cooperation, or the

51 eg the Agreement concluded by the Council of the European Union and the Republic of Iceland and the Kingdom of Norway concerning the latter's association with the implementation, application and development of the Schengen acquis [1999] OJ L176/36; Agreement between the European Union, the European Community and the Swiss Confederation on the Swiss Confederation's association with the implementation, application and development of the Schengen acquis [2008] OJ L53/52.

52 eg the Arrangement between the European Community, of the one part, and the Swiss Confederation and the Principality of Liechtenstein, of the other part, on the modalities of the participation by those States in the European Agency for the Management of Operational Cooperation at the External Borders of the Member States of the European Union [2010] OJ L243/4; see also Peers (n 20) 224.

53 Paula Garcia Andrade, Ivan Martin and Sergo Mananashvili, 'EU Cooperation with Third Countries in the Field of Migration' Study for the LIBE Committee (PE 536.469) (2015) 40–42.

54 See Monar (n 41) 57–58. For the full list of the agreements concluded by the EU in the AFSJ area, see European External Action Service, Treaties Office Database, Justice, Freedom and Security ‹http://ec.europa.eu/world/agreements/searchByActivity.do?parent=8528&xmlname=767&actName=Justice,%20freedom%20and%20security&printAcrivity=›.

55 See Rijpma (n 8) 314–15.

56 Protocol No 23 'On external relations of the Member States with regard to the crossing of external borders' annexed to the Treaties [2012] OJ C326/304. For a discussion regarding the possible interpretations of Protocol No 23; see Peers (n 20) 222–24.

57 See for an example Agreement between the European Union and the Republic of Cape Verde on the readmission of persons residing without authorisation [2013] OJ L282/15.

58 Protocol No 23 (n 56); see also Peers (n 20) 222–24, 287–88 and 588–89.

59 eg the Agreement between the European Community and the Islamic Republic of Pakistan on the readmission of persons residing without authorisation [2010] L287/52, art 17; Agreement between the European Union and the Republic of Cape Verde on the readmission of persons residing without authorisation [2013] OJ L282/15, art 19.

Global Approach to Migration.[60] Within the framework of these policies, enhanced operational cooperation on border control, as well the promotion of the EU *acquis* in this field in third countries are also sought. In this context, the so-called 'Global Approach to Migration',[61] adopted by the European Council was an action plan focusing initially on the African and the Mediterranean regions, and intended to introduce a 'balanced, global and coherent approach to migration' based on partnership, dialogue and cooperation.[62] Later, the Global Approach was extended to the eastern and south-eastern neighbourhood area,[63] and then further broadened and relabelled as the 'Global Approach to Migration and Mobility' (GAMM).[64] Within the Global Approach, Mobility Partnerships (MPs) and Common Agendas for Migration and Mobility (CAMMs) featuring a list of objectives related to migration (including border control) were concluded as legally non-binding instruments with the countries concerned.[65]

As regards enlargement, the relationship between the EU and the Western Balkan states, for instance, is covered by the Stabilisation and Association Process (SAP) entailing stabilisation and association agreements, financial assistance and EU secondary legislation instruments adopted under the European partnerships with these countries. Simply put, one important requirement within this framework is that candidates and potential candidates for EU accession should gradually adopt the EU *acquis*, with border management as one of the sectors concerned.[66] In the ENP area, association or partnership and cooperation agreements are concluded with the countries concerned, followed by action plans, as policy documents setting more concrete priorities and actions. In both categories of instruments, provisions are included with regard to immigration, readmission, visas and border management.[67] In this context, Frontex is involved in various GAMM processes, MPs, CAMMs and migration dialogues, and may provide technical assistance within the framework of Enlargement, ENP or development cooperation instruments.[68]

Thirdly, an important characteristic of the external dimension of border management is the emphasis on operational aspects. Thus, the Union has adopted a number

60 See Rijpma (n 8) 312–13; Andrade, Martin and Mananashvili (n 53) 23–35.

61 European Council, Presidency Conclusions, Brussels, 15–16 December 2005 (15914/05) point IV and Annex CI.

62 ibid para 8.

63 Commission, 'The Global Approach to Migration one year on: Towards a comprehensive European migration policy' (Communication) COM (2006) 735 final 7; Commission, 'Applying the Global Approach to Migration to the Eastern and South-Eastern Regions Neighbouring the European Union' (Communication) COM (2007) 247 final; Commission, 'Strengthening the Global Approach to Migration: Increasing Coordination, Coherence and Synergies' (Communication) COM (2008) 611 final.

64 Commission, 'The Global Approach to Migration and Mobility' (Communication) COM (2011) 743 final.

65 European Commission, Migration and Home Affairs, Global Approach to Migration and Mobility ‹https://ec.europa.eu/home-affairs/what-we-do/policies/international-affairs/global-approach-to-migration_en›; see also Andrade, Martin and Mananashvili (n 53) 28–29 and 30–35.

66 See Monar (n 41) 55–57; Andrade, Martin and Mananashvili (n 53) 35–37.

67 eg the Partnership and Cooperation Agreement between the European Communities and their Member States, of the one part, and Georgia, of the other part, signed on 22 April 1996 [2009] OJ L205/3, Title VIII.

68 See Andrade, Martin and Mananashvili (n 53) 44.

of binding, financial and soft law instruments intended to promote operational cooperation with third countries, exchanges of best practices, etc.[69] Next, with regard to joint operations at the external borders, return operations, operations in the high seas or in the waters of the third countries, the Member States always have a predominant role. The EU is financing or co-financing such operational activities and is involved in the coordination of such operations (mainly through Frontex), but it is the Member States' border control authorities which do the job.[70] Whereas the concrete operational activities at the external borders are also carried out within the framework of the EU instruments (agreements, working arrangements, policy initiatives), they are often based on agreements and arrangements between the Member States and the third countries concerned, although EU structures, such as Frontex, may also be involved.[71]

To conclude, the operational side of the external dimension for the management of the EU external borders is largely shaped at the executive level, through Member States' operational cooperation with third countries, and gradually through the international cooperation activities of the EU (in particular Frontex).[72] Although the EU is increasingly occupying this field of competence, it is unlikely that Member States will be deprived of their powers in the external sphere of border management, in particular with regard to bilateral operational cooperation. This is because in practice Member States may still be in a better position to establish operational cooperation with certain third countries.[73] This observation is particularly relevant for a proper understanding of the role of Frontex as a global actor.

5.3 Frontex's profile as an EU agency

5.3.1 Frontex's design and incremental evolution

The origins of Frontex can be traced back to the proposal advanced by the Commission to establish an External Border Practitioners Common Unit in order to bring together at EU level managers and practitioners of external border checks and surveillance from the Member States.[74] The Council endorsed the Commission's proposal and the Common Unit was created within the Council's Strategic Committee on Immigration, Frontiers and Asylum (SCIFA).[75] Composed of the heads of the border control services of the Member States, and assisted by the Council Working Party (SCIFA), the main aims of the unit were to promote the development of a common policy on the management of external borders and to ensure increased coordination between

69 In this respect, one should mention the EU Border management missions in third countries (ie the EU Border Mission in Moldova and Ukraine – EUBAM, and the EU Border Mission in Central Asia – BOMCA); see for details Rijpma (n 8) 327–32.

70 eg art 5 of Regulation 2016/1624.

71 See Rijpma (n 8) 341–42.

72 ibid 327.

73 ibid 355.

74 Commission, 'Towards integrated management of the external borders of the member states of the European Union'(Communication) COM (2002) 233 final 13–14.

75 Council, 'Plan for the management of the external borders of the Member States of the European Union' 14 June 2002 (10019/02) 12.

the activities of the border management authorities of the Member States.[76] Already in 2003, the Commission voiced criticism over the effectiveness of the Common Unit (also labelled as SCIFA+), and called for a new permanent Community structure which would be able to exercise the 'day-to-day management and co-ordination tasks and to respond in time to emergency situations'.[77] As a result, the Council replaced the existing structure with the Practitioners' Common Unit (PUC), composed solely of the heads of Member States' border guards' services and dealing only with operational aspects of border management.[78]

Soon thereafter, the Commission reacted to the call of the European Council to examine the creation of a stronger operational structure with a view to further '(. . .) enhance operational cooperation for the management of external borders'[79] and proposed the creation of an EU agency.[80] The establishment of an independent agency was considered by the Commission as the best means to increase effectiveness in the implementation of the EU policy on the management of the external borders, in particular through ensuring better coordination of the operational co-operation between the Member States as compared to previous institutional arrangements.[81] One year later, Regulation 2007/2004 establishing Frontex was adopted by the Council and, since October 2005, the Agency became fully operational.[82] The Agency was said to be more like a 'supranational panacea' as a reaction to previous intergovernmental arrangements (SCIFA+ and PUC), entailing coordination of administrative and operational action driven by Member States, rather than being delegated tasks previously exercised by the Commission or another EU institution.[83]

Article 1(1) of Regulation 2007/2004 made clear that Frontex's essential mission is to contribute '(. . .) to improving the integrated management of the external borders of the Member States of the European Union'. In so doing, the Agency was required to '(. . .) facilitate and render more effective (. . .)' the application of the EU *acquis* concerning the management of the external borders.[84] This translated into a double role for the Agency: (1) ensuring '(. . .) the coordination of Member States' actions in the implementation of the relevant EU measures, and (2) providing the Commission and the Member States with 'the necessary technical support and expertise in the management of the external borders'.[85] It is along these lines that the more detailed

76 ibid.
77 See Commission, 'On the development of a common policy on illegal immigration, smuggling and trafficking of human beings, external borders and the return of illegal residents' (Communication) COM (2003) 323 final 7–8.
78 Council, 'Effective management of the external borders of the EU Member States' (Conclusions), Brussels, 5 June 2003 (10059/03); European Council, Presidency Conclusions, Thessaloniki, 19/20 June 2003 (11638/03) 4.
79 European Council, Presidency Conclusions, 19/20 June 2003 (n 78).
80 Commission, 'Proposal for a Council Regulation establishing a European Agency for the Management of Operational Co-operation at the External Borders' COM (2003) 687 final.
81 ibid 4 and 7. For a more detailed discussion regarding the reasons behind the creation of Frontex, see Rijpma (n 4) 90–92.
82 Commission, 'Report on the evaluation and future development of the FRONTEX Agency' (Communication) COM (2008) 67 final 2.
83 See Rijpma (n 4) 88.
84 Art 1(2) of Regulation 2007/2004.
85 ibid art 1(2) and (3).

tasks of Frontex have been designed. According to the list provided by the original version of Article 2(1) of the former Frontex Regulation, the Agency was tasked with:

(a) coordinating operational cooperation between Member States in the field of the management of external borders
(b) assisting Member States in the training of national border guards
(c) carrying out risk analyses
(d) following up on the development of research relevant for the control and surveillance of external borders
(e) assisting Member States in circumstances requiring increased technical and operational assistance at external borders
(f) providing Member States with the necessary support in organising joint return operations.

According to Rijpma, the tasks assigned to Frontex could be roughly grouped into two categories: (1) technical and information assistance tasks (b, c, d, and potentially e), and (2) tasks of a more operational nature (a, f, and potentially e), which distinguishes this body from most EU agencies. Specifically with regard to the operational nature of the Agency, it has been emphasised that Frontex was essentially coordinating and supporting operational cooperation between the competent authorities of the Member States.[86] Hence, Frontex rather had the profile of a 'network agency', setting up, managing and boosting a network of border authorities from the Member States.[87]

Soon after Frontex became operational, its mandate had been extended by the so-called 'RABIT Regulation',[88] which enabled the Agency to deploy rapid border intervention teams to Member States. The remote aim of this mechanism was to increase solidarity and mutual assistance between the Member States.[89] Such rapid border intervention teams were composed of personnel, which the Member States made available in a rapid pool for such operations,[90] and were to be deployed in exceptional circumstances based on a request by a Member State.[91] Whilst Frontex had a primary role in deciding on the deployment of a team, setting up the operational plan and monitoring the implementation of the operational plan,[92] the teams were nevertheless under the instructions of the host Member State.[93]

The application of Frontex's legal framework revealed important shortcomings and limitations especially on the operational side of the Agency, in parallel with an insufficient level of support and solidarity of the Member States.[94] This led to a new amendment of the former Frontex Regulation in 2011, with a view to further clarifying and extending the mandate of the Agency. In brief, some of the main developments introduced by Regulation 1168/2011 concerned:

86 Rijpma (n 8) 259.
87 ibid 259–60.
88 Regulation 863/2007 (n 32).
89 ibid recital (6) of the preamble.
90 ibid recital (8) preamble and art 4(2).
91 ibid art 12(5), inserting arts 8a–8h in Regulation 2007/2004.
92 ibid.
93 ibid arts 5 and 10.
94 See Commission, 'Impact Assessment' (n 3) 11–12.

(1) specific provisions on the processing of personal data, including the possibility to transfer personal data to Europol or other EU law enforcement agencies
(2) tasks regarding the establishment and operation of information systems, including within the European border surveillance system
(3) a strengthened coordinating role for Frontex as regards joint return operations[95]
(4) a co-leading role for the Agency regarding joint operations and pilot projects[96]
(5) the possibility for Frontex to buy or lease its own equipment (cars, vessels, helicopters, etc.) or to buy such equipment in co-ownership with a Member State.[97]

What is more, the amending regulation established a compulsory mechanism for Member States to second national border guards and make available equipment to the Agency.[98] Furthermore, Regulation 1168/2011 introduced the European Border Guard Teams as the common name for teams deployed during Frontex operations (not only rapid border interventions, but also joint operations and pilot projects). It is noteworthy that these teams are to be made up of not only personnel assigned by the Member States to the national pool of border guards, but also by more semi-permanent staff seconded by the Member States to Frontex for a certain period.[99]

It should be further added that, the information-related tasks of Frontex were further expanded by the Eurosur Regulation.[100] Moreover, specific coordination tasks were granted to the Agency by Regulation (EU) 656/2014 in the context of operational cooperation pertaining to the surveillance of the external sea borders.[101]

With the new Frontex Regulation, the Agency has been recently consolidated and rebranded as the European Border and Coast Guard Agency.[102] Among others, the 'new Frontex' enjoys a stronger role in return operations and interventions,[103] monitors

95 Art 2(1) of Regulation 2007/2004 (as amended by Regulation 1168/2011); see also Commission, 'Impact Assessment' (n 3) 41.
96 Art 3a of Regulation 2007/2004 (introduced by Regulation 1168/2011).
97 ibid art 7.
98 ibid art 3b; see also Commission, 'Impact Assessment' (n 3) 41. Thus, once the Agency and a Member State agree on an annual plan, this Member State should on request by Frontex make the border guards and the equipment available to Frontex as described in the annual plan, unless this would seriously affect the discharge of national tasks.
99 Art 3b of Regulation 2007/2004 (introduced by Regulation 1168/2011).
100 Regulation (EU) 1052/2013 of the European Parliament and of the Council of 22 October 2013 establishing the European Border Surveillance System (Eurosur) [2013] OJ L295/11. In addition to setting the tasks of Frontex within the framework of EUROSUR, this Regulation also includes interesting provisions on international cooperation by the Agency (art 18 covers the exchange of confidential information with international organisations and also provides for coordination with EEAS, whilst art 20 allows the Agency to support the cooperation between Member States and third countries).
101 Regulation (EU) 656/2014 of the European Parliament and of the Council of 15 May 2014 establishing rules for the surveillance of the external sea borders in the context of operational cooperation coordinated by the European Agency for the Management of Operational Cooperation at the External Borders of the Member States of the European Union [2014] OJ 2014 L189/93.
102 However, recital (11) of the preamble of Regulation 2016/1624 makes clear that the Agency '(. . .) will continue to be commonly referred to as Frontex'.
103 Arts 27–33 of Regulation 2016/1624.

the capacities of Member States to face challenges at the external borders[104] and exercises specific powers at 'hotspot areas of Member States' external borders[105] and in situations requiring urgent action,[106] may deploy liaison officers in the Member States, acquires enhanced tasks regarding the setting up and deployment of European Border and Coast Guard teams,[107] and has at its disposal a rapid reaction pool of at least 1,500 border guards.[108]

While these amendments undoubtedly mark the growing importance of Frontex in managing the Union's external borders, nevertheless the *status quo* in this field, marked by the prominent role of the Member States, has not fundamentally changed. Thus, without underestimating the operational role of Frontex, it is important, for the sake of clarity, to observe the legal limits set in the mandate of the Agency, as well as the task division between Frontex and its national counterparts. First, both the old and the new Frontex founding acts are clear in stipulating that the primary responsibility for the control and surveillance of external borders lies with the Member States.[109] This means that Frontex will not carry out border checks or apprehensions of irregular migrants, but the national border guards will. Moreover, the (joint) operations at the external borders are carried out by the border guard authorities of the Member States using their own resources. It is true that Frontex may co-finance such operations and may increasingly assist with its own technical equipment the Member States, is involved in the planning phase and may participate in missions as an observer, but, in the coordination and execution of joint operations, the emphasis is on the Member States rather than on Frontex. Secondly, both old and new Frontex regulations explicitly include the possibility for the Member States to pursue their own operational cooperation together with other Member States and third countries, without necessarily involving Frontex.[110] In so doing, Member States are required to abide by the requirements of the principle of loyal cooperation[111] and just report on their activities to the Agency, but the fact remains that Member States (and not Frontex) are the main operational actors on the ground of border management.

5.3.2 Governance of Frontex

Keeping in line with the standard model of an EU decentralised agency,[112] the leading structure of Frontex consists of a collegiate body (a management board) and an executive organ (executive director).

104 ibid art 13.
105 ibid art 18.
106 ibid art 19.
107 ibid arts 20–25.
108 ibid art 20.
109 See recital (4) of the preamble and art 1(2) of Regulation 2007/2004, and art 5 of Regulation 2016/1624.
110 See art 2(2) of Regulation 2007/2004 and art 8(2) of Regulation 2016/1624. See also Peers (n 20) 217–18.
111 According to art 8(2) of Regulation 2016/1624 the Member States '(. . .) shall refrain from any activity which could jeopardise the functioning of the Agency or the attainment of its objectives'.
112 Joint Statement of the European Parliament, the Council of the EU and the European Commission on decentralised agencies of 19 July 2012 (Common Approach on EU agencies) 5–6

The management board comprises one representative from each Member State plus two representatives from the Commission.[113] The management board is chaired by a chairperson and a deputy chairperson elected from among the members of the management board for a term of office of four years, which can be extended once.[114] The main powers and tasks of the management board are very similar to those of the similar body in other EU agencies. These include *inter alia*:[115] (1) appointing the executive director and the deputy executive director and exercising disciplinary authority over them; (2) adopting the multiannual programming and the annual work programme of the Agency;[116] (3) adopting the Agency's annual activity report; (4) adopting the budget of the Agency and fulfilling other tasks related to the budget; and (5) establishing its own rules of procedure and procedures for decision-making by the executive director; (6) establishing the organisational structure of the Agency and the staff policy. Additionally, the management board is entrusted with some specific tasks related to operational aspects of the Agency's activities, such as: (a) adopting a technical and operational strategy for the European integrated border management; (b) adopting decisions on the nature and terms of the deployment of liaison officers in Member States; (c) adopting decisions on the profiles and the overall number of border guards or other relevant staff to be made available for the European Border and Coast Guard teams; (d) appointing the Agency's fundamental rights officer.[117]

The executive director is the 'face' and the manager of the Agency. The executive director is appointed by the management board on a proposal by the Commission for a five-year mandate, renewable once.[118] The executive director takes the most important decisions with regard to the daily management of the Agency and s/he is deemed to act fully independently in the performance of his/her duties.[119] In particular, the executive director prepares and implements the decisions and programmes adopted by the management board, takes the appropriate decisions in order to ensure the functioning of the Agency, exercises the powers of appointing authority with respect to the staff of the Agency, prepares and implements the budget and the work programme of the Agency, prepares the Agency's annual activity reports.[120] Notably, on the operational side the executive director draws up operational plans (together with the host or requesting Member State) for joint operations, pilot projects, and rapid interventions, and ensures the implementation thereof,[121] examines the request for assistance of a Member State for migration management support teams, may withdraw financing of activities in the context of joint operations, or rapid border interventions or migration management support team deployment, etc.[122]

‹https://europa.eu/european-union/sites/europaeu/files/docs/body/joint_statement_and_common_approach_2012_en.pdf›.

113 Art 63(1) of Regulation 2016/1624.

114 ibid art 65.

115 ibid art 62(1).

116 ibid art 64.

117 ibid art 62(1).

118 ibid art 69.

119 ibid art 68(1).

120 ibid art 68(3).

121 ibid art 68(3) in combination with arts 16–17 and 33.

122 ibid art 68(3).

The executive director is accountable to the management board,[123] which entails that ultimately s/he can be dismissed.[124] In this context, the duty of the executive director to prepare annual activity reports and to submit them to the management board can be seen as an aspect of this accountability relationship. Another aspect of the accountability of the executive director, and of the Agency more broadly, is the possibility laid down by the Frontex Regulation for the Council and the European Parliament to invite the executive director to report on the performance of his/her duties.[125]

5.4 Frontex's international dimension

5.4.1 Frontex's international cooperation legal framework and practice under Council Regulation 2007/2004

5.4.1.1 Mandate, tasks and instruments

Frontex's international dimension is to be seen against the background of the EU external border management policy and in particular as '(. . .) a key component of the integrated border management model'.[126] Two main directions pursued by Frontex in its international cooperation activities could be distilled based on its former Founding Regulation.[127] One concerning the facilitation of cooperation between the Member States and third countries. The other one concerns the direct cooperation established between Frontex and the relevant third countries and international organisations.[128] In so doing, Frontex was expected in particular to support the implementation of joint operations, to '(. . .) enhance the added value of risk analysis and support capacity building in third countries'.[129]

Articles 13–14 of Regulation 2007/2004 provided the general legal framework for Frontex's international cooperation activities. It is relevant to note that these legal provisions had been considerably expanded by Regulation 1168/2011, in line with a series of developments in the Union's relevant policy areas and in the international cooperation practice of the Agency.[130] A preliminary observation is that, from the very

123 ibid art 68(4).

124 According to art 69(2) of Regulation 2016/1624, the dismissal of the executive director mirrors the appointment procedure (ie decision of the management board on a Commission proposal).

125 ibid art 68(2).

126 Commission, 'Impact Assessment' (n 3) 14; see also Carrera (n 48) 25.

127 See also Violeta Moreno-Lax, 'Frontex as a Global Actor: External Relations with Third Countries and International Organisations' in Marianne Dony (ed), *La Dimension Externe de l'Espace de Liberté, Sécurité et de Justice au Lendemain de Lisbonne et de Stockholm: un Bilan à Mi-parcours* (Éditions de l'Université de Bruxelles, 2012) 172–73.

128 Commission, 'Impact Assessment' (n 3) 14; see also COWI, 'External Evaluation of the European Agency for the Management of Operational Cooperation at the External Borders of the Member States of the European Union' (Final Report) January 2009 61–62.

129 Commission, 'Impact Assessment' (n 3) 14; see also Moreno-Lax (n 127) 168.

130 Moreno-Lax (n 127) 174.

beginning, the legislator decided to make a distinction between the cooperation the Agency may enter into with international organisations (Article 13) and that with third countries (Article 14).

The main instrument through which the Agency formalised cooperation with its partners was always labelled as a 'working arrangement' in the former Frontex Regulation. Regardless of whether the partner is an international organisation or a competent authority of a third country, all working arrangements: (1) may cover only issues within the mandate of Frontex (as defined by its Founding Regulation) and (2) must be concluded 'in accordance with the relevant provisions of the TFEU'.[131] Whereas Articles 13 and 14 of Regulation 2007/2004 did not explain which provisions of the TFEU are 'relevant' for this purpose, it may be assumed that mostly the provisions of Part Five of the TFEU on the Union's external action were envisaged.

Specifically with regard to the cooperation between Frontex and relevant international organisations, Regulation 1168/2011 introduced a duty on behalf of the Agency to inform the European Parliament of the working arrangements entered into.[132] Another novelty brought out by the 2011 Amending Regulation was the possibility for international organisations to participate in the activities of Frontex pertaining to joint operations and pilot projects, risk analysis, and training. Last but not least, Regulation 1168/2011 expanded the Agency's possibilities as regards the processing of personal data during the performance of its tasks.[133] While in principle the Agency was precluded from transferring personal data to third countries and international organisations, exceptions were allowed arguably in the context of return operations.[134] As illustrated by the Agency's international cooperation practice, exchange of personal data with the competent authorities of third countries is subject to a special agreement between the Agency and its partner.[135] Such an agreement should include at least adequate data protection safeguards, and be subject to prior consultation of the European Data Protection Supervisor (EDPS).[136] It should be further noted that recently the Eurosur Regulation further extended the possibility for the Agency to process personal data for the purpose of detecting, identifying and tracking vessels,[137] and included specific provisions regarding the cooperation between Frontex and international organisations with a view to exchanging information (including confidential information) within the scope of the Eurosur system.[138] Under the Eurosur Regulation, the conclusion of a working arrangement with the relevant international organisation is a mandatory condition for enabling such cooperation.[139]

The core of Frontex's international cooperation was dealt with in Article 14, which provided a good illustration of the position of the Agency on the edge of the

131 Arts 13 and 14(2) of Regulation 2007/2004.
132 ibid art 13.
133 ibid arts 11a–11c.
134 ibid art 11b.
135 Working Arrangement between Frontex with Kosovo (2016) ‹https://frontex.europa.eu/assets/Key_Documents/Working_Arrangements/WA_with_Kosovo.pdf›.
136 See art 11a of Regulation 2007/2004.
137 Art 11ca of Regulation 2007/2004 and art 13(2) of Regulation (EU) 1052/2013.
138 Art 18 of Regulation (EU) 1052/2013.
139 ibid art 18(5).

competences of the Member States and of the European Union in the area of border management. The provision covered comprehensively the double position of Frontex in establishing direct cooperation with third countries, as well as a facilitator and a supporter of the cooperation between the Member States and third countries.[140] As regards the latter aspect, although the Agency was acting mostly for the benefit of the Member States, it was required to do so for the fulfilment of its tasks and within the framework of the external relations policy of the Union.[141] In the same vein, the Member States could include provisions concerning the role and competence of Frontex in their bilateral agreements with third countries, but at the same time such agreements had to be complementary to the activities of the Agency.[142]

As concerns specifically the direct cooperation between Frontex and third countries, there were several distinct, although not necessarily mutually exclusive, aspects and instruments attached to that. Most significantly, the working arrangements which Frontex could conclude with the competent authorities of third countries were gauged as formal cooperation instruments of a technical nature.[143] Next, since 2011, the Agency could deploy its own liaison officers (LOs) in third countries and it could also receive liaison officers from third countries. Liaison officers could only be deployed in third countries complying with 'minimum human rights standards', with the approval of the management board, and with priority being given to countries of origin and transit regarding illegal migration.[144] The main task of Frontex's liaison officers was to establish and maintain contacts with the competent authorities of the authorities of the third countries in order to promote the fight against illegal migration and the return of the illegal migrants.[145] Another novelty introduced by the 2011 Amending Regulation was the possibility for Frontex to launch and finance technical assistance projects in third countries under the instruments supporting Union's external relations policy as a means for the Agency to '(. . .) more proactively support capacity building in those countries'.[146] Whereas deployment of liaison officers and technical projects could also take place within the framework of working arrangements concluded between Frontex and the relevant third countries,[147] pursuing these instances of direct cooperation separately is not excluded.[148] Last but not least, according to Article 14(8),

140 ibid art 14(1) and (2)–(5).
141 ibid art 14(1).
142 ibid art 14(7), referring to art 2(2).
143 ibid art 14(2).
144 ibid art 14(3).
145 ibid art 14(4).
146 Commission, 'Impact Assessment' (n 3) 18.
147 See COM (2012) 590 final (n 36) 2.
148 Interview 31 with a Commission official, Brussels (26 June 2013). In practice, the Agency has already approved the deployment of LOs in in Turkey and Serbia (‹https://frontex.europa.eu/media-centre/news-release/frontex-to-deploy-liaison-officer-in-western-balkans-r8CFKb›), and is further planning to deploy an LO in Niger (‹https://frontex.europa.eu/media-centre/news-release/frontex-executive-director-on-official-visit-to-niger-6LTRB6›). Whereas Frontex has a working arrangement with Turkey, and the LO deployed in Serbia could be covered arguably under the working arrangement between Frontex and MARRI, there is no working arrangement between Frontex and Niger yet; the management board has given a mandate to the executive director to negotiate a working arrangement with Niger (Management Board Decision 5/2017),

the conclusion of working arrangements, as well as the deployment of liaison officers required the *prior* opinion of the Commission and was subject to a duty to inform the European Parliament. Another aspect pertaining both to direct cooperation pursued by Frontex and to the facilitation of cooperation carried out by Member States concerned the participation of third countries in the activities of Frontex, subject to identical conditions as in the case of international organisations.[149]

Two concluding observations can be advanced on the basis of the previous sketch of Frontex's international cooperation legal mandate, tasks and instruments. First, the functionalist vision, according to which the international cooperation is instrumental in the core role and tasks of the Agency, also applied to Frontex. In this respect, the core mandate of the Agency delimited the scope of the cooperation which can be pursued by Frontex. This, on the one hand, translates into international cooperation activities related to operational cooperation (joint and return operations), risk analysis and training, etc. On the other hand, the international cooperation pursued by Frontex must illustrate properly the position of the Agency within the EU setting. It is in this context that the working arrangements concluded by Frontex are considered to be purely technical instruments for cooperation, whereas the Member States can still conclude agreements with third countries which contain provisions relating to Frontex. Secondly, being only one of the players in the EU border management area, one may expect Frontex's international cooperation priorities and actions to be influenced by or subject to controls by other actors, in particular the Commission, the Council, and the Member States. The presence of various actors in this area also raises the question of how Frontex's international activities are coordinated with those of other relevant EU players.

5.4.1.2 The procedure for Frontex's working arrangements

The procedure for Frontex's working arrangements was adopted by the management board in 2006[150] and, with one important difference, it laid down the same steps for the negotiation and conclusion of the working arrangements with both third countries and international organisations.

First, there was a preparatory phase in which the executive director produced a draft mandate for negotiation with the international organisation or the third country concerned. At this stage, an important distinction was made between the international organisations and third countries, in that Frontex only had a formal duty to consult the Member States and the Commission in the latter case with a view to ensuring that their input is taken into account in the negotiation process.[151] Secondly, the management board approved the draft mandate, including the guidelines that must be observed during the negotiation process.[152] Thirdly, the executive director, supported

one of the main tasks of the Frontex LO deployed in that country being to support the negotiation process.

149 See art 14(6) of Regulation 2007/2004.

150 Decision of the Management Board of Frontex 11/2006 of 01 September 2006 laying down the procedures for negotiating and concluding working arrangements with third countries and international organisations.

151 ibid art 2(1).

152 ibid art 2(2).

by the Agency's relevant internal units entered into negotiations with the competent authorities of the third country concerned or with the respective international organisation. Fourthly, when a draft working arrangement had been agreed upon by the parties, the executive director had to ask for the Commission's opinion.[153] Interestingly, whereas in the Frontex Regulation the requirement to obtain Commission's opinion was only explicitly mentioned for third countries, the 2006 Decision of the Frontex management board did not seem to discriminate between third countries and international organisations with regard to this particular aspect.[154] Next, the draft working arrangement and the Commission's opinion were submitted to the management board, which adopted the final version with an absolute majority of its members with a right to vote.[155] Finally, the working arrangement was signed by the executive director and eventually co-signed by the chair of the management board.[156]

Although this does not appear to pertain solely to the procedure for the negotiation and conclusion of the Agency's working arrangements, the 2006 Frontex Management Board Decision also formalised a specific duty of the executive director to report to the management board regularly on the external relations with third countries and international organisations.[157] This latter aspect, together with the detailed procedure for the negotiation and the conclusion of working arrangements reveals an important role for the management board in Frontex's international cooperation. In view of the composition of the management board, this means that ultimately there is an important role for the Member States and the Commission.

5.4.1.3 Frontex's international dimension in practice

5.4.1.3.1 SETTING THE INTERNATIONAL COOPERATION PRIORITIES AND ACTIONS

The mid- to long-term strategy of Frontex is outlined in the multiannual plan, prepared by the executive director and adopted by the management board. This programme covers a period of five years and is updated on an annual basis.[158] It sets forth the key objectives and the main activities foreseen to attain them, thereby providing the basis for more detailed planning documents, such as the annual work programmes, action plans, and operational plans.[159] The multiannual plan normally includes the key strategic elements of the international cooperation envisaged by the Agency in fulfilling its core mandate.[160] It should be noted that as of 2016, the multiannual plan and the

153 ibid art 2(4).
154 ibid, art 2(4).
155 ibid, art 2(5).
156 ibid, art 2(6).
157 ibid, art 3.
158 eg Frontex Multi Annual Plan 2010–2013 5–6 (obtained on author's request).
159 ibid.
160 For instance, Section 3.6 of Frontex's Multi Annual Plan 2010–2013 covered the international dimension of the Agency quite in detail by (1) highlighting the main directions and means for international cooperation; (2) setting priorities with regard to the third countries with whom cooperation is foreseen; and (3) by displaying sensitivity with regard to the relevant EU policy and political context. Lately, the Multi Annual Programming Document 2016–2019 (at 17 and 36–39), and the Multi Annual Programming Document 2017–2019 (at 17, 35–37 and 73–76)

annual work programme of the Agency are integrated within one single document called Frontex's Programming Document.[161] Strikingly, unlike other agencies like Europol, Frontex did not have so far a separate comprehensive external relations strategy. The latest evaluation of the Agency signalled that international cooperation remains an area of significant improvement and recommended in particular that Frontex adopts a strategy regarding cooperation with third countries as a means to enhance its international dimension.[162] As a result, the Agency's Work Programme 2017 foresees the development and implementation of a third-country strategy enabling Frontex 'to better prioritise its activities in the external dimension'.[163]

The strategic planning of Frontex's international cooperation can be described as a mix of operational needs and wider policy-political considerations. From the technical-operational perspective, the priorities for international cooperation are mainly risk-analysis driven. Risk analysis is an internal tool which enables Frontex to assess threats and developments at the Union's external borders, informing the overall planning of the Agency's activities. From the policy-political side, the main priorities regarding international cooperation are set based on a wider scale, in the AFSJ area or in the EU external relations area, and different actors are involved, such as the Member States, the Council, the Commission, and the EEAS.[164] As such, Frontex's international cooperation is influenced by broader political processes and at times the Agency becomes part of larger EU political processes, like Mobility partnerships, enlargement and neighbourhood policies.[165]

There are several ways in which it is ensured that the Agency is up to date and follows the policy-political considerations relevant for its international cooperation dimension. First, the Member States and the Commission, represented in the management board, shape the strategic planning of the Agency and monitor its implementation. Secondly, Frontex maintains constant formal and informal contacts with the Commission (in particular with the 'mother' DG Home), the Council, and the EEAS, although in the latter case it appears that the interactions are at an early stage.[166] In this way, Frontex is made aware of the developments in EU external action area and may also be asked to report on the progress of its international cooperation activities.

outlined the Agency's international cooperation strategic objectives and actions in a rather straightforward manner.

161 Art 62(2)(j) in combination with art 68(3)(c) of Regulation 2016/1624; see Frontex Single Programming Document 2016–2019 ‹https://frontex.europa.eu/assets/Key_Documents/Programming_Document/2016/Programme_of_work_2016.pdf›; Frontex Programming Document 2017–2019 ‹https://frontex.europa.eu/assets/Key_Documents/Programming_Document/2017/Programme_of_work_2017.pdf›.

162 Ramboll and EurAsylum, External evaluation of the Agency under art 33 of the Frontex Regulation (Final Report) July 2015, 101 and 110 ‹https://frontex.europa.eu/assets/Publications/General/Final_Report_on_External_Evaluation_of_Frontex.pdf›.

163 Frontex Programming Document 2017–2019, 74.

164 See also COWI Report 2009, noting the view of several Member States according to which the Agency should '(. . .) remain focused on the practical and operational cooperation issues (. . .) leaving the politics to the Member States and the Commission', COWI (n 128) 63.

165 Interview 28 (phone) with a Frontex official (27 November 2012); see also Frontex's general reports, programming documents and annual work programmes, available at ‹https://frontex.europa.eu/about-frontex/key-documents/›.

166 Interview 1 with a Frontex official, Warsaw (4 March 2012).

Thirdly, while the Agency enjoys a certain degree of freedom in pursuing its international cooperation agenda, it appears that, whenever the changes in the EU political climate so require, Frontex may be compelled by the main political actors in the external relations of the EU to adjust its priorities and activities accordingly. This may at times entail adjusting the list of priority countries, stepping up the negotiation or conclusion of a working arrangement with a third country cooperation,[167] or suspending its implementation, etc.[168]

On a more general level, one may conclude that the capacity of Frontex to set and pursue its international cooperation strategy is subject to a double limitation. First, the scope of cooperation is limited to operational issues with the exclusion of political aspects. Secondly, the degree of independence enjoyed by the Agency seems rather limited, but instead it seems heavily dependent on other EU actors, in particular the Commission and the Member States.

5.4.1.3.2 FRONTEX'S WORKING ARRANGEMENTS

According to Frontex's legal framework the most important instrument formalising the relationship between the Agency and its international partners is the working arrangement.[169] Except perhaps for the instances in which Frontex participates in wider EU external relations initiatives and supports bilateral cooperation between Member States and third countries, most of the formal and informal international cooperation activities and instruments by Frontex are either aimed at concluding a working arrangement or are carried out within the framework of such an instrument.

Types and terminology

In a relatively short period, the Agency concluded more than twenty working arrangements with non-EU partners. Following the formal distinction between third country cooperation and cooperation with international organisations made in Articles 13–14 of the former Frontex Regulation, as well as the templates used in practice by Frontex,[170] two types of working arrangements concluded by the Agency can be distinguished accordingly. One type concerns the working arrangements with third countries (Type 1), whereas the other type consists of the working arrangements concluded with international organisations (Type 2).[171] Most working arrangements have been

167 See for an example COWI (n 128) 63.

168 Interview 33 (phone) with a Council official (2 July 2013); Interview 31 with a Commission official, Brussels (26 June 2013); Interviews 1 and 2 with Frontex officials, Warsaw (4 March 2013).

169 According to the latest external evaluation of the Agency, 'Frontex pursues the signing of working arrangements as its preferred option for establishing a framework for cooperation with different third countries', Ramboll and EurAsylum (n 162) 55.

170 Interviews 28 with Frontex officials (phone) (27 November 2012) and 2, Warsaw (4 March 2013).

171 See Annex 4 'Examples of Frontex's working arrangements'.

concluded with third countries[172] and few with international organisations.[173] In this context, the term 'working arrangement' covers all the formal international cooperation instruments concluded by the Agency with third countries and international organisations, regardless of the different titles used in practice for some of the instruments.[174]

It is important to note that, according to the former Frontex Regulation, Type 1 working arrangements were concluded with the competent authorities of third countries meaning, in principle, the authority competent for border management in the relevant country. However, in practice there is some variety, because the issue of the competent authority depends on the internal system and rules of each particular country. Moreover, in some countries there may be several authorities and bodies with powers in the border management area. In general, Frontex concludes working arrangements either directly with the specialised border guard service or body[175] or with the relevant ministry, usually the ministry of the interior.[176]

With regard to Type 2 working arrangements, some difficulties arise concerning the qualification as 'international organisations' of the Agency's partner organisations. Bearing in mind that the concept of an 'international organisation'[177] is not unequivocal,

172 According to Frontex's website, eighteen working arrangements have been concluded so far with competent authorities from third countries ‹https://frontex.europa.eu/about-frontex/key-documents/?category=working-arrangements-with-non-eu-countries›; see also Frontex Programming Document 2017–2019 (n 161) 75. Working arrangements have been concluded with the following third countries (listed in chronological order): Russian Federation, Ukraine, Moldova, Georgia, former Yugoslav Republic of Macedonia (FYROM), Serbia, Albania, Bosnia and Herzegovina, USA, Montenegro, Belarus, Canada, Cape Verde, Nigeria, Armenia, Turkey, Azerbaijan and Kosovo.

173 Working arrangements have been concluded with the United Nations Commissioner of Refugees (UNHCR); International Organisation for Migration (IOM); Interpol; CIS Border Commandants' Council; the Migration, Asylum, Refugees Regional Initiative (MARRI) Regional Centre in the Western Balkans; the International Centre for Migration Policy Development (ICMPD); the Democratic Control of Armed Forces (DCAF); the United Nations Office on Drugs and Crime (UNODC). It should be noted that due to the specific features of the partner organisation, the working arrangements with CIS Border Commandants' Council and MARRI Regional Centre in Western Balkans are mentioned on the Frontex website under the heading 'Cooperation with third countries' ‹https://frontex.europa.eu/partners/non-eu-countries/›.

174 eg Frontex concluded a 'memorandum of understanding' with the Turkish Ministry of Foreign Affairs and 'terms of reference' with the Russian Border Guard Service; further, the Agency concluded exchanges of letters with IOM, UNCHR and ICMPD, and a 'memorandum' with the Coordination Service of the CIS Border Commandants' Council.

175 See eg State Border Committee of Belarus; Border Guard Service of the Republic of Moldova; the Border Guard Service of the Federal Security Service of the Russian Federation; the State Border Guard Service of Ukraine; Canada Border Services Agency ‹https://frontex.europa.eu/about-frontex/key-documents/?category=working-arrangements-with-non-eu-countries›.

176 See eg Ministry of Internal Affairs of the former Yugoslav Republic of Macedonia; Ministry of Internal Affairs of Georgia; Ministry of Interior of Republic of Serbia; the United States Department of Homeland Security; Ministry of Security of Bosnia and Herzegovina ‹https://frontex.europa.eu/about-frontex/key-documents/?category=working-arrangements-with-non-eu-countries›.

177 Article 2(1)(i) of both the 1969 and the 1986 Vienna Conventions define an international organisation as 'an intergovernmental organisation'. On the contrary, the Union of International Associations (UIA) adopts a broad definition for the purpose of its Yearbook of International

one may arguably include here Interpol, the International Organisation for Migration (IOM), the United Nations Commissioner of Refugees (UNHCR), and the United Nations Office on Drugs and Crime (UNODC). However, the legal status of the Coordination Service of the Commonwealth of Independent States (CIS) Border Troop Commanders Council, the Migration, Asylum, Refugees Regional Initiative (MARRI) Regional Centre in the Western Balkans, the International Centre for Migration Policy Development (ICMPD), and the Democratic Control of Armed Forces (DCAF) is not very clear.[178] One may thus conclude that Frontex's current practice regarding working arrangements is based on quite a broad interpretation of the term 'international organisation' in Article 13 of the former Founding Regulation.[179]

Wording, content and structure

The working arrangements concluded by Frontex are by and large rather brief documents. In general, they comprise a preamble and the main part or the content of the instrument. Unlike the working arrangements concluded by EASA, those enacted by Frontex do not usually include Annexes. A preliminary observation is that, in practice, Frontex seems to be using two general templates for the working arrangements concluded, in line with the delineation between Type 1 (third countries) and Type 2 (international organisations) made earlier in this chapter. Depending on the circumstances, these templates are adapted slightly for each partner or group of partners.[180] In exactly the same way as EASA's working arrangements, the provisions of Frontex's working arrangements are not structured in articles, but they are in numbered paragraphs, with the only exception being the working arrangement with Interpol.

The preambles of both Type 1 and Type 2 working arrangements are rather brief and usually provide an overview of the background, reasons and objectives of the relationship formalised between Frontex and its partner. Some working arrangements include a formulation according to which Frontex and the partner organisation or third country authority 'agree' to establish operational cooperation.[181] For the remaining working arrangements, a slightly different wording is used. In a few cases, the working arrangement provides that the parties 'have reached the following

Organisations. In this respect, the concept of 'international organisation' covers a broad range of organisations and entities categorised in different types featuring different levels of 'internationality', Union of International Associations/The Yearbook of International Organizations/What types of organisations are included in the Yearbook ‹http://www.uia.org/yearbook?qt-yb_intl_orgs=3#yearbook_pages-page_yb_faq-4›. According to Schermers and Blokker, international organisations are '(. . .) forms of cooperation: (1) founded on an international agreement; (2) having at least one organ with a will of its own; and (3) established under international law', Henry G Schermers and Niels M Blokker, *International Institutional Law. Unity within Diversity* (Revised 5th edn, Martinus Nijhoff Publishers 2011) 36–37.

178 For a more general discussion regarding the legal status of such international bodies, see Ian Brownlie, *Principles of Public International Law* (7th edn, OUP 2008) 66–67.

179 Article 1 of Decision 11/2006 of the Management Board of Frontex defines international organisations as 'organisations of international scope or character competent in matters covered' by the Frontex Regulation.

180 Interviews with Frontex officials 28 (phone) (27 November 2012) and 2, Warsaw (4 March 2013).

181 With the 'Enlargement' countries, Nigeria, Cape Verde, Kosovo and Interpol.

understanding',[182] 'have reached a common understanding',[183] or 'have arrived at the present arrangements'.[184]

The large majority of the working arrangements concluded by Frontex are structured according to headings covering the different aspects of the cooperation foreseen between the Agency and its partner.[185] As regards the language used in the main body of the Frontex's working arrangements it should be noted that Type 1 working arrangements feature provisions characterised by the use of 'may' in combination with 'will' and sometimes 'shall'[186] clauses. Type 2 working arrangements, except for the memorandum with CIS Border Commandants' Council, are characterised by a more extensive use of 'will/shall/must' clauses. Additionally, in the working arrangements with DCAF, ICMPD, IOM, Interpol, MARRI RC, UNHCR, and Moldova, Frontex and its partner are referred to as 'parties'.

The working arrangements with third countries (Type 1) normally begin with listing the guiding principles and objectives underpinning the cooperation between the parties. The principle underlying the relationship between Frontex and its partner mentioned in most working arrangements is the 'gradual development towards a sustainable partnership'. In the working arrangements concluded with the Nigerian Immigration Service, with the Armenian National Security Council, with the Ministry of Interior of Kosovo, and with the Turkish Ministry of Foreign Affairs 'full respect for human rights' is added as an essential principle for cooperation.[187]

The objectives for cooperation are linked to Frontex's legal mandate. There is some variation between the working arrangements, but the common lines can be distilled. In Type 1 working arrangements, the primary umbrella objectives put at the top of the list consist of the countering of illegal/irregular migration, related cross-border crime, and strengthening of border security/management. This is usually followed by more concrete derived objectives such as: developing good relations and mutual trust between Frontex/border guards of the Member States and the other party; facilitating measures taken by the parties, etc. In Type 2 working arrangements, the objectives for cooperation are usually phrased concisely and in general terms. There are different formulations, but the overall objective pertains to establishing a framework, strengthening or enhancing the cooperation between the two partners in the field of border management related activities, such as integrated border management projects, exchange of information and expertise, assistance and the development of best practices.[188] Apart from objectives and principles, all of the Frontex's working arrangements include provisions regarding the modalities in which the daily contacts

182 ie MARRI and Canada.

183 ie USA.

184 ie Armenia, Belarus, Georgia, Moldova, Russian Federation, Ukraine.

185 Exceptions are the memorandum with CIS Border Commandants' Council and the MoU with Turkey.

186 For instance, the working arrangement with Kosovo provides that: 'Frontex and the Ministry of Internal Affairs shall take all necessary measures to ensure adequate confidentiality of the information received under the present Working Arrangement'.

187 On the occasion of the 12th meeting of the Frontex Consultative Forum on Fundamental Rights (Warsaw, 2 February 2017) it has been suggested that Frontex working arrangements which do not contain a 'human rights' clause need to be updated.

188 See in particular the working arrangements with DCAF, ICMPD, Interpol, IOM, UNODC, UNHCR.

between the Agency and its partner are established, with a view to implementing the cooperation enabled by the working arrangement.

With some variations, Type 1 working arrangements list the following core areas for cooperation: risk analysis; training; research and development; joint operations (including in some cases, joint return operations);[189] and operational interoperability between the competent authorities of the Member States and those of the relevant third countries. The practical modalities for implementing the cooperation between the parties cover: exchanges of information (especially in the area of risk analysis); exchange of analytical products and training tools; exchanges of best practices;[190] active participation;[191] the participation of observers from one competent authority (usually the one from the third country) in various activities of the other authority;[192] the secondment of personnel to Focal Point Offices; and the participation in various projects launched by Frontex. This provides a rather extensive picture of the 'cooperation toolbox' available under the working arrangements with the competent authorities of third countries.

Some working arrangements[193] include provisions regarding the financial aspects of the cooperation between the parties. Most of these working arrangements include a standard clause providing for the possibility for Frontex to finance the participation of the competent authority of the third country concerned in the activities coordinated by the Agency (eg joint operations). The financing is made available by Frontex in accordance with its own rules, as laid down in the Frontex financial regulation and the EU financial regulations. The working arrangements usually refer further to separate agreements between Frontex and its partners specifying the detailed terms and conditions in each particular case. In a few cases, however, the working arrangement mentions explicitly the conclusion of a separate financing framework agreement on these issues.[194] According to Rijpma, such financing framework agreements are similar to the financial partnership agreements concluded by the Commission with third countries.[195] Finally, but still importantly, few working arrangements[196] prescribe explicitly the conclusion of a separate security agreement or protocol concerning the detailed requirements and procedures with respect to the exchange of classified information. What is more, the working arrangement with Kosovo is the first to mention explicitly the possibility to exchange personal data between the Agency and its third country counterpart,[197] and it is likely that similar provisions regarding the

189 ie all Western Balkan countries, Turkey, Nigeria, Capo Verde, Canada and USA.

190 eg working arrangements with Canada and USA.

191 eg the working arrangement with Nigeria mentioning Frontex coordinated joint operations conducted with the participation of Nigerian competent authorities (para 4.7), as well as the active participation of the Nigerian authorities in Frontex coordinated joint return operations (para 4.9).

192 eg meetings of the Frontex Risk Analysis Network, joint operations, return operations.

193 ie the working arrangements with the Western Balkan countries, Turkey, Nigeria, Cape Verde, Armenia, Belarus, Georgia, USA and Kosovo.

194 Working arrangements with Armenia, Nigeria and Turkey.

195 Rijpma (n 8) 334.

196 Working arrangements with Armenia, Nigeria and Kosovo.

197 The exchange of personal data is made subject to a specific arrangement/agreement between the parties to the working arrangement.

exchange of personal data will be included in the future working arrangements concluded with third countries.

As regards the working arrangements with international organisations (Type 2), the rule of thumb regarding the information exchange seems to be that personal data is excluded from the scope of cooperation. Furthermore, some working arrangements also specify that the exchange of sensitive operational data is excluded[198] or it is allowed only in specific circumstances.[199] On the other hand, exchange of data classified as 'confidential' is possible in principle subject to specific confidentiality requirements and procedures.[200] Next, unlike the working arrangements with third countries, the cooperation entered into with international organisations does not normally cover core operational activities.[201] Finally, except for MARRI,[202] the working arrangements with international organisations do not include explicit provisions regarding the financing by Frontex of activities carried out by the partner organisation.

The final provisions of all Frontex's working arrangements cover the entry into force, the amendment procedure and the termination of the cooperation instrument (see Annex 4: Examples of Frontex's working arrangements). Additional aspects usually dealt with in most of the Type 1 and Type 2 working arrangements are the language and the interpretation of the instrument, and the procedure for solving disagreements and conflicts regarding the interpretation and the application of the working arrangement. Importantly, most of Frontex's working arrangements include specific provisions regarding their legal status and effects. Some of the working arrangements include dispute settlement clauses.[203] They are usually brief and simply stipulate that disagreements between the parties are to be solved by negotiations.[204] Sometimes the working arrangement includes provisions establishing the prevailing language version of the instrument in the case of a disagreement between the parties regarding the interpretation of the instrument.[205] What is more, few working arrangements provide for the possibility to suspend fully or in part the application of the instrument in case of disagreement.[206]

Type 1 working arrangements include a standard provision that they are not to be considered an international treaty or a document having effect under international law and that their implementation shall not be regarded as the fulfilment of international obligations by the EU,[207] its institutions[208] and its Member States[209] in relation to the

198 eg MARRI.
199 eg IOM and Interpol.
200 Working arrangements with DCAF, Interpol and IOM.
201 Only the working arrangements with Interpol (art 5) and MARRI (on the issue of the MARRI operational contact point) seem to cover activities marginally related to joint operations.
202 Even in this case, the working arrangement stipulates that Frontex may finance activities carried out by the MARRI member states (not MARRI as such).
203 Bosnia and Herzegovina, CIS, DCAF, Georgia, ICMPD, IOM, Moldova, Montenegro, Serbia, Turkey, Ukraine, UNODC and UNHCR.
204 DCAF, ICMPD, IOM, Turkey, UNODC and UNHCR.
205 Bosnia and Herzegovina CIS, Georgia, Moldova, Montenegro, Serbia and Ukraine.
206 UNODC and, most recently, Kosovo.
207 Including eg Belarus, Georgia, Russia and Ukraine.
208 Armenia, Bosnia and Herzegovina, Cape Verde, Macedonia, Montenegro, Nigeria, Turkey and Serbia.
209 Moldova.

third country concerned. The working arrangements with Canada and the USA feature a slightly different phrasing by specifying that the instrument 'does not create binding obligations under international law' and that, furthermore, 'it is not intended to create or confer any right, privilege, or benefit on any person or party, private or public'. It should be noted that these working arrangements also include some sort of a 'limiting clause' specifying that the parties are not precluded from entering in other forms of cooperation.

By comparison, Type 2 working arrangements do not include such explicit limitations. Yet, some of these working arrangements include details relevant for their status and effects. In the working arrangements with DCAF and MARRI it is stipulated that the termination of the working arrangement '(. . .) will not affect any benefits or obligations arising from its application before such termination'. In the working arrangement with UNODC, a right for the parties to suspend their obligations under that arrangement is included, and it is stated that 'No waiver, change, or modification in the working arrangement is valid or binding unless agreed to in writing and signed by all parties'. Moreover, it mentions that specific activities or obligations within the framework working arrangement requires '(. . .) the conclusion of separate agreements'.[210]

The procedure for the negotiation and conclusion of working arrangements

Few practical aspects regarding the procedure for the negotiation and conclusion of the working arrangements enacted so far by the Agency under the former Frontex Regulation are worth being mentioned for the purpose of our analysis. Thus, it appears that there is a slight difference between the international organisations and third countries in the preparatory phase of the procedure. When negotiation of a working arrangement with a third country is foreseen, even before asking the mandate from the management board, the executive director must already have entered into consultations with the Member States and with the Commission.[211] This difference in practice has been explained on the ground that the relationship with third countries is a 'more sensitive' issue at the EU level, which prompts the need for exchanges of views with the Commission at a very early stage.[212] The practical relevance of the consultation with the Commission at this stage seems to be quite significant, in that if there were objections or reservations from the Commission's side, the executive director would not even ask a mandate from the management board.[213] As for the need for Frontex to consult with the Member States, this rests on the fact that the latter might also have cooperation in place with the third country concerned which must not be jeopardised by Frontex, and based on which the Agency could also build its relationship with that third country.[214]

Next, it appears that consultations with the Commission took place not only in the preparatory phase and before submitting the text of the working arrangement

210 Working arrangement with UNODC.
211 Interview 28 (phone) with a Frontex official (27 November 2012).
212 ibid.
213 Interview 43 (phone) with a Frontex official (18 December 2012).
214 Interview 1 with a Frontex official, Warsaw (4 March 2013).

for approval to the management board, but also anytime during the negotiation phase, as necessary. This was done informally and took place, for instance, when the Agency encounters certain difficulties or obstacles during the negotiations. In such circumstances, by liaising with the Commission, the Agency sought guidance on how to deal with the matter or to be updated on the relevant developments at the EU level.[215] An important element of the relationship between the Commission and Frontex that was revealed during interviews is that whenever higher policy or political considerations required, the Commission urged the Agency to step up or speed up the negotiation and conclusion of a working arrangement, and it became apparent that the Commission's voice was always followed in the end.[216] This provides further support for the view that the Commission had a more authoritative position in practice as regards the process of the negotiation and the conclusion of the working arrangements than the mere opinion mentioned in Article 14(8) of the former Frontex Regulation.

One last practical aspect concerns the adoption of the working arrangement by the Agency's management board. Whilst, according to the formal procedure, the adoption of working arrangements required an absolute majority of its members with a right to vote, it appears that in practice consensus was sought in the management board with regard to the working arrangements.[217] This means that, even if it was possible to reach technically an absolute majority, the adoption of the working arrangement would still be delayed to make the necessary arrangements until the wishes of all the members of the management board were accommodated, so that the instrument was passed with no objections. Under such a scenario, one may assume that, in practice, if the Commission or the Member States would oppose a certain working arrangement, in the end the instrument will not be adopted by the management board.

5.4.2 Frontex's international dimension according to the new Frontex Regulation

Regulation 2016/1624 essentially keeps the international cooperation framework under the former Frontex Regulation. It thus, re-emphasises facilitation of cooperation between the Member States and third countries, and direct cooperation with third country authorities and international organisations as the main dimensions of the Agency's international cooperation. It further confirms the instrumental nature of the Agency's international dimension, and the obligation of Frontex to act in compliance with the EU legal and policy framework, in particular in the field of Union's external relations. The new Frontex Regulation also maintains the formal delineation between cooperation with international organisations (Article 52) and cooperation with third countries (Article 54), the latter being the centre of gravity of the Agency's international cooperation activities. The main instrument for international cooperation with both categories of partners remains the working arrangement, no additional

215 Interview 43 (phone) with a Frontex official (18 December 2012) and Interview 31 with a Commission official, Brussels (26 June 2013).

216 Interview 28 (phone) with a Frontex official (27 November 2012); Interview 2 with a Frontex official, Warsaw (4 March 2013); and Interview 31 with a Commission official, Brussels (26 June 2013). Apparently, this can go quite far, even after the working arrangement has been approved, but it is not yet signed by the executive director.

217 Interview 2 with a Frontex official, Warsaw (4 March 2013).

clarifications being made with regard to the legal nature of these instruments. Additionally, the provisions regarding the Agency's liaison officers in third countries,[218] the participation of observers from third countries and international organisations in the activities of the Agency,[219] the possibility to launch and finance technical assistance projects in third countries,[220] and the involvement of Frontex in the implementation of bilateral agreements between the Member States and third countries[221] are largely similar to those in the former Frontex Regulation.

However, Regulation 2016/1624 also features a number of notable adjustments and novelties as compared to the former Frontex Regulation. Regarding specifically Frontex's main cooperation instruments, a novel procedural element consists of subjecting, similarly to EASA, the Agency's working arrangements with both international organisations and competent authorities from third countries to Commission's *prior* approval.[222] Next, the new Frontex Regulation provides explicitly for the approval of the management board as regards the Agency's working arrangements with third countries.[223] While this is no absolute novelty as the Agency's internal procedure already included this step, this provision, however, formally aligns the Agency with para 25 of the Common Approach on EU agencies as far as the procedure for concluding working arrangements with third countries is concerned.[224]

Other changes aim at increasing the democratic accountability for the Agency's international cooperation actions. Thus, the new Frontex Regulation extends the scope of the Agency's duty to inform the European Parliament to all aspects of international cooperation with third countries.[225] In the same vein goes the obligation imposed on the Agency to include in annual reports an assessment of the cooperation with third countries.[226] The latter provision again seems partly to formalise existing institutional practices as Frontex already included in its annual reports a section covering cooperation activities with both third countries and international organisations.[227] What is more, as regards specifically the working arrangements with third countries, the new Frontex Regulation stipulates the duty to inform the European Parliament *before* such an instrument is concluded.[228] As far as the working arrangements with

218 Art 55 of Regulation 2016/1624.

219 ibid arts 52(5) and 54(7).

220 ibid art 54(9).

221 ibid art 54(10).

222 ibid arts 52(2) and 54(2). This entails that the Agency's internal acts concerning the procedure for negotiation and conclusion of working arrangements need to be adjusted accordingly.

223 ibid art 62(2)(z).

224 Interestingly, unlike the Agency's internal procedure, the management board's approval under the new Frontex Regulation does not seem to cover working arrangements with international organisations.

225 Under the former Frontex Regulation, this formally covered only the Agency's working arrangements with third countries and liaison officers.

226 Art 54(11) of Regulation 2016/1624.

227 eg Frontex, General Activity Report 2014 12–15 ‹https://frontex.europa.eu/assets/Key_Documents/Annual_report/2014/General_Report_2014.pdf›; Frontex, General Activity Report 2015 16 ‹https://frontex.europa.eu/assets/Key_Documents/Annual_report/2015/General_Report_2015.pdf›.

228 Art 54(2) of Regulation 2016/1624. This does not seem to be the case for the working arrangements with international organisations, where art 52(2) merely reproduces Agency's duty, laid down also in the former Frontex Regulation, to inform the European Parliament in every case.

international organisations are concerned, the new Frontex Regulation merely confirms existing practice by providing explicitly for the possibility and conditions for exchanging classified information.[229]

More developments are brought by the new Frontex Regulation with regard to the relationship between the Agency and third countries. In this respect, the new legal framework further brings Frontex in line with para 25 of the Common Approach on EU agencies and is accommodating practical concerns concerning the consistency of the Agency's international actions with the EU external action, by providing for coordination with EU delegations.[230] Yet another formalisation of existing practice entails the duty imposed on the Agency to contribute to the implementation of relevant international agreements between the EU and third countries within the framework of Union's external relations policy.[231] Next, the new Frontex Regulation also brings about a genuine extension of the Agency's international dimension. This concerns the possibility for the Agency to carry out actions on the territory of a third country, as part of joint operations organised in circumstances requiring increased technical and operational assistance, and entailing cooperation between Member States and third countries.[232] In such circumstances, the details of the participation of the Agency's staff in joint operations carried out on the territory of third countries will be subject to a status agreement concluded between the EU (not the Agency) and the third country concerned.[233] As for the possibility for the Member States to 'use' Frontex in their cooperation with third countries based on bilateral agreements, this requires the Agency's agreement, must be in accordance with the Frontex Regulation, and the Member States have a duty to notify the Commission.[234] Last but not least, the new Frontex Regulation essentially maintains the previous legal regime as regards the processing of personal data by Frontex during the performance of its tasks, but further adjusts it in line with the Agency's consolidated mandate.[235]

Overall, while the new Frontex Regulation definitely reinforces the Agency's international profile, it maintains at the same time the basic principles and instruments for international cooperation under the former Frontex Regulation though it brings them up to date by formalising various practical developments and addressing certain legal concerns.

5.5 Frontex on the global scene: a legal assessment

5.5.1 The twilight legal nature of Frontex's working arrangements

The legal nature of Frontex's working arrangements needs to be determined in light of the criteria for international binding agreements provided in this study – ie the wording and substance/content of the instrument, as well as the particular

229 Art 52(4).
230 Art 54(2). A similar duty to coordinate closely with the relevant EU delegations is laid down for the Agency's liaison officers deployed in third countries: ibid art 55(3).
231 ibid art 54(8).
232 ibid art 54(3).
233 ibid art 54(4).
234 ibid art 54(10).
235 Arts 45–49.

circumstances (context) surrounding the negotiation and conclusion of the instrument – and along the indicators corresponding to each criterion.[236]

The procedure for the negotiation and conclusion of the working arrangements is quite elaborate and formalised. In practice, the full completion of the procedure for each working arrangement normally took more than one year.[237] Significantly, the procedure for Frontex's working arrangements required so far two formal decisions to be adopted by the management board: one adopting the draft mandate and authorising the executive director to negotiate the working arrangement and another one adopting the final version of the working arrangement. This can be taken as an indicator of the importance attached to these formal cooperation instruments in the legal framework of the Agency. However, unlike 'ordinary' treaties, Frontex's working arrangements are not concluded with the head of state or government of the third country concerned and do not require an internal ratification procedure in the third country concerned. Moreover, Frontex's working arrangements are not registered with the UN, nor are they published in the Official Journal of the European Union, but are available on the Agency's website instead.[238] Yet, the fact that Frontex's working arrangements are available only via the Agency's website does not automatically mean that these instruments are not binding.

Next, the content and practical implementation of Frontex's working arrangements leave a mixed impression as regards their legal effects. First, a blended language, combining more prescriptive terms like 'agree', 'shall', 'will', 'must' with softer 'may' and 'endeavour' language is used both in Type 1 and Type 2 working arrangements. The intermingling of clauses regarding entry into force, interpretation, amendment, termination, respect for human rights, suspension of obligations[239] and preservation of the rights and duties resulting from the application of the instrument,[240] with provisions denying legal effects under international law have a similar result.[241]

Secondly, the cooperation that may be or is actually carried out in the implementation of Frontex's working arrangements contributes to the blurred picture. In this respect, in practice, Frontex normally establishes action plans or cooperation plans[242] with its partners with a view to implementing the working arrangement. These documents may envisage broader cooperation or specific projects, and they provide for the common actions envisaged by the partners and for the division of tasks, including the required resources to carry out the planned actions.[243] On the one hand, the cooperation with third country authorities and international organisations often materialises

236 See ch 2, Box 2.1: Criteria and indicators for identifying international binding agreements.

237 Interview 1 with a Frontex official, Warsaw (4 March 2013).

238 As of end June 2015, the working arrangements with third countries (Type 1) and the Type 2 working arrangements with CIS Border Troop Commanders Council and the MARRI Regional Centre were available on Agency's website. The remaining Type 2 working arrangements were obtained from the Agency at the author's request.

239 Working arrangement with UNODC.

240 Working arrangements with DCAF and MARRI.

241 Working arrangements with third country authorities.

242 See Frontex, Programme of Work 2012 68–69 ‹https://frontex.europa.eu/assets/Key_Documents/Programming_Document/2012/frontex_pow_2012.pdf›; Frontex Single Programming Document 2016–2019 (n 161) 38.

243 Confirmed more generally during Interview 43 (phone) with a Frontex official (18 December 2012) and partly in Interview 7 with a Frontex official, Warsaw (5 March 2013).

in rather light forms. This covers exchanges of best practices, representation in organisations and events of common interest and, most notably, cooperation in the area of training.[244] In this context, concerns were voiced by a Frontex official pointing to the lack of incentives such forms of cooperation may provide especially for third countries.[245] On the other hand, under the working arrangements, more substantive cooperation and responsibilities may be put in place, such as the exchange of confidential information and even personal data as illustrated by the working arrangement with Kosovo, or participation in joint operations or activities together with the related financial aspects.[246] The legal and practical relevance of such cooperation is illustrated by the clauses included in some working arrangements regarding the conclusion of separate security agreements, financing framework agreements or simply agreements on these issues.[247]

The prevailing opinion regarding the nature of the working arrangements concluded by Frontex is that they are not treaties under international law.[248] Similarly, Frontex officials and also officials from the Commission and the Council pointed out that these instruments cannot be considered as treaties. In this context, a Council official emphasised that the cooperation undertaken under working arrangements cannot be considered as 'something comparable to the legally binding agreements that the EU is engaging at the level of Council'.[249] In particular for the working arrangements concluded with third countries (Type 1), this qualification appears to find strong support in the instrument itself, based on the special clause regarding its legal status.[250] With regard to international organisations (Type 2 working arrangements), such a view may find some support in the 'limiting' clause inserted in such instruments, as

244 Access of third countries to Frontex training products are mentioned as a typical result of the signing of a working arrangement, Frontex' Programme of Work 2014 127 ‹https://frontex.europa.eu/assets/Key_Documents/Programming_Document/2014/PoW_2014_EN.pdf›; see also COWI (n 128) 63.

245 Interview 1 with a Frontex official, Warsaw (4 March 2013).

246 Whereas information regarding the Frontex international cooperation on these particular aspects is very scarce, interviews with Frontex officials provided more detailed insights and concrete examples of how the Agency carries out such activities, Interviews with Frontex officials 1, Warsaw (4 March 2013) and 7, Warsaw (5 March 2013).

247 Armenia, Azerbaijan, Nigeria (both security protocols and financial framework agreements); Belarus, Cape Verde, Georgia, Turkey, Western Balkan countries (only agreements on financing participation of the third country authority in Frontex activities); Canada, Interpol, USA, UNODC (agreements on financial aspects on a case-by-case basis); ICMPD and IOM (special arrangements regarding participation and financial aspects regarding the implementation of common projects).

248 See Rijpma (n 8) 333; Melanie Fink, 'Frontex Working Arrangements: Legitimacy and Human Rights Concerns regarding Technical Relationships' (2012) 28 *Utrecht Journal for International and European Law* 20, 27; Andrade, Martin and Mananashvili (n 53) 44–45; COWI (n 128) 63. This view seems to be shared also by Vara, although he appears to take a somewhat mixed approach when emphasising that Frontex working arrangements have important implications for human rights and that, for this reason, these instruments should be subject to the prior approval of the European Parliament, Juan S Vara, 'The External Activities of AFSJ Agencies: The Weakness of Democratic and Judicial Controls' (2015) 20 EFAR 115, 136.

249 Interview 33 (phone) with a Council official (2 July 2013).

250 See Andrea Ott, Ellen Vos and Florin Coman-Kund, 'EU Agencies on the Global Scene: EU and International Law Perspectives' in Michelle Everson, Cosimo Monda and Ellen Vos (eds), *European Agencies in between Institutions and Member States* (Kluwer Law International 2014) 111.

well as in the observation that in practice the cooperation entered into seems to be of a very limited scope.

Additional arguments are that the working arrangements do not have effects upon third parties[251] and that Frontex, as an independent agency with a very limited mandate, cannot conclude binding international agreements within the EU constitutional framework.[252] Moreover, the only effect in practice when such instruments are breached is the termination of the arrangement.[253] Instead, the working arrangements concluded by Frontex have been given different labels, such as non-binding 'letters of intent',[254] 'technical agreements',[255] 'one step lower' than the treaties,[256] 'administrative level agreements',[257] non-binding 'cooperation agreements',[258] 'legal instruments that allow for operational cooperation'.[259] These labels seem to convey the idea that the working arrangements are rather light instruments for low level technical cooperation that may entail some relevant practical consequences. As such, they are considered to be flexible instruments because they may be amended easily and stopped whenever necessary with no further impact.[260]

However, the analysis undertaken previously reveals that the view according to which the working arrangements concluded by Frontex are mere non-binding instruments for technical cooperation does not take account of all the complexities surrounding these instruments. The analysis of Frontex's working arrangements based on their wording, content and surrounding circumstances revealed that these instruments may entail limited legally binding effects. It is interesting to note that the legal effects discussed in this context can be identified not only in the working arrangements with international organisations, but particularly in those with third countries, in spite of the clause included in the latter that they are not international treaties, and do not entail international obligations on behalf of the EU. As regards Type 1 working arrangements, legal effects are likely to result in particular from the provisions relating to the exchange of information, cooperation in joint operations, technical assistance projects, financial provisions. As for Type 2 working arrangements, in particular the provisions regarding the exchange of information and common projects entail legal effects.

Moreover, the clause according to which the parties must afford full respect to human rights, which entails that, after all, individuals may be affected by the cooperation between the parties,[261] is included in some of the working arrangements with the competent authorities of third countries, and will likely be inserted in all Frontex's working arrangements. The latest working arrangements concluded by Frontex with

251 See Fink (n 248) 30.
252 Interview 31 with a Commission official, Brussels (26 June 2013).
253 ibid.
254 COWI (n 128) 63.
255 Rijpma (n 8) 334.
256 Interview 43 (phone) with a Frontex official (18 December 2012).
257 Interview 28 (phone) with a Frontex official (27 November 2012).
258 Interview 31 with a Commission official, Brussels (26 June 2013). With regard to the use of the term 'working arrangement' the interviewee took the view that normally 'in the European jargon it means that it's very limitative (. . .) is only to work together on certain issues'.
259 Interview 33 (phone) with a Council official (2 July 2013).
260 Interview 31 with a Commission official, Brussels (26 June 2013).
261 See Fink (n 248) 35.

a third country authority[262] also add to the 'human rights' clause a duty to respect relevant international laws and principles. In the same vein goes the 'exchange of personal data' clause in the working arrangement with Kosovo, and which will likely be included also in other working arrangements. Last but not least, the formal procedure for negotiating and concluding these instruments, as well as the inclusion of clauses regarding entry into force, amendment and termination, provide further indications that they contain commitments that are taken seriously by the parties.

Clauses in Frontex's working arrangements indicating legal commitments between the parties

Type 1 working arrangements:

Box 5.1 Working arrangement on establishing operational cooperation between the European Agency for the Management of Operational Cooperation at the External Borders of the Member States of the European Union (Frontex) and the Ministry of Internal Affairs of Kosovo, 2016

1. BASIC PRINCIPLES

(. . .)

(iii) In the implementation of the intended cooperation, Frontex and the Ministry of Internal Affairs afford full respect for human rights, enshrined in international laws and principles, in particular they shall ensure that the rights of persons in need of international protection and other vulnerable groups are respected during all joint activities.

(. . .)

3. CONTENTS

(. . .)

(iv) The exchange of classified information or intelligence, is object of a separate security arrangement/agreement to be adopted by Frontex and the Ministry of Internal Affairs of Kosovo.

(. . .)

(ix) Frontex may invite representatives of the competent authorities of Kosovo to participate in joint operations as observers upon mutual agreement. Participation in joint operations may take place only upon agreement of the host EU Member State.

(. . .)

262 Azerbaijan and Kosovo.

5. FINANCIAL ASPECTS

The participation of the competent authorities of Kosovo in activities coordinated by Frontex may be financed by Frontex in line with the regulatory framework in place.

(. . .)

7. CONFIDENTIALITY OF INFORMATION AND PROTECTION OF PERSONAL DATA

(i) Frontex and the Ministry of Internal Affairs shall take all necessary measures to ensure adequate confidentiality of the information received under the present Working Arrangement. They shall use this information only for the exercise of their responsibilities related to the border management as defined by the present Working Arrangement. They agree to take all necessary measures either to prevent or to end any situation of conflict of interest that may compromise the impartial and objective performance while collecting, processing or sharing information received under the present Working Arrangement.

(ii) The exchange of personal data, if required for the implementation of this Working Arrangement, will be object of a specific arrangement/agreement to be adopted by Frontex and the Ministry of Internal Affairs of Kosovo.

8. COMING INTO EFFECT, AMENDMENTS AND TERMINATION

(i) The present Working Arrangement shall come into effect on the day following its signature.

(ii) Frontex and the Ministry of Internal Affairs may amend the present Working Arrangement based on their mutual consent.

(iii) In case of disagreement on the interpretation and implementation of this Working Arrangement, Frontex and the Ministry of Internal Affairs shall meet and undertake genuine and good faith negotiations with a view to resolving the dispute or difference. In the meantime, the implementation of the article/articles subject to disagreement will be suspended.

(iv) The present Working Arrangement shall continue to be in effect unless terminated upon written notification of 90 days' minimum notice either by Frontex or by the Ministry of Internal Affairs

Type 2 working arrangements:

Box 5.2 Working arrangement in the form of an exchange of letters between European Agency for the Management of Operational Cooperation at the External Borders of the Member States of the European Union (Frontex) and Migration, Asylum, Refugees, Regional Initiative (MARRI) Regional Centre, 2011

(. . .)

Implementation modalities

- Both parties take appropriate measures to ensure effective cooperation and liaison by appointing contact points in respect of the implementation of this working arrangement.

(. . .)

- Each party shall bear the costs of any expenditure - including travel and subsistence - related to the attendance at respective management or high-level meetings. However, the participation of the MARRI Member States in Frontex coordinated operational activities may be financed by Frontex under the terms and conditions applied by Frontex. Details of such terms and conditions must be agreed separately on a case-by-case basis.

(. . .)

Termination

Either Party may terminate the present working arrangement at any time by providing written notification to the other Party. Termination shall take effect three months after the date of receipt of the notification by the other Party, unless the notification specifies a later date or the notification is rescinded prior to the specified date.

Termination of this working arrangement will not affect any benefits or obligations arising from its application before such termination.

This raises the question as to how Frontex working arrangements can be legally qualified in view of their paradoxical profile, blending the care to avoid portraying them as international treaties with the legal effects such working arrangements may actually entail under international law. Several scenarios may be advanced to solve this conundrum.

First, with regard to the working arrangements with third countries (Type 1), it is necessary to address the relevance of the clauses in the working arrangements that state that the instrument is not an international treaty and that it does not entail the fulfilment of international obligations on behalf of the EU. Whereas such clauses provide a strong indication as to the intention of the parties not to bind themselves, under international law they are not alone determinative of the legal nature of the instrument concerned.[263] Such a determination results from an overall analysis of the wording, content and surrounding circumstances of the respective instrument. The Commission took a similar view in its Vademecum on the EU External Action when emphasising that such a provision is not sufficient '(. . .) to express the real intentions of the signatories, which result from an analysis of the wording, content and purpose of the instrument'.[264] This would not necessarily be the case with the working arrangements concluded with international organisations (Type 2) because the 'limiting clause' included therein can be interpreted as only delineating the scope of application of the instrument (not anticipating on its legal nature).[265]

Secondly, the working arrangements could be some other kind of agreements entailing legally binding effects, which are nevertheless different than those in an international treaty. The argument could be made that the working arrangements are binding agreements that are not governed by international law, because the parties apply their own domestic rules and not international law.[266] However, the argument can be made that the mere fact that the working arrangements involve a trans-boundary element, in that they are concluded between actors mandated to pursue international cooperation, triggers the application of international law even if the parties agree to apply their own domestic rules.[267] Moreover, in view of the particular area and modalities in which working arrangements are implemented (especially those concluded with third countries) relevant international law is likely to become applicable.[268] In this respect, a Frontex official took the view that some aspects of the Frontex's working arrangements '(. . .) are governed by international provisions', together with relevant EU law and the domestic law of the partner concerned, and that their application may entail '(. . .) the launching of some kind of international procedure'.[269] This view seems to be confirmed by the latest working arrangements concluded by Frontex with the competent authority from Azerbaijan and Kosovo, which explicitly include a duty for the parties to respect international law.

Thirdly, Frontex's working arrangements could be qualified as non-binding or soft law instruments, although the analysis of these instruments shows that they may still entail legal effects under international law. In an attempt to solve this conundrum, one may assume for instance that such agreements, even if not legally binding, might nevertheless contain 'undertakings taken seriously' by the parties, which may trigger the application of the estoppel principle (based on 'expectations of continued observance by the parties').[270] In this context, one should add that soft law instruments

263 See ch 2, 2.3.1: The concept of 'international agreement'.

264 Commission, *Vademecum on the External Action of the European Union*, SEC (2011) 881/3 53.

265 For the view that the legal nature of a specific international cooperation instrument is to be established by considering the content and wording of the instrument as a whole, not on the basis of a specific clause, see *Vademecum on the External Action* (n 264) 52–53.

266 See Anthony Aust, *Modern Treaty Law and Practice* (CUP 2013) 17–18.

267 See Philippe Gautier, 'Article 1' and 'Article 2' in Olivier Corten and Pierre Klein (eds), *The Vienna Conventions of the Law of Treaties. A Commentary* (vol I, OUP 2011) 41.

268 See Fink (n 248) 33–35.

269 Interview 7 with a Frontex official, Warsaw (5 March 2013).

270 Oscar Schachter, 'The Twilight Existence of Non-binding International Agreements' (1977) 71 AJIL 296, 303–304. However, according to Schmalenbach, '[t]here is strong disagreement

are said to be legally relevant, in particular when they contain (administrative) 'rules and technical standards' for the implementation of treaties and other binding international instruments.[271] A recent trend is to consider soft law as a form of commitment situated in a continuum between non-legal positions and legally binding commitments.[272] Thus, it is posited that there are different degrees of 'bindingness' distinguishing not only hard law from soft law, but also different forms of soft law.[273] According to these delineations, in view of their specific features, Frontex's working arrangements could probably be qualified as 'binding instruments with a soft dimension' or as 'non-binding norms having legal relevance'.[274] Such a theoretical underpinning is appealing as it strives to grasp and explain the complexities of the current normative realities. However, it requires further conceptual clarity and more precise criteria in order to delineate between binding and non-binding, hard law and soft law.[275] One may also wonder what the practical relevance of using these categories is, as far as the legal effects resulting from Frontex's working arrangements are concerned.

Accordingly, the author takes the view that Frontex's working arrangements qualify as specific international agreements of a technical-administrative nature entailing limited legal effects. As such, Frontex's working arrangements set up technical and operational cooperation with competent authorities from third countries and international organisations on border management issues within the mandate of the Agency, as established by its Founding Regulation. A specific feature of Frontex's working arrangements is that they are like rather light framework agreements which lay down the foundations of the cooperation between the parties. Within this framework, the partners keep options open to maintain their cooperation at a basic level or to establish more enhanced cooperation through specific agreements. However, this feature is not as such to turn Frontex's working arrangements into non-binding instruments. In this regard, it has been pointed out that the fact that international cooperation instruments '(. . .) have little substance, 'hard' obligations or enforcement mechanism does not affect their treaty status'.[276] In this context, an instrument including obligations which confer wide discretion on the parties (eg duties to consult or negotiate) may still qualify as a binding international agreement.[277] Finally, the specific agreements

among scholars whether non-legally binding agreements can produce legal consequences via the principle of estoppel', Kirsten Schmalenbach, 'Article 2. Use of Terms' in Oliver Dörr and Kirsten Schmalenbach (eds), *Vienna Convention on the Law of Treaties. A Commentary* (Springer 2012) 43.

271 Alan E Boyle, 'Some Reflections on the Relationship of Treaties and Soft Law' (1999) 48 ICLQ 901, 905; see also Linda Senden, *Soft Law in European Community Law. Its Relationship to Legislation* (Hart Publishing 2004) 106.

272 See Fabien Terpan, 'Soft Law in the European Union. The Changing Nature of EU Law' (2015) 21 *European Law Journal* 68.

273 ibid 70–76.

274 For the use of these categories, see Terpan (n 272) 70–72.

275 For a view rejecting the category of 'soft law' agreements in international law, see Kal Raustiala, 'Form and Substance in International Agreements' (2005) 99 AJIL 581.

276 Aust (n 266) 18.

277 Hersch Lauterpacht, *Yearbook of the International Law Commission* (1953), vol II 97; Gautier (n 267) 44.

which further advance the cooperation between the Agency and its partners are still to be concluded within the framework of the 'umbrella' working arrangement.

Whilst the new Frontex Regulation does not bring fundamental changes as far as the legal nature of the Agency's working arrangements is concerned, some of the elements of the new legal regime seem to offer additional indications as to the increased significance attached to these instruments. Such are the upgrading of Commission's formal role from *prior* opinion, under the former Frontex Regulation, to *prior* approval of the Agency's working arrangements under the new Frontex Regulation, the express duty imposed on the Agency to inform the European Parliament before concluding a working arrangement with a third country, as well as the requirement that Frontex coordinates with EU delegations. This reinforcement of the supervisory mechanisms concerning Frontex's most important international cooperation instruments suggests growing awareness as to the legal consequences that such instruments might entail.

5.5.2 The status of Frontex as a global actor

5.5.2.1 On the international plane

The issue of the legal status of Frontex as a global actor entails determining whether the Agency can become a subject of international law in its own right, equipped with its own international legal personality or whether it is rather an agent of the EU and/or its Member States. In accordance with the criteria elaborated on in this study, assessing whether Frontex has international legal personality requires that the Agency has: (1) organisational distinctiveness; (2) separate will, so that it can be perceived as an entity detached from its creators; and (3) powers which it can exercise on the international plane.[278] Relevant indicators in this respect are Frontex's legal framework and its international cooperation practice. An additional indicator is the recognition of the Agency as a subject of international law by other subjects of international law (partners and non-partners).

Frontex appears to fulfil the first condition, since the Agency has been set up as an independent organisation, equipped with legal personality, with leading organs and an elaborated internal structure, with its own human and financial resources.[279] Furthermore, the former Frontex Regulation equipped the Agency with international cooperation tasks, including the capacity to conclude working arrangements with the competent authorities of third countries and international organisations. The Agency has exercised these powers in practice, as evidenced by its international cooperation record comprising more than twenty working arrangements, mostly with competent authorities from third countries, but also with various international organisations. The analysis of Frontex's working arrangements revealed that they qualify as specific international agreements of a technical-administrative nature entailing limited legal effects. Accordingly, one may conclude that Frontex also fulfils the third condition for international legal personality.

278 See ch 2, Box 2.2: Checklist international legal personality of semi-autonomous organs established by states and international organisations.

279 It should not be forgotten, however, that most of the resources of the Agency are in the form of a subsidy from the EU budget.

However, as in the case of EASA, it is maintained that Frontex does not display sufficient independence when pursuing international cooperation for it to be considered to have a separate will as a global actor. As regards the recognition of Frontex as a distinct subject on the international plane, a definite conclusion requires further empirical research. The Agency managed in a relatively short period of time, since it became operational, to conclude numerous working arrangements with various international organisations and competent authorities of third countries, in addition to pursuing cooperation within the framework of agreements between the Member States and third countries. This may be an indicator of the recognition of the role of Frontex as a sort of regional agency competent in border management issues. However, recognising Frontex as an entity of its own, active in the border management of the EU, but detached from the Union and its Member States is difficult to imagine. This aspect has been emphasised by Frontex officials, as well as by officials from the Council and the Commission, who further relied on this argument when expressing the view that the Agency does not have international legal personality. This view has even more weight as the Member States or the Union already have relevant arrangements or agreements in place covering border management issues, while the role of Frontex is to complement or facilitate the cooperation under those agreements.

That being said, it is more likely the case that Frontex is perceived by its partners as an agency acting on behalf of the Union and its Member States. The preliminary findings of the analysis of Frontex's working arrangements lend further support to this conclusion. In this respect, sometimes the preambles to working arrangements designate Frontex as a 'European Union Agency'[280] or as a 'body of the European Community'.[281] Additionally, the working arrangements with third countries explicitly mention the role of Frontex as a facilitator of cooperation between the third country competent authority and the border guard authorities of the Member States.[282]

Moreover, although Frontex has been granted formal autonomy by its former[283] and current Founding Regulations,[284] it is argued that the Agency does not have genuine independence in order to qualify as a distinct subject of international law. The Agency is heavily controlled by the Commission and the Member States *via* the management board, which adopts all the important strategic documents of the Agency and also approves the negotiating mandate, as well as the final text of Frontex's working arrangements. Moreover, this research revealed that the Commission had a much more authoritative position in practice as regards the negotiation and conclusion of the working arrangements than the mere consultative role enshrined in Article 14(8) of the former Frontex Regulation. Although in practice it appears that there were instances in which the executive director endeavoured to act more independently in international cooperation matters,[285] this tendency has always been kept under control in the end.

280 Working arrangement with UNODC.
281 Working arrangement with Interpol.
282 More empirical evidence is needed as regards the perception of Frontex by non-partners subjects of international law.
283 Art 15 of Regulation 2007/2004.
284 Art 56(3) of Regulation 2016/1624.
285 Interview 31 with a Commission official, Brussels (26 June 2013).

This has been ensured *via* the duties placed on the Agency to consult with the Member States and the Commission even before initiating any contacts with the partner envisaged, as well as by the mandate issued by the management board to the executive director regarding the negotiation of working arrangements and the prerogative of the former to approve the final instrument. Also, throughout the negotiation process and even after the approval by the management board, the Commission could interfere and request the Agency to step up or stop the negotiation process, or to delay the signing of the working arrangement as the case may be. The intervention of the Commission was motivated by the need to ensure that the Agency remained within the framework of the EU external policy, and in practice it was unlikely that the Agency would depart from the Commission's requests or opinion. Finally, in the process of the implementation of international cooperation, Frontex is dependent to a large extent on the Member States, which bear the main responsibility for carrying out joint operations at the external borders of the EU.

The conclusion of our analysis is that Frontex does not have international legal personality, but it acts on the global level mainly as an EU body.[286] This entails that, in principle, the Agency's actions on the international plane are to be attributed in the last instance to the Union itself. Yet, things become more blurred when Frontex is pursuing international cooperation within the framework of existing cooperation between the Member States and third countries.[287] Depending on the practical arrangements that such cooperation may entail, a complex agency relationship can arise in which Frontex would act both on behalf of the EU and on behalf of (some) Member States. These findings are further toughened by the new Frontex Regulation, which formally upgrades Commission's role with regard to the Agency's working arrangements, strengthens Frontex's democratic accountability, compels the Agency to coordinate with EU delegations and to implement Union's agreements with third countries, and further expands the Agency's tasks to support and coordinate cooperation between the Member States and third countries.

5.5.2.2 Within the EU: the principle of institutional balance and the Meroni *doctrine*

From an EU law perspective, Frontex's international dimension is subject to the requirements of the principle of institutional balance and of the *Meroni* doctrine. This assessment requires that Frontex's international cooperation tasks and actions: (1) are of executive nature; (2) remain within the boundaries of its mandate as defined by its regulatory framework; (3) are subject to conditions and supervisory mechanisms limiting the discretion of the Agency; and (4) do not encroach upon the powers vested in the EU institutions by the Founding Treaties, in particular in the Union's external action area.

286 For a similar view but based on different arguments, see Vara (n 248) 121.

287 See on the possibility for the Member States to 'borrow' the EU institutions for the purpose of implementing international agreements concluded outside the EU legal framework, Bruno de Witte and Tom Beukers, 'The Court of Justice Approves the Creation of the European Stability Mechanism outside the EU Legal Order: Pringle' (2013) 50 CML Rev 805, 843–47.

5.5.2.2.1 THE LEGAL FRAMEWORK AND INTERNATIONAL COOPERATION PRACTICE UNDER REGULATION 2007/2004

The starting point for the analysis is that Frontex is embedded in the institutional architecture of the Union as a technical-operational agency entrusted with some tasks in the field of EU border management. The international cooperation tasks and instruments entrusted to Frontex by its former Founding Regulation were clearly limited by and instrumental to the Agency's subject-matter competence.[288] Furthermore, the international cooperation entered into by Frontex was to take place '(. . .) in accordance with the relevant provisions of the TFEU'[289] and '(. . .) within the framework of the external relations policy of the Union'.[290] This indicates that, at least formally, Frontex's ability to pursue international cooperation was severely limited by its former founding act.

The international cooperation strategy and priorities, as well as the actual planning of the Agency are steered by the Commission and the Member States most obviously *via* their participation in the management board, but also in other more formal[291] and informal ways.[292] Moreover, the detailed procedure for negotiating and concluding working arrangements showed quite clearly how the Commission and the Member States were involved in different ways from the very beginning of the process. In this context, the empirical evidence obtained mainly from interviews with Frontex and Commission officials suggests quite an authoritative role for the Commission in its double capacity as a political institution and an EU external relations actor, in spite of the fact that the former Frontex Regulation only referred to 'a prior opinion of the Commission' solely for the working arrangements concluded with the competent authorities from third countries.[293] The analysis of the content and effects of the Frontex's working arrangements suggest that the cooperation pursued by the Agency is limited to technical-operational aspects and that, quite often, the practical outcome is more modest than what was allowed under the formal legal framework.[294] Furthermore, in pursuing international cooperation under its working arrangements, Frontex is heavily dependent on the Member States, especially where such cooperation entails the participation of the competent authorities of third countries in joint operations.[295]

From this perspective, it appears that Frontex's international dimension was of a limited scope and strictly restricted by the EU institutions (in particular, the Commission) and the Member States, precluding the Agency from enjoying a large measure of discretion. However, an element of the Agency's international dimension arguably raising concerns in particular in light of *Meroni* was the possibility left to the Member States to entrust Frontex with powers via their bilateral agreements with third

288 See arts 13–14 of Regulation 2007/2004.
289 ibid arts 13 and 14(2).
290 ibid art 14(1).
291 eg the prerogatives of the Commission in budgetary matters.
292 eg informal meeting/consultations with the Commission and the Member States, for instance, in the context of participation of the Agency in COSI or in the margin of various inter-ministerial meetings.
293 Art 14(8) of Regulation 2007/2004.
294 See also COWI (n 128) 63.
295 See art 14(6) of Regulation 2007/2004.

countries. Whilst the Member States' cooperation with third countries was said to be without prejudice to the Agency's mandate and complementary to the Agency's activities,[296] the lack of formal provisions regarding safeguards and oversight could lead to situations where Frontex would be delegated powers in breach of the *Meroni* requirements.

A problematic aspect of Frontex's international dimension pertains to the working arrangements concluded by the Agency, particularly in view of their qualification as (framework) international agreements of a technical-administrative nature entailing limited legal effects. This applies not only to the working arrangements concluded with international organisations but in particular to those concluded with the competent authorities of third countries, which may produce legal effects in spite of the clause denying their status as international treaties. As maintained more generally in Chapter 2 of this study, EU agencies' binding agreements, as a form of EU external administrative action, would not automatically disturb the institutional balance in EU external relations. In this context, it is essential that: (1) Frontex's working arrangements remain within the core mandate of the Agency, and are consistent with 'Article 218 TFEU' agreements and EU legislation; and (2) the Agency is subject to sufficient supervision and control, ensuring that the powers of the main actors in EU external action area are not affected.

The comprehensive analysis of Frontex's working arrangements reveals that these instruments establish cooperation on a technical level between the Agency and its counterparts with a view to ensuring the full implementation of the Agency's regulatory framework. The 2009 Frontex external evaluation emphasised clearly that the Agency remained '(. . .) focused on the practical and operational cooperation issues while leaving the politics to the Member States and the European Commission'.[297] In this context, Frontex's working arrangements were limited in three ways: (1) covering technical-operational cooperation issues strictly limited to the tasks of the Agency; (2) establishing quite light forms of cooperation, leaving the parties the discretion to pursue more enhanced cooperation in the future; (3) providing that some more substantive forms of cooperation such as information exchange or the financing of common actions must observe Frontex's legal framework.

The plethora of formal and informal controls enabling the Commission, the Council and the Member States to steer and oversee closely the Agency's international cooperation seemed to be capable of ensuring the required consistency with the overall priorities in the EU external action area and to preserve the Commission's role under Articles 17 TEU and 220 TFEU. In particular, the involvement of the Commission in Frontex's international cooperation, well beyond the *prior* opinion mentioned in Frontex's Regulation, provided an effective guarantee that the working arrangements of the Agency were in line with 'Article 218 TFEU' agreements and EU external relations priorities. In view of the qualification of Frontex's working arrangements as a form of EU external administrative action, preservation of institutional balance in EU external relations does not require the involvement of the Council and the European Parliament in the negotiation and conclusion of these instruments in accordance with their powers under Article 218 TFEU. In this context, the duty placed on the Agency

296 ibid art 2(2).
297 COWI (n 128) 63.

to merely inform the European Parliament about the working arrangements concluded with third countries and international organisations did not affect *per se* the powers of the European Parliament under Article 218 TFEU.[298] In light of these considerations, Frontex's working arrangements do not seem to breach the institutional balance in EU external relations.

5.5.2.2.2 THE NEW FRONTEX REGULATION

As already mentioned, the new Frontex Regulation largely maintains the design of the Agency's international dimension based on the previous legal framework. In general, the changes introduced by the new Frontex Regulation either align the Agency's international cooperation with its consolidated core mandate, or formalise existing institutional practices in the field of international cooperation.

Thus, similarly to Regulation 2007/2004, the new Frontex Regulation emphasises that international cooperation is ancillary to the Agency's core mandate, and that, furthermore, it must comply with EU law and policy, in particular with Union's external relations policy.[299] Next, one of the most significant novel elements of the Agency's international dimension – ie the possibility to carry out actions in third countries – is made subject to a status agreement concluded by the EU. What is more, the Agency's international dimension is formally aligned to the Common Approach on EU agencies by compelling Frontex to coordinate, including in the case of Agency's liaison officers, with the EU delegations. In the same direction goes the formalisation in the new Frontex Regulation of the management board's *prior* approval of the Agency's working arrangements with third countries. The new Frontex Regulation also consolidates the system of controls over Frontex's working arrangements by formally upgrading Commission's role in the procedure for the negotiation and conclusion of these instruments, and by inserting a duty to inform the European Parliament before concluding a working arrangement with a third country. These elements are reflected accordingly in the new management board's rules of procedure[300] setting the new procedure for the negotiation and conclusion of the Agency's working arrangements.[301] The new Frontex Regulation also addresses the concerns related to the possibility of the Member States to include provisions on the competence of the Agency in their bilateral agreements

298 In addition to that, according to Vara, the most important control the European Parliament has over the external activities of the AFSJ agencies (including Frontex) stems from its role as a budgetary authority, Vara (n 248) 129–30.

299 See arts 52, 54–55 of Regulation 2016/1624.

300 Management Board Decision 11/2017 of 30 March 2017 adopting the Rules of Procedures of the management board. The new rules of procedure repealed Management Board Decision 11/2006 laying down the procedures for negotiating and concluding working arrangements with third countries and international organisations.

301 Art 19 of Management Board Decision 11/2017. By comparison with Management Board Decision 11/2006, the new rules of procedure lay down a much more simplified formal procedure, which comprises the following steps: (1) the executive director must inform the management board of its intention to negotiate a working arrangement with a third country; (2) after negotiations and before submitting the working arrangement to the management board, the executive director must seek Commission's approval and inform the European Parliament; (3) approval of the working arrangement by the management board; (4) signing of the working arrangement by the executive director.

with third countries by securing the Agency's agreement to such provisions and by imposing on the Member States a duty to notify the Commission.

One potential problematic aspect raised by the new Frontex Regulation is that some of the above mentioned safeguards and mechanisms do not seem to cover cooperation with international organisations, though this gap could be covered by subsequent implementing acts and/or institutional practice, as illustrated by the procedure for the negotiation and conclusion of the Agency's working arrangements under the former Frontex Regulation.[302] Nonetheless, the elements of the new legal regime seem to indicate overall, perhaps even more clearly than before, that the Agency's international dimension, including its working arrangements, will likely comply with *Meroni* and institutional balance in EU external relations.

5.6 Conclusion

The examination of Frontex's international cooperation legal framework and practice indicates that the international dimension of Frontex is instrumental to the core mandate of the Agency and is embedded in the external dimension of the border management area. In this vein, both the former and current Frontex regulations explicitly made the scope of the international cooperation pursued by the Agency subject to its technical-operational role and tasks and, furthermore, made it dependent upon the EU external relations policy.

A review of Frontex's international cooperation practice indicates that the Agency's priorities and actions were shaped to a great extent through various formal and informal interactions with the Commission and the Member States. Thus, the procedure for the negotiation and conclusion of Frontex's working arrangements revealed the involvement of the Commission and of the Member States from the very beginning and throughout the whole process. In particular, the Commission has played quite an influential role in practice, well beyond the mere formal *prior* opinion mentioned in the former Frontex Regulation. Also, the implementation of cooperation under the working arrangements seemed to be very much dependent on the changes in the EU external policy climate, which meant in fact that the Commission urged the Agency to slow down or step up cooperation according to the circumstances.

A closer look at the content and effects of Frontex's working arrangements reveals quite a low-level cooperation, as well as the concern to avoid that these instruments, in particular those with third countries, are qualified as binding international agreements. However, the comprehensive analysis of the Frontex's working arrangements from an international law perspective provides support for the view according to which the working arrangements may create legal effects, albeit limited. This is true for the clauses regarding the exchange of information and related confidentiality duties, participation in and financing of joint and return operations, common technical assistance projects, and the human rights clause. Most of these rights and duties become active upon the conclusion of subsequent agreements between the parties, but nevertheless such instruments would be concluded within the framework and with a view

302 However, it should be noted that, unlike the Management Board Decision 11/2006, the new management board's rules of procedure do not say anything about the procedure for negotiating and concluding working arrangements with international organisations.

to implementing the 'mother' working arrangements. In view of their features, Frontex's working arrangements are included in the category of international agreements of a technical-administrative nature, as opposed to the high-level (political) agreements covered by Article 218 TFEU.

The analysis of Frontex's former legal framework and practice suggests that the Agency's international cooperation tasks and actions remained overall within the scope of its mandate and are subject to sufficient supervision and conditions, in line with the present day *Meroni* requirements. As to Frontex's working arrangements specifically, the examination of these instruments revealed that they establish cooperation on a technical level between the Agency and its partners with a view to ensuring the full implementation of its regulatory framework. The plethora of formal and informal controls enabling the Commission, the Council and the Member States to steer and oversee closely the Agency's international cooperation seemed to be capable of ensuring the required consistency with the overall priorities in the EU external action area and to preserve the Commission's role under Articles 17 TEU and 220 TFEU. In particular the involvement of the Commission in Frontex's international cooperation provided an effective guarantee that the working arrangements of the Agency were in line with Union's external relations policy and with 'Article 218 TFEU' agreements. Accordingly, Frontex's working arrangements concluded so far as technical-administrative agreements seem to be generally in line with *Meroni* requirements and the principle of institutional balance.

Regarding the Agency's legal status as a global actor, the plethora of formal and informal conditions and controls limiting Frontex's international cooperation indicates that the Agency did not act as an independent entity on the international plane. Accordingly, although it was equipped with legal personality and formal autonomy, as well as international cooperation tasks by its former Basic Regulation, Frontex did not have international legal personality. Instead, Frontex acted on the global level as an EU body entailing that, in principle, its actions are attributable in the last instance to the Union, although under certain circumstances the Agency may pursue cooperation both on behalf of the EU and of (some) Member States. Thus, considering that the legal status of Frontex on the international plane was that of an 'EU agent', contrary to the Common Approach on EU agencies, its working arrangements are to be considered as being concluded ultimately on behalf of the Union.

The new Frontex Regulation largely maintains the design of the Agency's international dimension based on the previous legal framework, but at the same time it also expands Frontex's international cooperation 'toolbox' while reinforcing on paper the system of safeguards and controls over the Agency's international activities, including the working arrangements with third countries and international organisations. This suggests that, perhaps even more than before, Frontex will continue to pursue international cooperation as an 'EU agent', and that its international dimension will likely be in line with *Meroni* and institutional balance in external relations.

6 The case of Europol

6.1 Introduction*

Europol is one of the few EU agencies whose international cooperation record consists of cooperation agreements concluded with third countries and international organisations. From this perspective, Europol could be seen as an 'exemplary' case for the outer limits that EU agencies' international cooperation may reach. Europol is a peculiar EU agency acting within a specific legal-policy environment, and having the 'pedigree' of an intergovernmental body established by the Member States *via* a convention.[1] This 'intergovernmental pedigree' has been reflected also in the legal framework based on Council Decision 2009/371/JHA (Europol Council Decision)[2] as regards the Agency's international cooperation. The new Europol Regulation,[3] applicable as of 1 May 2017, redesigns the Agency's international cooperation framework. Arguably, one important change concerns Europol's international cooperation instruments, in that the Agency will conclude in the future working and administrative arrangements instead of cooperation agreements as provided by the Europol Council Decision. However, according to the new Europol Regulation, the legal framework based on Council Decision 2009/371/JHA remained in force until 1 May 2017[4] and, moreover, the rules and measures adopted by the Agency's management board based on the former Europol Council Decision remain in force also after 1 May 2017.[5] Importantly, the new Europol Regulation also preserves the validity of Europol's cooperation agreements concluded *prior* to 1 May 2017.[6]

Against this background the aim of this chapter is twofold. The first aim is to provide an assessment of Europol's international dimension based on its former legal

* Florin Coman-Kund, 'Europol's International Cooperation between "Past Present" and "Present Future": Reshaping the External Dimension of EU Police Cooperation' (2018) 1 *Europe and the World* (forthcoming).

1 Convention based on art K.3 of the Treaty on the European Union, on the establishment of a European Police Office (Europol Convention) [1995] OJ C316/1.

2 Council Decision 2009/371/JHA of 6 April 2009 establishing the European Police Office (Europol) [2009] OJ L131/37.

3 Regulation (EU) 2016/794 of the European Parliament and of the Council of 11 May 2016 on the European Union Agency for Law Enforcement Cooperation (Europol) and replacing and repealing Council Decisions 2009/371/JHA, 2009/934/JHA, 2009/935/JHA, 2009/936/JHA and 2009/968/JHA [2016] OJ L135/53.

4 Art 77(2) of Regulation 2016/794.

5 ibid art 76.

6 ibid art 71(2).

framework and its international cooperation practice. This is motivated by the fact that Europol's international instruments concluded under the former legal framework remain valid bases for cooperation, but also by the fact the new Europol Regulation amends the Agency's international dimension in response to perceived legal problems and shortcomings rooted in the Europol Council Decision. Hence, it is examined whether Europol's international cooperation mandate, tasks and activities under the former Europol Council Decision were fully compatible with Union's constitutional framework and principles, in particular after Lisbon. Secondly, the chapter offers a fresh appraisal of Europol's redesigned international dimension based on the new Europol Regulation with a view to mapping prospectively its legal effects and potential problems regarding Europol's operation as a global actor, and to assess the way in which it addresses crucial aspects of the Agency's international cooperation as compared to the former Europol legal framework.

The chapter begins with an overview of the legal-policy context relevant for the study of Europol as a global actor (section 6.2). This encompasses sketching the relevant legal and institutional framework in the area of police cooperation and focusing on the external dimension of the EU police cooperation area, in order to understand the wider framework of Europol's international activities. Additionally, the evolution and design of the Agency's general mandate are mapped out in order to understand Europol's profile (section 6.3). Subsequently, the international dimension of the Agency according to the Europol Council Decision is scrutinised addressing both the formal legal framework for the Agency's international cooperation and its international practice. Next, Europol's international dimension according to the new Europol Regulation is examined (section 6.4). Section 6.5 provides an assessment of Europol's international dimension with regard to the legal nature and effects of its international cooperation instruments, the legal status of the Agency as a global actor, and as concerns the compatibility of its international dimension with the Union's relevant legal-institutional framework.

6.2 The policy and legal-institutional environment of Europol

6.2.1 Union's legal and institutional framework in the police cooperation area

As is the case for Frontex, the *legal-policy context* relevant for analysing Europol is the former Justice and Home Affairs (JHA) area, now the Area of Freedom, Security and Justice (AFSJ), which includes, among other fields, police cooperation in criminal matters. As one may expect, police cooperation between the Member States had been established at the European level well before it was formalised for the first time by the TEU. Police cooperation used to take place in an informal intergovernmental setting, when the representatives of the Member States would meet secretly in *ad hoc* committees, and would adopt decisions and carry out activities away from the public eye and legal scrutiny.[7] By including police cooperation in the 'third pillar', the Treaty of

7 See Steve Peers, 'Governance and the Third Pillar: The Accountability of Europol' in Deirdre M Curtin and Ramses A Wessel (eds), *Good Governance and the European Union. Reflections on Concepts, Institutions and Substance* (Intersentia 2005) 254. See also Conny Rijken, 'Legal and

Maastricht maintained its intergovernmental nature, while, at the same time, it subjected this field to a more formalised institutional framework, mechanisms and instruments.[8] At the same time, the TEU referred explicitly to a European Police Office (Europol) for the purpose of organising an EU-wide system for information exchange, but it did not specify further its legal status and tasks.[9] The dominant actors with regard to decision-making and implementation were clearly the Member States and the Council, while the European Parliament and the Commission were assigned a rather 'decorative' role.[10] The TEU listed joint actions, joint positions, and, especially relevant for Europol, conventions as the formal decision-making instruments in the JHA area.[11] All these instruments were to be adopted by the Council acting unanimously.[12] Additionally, the conventions needed to be adopted by the Member States according to their constitutional requirements.[13]

The Treaty of Amsterdam gave a boost to police cooperation, although this field remained within the diminished 'third pillar'.[14] Closer cooperation between police forces, customs authorities and other authorities of the Member States, both directly and through Europol, was seen as instrumental for achieving a high degree of safety within the area of freedom, security and justice.[15] The Treaty of Amsterdam was more concrete than that by providing the lines along which such cooperation should be enabled. Those included: (1) operational cooperation between the competent authorities of the Member States with regard to the prevention, detection and investigation of criminal offences; (2) collection, storage, processing, analysis and exchange of information, particularly through Europol; (3) cooperation in training, exchange of liaison officers, secondments, equipment and research; and (4) evaluation of investigative techniques in relation to the detection of serious organised crime.[16] Moreover, with regard to Europol specifically, the Treaty tasked the Council with advancing cooperation through this structure and enacting a series of measures and actions in order to enable it to fulfil its role.[17] These provisions introduced by the Treaty of

Technical Aspects of Co-operation between Europol, Third States, and Interpol' in Vincent Kronenberger (ed), *The European Union and the International Legal Order: Discord or Harmony?* (Asser Press 2001) 578–79.

8 ex art K 1 TEU. See Peers (n 7) 254.

9 ex art K 1 TEU.

10 See Peers (n 7) 254. Thus, the Commission kept a right of initiative together with the Member States in some of the JHA cooperation areas, excluding, however, the area of police cooperation. The European Parliament was granted a general right of information and consultation (on principal aspects), as well as the possibility to ask questions and make recommendations (ex art K 6 TEU).

11 ex art K 3(2) TEU.

12 ex art K 4(3) TEU.

13 ex art K 3(2)(c) TEU.

14 The 'leftovers' of the third pillar were included in Title VI TEU 'Provisions on Police and Judicial cooperation in criminal matters', whereas asylum, migration, border controls and judicial cooperation in civil matters became Title IV TEC. See on this Steve Peers, *EU Justice and Home Affairs Law* (OUP 2011) 18; Georges Rauchs and Daniel J Koenig, 'Europol' in Daniel J Koenig and Dilip K Das (eds), *International Police Cooperation. A World Perspective* (Lexington Books 2001) 47–48.

15 TEU art 29 (ex K 1). See also Alexandra de Moor and Gert Vermeulen, 'The Europol Council Decision: Transforming Europol into an Agency of the European Union' (2010) 47 CML Rev 1089, 1091.

16 Art 30(1) TEU (ex art K 2).

17 Art 30(2) TEU. See also Peers (n 14) 865.

Amsterdam need to be seen in a wider context and require one step back to 1995 when a Convention establishing Europol had been drawn up by the Council and was being adopted by the Member States under Article K 3 TEU. Last but not least, the Treaty of Amsterdam slightly consolidated the position of the Commission and of the European Parliament in the area of police cooperation.[18] The Commission was granted a right of initiative in this field,[19] whereas the European Parliament's right of consultation was further enhanced.[20]

The Lisbon Treaty brought the fields from the former 'third pillar' within Title V of the TFEU, together with the other elements of the AFSJ.[21] The impact on the area of police cooperation is important since it became a shared competence,[22] and all regular EU instruments and decision-making procedures are applicable in this field. This entails *inter alia* a stronger role for the European Parliament, in particular when the ordinary legislative procedure is used, and full jurisdiction for the CJEU. It should be noted, however, that Protocol 36 on Transitional Provisions preserved the effects of the measures that were adopted before the entry into force of the Lisbon Treaty under former Title VI TEU, and exempted them from the full jurisdiction of the CJEU and from the Commission's powers under the infringement procedure for a period of five years.[23] Moreover, the provisions of Chapter 5 'Police cooperation' (Articles 87–89 TFEU) feature some intergovernmental elements. This is obvious in particular for operational cooperation issues, with regard to which all relevant measures are subject to a special legislative procedure requiring unanimity in the Council and where the European Parliament is only consulted.[24] Another intergovernmental twist concerns the external dimension of the AFSJ (including police cooperation), in which the Member States still have the possibility to conclude international agreements on their own.[25]

18 See Estella Baker and Christopher Harding, 'From Past Imperfect to Future Perfect? A Longitudinal Study of the Third Pillar' (2009) 34 EL Rev 25, 31 and Peers (n 7) 255.

19 Art 34(2) TEU (ex art K 6); see also Peers (n 14) 25.

20 Except for the common positions, the European Parliament had to be consulted with regard to all the instruments adopted within the 'third pillar', art 39 TEU (ex art K 11); see also Peers (n 14) 25.

21 Title V 'Area of Freedom, Security and Justice' of the TFEU comprises five chapters: 1. General Provisions; 2. Policies on border checks, asylum and immigration; 3. Judicial cooperation in civil matters; 4. Judicial cooperation in criminal matters; 5. Police cooperation.

22 Art 4(2)(j) TFEU.

23 Protocol (No 36) on Transitional Provisions, arts 9–10. For a detailed analysis regarding the legal implications of Protocol 36, see Peers (n 14) 61–64. The five-year transitional period ended officially on 1 December 2014; see also Valsamis Mitsilegas, Sergio Carrera and Katharina Eisele, 'The End of the Transitional Period for Police and Criminal Justice Measures Adopted before the Lisbon Treaty. Who Monitors Trust in the European Justice Area? Study for the LIBE Committee (PE 509.998) 2014 8 ‹http://www.europarl.europa.eu/RegData/etudes/STUD/2014/509998/IPOL_STU%282014%29509998_EN.pdf›.

24 Arts 87(3) and 89 TFEU; see also Peers (n 14) 43 and 869–71.

25 See Declaration 36 on Article 218 of the Treaty on the Functioning of the European Union concerning the negotiation and the conclusion of international agreements by Member States relating to the area of freedom, security and justice (2012) OJ C326/351. However, agreements concluded by the Member States in the AFSJ need to abide by the requirements derived from the principle of sincere cooperation; in particular, they must be without prejudice to the Union's exclusive external competence and should not deviate from EU law, see Peers (n 14) 129.

Just like in the case of Frontex,[26] the *policy context* relevant for assessing Europol encompasses the five-year multiannual programmes which set Union's agenda in the AFSJ.[27] Since the very beginning, these planning instruments have also addressed the priorities and milestones for the police cooperation area, and within this field, also for Europol.[28] Within this framework,[29] there are other important policy-political instruments affecting Europol's annual and multiannual strategy and activities such as the Union's Internal Security Strategy[30] and the EU Policy Cycle setting Union's priorities for the fight against serious and organised crime.[31]

As regards the *actors* involved in the police cooperation area the situation is very similar to that of Frontex.[32] Thus, on the policy level, the main actors involved are the Council (the JHA Council), the European Council,[33] and the Commission. As concerns legislative decision-making and implementation, the Council and the Commission are again the main players, whereas the European Parliament gained an enhanced legislative role, subject to variations depending on whether the particular measure is adopted according to the ordinary[34] or to a special[35] legislative procedure.

26 See ch 4.

27 Including the Tampere Programme (1999); the Hague Programme (2004); the Stockholm Programme (2009); and the 'Strategic guidelines' for the AFSJ (2014).

28 See Peers (n 14) 866–68. For instance, the 'Strategic guidelines' for the AFSJ area between 2015–2020 call for a reinforced coordination role of Europol in the police cooperation area, in particular with regard to the review of the EU internal security strategy, the improvement of cross-border information exchanges, and the development of a comprehensive approach to cyber security and cybercrime – European Council, Conclusions, 26/27 June 2014 (EUCO 79/14) 5.

29 For instance, the Stockholm Programme called for the definition of a '(. . .) comprehensive Union internal security' encompassing 'stringent cooperation between the Union agencies including further improving the information exchange'. This broad objective has been implemented in the first place through the Union's Internal Security Strategy (ISS) adopted by the Council in 2010. This document lists the common threats as well as principles and strategic guidelines to address such threats. Whereas most of these threats relate to terrorism and criminality, an essential element to implement the ISS further is the EU Policy Cycle for organised and serious international crime. This was conceived as a four-step instrument aimed at dealing with criminal threats. It includes both policy (policy development, as well as policy setting and decision-making by the Council) and operational aspects (threat assessments and operational action plans) and involves various actors, see Joanna Parkin 'EU Home Affairs Agencies and the Construction of EU Internal Security' (2012) CEPS Paper 53/2012 3–5 ‹https://www.ceps.eu/system/files/No%2053%20JP%20EU%20Home%20Affairs%20Agencies.pdf›.

30 The first EU Internal Security Strategy had been adopted by the Council in 2010; a renewed ISS for the period 2015–2020 has been approved by the Council in 2015, see Council, 'Draft Conclusions on the Renewed European Union Internal Security Strategy 2015–2020', Brussels, 10 June 2015 (9798/15).

31 The first EU Policy Cycle has been adopted for a period of two years, see Council, 'Draft Conclusions on setting the EU's priorities for the fight against organised crime between 2011 and 2013', Brussels, 6 June 2011 (11050/11). The next EU Policy Cycles have been adopted for a four-year period (between 2014–2017 and between 2017–2021), see Europol Programming Document 2017–2019 8 ‹https://www.europol.europa.eu/publications-documents/europol-programming-document›.

32 See ch 4.

33 eg art 68 TFEU.

34 eg Arts 87(2) and 88(2) TFEU.

35 Arts 87(3) and 89 TFEU.

Two additional observations are relevant in the context of police cooperation. First, the standing committees set up within the Council, such as CATS, COSI, Enforcement Working Party (ENFOPOL), Counter-terrorism Coordinator (CTC)[36] are influential in shaping EU policy and the legal agenda, and they may be seen as reinforcing the intergovernmental trend in the police cooperation area.[37] Secondly, the Member States remain core actors in the police cooperation area, as they are involved in policy-making, legislation and the implementation of Union's policies and measures in AFSJ.

6.2.2 The international (external) dimension of the Union's police cooperation area

As already mentioned, the objectives set in the AFSJ cannot be fully achieved only by internal measures and actions.[38] This has prompted the gradual development of an external dimension to the AFSJ that is instrumental to the attainment of its objectives as formalised in the Founding Treaties and further elaborated in various policy and legal instruments.[39]

Several general aspects characterising the external dimension of the overall AFSJ and, as such, also applicable to the police cooperation field, are relevant here. First, like with border management, the starting point for discussing international aspects in the police cooperation area are the multiannual programmes covering the overall AFSJ area,[40] together with the 2005 Strategy regarding specifically the external dimension of the AFSJ.[41] In order to ensure in particular cooperation with third countries, the Strategy lists key priorities, underlying principles, tools and mechanisms, as well as task division and interactions between the actors and structures involved. Another component of the external dimension of AFSJ, also touching upon the field of police cooperation are the strategic documents and action plans dealing with specific third countries and groups of third countries.[42] Such specific policy documents and action plans are set up in the framework of other EU external policies, such as enlargement, neighbourhood, or development cooperation, and they also enable cooperation in the area of prevention and combating crime.[43]

36 See Jörg Monar, 'The External Dimension of the EU's Area of Freedom, Security and Justice. Progress, Potential and Limitations after the Treaty of Lisbon' (2012) 1 Sieps 38–39 ‹http://www.sieps.se/en/publications/2012/the-external-dimension-of-the-eus-area-of-freedom-security-and-justice-20121/Sieps_2012_1›; Jorrit J Rijpma, 'Hybrid Agencification in the Area of Freedom, Security and Justice and its Inherent Tensions: The Case of Frontex' in Madalina Busuioc, Martijn Groenleer and Jarle Trondal (eds), *The Agency Phenomenon in the European Union: Emergence, Institutionalisation and Everyday Decision-making* (Manchester University Press 2012) 86.

37 Monar (n 36) 38. See specifically on COSI, Rijpma (n 36) 86.

38 See ch 4.

39 See Commission, 'Strategy on the External Dimension of the Area of Freedom, Security and Justice' (Communication) COM (2005) 491 final. See also Juan S Vara, 'The External Dimension of the Area of Freedom Security and Justice in the Lisbon Treaty' (2008) 10 European Journal of Law Reform 577–78.

40 Monar (n 36) 50.

41 Council, 'A Strategy for the External Dimension of JHA: Global Freedom, Security and Justice', 6 December 2005 (15446/05) 5. The Strategy also entrusts Europol and other AFSJ agencies with the task of enhancing appropriate operational cooperation with priority countries (p. 7).

42 See also ch 4.

43 Monar (n 36) 53–55 and 60–67.

Secondly, there are important legal aspects which impact upon the external dimension of the AFSJ and they also implicitly affect police cooperation. The Union has already concluded a number of multilateral and bilateral agreements dealing specifically or incidentally with AFSJ matters.[44] Such formal cooperation instruments establish various frameworks of cooperation with third countries and international organisations and need to be taken into account by the actors involved in the AFSJ.

Thirdly, as regards the EU actors involved in the AFSJ external dimension, the picture is very complex. However, in an attempt to capture the main elements, in particular in the context of police cooperation, one may discern the Council (the JHA Council), the Commission and the Member States as steering actors, followed by EU agencies as supportive actors on the technical-operational level, and more marginally the High Representative, the EEAS, and the European Parliament.[45] The Member States remain very much present, not only indirectly, through their representatives in the Council or in the management boards of the relevant EU agencies,[46] but also as actors on their own. In relation to this, it must be recalled that the Member States remain competent to conclude international agreements on AFSJ matters.[47] Good examples of such agreements, relevant particularly for the area of police cooperation, are the mutual legal assistance (MLA) treaties concluded by various Member States with third countries.[48] The persistence of such agreements appears to be motivated by the fact that, in spite of the developments at EU level, most operational powers and capacities remain with the Member States, and this also illustrates quite clearly the limits of the external dimension of AFSJ.[49]

Finally, a few specific features of the external dimension of the field of police cooperation need to be mentioned briefly for providing a more complete overview of the context relevant for Europol's international dimension. One such feature is the setting of strategic priorities through a mix of policy and operational instruments. For instance, the EU Policy Cycle, adopted by the Council since 2011 and defining 'a range of external objectives in relation to internal priorities'[50] is based on the Organised Crime Threat Assessment (OCTA) and, more recently, on the Serious and Organised Crime Threat Assessment (SOCTA), which is an operational instrument prepared by

44 Jörg Monar, 'The EU's Growing External Role in the AFSJ Domain: Factors, Framework and Forms of Action' (2014) 27 Cambridge Review of International Affairs 147, 159–64; see also Vara (n 39) 577–82.

45 See Council, '2011 JHA External Relations Trio Programme', 4 July 2011 (12004/11) 23; Council, 'A Strategy for the External Dimension of JHA' (n 41) 7–8. The European Parliament, however, had made use at times of its post-Lisbon reinforced 'external relations' prerogatives, for instance, by rejecting on 11 February 2010 the so-called SWIFT Interim Agreement between the EU and USA granting access to US law enforcement authorities to financial data managed by the international SWIFT bank consortium; for more details see Monar (n 44) 147, 156.

46 The following EU agencies are involved in the AFSJ: Europol, Eurojust, Cepol, Frontex, EASO, eu-LISA, but also FRA, ENISA, EMCDDA, ETF; see Commission, 'The Global Approach to Migration and Mobility' (Communication) COM (2011) 743 final 10.

47 See Monar (n 36) 59–60.

48 ibid 59. Monar offers also a concrete example of an agreement concluded in 2008 between Germany and US on access to biometric data and spontaneous sharing of data regarding known and suspected terrorists: Monar (n 44) 162.

49 ibid 60.

50 ibid 52.

Europol.[51] Another important element of the external dimension in the field of police cooperation consists of the specific agreements concluded by the EU with third countries regarding cooperation on criminal justice and law enforcement.[52] Yet another distinctive element of the external dimension of police cooperation are the numerous cooperation agreements concluded by Europol with third countries and international organisations with a view in particular to implement the exchange of various types of information.

6.3 Europol's profile as an EU agency

6.3.1 Europol's legal design and incremental evolution

The official genesis of Europol can be traced back to the Treaty of Maastricht, which provided for an explicit legal basis to set up a European Police Office (Europol) in the framework of an EU system of exchanging information in the field of police cooperation.[53] The next step was the creation of the Europol Drugs Unit (EDU) by ministerial agreement,[54] which became operational in 1994. Designed as a non-operational unit devoid of legal personality, EDU had as its main function to ensure information exchange (including personal information) on drug trafficking and money laundering among the Member States.[55] The mandate of the EDU was extended twice, in 1995[56] and 1996,[57] before being replaced by Europol.

Europol was established on the basis of Article Kl TEU by the 1995 Europol Convention[58] and became operational on 1 July 1999. This prompted the conclusion that Europol was not really an EU agency but a 'fully fledged international organisation' equipped with 'full legal personality, including the capacity to enter into binding agreements under international law'[59] or at least a 'European organisation *sui generis*

51 See, for instance, Council, 'Draft Conclusions', 6 June 2011 (n 31) 1; Europol's OCTAs and SOCTAs are available at ‹https://www.europol.europa.eu/activities-services/main-reports/serious-and-organised-crime-threat-assessment%20-%20fndtn-tabs-0-bottom-2?rt[]=283›.

52 See Monar (n 36) 58. Such are the mutual legal assistance agreements concluded with USA and Japan, the Terrorist Finance Tracking Programme (TFTP) Agreement between USA and EU, and the Passenger Name Record (PNR) Agreements with USA, Australia and Canada.

53 ex art K 1 TEU.

54 Ministerial agreement on the establishment of Europol Drugs Unit (2 June 1993). See also the preamble of Joint Action 95/73/JHA of 10 March 1995 adopted by the Council on the basis of Article K.3 of the Treaty on European Union concerning the Europol Drugs Unit [1995] OJ L62/1.

55 Ministerial agreement on the establishment of Europol Drugs Unit (2 June 1993); see also Peers (n 14) 931.

56 Joint Action 95/73/JHA.

57 Joint Action 96/748/JHA of 16 December 1996 adopted by the Council on the basis of Article K.3 of the Treaty on European Union extending the mandate given to the Europol Drugs Unit [1996] OJ L342/4.

58 The Europol Convention can be best described as an intergovernmental agreement concluded by the Member States within the framework of the EU; see Rijken (n 7) 582–83.

59 Dick Heimans, 'The External Relations of Europol – Political, Legal and Operational Considerations' in Berndt Martenczuk and Servaas van Thiel (eds), *Justice, Liberty and Security: New Challenges for EU External Relations* (VUBPRESS 2008) 369.

of the EU'.[60] The centre of gravity of Europol's mandate was on information processing and exchange tasks.[61] Although the tasks of Europol have been gradually expanded including the possibility to participate in joint investigation teams (JITs), this body remained essentially a non-operational support organisation for the enforcement authorities of the Member States.[62] This role of Europol has been enabled in particular through the liaison officers (LOs) posted by the Member States at Europol's headquarters, as well as through the Europol National Units established in the Member States as an interface between this body and the national competent authorities.[63]

After ten years of operation as an intergovernmental body, Europol's legal framework had been replaced by Council Decision 2009/371/JHA (Europol Council Decision). This was an important milestone in the evolution of Europol with implications for its legal status and operation. Most notably, although it kept its legal personality, Europol is transformed into an EU agency, entailing that it is financed from the EU budget and subjected to all relevant EU rules.[64] However, with regard to its mandate and main tasks, its governance and control, the Europol Council Decision implemented overall cosmetic changes.[65] The same holds for the international dimension of Europol. The Europol Council Decision together with the relevant implementing measures[66] basically maintained the *status quo* from under the Europol Convention, including the Agency's capacity to conclude agreements with third countries and international organisations.[67]

An element impacting upon the current and future evolution of Europol, in particular as regards international cooperation, is the entry into force of the Lisbon Treaty. Whereas Protocol 36 attached to the TFEU still allowed the Agency to operate under its legal framework based on the Europol Council Decision, Article 88 TFEU (Europol's Treaty legal basis) ensures that in the future the legal framework of the Agency would be determined by regulations adopted by the Council and the European Parliament according to the ordinary legislative procedure. It should be also noted that Article 88(2)(a) TFEU foresees Europol's international dimension closely linked to the Agency's tasks regarding data collection, processing and exchange.

Both the former Europol Council Decision[68] and Article 88(1) TFEU emphasise Europol's function as a supportive structure for the enforcement authorities of the Member States. Europol is designed as an assisting body of the real operational actors at the state level, and not as a 'European FBI' with fully fledged investigative

60 Rijken (n 7) 583.
61 Heimans (n 59) 369–70.
62 ibid.
63 ibid.
64 Peers (n 14) 932.
65 Such were, for instance, the possibility for Europol to establish new systems processing data (art 10), and the introduction of the Agency's task to provide analytical support to Member States in connection with major international events (art 5(1)(e)), see for more details Moor and Vermeulen (n 15) 1097–104 and 1120–21.
66 Council Decision 2009/934/JHA of 30 November 2009 adopting the implementing rules governing Europol's relations with partners including the exchange of personal data and classified information, [2009] OJ L325/6, and Council Decision 2009/935/JHA of 30 November 2009 determining the list of third States and organisations with which Europol shall conclude agreements [2009] OJ L325/12.
67 Moor and Vermeulen (n 15) 1121.
68 Art 3 of the Europol Council Decision.

and enforcement powers. Compared to the previous situation, the current Europol Council Decision extends the scope of the Agency's competence from 'organised' to 'serious crime',[69] although the latter is not defined. This introduces a certain degree of ambiguity as to the precise scope of the *ratione materiae* competence of the Agency.[70]

The main tasks entrusted to Europol by the former Europol Council Decision could be divided into three main categories: information related tasks;[71] strategic analysis and threat assessment tasks;[72] and semi-operational tasks[73] (eg the possibility to ask competent authorities of the Member States to initiate investigations and to participate in joint investigation teams).[74] Of all the three categories, the information-related tasks define the 'core business' of the Agency.[75] In particular, the ability to facilitate the exchange of information between the Member States, to exchange information with third countries and international organisations, as well as the capacity for information processing confer added value on Europol.[76]

The new Europol Regulation based on Article 88 TFEU maintains the core principles upon which the role and functioning of Europol are premised, but also brings some noteworthy novelties. First, it expands Europol's *ratione materiae* competence by supplementing the list of serious crimes, and by adding 'forms of crime which affect a common interest covered by a Union policy'.[77] Secondly, it enhances Europol's operational capacity by formalising the Agency's power to set up specialised centres for combating crime such as the European Cybercrime Centre, and by enabling the Agency to make internet referrals to online service providers.[78] Thirdly, it further consolidates Europol's core information-related tasks by establishing an obligation for the Member States to provide information to the Agency.[79] Fourthly, it aims to strengthen through the involvement of the European Data Protection Supervisor (EDPS) the supervision over Europol's processing of personal data,[80] and to increase parliamentary supervision over Europol's activities.[81] Overall, the new Regulation can be seen as an important step towards transforming Europol from a 'special' agency into a 'regular' EU agency, entailing also a more influential role for the Commission.[82]

69 ibid art 4(1).

70 See Moor and Vermeulen (n 15) 1121; Elspeth Guild, Sergio Carrera, Leonhard den Hertog and Joanna Parkin, 'Implementation of the EU Charter of Fundamental Rights and its Impact on EU Home Affairs Agencies. Frontex, Europol and the European Asylum Support Office' Study for the European Parliament, Committee on Civil Liberties, Justice and Home Affairs (LIBE) (PE 453.196/2011) 26 ‹http://www.europarl.europa.eu/meetdocs/2009_2014/documents/libe/dv/02_study_fundamental_rights_/02_study_fundamental_rights_en.pdf›.

71 Art 5(1)(a)–(c) and (e) of the Europol Council Decision.

72 ibid art 5(1)(f).

73 ibid arts 5(1)(d) and 6.

74 See Guild and others (n 70) 27–29.

75 Moor and Vermeulen (n 15) 1099.

76 Guild and others (n 70) 27.

77 See Annex I and art 3(1) of Regulation 2016/794.

78 ibid art 4(1)(l) and (m).

79 ibid recital (13) and art 7(6).

80 ibid recitals (50)–(54) and art 43.

81 ibid recital (58) and arts 51–52.

82 See, for instance, arts 12 and 68 of Regulation 2016/794.

6.3.2 Governance of Europol

The leading structure of Europol consists formally of the management board and the director. The management board is the organ responsible for '[t]he greater part of the steering of the agency',[83] and is composed of one representative of each Member State plus one representative of the Commission.[84] With some idiosyncrasies, the main powers and tasks of the Europol management board are very similar to those of other EU agencies. In this regard, it should be noted that the management board can only adopt a list of candidates for the post of director and deputy directors, which is then submitted to the Council for the final appointment decision.[85] The management board fulfils the normal tasks that similar organs fulfil in other EU agencies. For example, it adopts: (1) Europol's strategy; (2) the Agency's annual activity report and its annual work programme; (3) the financial regulation and rules regarding the staff of the Agency; (4) the budget of the Agency and fulfils other tasks related to the budget; and (5) its own rules of procedure and other internal rules.[86]

The director is in charge of the daily management of the Agency. In particular, s/he prepares and implements the decisions adopted by the management board. Furthermore, s/he takes the appropriate decisions in order to ensure the functioning of the Agency, exercises the powers of appointing authority with respect to the staff of the Agency, prepares and implements the budget and the work programme of the Agency.[87] The executive director is accountable to the management board,[88] though s/he can be dismissed only by the Council. Notably, the director is required to report regularly to the management board as concerns the implementation of Europol's priorities,[89] and has a duty to prepare the annual activity reports and to submit them to the management board.[90]

A particular feature of Europol's governance, compared to most EU agencies, was the Joint Supervisory Body (JSB). Established as an independent body outside the structure of the Agency, the JSB was Europol's data protection control authority.[91] It was composed of representatives of national supervisory bodies, and its main task was to review all the relevant activities of the Agency in order to ensure that the rights of the individuals are not violated by the storage and processing of data held by the Agency.[92] It should be added that JSB also played an important role concerning all international cooperation activities of Europol involving personal data and particularly

83 Moor and Vermeulen (n 15) 1113; Peers (n 14) 932.
84 Art 10 (1) of Regulation 2016/794.
85 ibid arts 11(1)(j) and 54(2).
86 ibid art 11(1).
87 ibid art 16(5).
88 ibid art 16(1).
89 ibid art 11(1)(o).
90 ibid art 11(1)(g). In practice, it appears that in the past the fulfilment of the reporting duties by the director has been treated quite strictly by the management board, with reports being rejected, redrafted and then rejected again, see Madalina Busuioc, Deirdre Curtin and Martijn Groenleer, 'Agency Growth between Autonomy and Accountability: the European Police Office as a 'Living Institution' (2011) 18 *JEPP* 859, 859–60.
91 Heimans (n 59) 371.
92 Art 34 of the Europol Council Decision.

in preparing Europol's operational agreements.[93] With the new Europol Regulation, the role of the JSB has been taken over by the EDPS.[94]

6.4 Europol's international dimension

6.4.1 Europol's international cooperation legal framework and practice under Council Decision 2009/371/JHA

6.4.1.1 Mandate, tasks and instruments

The legal framework for Europol's international cooperation activities was provided primarily by Article 23 of the Europol Council Decision complemented by Council Decision 2009/934/JHA. Article 23(1) Europol Council Decision stipulated clearly that Europol's international cooperation activities were instrumental to the core mandate and tasks of the Agency.

The following paragraphs of Article 23 indicated, with more precision, the core elements of Europol's international dimension. First, it was made clear that the essential way for the Agency to formalise its relationship with partners outside the EU was by concluding cooperation agreements. Various scenarios were also dealt with regarding the possibility to exchange information related to crimes within the Agency's competence with non-EU recipients, subject to quite restrictive conditions, before the entry into force or even in the absence of an agreement. Secondly, this provision exhibited that exchange of information was the main concern of such instruments.[95] Furthermore, Council Decision 2009/934/JHA touched mostly on the issue of information exchange between Europol and its external partners.[96] Additionally, it introduced a distinction between operational and strategic agreements concluded by Europol with its partners, depending on the information which could be exchanged under each type of instrument.[97] Thirdly, the Europol Council Decision provided two important limitations on Europol's international cooperation. Thus, according to Article 23(2) in combination with Article 26(1) of the Europol Council Decision the Agency was bound to conclude agreements only with third countries and international organisations put on a 'list' drawn up by the Council, on the proposal of Europol's management board.[98] Furthermore, Article 23(2) subjected each Europol's agreement to *prior*

93 ibid art 23.

94 Art 43 of Regulation 2016/794. The EDPS has been established on the basis of Regulation (EC) 45/2001 on the protection of individuals with regard to the processing of personal data by the Community institutions and bodies and on the free movement of such data [2001] OJ L8/1.

95 Art 23(3)–(9) of the Europol Council Decision.

96 Title III, arts 8–20 of Council Decision 2009/934/JHA; 13 of the 21 articles of the Decision were concerned with conditions and details regarding receipt and transmission of information by Europol including onward transmission of data, correction and deletion of information and personal data, responsibility for the transmission of data.

97 Art 1(g) and (h) of Council Decision 2009/ 934/JHA. Whereas strategic agreements allow exchanging various kinds of information regarding crimes within Europol's mandate except for personal data, operational agreements include also the exchange of personal data.

98 The 'list' took the form of Council Decision 2009/935/JHA, and included initially 25 third countries and 3 organisations. The Council list was amended in May 2014, when four third countries were added (Brazil, Georgia, Mexico and the United Arab Emirates) – see art 1 of

approval by the Council. This originates in the Agency's intergovernmental 'pedigree' under the old Europol Convention,[99] and seems to reflect Council's role regarding EU treaty-making, as well as the need to rationalise Europol's international cooperation '(. . .) in order to ensure consistency with the general policy of the Union'.[100]

6.4.1.2 The procedure for Europol's cooperation agreements

As to the internal processes enabling Europol to fulfil its international cooperation mandate, the procedure for negotiating and concluding international agreements was to be ranked at the top. Essential elements of the procedure for negotiating and concluding Europol's international agreements were mentioned in Article 23 of the Europol Council Decision, but the detailed procedural steps were listed in Articles 5–6 of Council Decision 2009/934/JHA. The procedure included the following milestones with regard to all Europol's agreements:

- the negotiations with a third country or international organisation included on the Council's 'list' were carried out by the executive director, supported by the relevant internal units of Europol[101]
- after the conclusion of negotiations, the executive director had to submit the draft agreement to the management board for endorsement[102]
- the draft agreement endorsed by the management board was then submitted to the Council for approval (which decided after having consulted the management board)[103]
- the agreement was concluded (signed by the executive director) after Council's approval.[104]

Whereas for strategic agreements the steps mentioned previously were sufficient, for operational agreements there were additional procedural requirements.[105] First, before initiating negotiations, Europol had to carry out 'an assessment of the existence of an adequate level of data protection ensured by the third party'.[106] This assessment was forwarded to the management board, which sent it to the Joint Supervisory Body (JSB) for an opinion. After receiving the opinion of the JSB, the management board decided whether to authorise the executive director to start negotiations on an operational agreement.[107] Secondly, after the negotiations, the draft agreement was

Council Implementing Decision 2014/269/EU of 6 May 2014 amending Decision 2009/935/JHA as regards the list of third states and organisations with which Europol shall conclude agreements, [2014] OJ L138/104.

99 See in particular art 42 of the Convention, and Council Act of 3 November 1998 laying down rules governing Europol's external relations with third States and non-European Union related bodies, [1999] OJ C26/19.

100 See recital (18) of the preamble to the Europol Council Decision.

101 Art 6(1) and (2) of Council Decision 2009/934/JHA.

102 ibid art 6(3).

103 ibid art 6(4).

104 ibid art 6(4). After Lisbon, the approval has taken the shape of a Council implementing decision.

105 See Emma Disley, Barrie Irving, William Hughes and Bhanu Patruni, 'Evaluation of the implementation of the Europol Council Decision and of Europol's activities' (Technical report), RAND Europe (2012) 113 (RAND Report).

106 Art 5(4) of Council Decision 2009/934/JHA.

107 ibid art 6(1).

submitted to the management board, which asked again for the opinion of the JSB, this time on the draft agreement.[108] The opinion of the Joint Supervisory Body was to be taken into account both by the management board when endorsing the draft agreement and by the Council when approving the agreement.[109]

What also needs to be mentioned with regard to all agreements concluded by Europol with third countries and international organisations was the duty imposed on the executive director to report regularly to the management board 'on the state of play of ongoing negotiations'.[110] The Council Decision establishing the 'list' of Europol's partners added to that a duty for the director to submit to the management board a progress report every six months with regard to the ongoing negotiations with third parties.[111] On top of the procedure for the conclusion of international agreements described above, these provisions further support the picture of a *quasi*-omnipotent management board which exercised crucial powers with regard to Europol's most important international cooperation instruments.

6.4.1.3 Europol's international dimension in practice

6.4.1.3.1 SETTING THE INTERNATIONAL COOPERATION PRIORITIES AND ACTIONS

Similar to other EU agencies, Europol's priorities are framed in a multiannual document adopted by the management board. The initial document laying down the Agency's multiannual strategic objectives post-Lisbon was 'Europol Strategy 2010–2014',[112] a new strategy having been adopted for the period 2016–2020.[113] Europol's priorities in the area of international cooperation are further developed in specific multiannual external strategies. Post-Lisbon, the Agency's international cooperation actions have been guided by Europol External Strategy 2010–2014.[114] Europol External Strategy 2010–2014 emphasised the supportive role of the Agency's international cooperation in its core business. Additionally, the Strategy highlighted the need for compliance of Europol's international dimension with the Union's overall objectives integrated within the external dimension of the AFSJ area.[115] Recently, a new external strategy defining the focus and steps to be taken towards enhancing cooperation with third countries and international organisations has been endorsed by the Europol's management board for the period 2017–2020.[116] The new strategy emphasises *inter alia* the

108 ibid art 6(3).
109 ibid art 6(3) and (4).
110 ibid art 7.
111 ibid art 1(3).
112 Europol Strategy 2010–2014 ‹https://www.europol.europa.eu/content/press/european-eod-network-meets-during-cyprus-presidency-1767›.
113 Europol Strategy 2016–2020 (2015) EDOC# 796794v19B ‹https://www.europol.europa.eu/content/europol-strategy-2016-2020›.
114 Europol External Strategy 2010–2014 (2010) EDOC # 434663. Pre-Lisbon, Europol had adopted own two-year external strategies starting with 2004; see Gregory Mounier, 'Europol: A New Player in the EU External Policy Field?' (2009) 10 Perspectives on European Politics and Society 582, 590.
115 Europol External Strategy 2010–2014 (n 114) 4.
116 Europol External Strategy 2017–2020 (2016) EDOC#865852v3.

essential role of various relevant EU policy documents such as the EU Global Strategy for the European Union's Foreign and Security Policy, the European Agenda in Security and the European Agenda on Migration in shaping Europol's external relations strategy.[117]

The overall planning of Europol's priorities concerning international cooperation could be depicted as mainly being operationally-driven, but also subject to policy-political influences.[118] First, although driven mostly by operational needs, setting the Agency's priorities was tightly restricted and controlled by the Council, and the Member States *via* the management board. As shown previously, while the freedom of Europol to conclude cooperation agreements was curtailed *ab initio* by the Council's 'list', the Agency's international cooperation priorities need to be endorsed by the Member States *via* the management board. Furthermore, the main mission of Europol according to the Europol Council Decision and its own perception was still to support the Member States, whilst the Agency was heavily dependent on the input coming from the latter for fulfilling its main task as an 'EU criminal information hub'.[119] In these circumstances, the preferences and operational needs of the Member States could not be easily discarded by the Agency, and the information exchange and consultations between the parties on a regular basis ensure that such needs and requirements are given consideration.

Secondly, the consistency between Europol's international cooperation priorities and the Union's operational and political needs and priorities including taking into account the sudden changes in the EU external action,[120] was guaranteed mainly by the Commission by virtue of its role to ensure[121] the management and consistency of Union's external relations.[122] Furthermore, Europol was briefed on the relevant EU priorities through its participation in Council committees such as JAIEX, COSI and CATS.[123] In this context, the Agency has been urged in practice by the Commission or the Council, based on wider policy/political considerations,[124] either to give priority to a certain third

117 ibid 1.

118 According to a Europol official, 'the setting of Europol's international strategy is a mix of (politically) predetermined elements and of operationally driven considerations', Interview 5, The Hague (29 January 2013).

119 See Europol Strategy 2010–2014 (n 112). See also Martijn Groenleer, *The Autonomy of European Union Agencies. A Comparative Study of Institutional Development* (D Phil thesis, Leiden University 2009) 296–99; Busuioc, Curtin and Groenleer (n 90) 861. According to a Europol official '(. . .) basically 99% of the information processed by the Agency comes from the Member States; as a result, the Agency has to support the Member States', Interview 13, The Hague (1 July 2013).

120 Interview 13 with a Europol official, The Hague (1 July 2013).

121 Arts 17(1) and 21(3) TEU.

122 This is in line with the Common Approach on EU agencies providing for Commission's role to oversee EU agencies' international cooperation, Joint Statement of the European Parliament, the Council of the EU and the European Commission on decentralised agencies of 19 July 2012 (Common Approach on EU agencies) para 25 ‹https://europa.eu/european-union/sites/europaeu/files/docs/body/joint_statement_and_common_ approach_2012_en.pdf›.

123 In these committees, the Agency normally informs the players on the progress of its international cooperation activities and strategy, but it may also receive input from the Commission and the Member States, Interview 13 with a Europol official, The Hague (1 July 2013).

124 An example pertains to the visa liberalisation process between the EU and certain third countries where one of the requirements was the conclusion of a cooperation agreement between that country and Europol, Interview 13 with a Europol official, The Hague (1 July 2013).

country or to postpone or speed up negotiations or the conclusion of an agreement. However, at times these policy-political priorities may have clashed with Europol's legal framework for international cooperation, for instance, when the Agency was asked to conclude an agreement with a third country which was not on the Council's 'list'.[125]

The previous account suggests that Europol's discretion was rather limited because of the restrictions laid down in the Agency's legal framework and the constraints imposed by its operational and political environment.[126]

6.4.1.3.2 EUROPOL'S FORMAL INTERNATIONAL COOPERATION INSTRUMENTS

Europol's former legal framework emphasised the cooperation agreements with third countries and international organisations as a central element of the international cooperation carried out by the Agency.[127] Furthermore, although they were not explicitly mentioned by its legal framework, Europol also concluded memoranda of understanding (MOUs) or arrangements with third countries and international organisations. As a rule, such instruments were enacted on the basis of the 'mother' cooperation agreements between the Agency and the third party concerned, and were intended to ensure the implementation thereof.[128] Interestingly, for the same purposes, sometimes the main cooperation agreements concluded by Europol required the conclusion of further special 'agreements' between the contracting parties.[129]

The (main) cooperation agreements

Terminology and types:

As mentioned previously, Council Decision 2009/934/JHA categorised Europol's cooperation agreements into two sub-categories: strategic and operational. Whilst the scope of Europol's strategic agreements is more limited in that they allow for the exchange of information, except for personal data, operational agreements also cover personal data. Put simply, the two types of agreements provide the 'toolbox' allowing

125 Such an example is the Commission's request to Europol to conclude a cooperation agreement with Andorra based on the Monetary Agreement 2011 concluded by the EU (represented by the Commission) with Andorra, although this third country was not included on the Council's 'list'; see art 8(1)(c) of Monetary Agreement between the European Union and the Principality of Andorra (2011) OJ C369/01. This awkward situation has been acknowledged during interviews with officials from Europol, the Council and the Commission.

126 See Busuioc, Curtin and Groenleer (n 90) 862.

127 Information exchange was also possible pending the entry into force or even in the absence of a cooperation agreement, but this was seen as the exception and was subject to important limitations and safeguards, see art 23 of the Europol Council Decision, in particular paragraphs (3)–(6) and (8). A Europol official admitted that personal information had been exchanged only a few times with the USA in the absence of a cooperation agreement in the aftermath of the 9/11 terrorist attacks, Interview 13, The Hague (1 July 2013).

128 Interviews 5 and 13 with Europol officials, The Hague (29 January and 1 July 2013).

129 The special implementing agreements concluded by Europol with its partners on the basis of the framework cooperation agreement, as well as the memoranda of understanding are not available on the Agency's website.

Europol to use one instrument or another depending on the level of trust in its partners: strategic agreements to establish formal cooperation with partners whose data protection system or human rights record might be problematic,[130] and operational agreements with close partners.

According to its own website,[131] Europol concluded 24 agreements: 21 with third countries, and 3 with the organisations mentioned by Council Decision 2009/935/JHA establishing the list of Europol's partners.[132] The same source indicates that Europol had concluded 18 operational agreements (17 with third countries[133] and one with Interpol) and 6 strategic agreements (4 with third countries[134] and the remaining two with UNODC and WCO). The Operational and Strategic Agreement with Liechtenstein was the first agreement fully initiated, negotiated and concluded under the Europol Council Decision.[135] Shortly before the entry into force of the new Europol Regulation, new operational and strategic agreements have been signed with Ukraine[136] and Georgia;[137] furthermore, strategic agreements have been concluded with the United Arab Emirates,[138] Brazil[139] and China.[140]

Wording, content and structure:

The wording of both strategic and operational agreements is characterised by prescriptive 'shall/will' clauses. Regarding the structure, both strategic and operational agreements include a preamble, a main body, and usually one or more annexes. The provisions of all the cooperation agreements are structured in articles.

130 Heimans (n 59) 382.

131 The list of cooperation agreements is available at Europol/Partners/External Cooperation ‹https://www.europol.europa.eu/content/page/external-cooperation-31›.

132 Interpol, United Nations Office on Drugs and Crime (UNODC) and World Customs Organisation (WCO).

133 Albania, Australia, Bosnia and Herzegovina, Canada, Colombia, Former Yugoslav Republic of Macedonia (FYROM), Georgia, Iceland, Liechtenstein, Moldova, Monaco, Montenegro, Norway, Serbia, Switzerland, Ukraine and the USA (Supplemental Agreement 2002).

134 China, Russian Federation, Turkey; though the 2001 agreement between USA and Europol is included under 'operational agreements' on Europol's website, for the purpose of this study it has been included in the category of 'strategic agreements' in view of its specific features.

135 Signed on 7 June 2013. The operational agreements concluded afterwards follow a similar format.

136 The Agreement on Operational and Strategic Cooperation with Ukraine has been signed on 14 December 2016, Europol/Newsroom ‹https://www.europol.europa.eu/newsroom/news/europol-and-ukraine-sign-agreement-to-tackle-cross-border-crime›. This agreement has replaced the previous strategic agreement between Ukraine and Europol.

137 The Agreement on Operational and Strategic Cooperation with Georgia has been signed on 4 April 2017, Europol/Newsroom ‹https://www.europol.europa.eu/newsroom/news/europol-and-georgia-sign-agreement-to-tackle-cross-border-crime-and-terrorism›.

138 The strategic agreement with UAE was signed on 7 September 2016, Europol/Newsroom ‹https://www.europol.europa.eu/newsroom/news/europol-and-united-arab-emirates-join-forces-in-fighting-cross-border-crime›.

139 The strategic agreement with Brazil has been signed on 11 April 2017, Europol/Newsroom ‹https://www.europol.europa.eu/newsroom/news/today-brazil-and-europol-signed-agreement-to-expand-cooperation-to-combat-cross-border-criminal-activities›.

140 The strategic agreement with China has been signed on 19 April 2017, Europol/Newsroom ‹https://www.europol.europa.eu/newsroom/news/europol-and-people%E2%80%99s-republic-of-china-join-forces-to-fight-transnational-crime›.

Strategic agreements include standard provisions pertaining to the purpose and scope of cooperation, as well as to practical aspects aimed at enabling cooperation between the parties. The core part of the agreements deals mostly with the exchange of operational, strategic and technical information relating to the areas of crime within Europol's mandate. Rules on the detailed procedures for information exchange, specific limitations and requirements, as well as confidentiality duties are included. The exchange of classified information is usually allowed, subject to a detailed procedure included in an annex to the agreement or, in the case of the latest strategic agreements, in a separate memorandum of understanding.[141] Other aspects normally included in the core part of the agreements cover issues such as the exchange of expertise and trainings. Importantly, the agreements provide for the possibility to assign liaison officers (LOs), subject to a separate liaison agreement[142] or memorandum of understanding.[143]

The final provisions of the strategic agreements usually cover dispute settlement, amendment procedures, entry into force, termination of the agreement, and the relationship with other international cooperation instruments. The newest strategic agreements include liability provisions for damages caused to the other party or to an individual as a result of unauthorised or incorrect information processing. Regarding dispute settlement, the agreements provide for 'friendly' and flexible procedures consisting of consultations and negotiations between the parties. The agreements with WCO and UNODC, as well as the coming strategic agreements with third countries provide for the right of a party to suspend its obligations under the agreement in case of breaches by the other party.[144]

The entry into force of the agreements is usually linked to the date on which the third country notifies Europol about the completion of its own internal procedures. The agreements stipulate that Europol may consent to amendments only after approval by the Council, thereby re-confirming that the Agency does not act fully independently in its relationship with international partners. According to the standard procedure, the termination of the agreements requires a written notification and a three-month notification period.

In addition to the strategic agreements, the *operational agreements* include detailed provisions on the procedures and obligations of the parties concerning the exchange, processing and handling of *personal data*, including conditions and restrictions for the onward transmission of the data exchanged with third parties.[145] Next, the operational agreements lay down a right for the individuals and private entities to have access to personal data concerning them that is processed under the agreement.[146] In view of their important role in facilitating the exchange of information, the agreements include normally more detailed provisions on LOs.[147] Additionally, these agreements usually comprise more elaborated provisions on the liability of the contracting parties, in particular for the damages caused to individuals as a result of errors in the exchange and processing of personal data. Operational agreements feature dispute settlement

141 eg art 13 of the Strategic Agreement with China.
142 eg the Strategic Agreement with USA (2001).
143 eg art 9 of the Strategic Agreement with Brazil.
144 Art 6 of the Agreement with WCO and art 7 of the Agreement with UNODC.
145 eg arts 8–9 of the Agreement with FYROM.
146 ibid art 7.
147 ibid arts 14–15.

procedures comprising at least consultations and negotiations as well as the right for the contracting parties to suspend the application of the agreement,[148] while some provide for arbitration by a tribunal of arbitrators whose decision is final and binding.[149]

The procedure for the negotiation and conclusion of the cooperation agreements:

One important practical aspect related to the initiation, negotiation and conclusion of cooperation agreements was the duration of the whole process. Whilst for strategic agreements, which were less problematic, the duration of the procedure was fourteen months on average,[150] for operational agreements it usually took between three and five years.[151]

In practice, the initiation of contacts with potential partners started after receiving a request, which was normally channelled through the management board.[152] The process was initiated by sending a data protection questionnaire to the envisaged partner country or organisation in order to collect information with a view to determining whether there was an adequate level of data protection.[153] After receiving the input on the questionnaire, a data protection study visit or a confidentiality study visit was made by a Europol delegation to the country or organisation concerned.[154] Following the visit, a data protection report was drafted and sent to the management board, which further forwarded it to the Joint Supervisory Body (JSB) to give its opinion.[155] After receiving the JSB opinion on the data protection level in the country or organisation concerned, the management board decided whether to approve the report, which resulted in giving authorisation to the director of Europol to start negotiations. From a practical point of view, a positive assessment of the data protection report followed by the authorisation to start negotiations appeared to be the most critical stage in the procedure.[156] Another important aspect is that both JSB opinions (on the data protection report and on the draft agreement to be signed between the parties) seemed to be very influential in practice.[157]

148 eg art 22 of the Agreement with Liechtenstein.
149 eg art 18 of the Agreement with Monaco.
150 See Council, 'Proposal for a Regulation of the European Parliament and of the Council on the European Union Agency for Law Enforcement Cooperation and Training (Europol) and repealing Decisions 2009/371/JHA and 2005/681/JHA, Discussion paper on Europol´s agreements with third countries', 17 September 2013 (ST 13702/13 INIT) 2.
151 ibid. To take one example, the operational agreement concluded with Liechtenstein took almost five years, see also RAND Report (n 105) 113.
152 Interview 13, The Hague (1 July 2013).
153 RAND Report (n 105) 113.
154 ibid.
155 ibid. See for a practical example, the Opinion of the JSB on the data protection level in Liechtenstein, 6 February 2012 (Document 12/09).
156 'For us, that's the biggest step. If we have done this, then we will basically make it (. . .)' – Interview 13 with a Europol official, The Hague (1 July 2013).
157 This view was conveyed by a Europol official in particular with regard to the data protection reports mentioning that: '(. . .) JSB was always there, but formally, JSB only gave opinions (. . .) And of course the opinions were so strong that they couldn't ignore it, at least those who have to approve it' (ie *the agreement*) – Interview 13 with a Europol official, The Hague (1 July 2013).

Throughout the whole process (initiation, negotiations, conclusion) there were informal and formal interactions between the Agency and the Council, the Commission and the Member States. Regarding the relationship with the Commission, regular meetings have been reported to take place on working and high levels, along with an informal direct line of communication,[158] enabling the Commission to ask Europol to put more or less emphasis on one file or another according to the priorities in the EU external action area.[159] Although the interactions have been judged as positive from both sides, it has been conveyed that the Commission was a less influential actor than the Member States[160] and that sometimes there were coordination problems, especially because the Commission did not always communicate with Europol on wider initiatives and priorities.[161] Furthermore, Europol participated in the relevant Council working groups, in which the Agency reported on the status of negotiations, and sometimes was also seeking guidance and instructions on how to proceed in relation to a third country or another.[162]

A recent development regarding the procedure for the conclusion of Europol's agreements flowed from CJEU's judgment in Case C-363/14[163] concerning the action for annulment of Council Implementing Decision 2014/269/EU extending the Council's 'list'. In this judgment, the Court confirmed the possibility for the Council to adopt implementing acts under secondary law provisions within the former 'third pillar',[164] and established that Article 26(1)(a) of the Europol Council Decision represented a valid secondary legal basis for adopting such acts.[165] The Court also established a duty for the Council to consult the European Parliament based on former Article 39(1) TEU when adopting implementing acts under Article 26(1)(a) of the Europol Council Decision.[166] The Council gave an extensive interpretation to this consultation duty in that it applied to all implementing measures adopted under the old 'third pillar' framework, even in the absence of an explicit provision to that effect.[167] Accordingly, after September 2015, the Council implementing decisions adopted on the basis of Article 23(2) of the Europol Council Decision with a view to approving Europol's agreements with third countries were subject to *prior* European Parliament

158 Interview 5 with a Europol official, The Hague (29 January 2013).

159 Interview 35 (phone) with a Commission official, 1 October 2013.

160 ibid.

161 Interview 5 with a Europol official, The Hague (29 January 2013).

162 Interview 13 with a Europol official, The Hague (1 July 2013), and Interview 19 (phone) with a Council official (26 June 2013).

163 Case C-363/14 *Parliament v Council* EU:C:2015:579. In that case, the European Parliament argued essentially that the contested Council implementing decision had been adopted based on an invalid secondary law legal basis (ie art 26 of the Europol Council Decision), and that, moreover, European Parliament's prerogative to be consulted before the adoption of that decision had been breached.

164 See for previous cases on this matter, Joined Cases C-317/13 and C-679/13 *Parliament v Council* EU:C:2015:223, and Case C-540/13 *Parliament v Council* EU:C:2015:224.

165 Case C-363/14 *Parliament v Council* (n 163) paras 70–72.

166 ibid paras 82–85.

167 Council, 'Judgment of the Court of 10 September 2015 in Case C-363/14, European Parliament v Council for the European Union – legality of a Council implementing Decision based on the 2009 Europol Decision concerning the list of third states with which Europol can conclude cooperation agreements', 7 October 2015 (12035/15) 6.

consultation.[168] In short, this resulted in strengthening European Parliament oversight by adding an extra condition to the procedure for the negotiation and conclusion of the Agency's cooperation agreements laid down in Europol's former legal framework.

Memoranda of understanding, arrangements and subsequent agreements

On the basis of the 'mother' strategic and operational cooperation agreements, further instruments were concluded between Europol and the third country or organisation concerned. These were labelled 'memorandum of understanding', 'agreement' or 'arrangement', or 'exchanges of notes'[169] and were intended to implement various aspects of the cooperation covered by the main agreement.[170] Such instruments are not available on the Europol's website and are restricted from public access.[171] As a result, the succinct analysis of these instruments is based on indirect and secondary sources, such as the text of the basic cooperation agreements, interviews with Europol officials, information available on the Agency's website, and other public sources of information.

First, these implementing instruments normally cover issues such as: (1) the status, tasks, working methods, liability, and cases of conflict regarding LOs; (2) principles, obligations and procedures related to the exchange and processing of confidential information; (3) general terms on the assessment of specified types of information and specified sources;[172] (4) establishment and operation of a secure communication line.[173] As such, these instruments seem to include concrete rules and procedures of a rather technical and operational nature, giving substance to important elements of the cooperation between the parties mentioned, in a more general manner or at the level of principle, in the main cooperation agreement.

168 Council, 'Draft Council Implementing Decision (EU) 2015/ (. . .) approving the conclusion by Europol of the Agreement on Strategic Cooperation between the Federative Republic of Brazil and the European Police Office (Europol)', 19 October 2015 (12927/15) 1–2.

169 See art 10 of the Strategic Agreement with Russia. According to a Europol official, a separate agreement on confidentiality was concluded with Russia; it appears that Russia considered it to be an international agreement in that it underwent internal ratification process – Interview 5 with a Europol official, The Hague (29 January 2013).

170 Interviews 5, The Hague (29 January 2013) and 13, The Hague (1 July 2013).

171 The author attempted to obtain these documents through requests for access to documents but the Agency refused to grant access on the grounds that 'disclosure would undermine the protection of the public interest as regards the proper fulfilment of Europol's tasks and international relations as well as Europol's decision-making process and/or, the privacy and integrity of the individual'.

172 eg art 10(5) of the Agreement with FYROM, and art 10(5) of the Agreement Monaco.

173 eg arts 20 and 23 of the Agreement with Liechtenstein. According to one Europol official, the MoU on confidentiality with Liechtenstein has been considered by the latter third country to be an international agreement in that it underwent internal ratification process – Interview 5 with a Europol official, The Hague (29 January 2013). In 2011, the Agency has concluded a MoU on secure communication line with Interpol, Europol, 'Press Releases', 'Europol and Interpol agree joint initiatives to enhance global response against transnational crime', 12 October 2011 ‹https://www.europol.europa.eu/content/press/interpol-and-europol-agree-joint-initiatives-enhance-global-response-against-transnati›.

Secondly, it appears that in practice technical rules such as those related to LOs and exchange of confidential information were part of the negotiations for the main agreement. If such technical aspects were agreed upon during this process, they were included in the main agreement, most often as annexes.[174] If it was not possible to reach a consensus by the time the main agreement had been finalised, these issues were settled later through a MoU or an implementing agreement.[175]

Thirdly, an important difference between these implementing agreements and the main cooperation agreements lied in the procedure followed on Europol's side for the negotiation and conclusion of such instruments. Thus, it appears that, as a rule, these instruments were negotiated and concluded according to a simplified procedure in which the Council was not directly involved. The entire process took place between the director of the Agency, supported by the relevant internal structures, and the respective third country or organisation.[176] The management board was kept informed on the progress, whilst the Security Committee, which was attached to the management board, was more active in authorising the assessment of the adequacy of security measures and monitoring the process.[177] Compared to the procedure for the negotiation and conclusion of the 'normal' cooperation agreements, the overall simplified procedure could be characterised as largely lacking legal oversight, by leaving the Council out and involving the management board only to a limited extent.[178] This situation had been explained by the fact that this category of instruments comprises rules of a technical nature only implementing the provisions of the basic agreement endorsed by the management board and approved by the Council.[179] Pragmatic reasons justified apparently the choice for separate implementing agreements, adopted according to simplified and flexible procedures and dealing with technical aspects.[180]

6.4.2 The new Europol Regulation: redesigning Europol's international dimension

The new Europol Regulation substantively redesigns Europol's international dimension. This is dealt with mainly in Chapter V 'Relations with Partners' of Regulation

174 eg the Agreement with FYROM has a confidentiality agreement attached in Annex 1 'Exchange of classified information' and a liaison agreement in Annex 4 'Liaison Officers'.

175 Interview 13 with a Europol official, The Hague (1 July 2013).

176 ibid.

177 ibid.

178 Some operational agreements provide, however, for the Council's or management board's approval as regards some specific MoUs and implementing agreements. This is the case of the Agreement with Monaco – arts 13(3) and 20(1) – providing for the Council's approval as regards the subsequent confidentiality agreement concluded by the contracting parties, whereas the Agreements with Iceland, Norway and Switzerland subject the MoU on the assessment of specified types of information and specified sources to the management board's approval. It should be added that recent operational agreements (Liechtenstein, Albania and Serbia) provide for the conclusion of a MoU on confidentiality and information assurance, which does not require the Council's approval.

179 Interview 13 with a Europol official, The Hague (1 July 2013).

180 That is to leave out of the main agreement all the detailed technical rules which could have further delayed the negotiation process and to deal with these issues at a later stage, without repeating the whole procedure again, Interview 13 with a Europol official, The Hague (1 July 2013).

2016/794. Based on these provisions, Europol's international cooperation framework features several novelties which are worth being highlighted.

First, Europol is brought in line with other EU agencies, in that the Agency will formally establish cooperative relations with the competent authorities of third countries (instead of third countries as provided by the 'defunct' Europol legal framework).[181]

Secondly, there will no longer be Europol cooperation agreements. Although Europol's agreements concluded until 1 May 2017 will be preserved,[182] from that moment international agreements allowing the Agency to transfer personal data will be concluded according to Article 218 TFEU.[183] However, for the time being Europol's cooperation agreements remain the basis for future cooperation with third countries and international organisations.[184]

However, the Europol Regulation does not clarify whether and how the Agency will be involved in the negotiation of the relevant agreements foreseen under Article 218 TFEU. Article 11(2) of the Europol Regulation only enables the management board to make a suggestion to the Council to draw the attention of the Commission to the need for concluding an 'Article 218 TFEU' international agreement. From this provision, it can be inferred that the initialing of an international agreement allowing Europol to exchange personal data will not so much depend on the Agency anymore, but on the Council and the Commission. Furthermore, the application of the procedure for 'Article 218 TFEU' agreements will entail Council decisions concerning opening of negotiations, adopting negotiating directives, authorising the signing of and concluding the agreement, negotiations by the negotiator designated by the Council, and European Parliament consent.[185] Within this procedure, Europol representatives might eventually be involved either in the negotiating team or in the special consultation committee which may be designated by the Council in order to support the negotiator.[186] In any case, this represents an important shift in Europol's role in international cooperation, as compared to the Europol Council Decision, where the Agency was in the lead as regards the initiation, negotiation and conclusion of the cooperation agreements. This change largely reflects the Commission's view regarding the revision of Europol's international cooperation with a view to fully align it with the Lisbon Treaty and to increase coherence in the Union's external relations.[187]

Furthermore, one may wonder how effective the procedure laid down in Article 218 TFEU will be. Thus, political and non-specialised actors might not be sufficiently familiar with the specific and highly technical issues covered by the current Europol

181 See art 23(1) of Regulation 2016/794.

182 According to art 25(4) of Regulation 2016/794, the Commission will review all Europol's cooperation agreements by 14 June 2021 in particular with regard to data protection; based on this assessment, the Commission may then submit to the Council recommendations for the opening of negotiations for the conclusion of 'Article 218 TFEU' international agreements with a view to replace existing Europol agreements.

183 Art 25(1) and (4) of Regulation 2016/794.

184 Europol External Strategy 2017–2020 (n 116).

185 Art 218(6)(a) TFEU juncto art 88(2) TFEU.

186 Art 218(4) TFEU.

187 Moor and Vermeulen (n 15) 1107–108.

agreements. What is more, there might be a risk for wider political preferences in the Union's external action area being privileged to the detriment of Europol's operational priorities.

Besides, it is not very clear what kind of agreements will be concluded under Article 218 TFEU. One option would be to conclude special agreements concerning Europol's cooperation with a country or international organisation, in particular with regard to the exchange of personal data. Such instruments would be very much like the current Europol cooperation agreements. Another option could be the conclusion of framework agreements between the EU and the respective international partner covering various cooperation aspects, and including also Europol.

Thirdly, Europol is still allowed to conclude specific international cooperation instruments. In this respect, the Europol Regulation distinguishes between working arrangements and administrative arrangements in a way which evokes the demarcation between strategic and operational agreements under the old legal framework. The working arrangements are designed to cover cooperative relations, except for exchanges of personal data, and are explicitly characterised, in line with the Common Approach on EU agencies, as not being binding for the EU and the Member States.[188] Europol's administrative arrangements are intended to enable personal data exchanges by implementing 'Article 218 TFEU' agreements, cooperation agreements concluded by Europol before 1 May 2017, or the Commission's 'adequacy decisions' regarding the transfer of personal data, but, unlike the working arrangements, nothing is mentioned about their legal nature.[189] While on the face of it, the provisions of the new Regulation indicate that such instruments would probably qualify as soft law measures,[190] as it will be shown thereafter (in section 6.5) determining their legal nature requires a case-by-case analysis of each particular instrument in light of international law criteria.

It should be also noted that, unlike the Europol Council Decision, the new Regulation does not provide details regarding the procedure for the negotiation and conclusion of Europol's working and administrative arrangements, except that the management board decides on the conclusion of such instruments, and perhaps that the executive director must inform the management board on the intention to initial such arrangements.[191] As compared to Europol's cooperation agreements, the new international cooperation framework does not foresee Council's approval or European Parliament's compulsory consultation for the Agency's new international cooperation tools. Relevant acts implementing the Europol Regulation as well as the Agency's internal rules will probably provide the procedural details concerning the negotiation and conclusion of Europol's arrangements with international partners. In any case, these succinct procedural provisions regarding the negotiation and conclusion of Europol's international cooperation arrangements suggest that these instruments could be seen as the 'successors' of the Agency's MoUs, agreements and arrangements implementing the Europol's cooperation agreements under the former legal framework. What seems to be a constant feature of Europol's international dimension is the

188 Art 23(4) of Regulation 2016/794.

189 ibid art 25(1).

190 For a recent analysis of the concept of 'soft law' and of soft law instruments at EU level, see Fabien Terpan, 'Soft Law in the European Union: The Changing Nature of EU Law' (2015) 21 *European Law Journal* 68.

191 Arts 11(1)(r) and 23(3) of Regulation 2016/794.

oversight of the management board over the implementation of the Agency's external actions on the basis of regular reporting.[192]

Fourthly, the new Regulation enhances Commission's role with regard to Europol's international dimension. Most obviously, this is exhibited by formalising the Commission's 'adequacy decisions'[193] as one of the legal bases allowing the Agency to exchange personal data. As mentioned above, the implementation of such decisions may require the Agency to conclude specific administrative arrangements with competent authorities of third countries and international organisations,[194] and, moreover, Europol's executive director has a duty to report to the management board on the implementation of Commission's 'adequacy decisions'.[195] Additionally, Article 25(4) of the new Regulation further bolsters Commission's position by granting it the power to review Europol's 'surviving' cooperation agreements with a view to maintain or replace them with 'Article 218' agreements. In line with the Common Approach on EU agencies,[196] the new Regulation also introduced more generic tools, which enable arguably the Commission also to influence the Agency's international cooperation. This entails giving the Commission a say with regard to Europol's multiannual planning and annual work programmes,[197] as well as presumably the role assigned to the Commission as regards the periodic evaluation of the Agency.[198] Finally, but yet importantly, Europol's External Strategy 2017–2020 emphasises Europol's commitment to enhance the cooperation with the Commission and the European External Action Service when establishing contacts with third countries with which the Agency does not cooperate yet.[199]

Fifthly, the new Regulation enhances parliamentary scrutiny of Europol's international cooperation as compared to the former Europol Council Decision. A joint parliamentary scrutiny group (JPSG) bringing together members of the European Parliament and of national parliaments is established with a view to monitor Europol's activities.[200] For this purpose, the Europol Regulation imposes a duty on the chair of the management board, the executive director and other Europol officials to report before JPSG on the Agency's activities.[201] Moreover, an obligation is placed on Europol to transmit to JPSG various documents, including the administrative arrangements implementing the Union's international agreements or the Commission's 'adequacy decisions'.[202] The outcome of the monitoring carried out by the JPSG materialises in

192 Europol External Strategy 2017–2020 (2016) (n 116).

193 Based on Directive (EU) 2016/680 of the European Parliament and of the Council of 27 April 2016 on the protection of natural persons with regard to the processing of personal data by competent authorities for the purposes of the prevention investigation, detection or prosecution of criminal offences or the execution of criminal penalties, and on the free movement of such data, and repealing Council Framework Decision 2008/977/JHA [2016] OJ L119/89. According to art 36 in combination with recital 67 of the preamble of this directive, an 'adequacy decision' is a Commission decision determining that the third country or the international organisation in question 'ensures an adequate level of protection', which is 'essentially equivalent to that ensured within the Union'.

194 Art 25(1) of Regulation 2016/794.

195 ibid art 25(2).

196 See in particular paras 29 and 60 of the Common Approach on EU agencies (n 122).

197 Art 12(1) of Regulation 2016/794.

198 ibid art 68.

199 Europol External Strategy 2017–2020 (n 116).

200 Art 51(1) of Regulation 2016/794.

201 ibid art 51(2).

202 ibid art 51(3)–(4).

'conclusions' which are submitted to the European Parliament and the national parliaments.[203] Additionally, the European Parliament has the possibility to access non-classified and, under certain conditions, also classified information processed by or through Europol.[204] Nevertheless, two caveats should be mentioned both as regards the JPSG's monitoring and the European Parliament's access to Europol information. To begin with, access to information will be governed by the Agency's own rules regarding protection of non-classified and classified information, which could at least in theory enable Europol to restrict to a certain extent parliamentary scrutiny of its activities.[205] Next, the Europol Regulation does not provide anything concrete regarding the legal consequences of the scrutiny of Europol's activities.

Sixth, the supervision over Europol's processing of personal data is reinforced by replacing the JSB with the European Data Protection Supervisor (EDPS) with far-reaching tasks and powers.[206] In this respect, the EDPS is tasked to hear complaints, conduct inquiries, monitor and ensure the application of the relevant EU legal framework in order to protect natural persons with regard to processing of personal data by Europol.[207] The EDPS may *inter alia* warn or admonish Europol, compel the Agency to rectify, restrict, erase or destroy incorrectly processed personal data, ban Europol's processing operations, or refer a matter to the European Parliament, the Council, the Commission or the CJEU.[208]

Importantly, the new Regulation enables Europol to exchange personal data without having to rely on a Commission 'adequacy decision', an 'Article 218 TFEU' agreement, or a Europol cooperation agreement.[209] While this possibility represents an exception just like in the old Europol Council Decision,[210] it has arguably a broader scope, by covering explicitly both case-by-case transfers and sets of transfers of personal data, and features open-textured provisions[211] suggesting a lower threshold on effecting such transfers.[212] The safeguards designed by the new Regulation with regard to these derogatory situations entail a duty of the executive director to inform *ex post* the

203 ibid art 51(5).
204 ibid art 52.
205 ibid arts 51(4) and 52(1)–(2) juncto art 67.
206 ibid art 43.
207 ibid art 43(2).
208 ibid art 43(3).
209 ibid art 25 (5)–(7).
210 Art 23(6) and (8)–(9) of the Europol Council Decision allowed the executive director to transfer personal data to third countries and international organisations in the absence of a cooperation agreement only in two situations: (1) when this was 'necessary in individual cases for the purposes of preventing or combating criminal offences' within Europol's competence and (2) when it was considered that the transmission of the data was 'absolutely necessary to safeguard the essential interests of the Member States concerned within the scope of Europol's objectives or in the interests of preventing imminent danger associated with crime or terrorist offences', and after assessing the adequacy of the level of data protection afforded by the entities concerned
211 For instance, according to art 25(5)(d)–(e) of the Europol Regulation personal data can be transferred when necessary '(. . .) for the purposes of prevention investigation, detection or prosecution of criminal offences or the execution of criminal sanctions or (. . .) for the establishment, exercise or defence of legal claims relating to the prevention investigation, detection or prosecution of a specific criminal offence or the execution of a specific criminal sanction'.
212 For instance, according to art 25(6) of Regulation 2016/794 a set of transfers of personal data can be authorised by the management board in all the broadly defined instances in which transfers on a case-by-case basis are allowed.

management board and the EDPS, in case of individual transfers, and respectively the duty of the management board to act in agreement with the EDPS when authorising a set of transfers.

6.5 Europol on the global scene: a legal assessment

6.5.1 The legal nature of Europol's formal international cooperation instruments

The legal nature of Europol's international cooperation instruments needs to be determined in light of the criteria for international binding agreements followed in this study – ie the wording and substance/content of the instrument, as well as the particular circumstances (context) surrounding the negotiation and conclusion of the instrument – and along the indicators corresponding to each criterion.[213]

6.5.1.1 The legal framework and international cooperation practice under Council Decision 2009/371/JHA

Cooperation agreements

Whilst as of 1 May 2017 Europol will not be able to conclude cooperation agreements as provided by the Europol Council Decision, the agreements already concluded by the Agency by that date remain in force under the new legal framework and, therefore, assessing their legal nature is of relevance. The analysis of the relevant legal framework, procedure for the negotiation and conclusion, the content and effects supports the conclusion that Europol's cooperation agreements can be qualified as binding international agreements (see also the examples provided below and Annex 5: Examples of Europol's cooperation agreements).[214] This is most obvious with the operational agreements, which include clear obligations for the contracting parties in terms of data protection, information exchange and processing, rights for third parties affected, liability provisions, elaborated dispute settlement procedures, including sometimes arbitration clauses.

The strategic agreements are lighter in terms of the content of the cooperation and they resemble the working arrangements concluded by other EU agencies,[215] but still the procedure used, and the wording and content of their provisions suggest their binding nature.[216] Furthermore, in practice no distinction seems to be made between operational and strategic agreements in terms of their legal nature.[217] The qualification

213 See ch 2, Box 2.1: Criteria and indicators for identifying international binding agreements.

214 See also Juan S Vara, 'The External Activities of AFSJ Agencies: The Weakness of Democratic and Judicial Controls' (2015) 20 EFAR 115, 127 and 135.

215 In particular, the agreements with UNODC and WCO appear to entail light and limited forms of cooperation.

216 The strategic agreements with third countries include rather 'hard law' provisions on conditions for information exchange, confidentiality, liaison officers, and liability.

217 According to a Europol official all cooperation agreements concluded by the Agency, be they strategic or operational, have the same legal value under international law, Interview 5, The Hague

of Europol's cooperation agreements as binding international agreements triggers the application of the principle *pacta sunt servanda*, and international responsibility in case of breach of the duties under the agreement.[218]

Examples of standard clauses in Europol's cooperation agreements indicating legal commitments between the parties

Operational agreements:

Box 6.1 Agreement on operational and strategic cooperation between Montenegro and the European Police Office (Europol), 2014

(. . .)

Article 3

Areas of crime

1. The co-operation as established in this Agreement shall relate to all areas of crime within Europol's mandate as listed in Annex 1, including related criminal offences.

Article 4

Areas of cooperation

The cooperation may, additional to the exchange of information, in accordance with the tasks of Europol as outlined in the Europol Council Decision, in particular include the exchange of specialist knowledge, general situation reports, results of strategic analysis, information on criminal investigation procedures, information on crime prevention methods, participation in training activities as well as providing advice and support in individual criminal investigations.

(. . .)

Article 9

Liaison officers

1. The Parties agree to enhance the cooperation as laid down in this Agreement through the secondment of liaison officer(s) of Montenegro. Europol may at its own discretion, equally consider the secondment of liaison officer(s) to Montenegro.

(29 January 2013). However, according to Mounier, from a practical point of view only the operational agreements 'have a real added value for investigations', Mounier (n 114) 587.

218 See generally on this issue Duncan B Hollis, 'Defining Treaties' in Duncan B Hollis (ed.), *The Oxford Guide to Treaties* (OUP 2012) 14.

2. The liaison officers' tasks, rights and obligations, their number, and the costs involved, shall be governed by an exchange of letters.

Article 10

General provisions

1. Exchange of information between the Parties shall only take place for the purpose of and in accordance with the provisions of this Agreement.
2. The transmission of personal data and classified information by Europol must be necessary in individual cases for the purpose of preventing or combating the criminal offences referred to in Article 3.
3. Parties shall only supply information to each other which was collected, stored and transmitted in accordance with their respective legal framework and has not been manifestly obtained in violation of human rights. In this context Europol will in particular be bound by article 20(4) of the Council Decision of 30 November 2009 adopting the implementing rules governing Europol's relations with partners including the exchange of personal data and classified information.
4. Individuals shall have the right to access the information related to them transmitted on the basis of the present Agreement, and to have such information checked, corrected or deleted. In cases where this right is exercised, the transmitting Party will be consulted before a final decision on the request is taken.
5. Requests for public access to information transmitted on the basis of the present Agreement shall be submitted to the transmitting Party for their advice as soon as possible. The concerned information shall not be disclosed should the transmitting Party object to it.

Article 11

Transmission of personal data

1. Requests from the Parties for personal data must be accompanied by an indication of the purpose and reason for it.
2. In the absence of an indication as mentioned in paragraph 1, the Parties are not permitted to transmit personal data.
3. The Parties shall indicate at the moment of transmission of the personal data or before, the purpose for which the data were transmitted, and any restriction on its use, deletion or destruction, including possible access restrictions in general or specific terms. Where the need for such restrictions becomes apparent after the supply, Parties shall inform of such restrictions at a later stage.

4. The Parties shall determine without undue delay, no later than six months after receipt, if and to what extent the personal data which have been supplied are necessary for the purpose for which they were supplied and inform the transmitting Party thereof. The personal data must be deleted when the data is not necessary for the purpose for which they were transmitted.
5. The Parties are only permitted to transmit personal data revealing racial or ethnic origin, political opinions or religious or philosophical beliefs, or trade union membership and data concerning a person's health or sexual life if strictly necessary.
6. Europol shall keep a record of all communications of personal data under this Article and of the grounds for such communications.

Article 12

Use of the information

1. Information if transmitted with a purpose may be used only for the purpose for which it was transmitted and any restriction on its use, deletion or destruction, including possible access restrictions in general or specific terms must be respected by the Parties.
2. Use of information for a different purpose than the purpose for which the information was transmitted must be authorised by the transmitting Party.

Article 13

Onward transmission of the information received

1. Onward transmission of the information received by Montenegro shall be restricted to the competent authorities of Montenegro mentioned in Article 7 and shall take place under the same conditions as those applying to the original transmission. Any other onward transmission, including to third States and international organisations, must be consented to by Europol.
2. Onward transmission of the information received by Europol shall be restricted to the authorities responsible in the Member States of European Union for preventing and combating criminal offences and shall take place under the same conditions as those applying to the original transmission. Any other onward transmission, including to third States or international organisations must be consented to by Montenegro.

(. . .)

Article 16

Data security

The Parties shall ensure that the information exchanged or received are protected through technical and organisational measures. Such measures shall only be necessary where the effort they involve is proportionate to the objective they are designed to achieve in terms of protection, and will be designed to:

1) deny unauthorised persons access to data processing equipment used for processing personal data (equipment access control),
2) prevent the unauthorised reading, copying, modification or removal of data media (data media control),
3) prevent the unauthorised input of personal data and the unauthorised inspection, modification or deletion of stored personal data (storage control),
4) prevent the use of automated data- processing systems by unauthorised persons using data- communication equipment (user control),
5) ensure that persons authorised to use an automated data- processing system have access only to the personal data covered by their access authorisation (data access control),
6) ensure that it is possible to verify and establish to which bodies personal data may be or have been transmitted using data communication equipment (communication control),
7) ensure that it is possible to verify and establish which personal data have been input into automated data-processing systems and when and by whom the personal data were input (input control),
8) prevent the unauthorised reading, copying, modification or deletion of personal data during transfers of personal data or during transportation of data media (transport control),
9) ensure that installed systems may, in the event of interruption, be restored immediately (recovery),
10) ensure that the functions of the system perform without fault, that the appearance of faults in the functions is immediately reported (reliability) and that stored personal data cannot be corrupted by system malfunctions (integrity).

(. . .)

Article 19 Principles of security and confidentiality

Each Party shall:

1. protect and safeguard unclassified information subject to this Agreement and the Memorandum of Understanding referred to in Article 20, with the exception of information which is expressly marked or is clearly recognisable as being public information, by various measures including the obligation of discretion and confidentiality, limiting access to authorised personnel and general technical and procedural measures;
2. protect and safeguard classified information subject to this Agreement and the Memorandum of Understanding referred to in Article 20.

3. ensure that it has a security organisation, framework and measures in place. The Parties mutually accept and apply the basic principles and minimum standards implemented in their respective security systems and procedures to ensure that at least an equivalent level of protection is granted for classified information subject to this Agreement.
4. ensure that the promises where information subject to this Agreement is kept have an appropriate level of physical security in accordance with the respective legal framework of the Party.
5. ensure that access to and possession of information is restricted to those persons who by reason of their duties or obligations need to be acquainted with such information or need to handle it.
6. ensure that all persons who, in the conduct of their official duties require access or whose duties or functions may afford access to classified information shall be subject to a basic security screening in accordance with the respective legal framework of the Party.
7. be responsible for the choice of the appropriate classification level for information supplied to the other Party.
8. ensure that classified information subject to this Agreement keeps the classification level given to it by the originating Party. The receiving Party shall protect and safeguard the classified information according to its legal framework for the protection of classified information holding an equivalent classification level.
9. not use or permit the use of classified information subject to this Agreement except for the purposes and within any limitations stated by or on behalf of the originator, without the written consent of the originator;
10. not disclose or permit the disclosure of classified information subject to this Agreement to third parties, without the prior written consent of the originator.

(. . .)

Article 21

Liability

1. The Parties shall be liable, in accordance with their respective legal frameworks, for any damage caused to an individual as a result of legal or factual errors in information exchanged. In order to avoid its liability under their respective legal frameworks vis-à-vis an injured party, neither Party may plead that the other had transmitted inaccurate information.
2. If these legal or factual errors occurred as a result of information erroneously communicated or of failure on the part of the other Party to comply with their obligations, they shall be bound to repay, on request, any amounts paid as compensation under paragraph 1 above, unless the information was used by the other Party in breach of this Agreement.

3. The Parties shall not require each other to pay for punitive or non-compensatory damages under paragraphs 2 and 3 above.

Article 22

Settlement of disputes

1. All disputes which may emerge in connection with the interpretation or application of the present Agreement shall be settled by means of consultations and negotiations between representatives of the Parties.
2. In the event of serious failings of either Party to comply with the provisions of this Agreement, or a Party is of the view that such a failing may occur in the near future, either Party may suspend the application of this Agreement temporarily, pending the application of paragraph 1. Obligations inherent upon the Parties under the Agreement will nonetheless remain in force.

(. . .)

Article 25

Amendments and supplements

1. This Agreement may be amended in writing, at any time by mutual consent between the Parties. Any amendments must receive the approval by the Council of the European Union.
2. The Annexes to this Agreement, as well as the provisions of Article 3(3) may be amended through an Exchange of Notes between the Parties.
3. For Europol, without prejudice to paragraph 1, amendments to the Annexes of this Agreement may be agreed upon without the approval of the Council of the European Union. For Montenegro, amendments to the Annexes of this Agreement may be agreed upon without the approval of the Parliament of Montenegro.

Article 26

Entry into force and validity

This Agreement shall enter into force on the date on which Europol notifies Montenegro in writing through diplomatic channels that it has received and accepted notification of Montenegro that its internal ratification process has completed.

(. . .)

Article 28

Termination of the Agreement

1. This Agreement may be terminated in writing by either of the Parties with three months' notice.

2. In case of termination, the Parties shall reach agreement on the continued use and storage of the information that has already been communicated between them. If no agreement is reached, either of the two Parties is entitled to require that the information which it has communicated be destroyed or returned to the transmitting Party.

Strategic agreements:

Box 6.2 Agreement on cooperation between the European Police Office (Europol) and the Republic of Turkey, 2004

(. . .)

Article 2

Framework of cooperation

The Parties shall cooperate in accordance with the provisions of this Agreement provided that Europol acts within its legal framework and the Republic of Turkey observes its national legislation and international obligations.

Article 3

Exchange of expertise

In order to realise the purpose laid down in Article 1 of this Agreement the Parties shall cooperate in the following ways:

1. Exchange of strategic and technical information of mutual interest;
2. Exchange of law enforcement experience including the organisation of scientific and practice-oriented conferences, internships, consultations and seminars;
3. Exchange of legislation, manuals, technical literature and other law enforcement materials; and
4. Training.

(. . .)

Article 5

Request for assistance

1. Cooperation within the framework of this Agreement will be carried out on the basis of requests for assistance, or on the initiative of one of the Parties, if this Party presumes that such assistance is of interest to the other Party.

2. A request for assistance will be provided in writing. If any doubts emerge related to the authenticity or the contents of the request, an additional confirmation may be requested.

Article 6

Execution of requests

1. The requested Party shall take all necessary measures to ensure a prompt and complete execution of the request. The requesting Party shall be immediately notified about any circumstances that may hamper the execution of the request or considerably delay its execution.
2. The requested Party shall have the right to ask for any further data it considers necessary to duly execute the request.
3. At the request of the Party requesting assistance, the requested Party shall take all necessary measures to ensure confidentiality of the fact that the request was made, the contents of the request and any annexed documents, as well as the fact that it has provided assistance. The requested Party shall inform the requesting Party if it is not possible to execute the request while preserving its confidentiality. The requesting Party shall decide whether it is acceptable to execute the request under these conditions.
4. The requested Party shall inform the requesting Party of the results of the execution of the request at its earliest convenience.

Article 7

Confidentiality

1. Each Party shall take the measures necessary to protect the information received from the other Party, which are equivalent to those applied by the submitting Party to ensure its confidentiality. The correlation of such protection measures shall be determined by mutual consent between the Parties. The measures for the protection of information may be changed by the receiving Party upon request of the Party which submitted the information, or with its written consent, with due regard to the applicable regulations on confidentiality of the receiving Party.
2. The Party providing the information may stipulate conditions on its further use. Such conditions on the usage of information may only be eliminated with the written consent of the providing Party.
3. Information received in accordance with the present Agreement shall not be used without the consent of the providing Party for purposes other than those for which it was provided.

(. . .)

Article 9

Expenses

The Parties shall bear their own expenses which arise in the course of implementation of the present Agreement, unless otherwise agreed on a case-by-case basis.

Article 10

Settlement of disputes

All disputes which may emerge in connection with the interpretation or application of the present Agreement shall be settled by means of consultations and negotiations between representatives of the Parties.

Article 11

Amendments to and termination of the Agreement

This Agreement may be amended by mutual consent between the Republic of Turkey and Europol. Europol may only give its consent to amendments after the unanimous approval of such amendments by the Council of the European Union.

Article 12

Entry into force

The present Agreement shall enter into force on the following day of the receipt of the last notification by which the Parties inform each other that their respective legal requirements for its entry into force have been completed.

Memoranda of understanding, arrangements and subsequent agreements

The situation is more blurred with regard to the legal nature of the cooperation instruments concluded in the implementation of the main cooperation agreements, such as MOUs, arrangements and agreements.[219] First, Europol's legal framework did not provide details about such instruments. Secondly, these instruments were concluded according to a simplified procedure, which usually did not involve the Council and only included the management board. Thirdly, as a rule, such implementing

219 According to a Europol official, such instruments are not legally enforceable in the same way as a normal international agreement, Interview 5 with a Europol official, The Hague (29 January 2013).

instruments are not intended to affect third parties.[220] However, the purposes for which such instruments are used (eg confidentiality arrangements, liaison officers) indicate that they include detailed rules and duties between the parties.[221] As such, they are perceived as binding by the Agency and the third countries concerned, and some of the third countries have subjected these instruments to their internal ratification procedures.[222]

Accordingly, one cannot deny the legally binding nature of such instruments based on their content and the fact that they are derived from the 'mother agreement'. In view of these considerations, qualifying these instruments as legally non-binding does not accurately reflect the current practice as it minimises their real impact. Based on the information available, it appears that the provisions of these instruments are legally binding and enforceable between the contracting parties,[223] keeping in mind of course the meaning of these terms in the international law context.[224] Perhaps an adequate generic label for these instruments could be 'implementing agreement of the main cooperation agreement'.

Binding international agreements of a technical-administrative nature

Although in the case of Europol, the particular features of the Agency, the legal framework and overall setting make it much easier to qualify its cooperation instruments as binding international agreements,[225] they are nevertheless to be included in the category of technical-administrative agreements concluded on the international plane.

220 As explained by a Europol official, whereas the legal basis of such instruments is in the basic cooperation agreements, which are ratified and valid as law, the technical implementation of the agreements is done by means of instruments like MoUs, which are only binding between the parties, Interview 13 with a Europol official, The Hague (1 July 2013).

221 eg provisions on data security, provisions on costs, staff exchange – Interviews 5 and 13 with Europol officials, The Hague (29 January 2013 and 1 July 2013).

222 This seems to have happened with the separate agreement on confidentiality concluded with Russia, as well as with the MOU on confidentiality concluded with Liechtenstein on the basis of the main agreement – Interview 5 with a Europol official, The Hague (29 January 2013).

223 This binding character could result from the way in which the provisions of the instrument are drafted and its overall structure, or it could be traced back to the main agreement as suggested by a Europol official – Interview 13 with a Europol official, The Hague (1 July 2013).

224 In this respect, an interviewee emphasised that, even if there are liability provisions in the main agreement or in a MOU, it is not the point really to use them, but to try to reach a compromise, failing which the only effective sanction left in practice is to terminate the agreement: 'Of course these liability provisions are always there, but you don't do that. How would you do it, which court? The only thing you could do is stop the agreement, terminate it (. . .). That's it in essence (. . .) to talk to each other (. . .). There's no third party involved' – Interview 13 with a Europol official, The Hague (1 July 2013).

225 'Legally binding' must be understood here in the context of international law. This entails in any case, much less enforcement compared to a domestic legal system. Instead, the 'enforcement' of the agreement between the parties is ensured through the use of more cooperative and flexible mechanisms (negotiations and consultations, suspension of obligations, and sometimes arbitration). International agreements may feature more 'hard law' elements when they confer rights on third parties, which may be enforced by the latter before domestic or other designated courts.

In spite of being concluded at state level on behalf of the third country concerned,[226] these agreements have a very limited scope, which is in line with the mandate and legal framework of the Agency, and they lay down a very specific framework for technical and operational cooperation. As such, these agreements enable concrete cooperation between administrations without normally touching the political sphere of external relations. However, in external relations, the distinction between technical and politically sensitive issues is not always clear cut. Therefore, such global sectoral administrative action needs to be coordinated and consistent with the Union's wider political and policy directions in external relations.

6.5.1.2 The new Europol Regulation

At the moment of the writing, there were no working arrangements or administrative arrangements concluded yet between Europol and third countries or international organisations under the new Europol Regulation. Therefore, the assessment of these international cooperation instruments can only be prospective. Nevertheless, similarly to the cooperation instruments implementing the Agency's main cooperation agreements under the Europol Council Decision, the application of the criteria for binding international agreements to Europol's working and administrative arrangements which will be concluded under the new Regulation might conduce to the conclusion that some of them are legally binding instruments.[227] Hence, in spite of being labelled 'arrangements', if the wording, content of these instruments as well as the particular circumstances surrounding their negotiation and conclusion reveal the intention of the parties to create legally binding effects under international law they will likely qualify as binding international agreements.

6.5.2 The legal status of Europol as a global actor

6.5.2.1 On the international plane

To determine the legal status of Europol on the international plane, it must be examined whether the Agency qualifies as a subject of international law with its own international legal personality or whether it is rather an 'agent' of the EU and/ or its Member States. In accordance with the criteria devised in this study, assessing whether Europol has international legal personality requires that the Agency has: (1) organisational distinctiveness; (2) separate will, so that it can be perceived as an entity detached from its creators; and (3) powers that it can exercise on the international

226 However, the fact that these instruments were often signed by the competent ministry or the director of the national police suggests that at least some of them could be regarded differently from the regular treaties concluded by the state. More evidence is needed, but preliminary empirical insights indicate that in some cases the agreement has not been ratified by the competent legislative authority in the third country concerned (eg USA, Canada), which rather suggests that such agreements are considered to be executive or administrative agreements concluded at state level.

227 Presumably, this could be the case most obviously for the administrative arrangements concluded by Europol with a view to enabling exchanges of personal data.

plane.[228] Relevant indicators in this respect are Europol's legal framework and its international cooperation practice. An additional indicator is the recognition of the Agency as a subject of international law by other subjects of international law (partners and non-partners).

Before 2009, Europol had been categorised as an intergovernmental organisation with legal personality.[229] The 1995 Convention equipped Europol with legal personality,[230] its own organs[231] and international cooperation tasks to be exercised through the conclusion of agreements and other international cooperation instruments.[232] However, even when Europol used to work under an intergovernmental framework, the Council imposed important limitations and exercised significant formal controls in particular with regard to Europol's cooperation agreements. Moreover, the Member States played a steering role regarding Europol's international cooperation. That being said, in spite of being set up as a distinct intergovernmental body entrusted with limited powers which can be exercised on the international plane, it transpires that Europol was rather an operational structure acting on behalf of the Council and the Member States.

After 2009, Europol was still equipped with legal personality and could conclude cooperation agreements with third countries and international organisations. The transformation of Europol from an intergovernmental body into an EU body arguably had important implications regarding its legal status on the international plane. In this respect, from a formal-legal perspective, Europol is no longer an organisation established by the Member States *via* an international agreement, but rather it is an agency based on an instrument of EU secondary legislation, just like other European agencies. In line with the view taken in this study, Europol, as an EU agency, may still acquire a functionally limited international legal personality, provided that the requirements mentioned previously are met.

Under the old Europol Council Decision, the Agency had its own organisation, the capacity to conclude binding international agreements with third countries and international organisations, and a rich international cooperation practice.[233] Accordingly, one may conclude that the Agency fulfilled the first and the third conditions for international legal personality. However, it was not very likely that Europol acted independently from the EU and its Member States, so as to acquire a separate will as a global actor. Whereas the Agency had some degree of operational independence, nevertheless it had 'a political master'.[234] This illustrates that the legal status of Europol as a global actor was rather blurred, considering the fact that the Agency, as an EU body controlled by the Council and the Member States, continued to conclude its own international agreements.[235] Moreover, both Europol's former legal framework and

228 See ch 2, Box 2.2: Checklist international legal personality of semi-autonomous organs established by states and international organisations.

229 Peers (n 14) 932; Heimans (n 59) 369.

230 Art 26 of the Europol Convention.

231 ibid art 27.

232 ibid arts 26(3) and 42.

233 With this in mind, an EU official expressed the view that the Agency still has international legal personality, Interview (phone) with a Council official (26 June 2013).

234 Interview 5 with a Europol official, The Hague (29 January 2013).

235 See also Mounier (n 114) 587.

institutional practice indicated an increased role for the Commission in shaping the Agency's international cooperation, as well as enhanced scrutiny by the European Parliament as regards Europol's cooperation agreements. Also, when setting and implementing its international cooperation strategy, Europol needed to observe the operational and political priorities set by the main EU institutions, as well as the operational needs of the Member States.

In this context, whether Europol was sufficiently autonomous, formally and actually,[236] from the EU institutions and the Member States is highly questionable. It is rather the case that Europol remained an 'EU agent' in the area of international police cooperation, implying that its international agreements are concluded ultimately on behalf of the Union and its Member States. As regards the way in which Europol was perceived by its partners, the preliminary findings of this study, resulting from the analysis of Europol's cooperation agreements, further lend support to this conclusion.[237] Thus, the cooperation agreements concluded by Europol acknowledge the position of the Agency as an EU body controlled by the Council, and also supporting the Member States.[238] Based on this analysis, it is submitted that the Agency did not meet the 'separate will' condition under the former Europol legal framework. Accordingly, Europol did not have international legal personality, but it was acting on the global level rather as an EU body.[239] This entailed that, in principle, the Agency's actions on the international plane were to be considered as being carried out ultimately on behalf of the European Union.

This conclusion is further reinforced by the new Europol Regulation which removes the Agency's power to conclude its own cooperation agreements, makes Europol's international cooperation regarding personal data exchanges dependent upon 'Article 218 TFEU' agreements and upon Commission's adequacy decisions, and, on the face of it, further enhances involvement by the Commission and the European Parliament in the Agency's international cooperation activities. These elements provide a strong indication that Europol's legal status on the international plane remains that of an 'EU agent'.

6.5.2.2 Within the EU: the principle of institutional balance and the Meroni *doctrine*

Assessing Europol's international dimension against the principle of institutional balance and the delegation of powers within the EU requires that the tasks and actions of the Agency: (1) are of executive nature; (2) remain within the boundaries of its mandate as defined by its regulatory framework; (3) are subject to conditions and

236 See on the distinction between formal and actual autonomy Groenleer (n 119) 29–39.

237 In this respect, a Europol official suggested, while referring to a concrete example concerning the negotiation of a cooperation agreement with Russia, that agencies like Europol and Eurojust are ultimately perceived as working for the 'the same father and mother' (meaning the European Union) – Interview 13 with a Europol official, The Hague (1 July 2013).

238 More empirical evidence is needed as regards the perception of Europol by non-partners subjects of international law.

239 According to Mounier, Europol has never been an international actor and 'will probably never be', Mounier (n 114) 597. For a view suggesting that Europol still had international legal personality under the 2009 Council Decision, see Vara (n 214) 119–20.

supervisory mechanisms limiting the discretion of the Agency; (4) do not encroach upon the powers conferred by the Founding Treaties on the EU institutions, in particular in the Union's external action area.

6.5.2.2.1 THE LEGAL FRAMEWORK AND INTERNATIONAL COOPERATION PRACTICE UNDER COUNCIL DECISION 2009/371/JHA

In the field of police cooperation, Europol is a technical body playing a much more modest role than suggested by its name. Europol's discretion to set its international cooperation priorities seems rather limited because of the constraints imposed on the Agency in practice by its operational and political environment. The limited role of Europol as a global actor was also reflected in the Agency's legal framework for international cooperation,[240] and in its cooperation agreements. Europol's agreements primarily cover information exchange and processing, the competence of the Agency is delineated, essential requirements are included in line with Europol's legal framework regarding data protection, confidentiality and liaison officers. Overall, Europol's legal provisions on international cooperation, as well as its agreements and related activities were instrumental to attaining the main objectives set by the relevant legal framework, including Article 88(2) TFEU, and their scope and cooperation modalities remained seemingly within the core mandate of the Agency.

Particularly after Lisbon, the conclusion of binding international agreements by Europol posed arguably problems for the institutional balance in the EU external action area.[241] Whereas the legal regime established by the Europol Council Decision had been safeguarded under Article 9 of the Protocol 36 on Transitional Provisions, Europol's cooperation agreements remained a controversial issue. Thus, it could be maintained that 'Article 218 TFEU' agreements should have been used instead or, in the alternative, that in any case the legal framework concerning Europol's cooperation agreements did not account sufficiently for the Commission's role to ensure the Union's external representation under Articles 17(1) TEU and 220 TFEU, and for European Parliament's prerogatives under Article 218 TFEU.

Based on the previous analysis of Europol's agreements, we take the view that these instruments qualify as technical-administrative agreements outside the scope of Article 218 TFEU, and as such they do not automatically affect institutional balance in external relations. In our opinion, the CJEU judgment in Case C-363/14 provides further support for this view. In order to determine that amending the list of partners with whom Europol could conclude cooperation agreements was an issue of secondary importance which could be delegated by the legislator and exercised by an implementing act,[242] the Court looked closely at Europol's legal framework concerning international cooperation, including the procedure for negotiation and conclusion of its cooperation agreements.[243] In this respect the Court noted that Europol's international dimension

240 See art 23 of the Europol Council Decision.

241 Andrea Ott, Ellen Vos and Florin Coman-Kund, 'EU Agencies on the Global Scene: EU and International Law Perspectives' in Michelle Everson, Cosimo Monda and Ellen Vos (eds), *European Agencies in between Institutions and Member States* (Kluwer Law International 2014) 108.

242 Case C-363/14 *Parliament v Council* (n 163) para 57.

243 ibid paras 49–50 and 54–56.

is ancillary to the core activities of the Agency, and that the EU legislator had defined the framework within which Europol's international cooperation takes place.[244] What is more, the Court highlighted the possibility for Europol to conclude cooperation agreements as an essential element of this framework, and then indicated that the procedure for the negotiation and conclusion of these instruments provided sufficient safeguards preventing the transfer of personal data to third countries from interfering with fundamental rights.[245] From this it can be inferred that Europol's cooperation agreements as forms of Agency's ancillary international action, and taking place within the legal framework defined by the legislator were not precluded *per se* by Article 218 TFEU.

The legal provisions dealing with international cooperation established important formal conditions and controls concerning Europol's agreements. These included the Council's 'list', the role of the management board to authorise the negotiation of cooperation agreements and to endorse them, the approval of each cooperation agreement by the Council, as well as the authoritative opinions of the JSB on operational agreements. Insights from practice into the procedure for the negotiation and conclusion of Europol's agreements revealed additional informal supervisory mechanisms carried out by the Commission. Such formal and informal conditions and mechanisms appeared to be capable of ensuring consistency with Union's priorities in external relations, and to preserve Commission's role under Articles 17 TEU and 220 TFEU. Furthermore, the obligation undertaken recently by the Council to consult the European Parliament *prior* to approving Europol's cooperation agreements, together with the duty placed on the chair of the management board and of the director to inform the European Parliament on request[246] seemed sufficient to pass the *Meroni* conditions and the institutional balance test.

Accordingly, Europol's cooperation agreements are in line overall with *Meroni* and do not seem to disturb *per se* the institutional balance in EU external relations. Being concluded by an EU body acting on the global level, Europol's agreements are considered as being carried out ultimately on behalf of the European Union. This is in contrast with the Common Approach on EU agencies, stipulating that EU agencies cannot commit the Union to international obligations.[247]

6.5.2.2.2 THE NEW EUROPOL REGULATION

The legal framework established by the new Regulation marks arguably a weakening of Europol's role in international cooperation, in parallel with a partial enhancement of controlling mechanisms over the Agency's international dimension. While emphasising almost identically with the old Europol Council Decision the instrumental-ancillary nature of Europol's international cooperation,[248] the new Regulation also subdues the Agency's core international activities – ie exchange of personal data – to 'Article 218 TFEU' agreements and Commission's 'adequacy decisions'. The

244 ibid paras 49–50.
245 ibid paras 53–55.
246 Art 48 of the Europol Council Decision.
247 Para 25.
248 Art 23(1) of Regulation 2016/794.

Agency is merely left with the possibility to conclude administrative arrangements to implement the instruments providing the legal basis for international cooperation, or to conclude, on the matters covered previously by strategic agreements, working arrangements which are, however, qualified as non-binding for the EU and the Member States. At the same time, the new Regulation features increased scrutiny from the Commission and the European Parliament over Europol's international cooperation. As discussed, for the Commission this entails the possibility to assess Europol's 'surviving' cooperation agreements, getting involved in the Agency's annual and multiannual planning, and undertaking the periodic evaluation of the Agency. European Parliament's increased role vis-à-vis the Agency materialises most importantly in the monitoring of Europol's activities through the JPSG and the possibility to obtain access to Europol information. Additionally, Europol's international cooperation entailing exchanges of personal data is subject to EDPS's scrutiny and intervention powers. The previous points suggest that Europol's redesigned international dimension is likely to respect institutional balance in external relations and the *Meroni* doctrine.

However, several aspects of the new legal framework might become legally problematic. First, the fact that the new Regulation is elliptical as regards the involvement of the Council, the Commission and the European Parliament in the procedure for the negotiation and conclusion of Europol's new international cooperation instruments raises questions about the sufficiency of controlling mechanisms by the main EU institutions in light of *Meroni*. From this perspective, the new Regulation marks a step back as compared to the system of controls under the previous legal framework. While the most important Europol's international cooperation instruments will be concluded within the framework of existing international agreements or Commission's 'adequacy decisions', the lack of formal provisions with regard to controlling mechanisms ensuring that the Agency remains within its mandate and does not affect the powers of the institutions in the EU external action area remains a matter of concern according to the *Meroni* requirement concerning sufficient control. Arguably this concern is not sufficiently addressed by the Commission's involvement in the Agency's annual and multiannual planning nor by the duty to transmit *ex post* to the JPSG the administrative agreements concluded with third countries and international organisations.[249] According to Articles 17(1) TEU and 220 TFEU, and in line with the Common Approach on EU agencies, at least involvement and oversight by the Commission should be ensured in line with the role of the latter to ensure Union's external representation and consistency of EU policy. This could be shaped through institutional practices and/or formalised in relevant rules implementing the Europol Regulation, as well as through working arrangements between the Agency and the Commission.[250]

Secondly, with regard to the derogations enabling Europol to exchange personal data without having to rely on a Commission 'adequacy decision' or an existing international agreement, it remains to be seen whether the involvement of the EDPS

249 In our view, more effective oversight could have been ensured by including in the Europol Regulation a duty to inform the JPSG before an administrative agreement is concluded (*ex ante*) as this could prevent potential breaches by the Agency of its legal framework from taking place in the first place.

250 Common Approach on EU agencies (n 122) para 25.

will ensure sufficient supervision by limiting the Agency's discretion in exercising these powers in line with *Meroni*. Whereas the EDPS has important intervention powers regarding the exchange of personal data by the Agency, effective supervision will probably depend on the information provided by Europol as concerns individual and massive transfers of data.

6.6 Conclusion

The analysis of Europol's international cooperation framework and practice reveals an agency with an international dimension ancillary to its core tasks, and subject to various formal and informal conditions and controls, in particular by the Council, the Commission and the Member States. As such, Europol's international dimension under the former Europol Council Decision represented a specific form of EU administrative external action which was in line in principle with the institutional balance in external relations and with the present-day *Meroni* requirements. The same holds for Europol's binding cooperation agreements having a limited scope which revolves around the Agency's information-related tasks, and laying down a very specific framework for technical and operational cooperation. As a specific category of international agreements of a technical-administrative nature, these instruments appear to remain outside the scope of Article 218 TFEU, and to comply overall with the relevant EU legal framework.

Whereas Europol allegedly had its own international personality before becoming an EU agency,[251] the analysis of the legal framework under the Europol Council Decision revealed an Agency with a complex design, as well as a system of formal and informal conditions and controls limiting significantly its discretion in fulfilling its international cooperation tasks. Accordingly, even in an 'extreme' case like Europol, this Agency could not be said to have a sufficient degree of autonomy, which would allow it to acquire international legal personality. This entails that Europol's actions on the international plane were performed ultimately on behalf of the EU. As a result, and contrary to the Common Approach on EU agencies, Europol's cooperation agreements ultimately bind the Union under international law.

Regulation 2016/794 substantially redesigns Europol's international dimension while ensuring that the Agency's cooperation agreements remain valid bases for international cooperation under the new legal framework. The new Europol Regulation brings Europol's international dimension in line with that of other EU agencies, and attempts to improve the Agency's accountability for its international activities through increased parliamentary oversight, and *via* supervision by the EDPS. Quite significantly, the new Regulation removes the Agency's power to conclude cooperation agreements by replacing them with 'Article 218 TFEU' agreements. While in our view such a change was not imperative in order to ensure compatibility of Europol's international dimension with the current Treaty framework, it arguably downplays the role of Europol on the international plane. This suggests a more modest international dimension for Europol, which will probably respect institutional balance in external relations and the *Meroni* conditions, and entailing that the Agency will continue to operate as an 'EU agent' on the international plane.

251 See, however, the more nuanced view expressed by Rijken (n 7) 583.

Nevertheless, the application of the new Regulation also raises some interesting legal and practical questions regarding the legal nature and implications of Europol's working and administrative arrangements, as well as the supervision and controls over Europol's international cooperation powers and instruments. While on the face of it the new Regulation entails less formal powers for Europol, it also seems to offer new opportunities which might actually enhance the operational side of the Agency's international dimension, and which will probably raise legal concerns.

7 Cross-case study observations

7.1 Disclaimer

The general legal-analytical framework for assessing the EU agencies' international dimension developed in the general part of this study has been tested through in-depth case studies on EASA, Frontex and Europol. Whilst the careful selection of the three agencies was aimed at covering aspects of international cooperation that are common to the whole population of EU agencies, the use these findings to make generalisations beyond the case studies examined should be regarded with caution. EU agencies share a number of general features which distinguish them from the EU institutions and other EU bodies, but at the same time each agency has its own identity resulting from the peculiarities of its legal-policy framework. Moreover, the general examination of the international dimension of the EU agencies undertaken in Chapter 1 of this study revealed variations between these bodies with regard to the design of their international cooperation mandate and also with regard to their international cooperation practice. Accordingly, it cannot be claimed that the findings reached with regard to EASA, Frontex and Europol would apply *mutatis mutandis* to all EU agencies.

With this disclaimer in mind, the case studies aimed, nevertheless, at attaining a certain level of analytical generalisation. This entails that the case study findings obtained after applying the parameters of the general legal-analytical framework devised for examining the international dimension of the EU agencies, should feed this framework with fresh insights. This was expected to complement and fine-tune the general approach taken towards the international dimension of the EU agencies, to identify new areas of concern, and to create a stepping stone for more in-depth studies regarding the international cooperation of other EU agencies.

7.2 Cross-cutting observations

One cross-cutting case study observation is that the international dimension of EASA, Frontex and Europol seems to comply overall with the principle of institutional balance and the *Meroni* doctrine. The international dimension of the agencies examined appears to be instrumental to their core mandate and, at the same time, embedded in the external dimension of the relevant EU policies. While all three agencies display a certain degree of autonomy in setting priorities and planning actions in the area of international cooperation, in doing so they may not ignore the wider EU policy directions and actions in the external action area. This requires some flexibility on behalf of the agencies, in that they must be ready to adjust their international cooperation priorities and actions at any time in light of the sudden changes in the external dimension of the relevant policy area or in the Union's overall external relations.

It should be noted, however, that the relationship between the three EU agencies and the EEAS seems to be at an incipient stage, whilst the European Parliament has not been traditionally involved in their international dimension. Yet, the formal relationship and the informal interactions among these agencies and the Commission[1] as well as the Council appear to have ensured, in general, that they remain within the boundaries of their legal framework and that they follow the EU position in external relations. Although there are some differences between the agencies examined as regards the degree of involvement of the Commission and of the Council,[2] it appears that in all cases the controls and monitoring mechanisms put in place formally and informally were capable of ensuring overall that the agency's international cooperation is consistent with the Union's external relations policy. This is not, however, without some difficulties in practice, since, from an agency's perspective, the constant adjustment to the frequent changes in EU external policies is likely to endanger or compromise the agency's needs and efforts to pursue cooperation on a technical-operational level. Moreover, the case study research has revealed instances of lack of coordination and consistency between Union's external actions and EU agencies' international cooperation activities potentially leading to tensions between and within the international and EU legal orders.

This research reveals that, in addition to the EU institutions, the Member States may also play a role in shaping the international cooperation priorities and actions of the EU agencies. This becomes already apparent if one looks at the way in which the governance of the three agencies is designed, in particular the composition of agencies' management board. This is even more obvious in the case of Frontex and Europol, because these agencies rely to a great extent on the support of the competent authorities of the Member States in pursuing international cooperation in areas in which the EU competences are still 'light'.

The formal legal design of the international dimension of the EU agencies prompts several observations. To begin with, in all three cases the relevant legal framework covers in more or less detail the aims, instrumental nature, main directions and instances of agencies' international cooperation, the categories of partners with whom they may establish relations and the instruments through which international cooperation may be formalised, including various conditions and procedural aspects. In this respect, it should be noted that the two AFSJ agencies discussed here benefit of quite elaborated provisions on international cooperation as compared to EASA, one of the possible explanatory factors being that Frontex and Europol pursue international cooperation in rather specific and often sensitive policy areas.

The founding acts of all three agencies identified third countries and international organisations as the main categories of agencies' international partners. Whereas in the case of EASA and Frontex the founding acts specify that agencies' partners are effectively the corresponding competent authorities or agencies of third countries, the

1 In particular the agency's 'mother' DG.

2 In this regard, it should be noted that EASA has a very close relationship with the Commission, Frontex has extensive interactions both with the Commission and the Council, whereas Europol traditionally had a close relationship with the Council, although the Commission has been increasingly involved in Europol's activities, especially after Europol became an EU agency, and even more after the adoption of the new Europol Regulation.

former Europol Council Decision referred to 'third countries', entailing that Europol could in theory establish relationships on a higher governmental level. This situation has changed under the new Europol Regulation, which aligns Europol to the other two agencies by establishing the authorities of third countries as the Agency's international partners. Regarding the legal design of the relationship between each agency and its international partners, in the case of EASA and Europol the founding acts appear to construe common provisions for both categories of international partners, whilst Frontex's founding acts mark a clear distinction between the cooperation with third countries and that with international organisations. In practice, however, especially when it comes to 'international organisations' in a broad sense, there are instances where the agencies examined establish cooperation with entities with a rather unclear legal status, Frontex's working arrangements with MARRI, the CIS Border Troop Commanders Council, ICMPD or DCAF being illustrative in this respect.

An interesting aspect reflected in particular in the legal design of the international dimension of EASA and Frontex is their role in supporting not only the Union's external action, but also the international cooperation pursued by the Member States. The support provided by EASA and Frontex to the Member States can be far-reaching, such as the issuing of airworthiness certificates on behalf of Member States in the application of their international agreements with third countries,[3] in the case of EASA, or having international agreements between a Member State and a third country that include provisions regarding the role of the agency,[4] as is the case with Frontex. This is a peculiar situation where an EU body is enabled by EU secondary legislation to act on the international plane on behalf of a Member State. In the case of Europol, the provisions in the founding act dealing specifically with international cooperation do not provide explicitly for assistance to the Member States, but this can be derived from the Agency's general role to '(. . .) support and strengthen action by the competent authorities of the Member States and their mutual cooperation (. . .)' enshrined in Article 3(1) of the Europol Regulation. This phenomenon could be explained by the fact that these EU agencies are active in policy areas belonging to the domain of 'shared competences' in which there is a mismatch between the powers acquired 'internally' by the Union and the external projection of these powers on the international plane. Though the EU exercised important competences in the field of aviation safety or border management, on the international plane, it is still the Member States who are full members of the ICAO, or have concluded important international agreements with third countries.

Two of the EU agencies examined (ie Frontex and Europol) have recently been reformed by way of new founding regulations, whilst at the time of writing, a new EASA regulation was awaiting adoption by the EU legislator. In this respect, Europol has been the agency incurring by far the most significant changes as regards its international dimension. This is arguably because, although post-Lisbon Europol could maintain its rather specific international cooperation framework under Article 9 of Protocol 36, the aim of the new Europol Regulation was to bring Europol as much as much as possible into line with other EU agencies. In this vein, the new Europol Regulation redesigned the Agency's formal international cooperation instruments in

3 See arts 12, 17 and 20 of Regulation 216/2008.
4 See art 54(10) of Regulation 2016/1624.

line with the Common Approach on EU agencies, and has arguably enhanced control and supervision over Europol's international activities, in particular by the Commission, the European Parliament and the EDPS. The trend towards streamlining agencies' formal international cooperation instruments, as well as the system of controlling and supervisory mechanisms over their international activities is also displayed by the new Frontex Regulation.

Regarding the formal international cooperation instruments that may be concluded by the EU agencies with their partners, in the case of EASA and Frontex, the founding regulations have always employed the label 'working arrangement'. The case of Europol was different as under the former Europol Council Decision, this agency could conclude strategic and operational agreements. As discussed, the new Europol Regulation further aligns Europol to most EU agencies by enabling the Agency to enact only working and administrative arrangements. The examination of the international practice of the three agencies prompts, however, two interesting observations. First, EASA and Frontex enact sometimes instruments labelled slightly differently than in the agencies' founding acts, such as 'technical arrangement', 'memorandum' or 'exchange of letters', but which are nevertheless considered as equivalent to the agencies' formal international cooperation instruments enshrined in their legal framework. These instruments do not raise special legal problems as they are fully subject to the substantive and procedural legal framework concerning agencies' formal international cooperation instruments. Second, the international cooperation practice of all three agencies features instruments (arrangements, agreements, MOUs, implementing procedures, etc) which fulfil seemingly different functions as compared to the formal international cooperation instruments referred to in agencies' founding acts. Such instruments are routinely used to prepare the ground for international cooperation instruments enshrined in agencies' founding acts, or to ensure their implementation. They are not usually mentioned expressly in the agencies' founding acts, and they are concluded in accordance with rather simplified and not always very transparent procedures. The use of such instruments may raise questions regarding the compliance with institutional balance in external relations and with the *Meroni* requirements.

The working arrangements and agreements concluded by EASA, Frontex and Europol are regarded by the EU agencies as forms of international cooperation, although of a practical and technical nature and sometimes not at the same level as a 'treaty'. Although such 'agreements' are concluded with due observance and in the implementation of the 'domestic' legal framework of the contracting parties, both in the EU agencies' legal framework and in practice, they seem to be perceived as international cooperation, not as some sort of 'domestic' agreements. In any case, even the explicit clauses included in such agreements with regard to the application and non-affectation of the domestic law or of the provisions of other international agreements applicable to the contracting parties are not as such to transform the nature of the instrument from 'international' into something else. The case of Europol's cooperation agreements is slightly different as there are no difficulties in general in considering these instruments as binding international agreements.

The analysis of the content, wording and structure of the international cooperation instruments concluded by EASA, Frontex and Europol revealed that they can be qualified as binding instruments or, at least, as including limited substantive and procedural obligations. The cooperation instruments with (the competent authorities of) third countries usually foresee more substantive cooperation than those concluded with various international organisations. Overall, the formal cooperation instruments concluded by EASA, Frontex and Europol have a treaty-like structure and wording. These instruments usually feature a prescriptive language, laying down more or less detailed rights and duties for the contracting parties and sometimes also for third parties. Moreover, these instruments include standard provisions regarding the entry into force, amendment, termination, sometimes suspension of their application and repealing of previous instruments.

Europol's agreements, in particular those covering personal data exchanges, comprise quite detailed provisions regarding the rights of third parties and liability in case of non-compliance with the terms of the agreement. EASA's working arrangements pertaining to cooperation with regard to certification and design approvals are the most obvious example of the Agency's agreements entailing binding legal effects, whereas other working arrangements seem to include at least limited procedural and substantive obligations. Frontex's working arrangements suggest quite a low-level cooperation and, in particular, the working arrangements with the competent authorities of third countries bespeak the concern to avoid taking these instruments as binding international agreements. However, the overall analysis of the wording and content of Frontex's working arrangements suggests that these instruments are still capable of giving rise to limited legal rights and obligations. Most of these rights and duties would become active upon the conclusion of subsequent agreements between the parties, but nevertheless such instruments would occur within the framework and with a view to implementing the existing working arrangements. Inconclusive evidence suggests that framework financial agreements and other implementing cooperation instruments may have been adopted by Frontex. In this regard, it is important to undertake further research to gain insight into the subsequent agreements concluded by this Agency with its partners within the framework of its working arrangements.

The procedure for the negotiation and conclusion of EU agencies' international cooperation instruments lends further support to the view that these are considered as more than mere non-binding instruments. EASA, Frontex and Europol have quite formalised procedures which include, in addition to the relevant internal structures, the main organs of the agency (ie the executive director and the management board). EASA is a special case as the management board does not seem to be formally involved in the procedure. In practice, the initiation, negotiations and conclusion of these instruments often require significant resources and take a significant period of time, ranging from one to several years. Considering these circumstances, it seems reasonable to assume that the agencies examined do not enter into long negotiations and complex procedures solely to attain something which does not involve any commitment on behalf of the parties.[5]

It should be noted, however, that the preliminary examination of the international practice of the three EU agencies suggests that the 'enforcement' of the formal international cooperation instruments entered into materialises usually in informal or formal negotiations or consultations, the suspension of the application of the agreement, and, ultimately, in cessation of the cooperation. Even in the case of Europol's agreements with third countries and international organisations, it appears that in practice the formal liability and dispute settlement provisions were rarely, if ever, used. This does not mean, however, that the agreements enacted by the three EU agencies are not binding in terms of the international law principle *pacta sunt servanda*,

5 See Jan Klabbers, *The Concept of Treaty in International Law* (Kluwer 1996) 256.

but rather that the bindingness of such instruments, in particular from an enforcement perspective, needs to be seen differently in the international law context, still characterised by a strong consensual character.

The overall analysis of the working arrangements concluded by EASA and Frontex, as well as of the strategic and operational agreements concluded by Europol allows concluding that these instruments have a very limited scope and remain overall within the core mandate of the EU agencies. These international cooperation instruments provide a very specific framework for technical and operational cooperation, and are intended to enable the respective agency to implement its regulatory framework.

In line with the distinction made in the general part of this study between the so-called 'legislative' external action and administrative external action, the author is of the opinion that, in view of their features, these international cooperation instruments are to be included in the category of international agreements of a 'technical-administrative' nature. As shown, the current international practice features numerous agreements on a technical-administrative level that are concluded between various authorities of states and international organisations, in addition to the treaties concluded at the highest level according to formalised procedures involving the most important political institutions.

The working arrangements concluded by EASA and Frontex with the competent authorities of third countries obviously fit this format. In spite of being concluded usually at 'state level', Europol's cooperation agreements are also to be included in the category of 'technical-administrative' agreements in view of their very limited scope and the low-level cooperation involved. The legal nature of Europol's working and administrative arrangements concluded with competent authorities of third countries and international organisations under the new Europol Regulation remains still to be clarified as there was no Agency practice at the moment of writing. Yet, a preliminary analysis of these instruments on the basis of the new legal framework suggests that they are very similar to Europol's cooperation instruments implementing the Agency's main cooperation agreements under the former Europol Council Decision. This entails that some of them could actually qualify as legally binding administrative agreements.

In line with the view taken in Chapter 2 of this study, within the EU legal system, such technical-administrative agreements reflecting external administrative cooperation do not necessarily affect the institutional balance in external relations, if they are outside the scope of Article 218 TFEU, comply with 'Article 218' agreements and with EU legislation, and do not entrench on the Commission's powers under Articles 17 TEU and 220 TFEU. In light of the *Meroni* doctrine, it is required that the technical-administrative agreements concluded by EASA, Frontex and Europol remain within the boundaries of the EU agencies' mandate, and that there are sufficient conditions and supervision limiting the discretion of the agency.

The case study research suggests that the formal international cooperation instruments concluded by EASA, Frontex and Europol comply overall with the above-mentioned parameters. EASA's working arrangements with the competent authorities of third countries cover technical cooperation matters within the mandate of the Agency, whereas the initiation, negotiation and conclusion of the instruments appears to be steered closely by the Commission. Also, Frontex's working arrangements with international organisations and the competent authorities of third countries appear to cover technical-operational cooperation aspects falling within the Agency's regulatory framework. Although at times Frontex had seemingly made attempts to pursue international cooperation more independently, both the relevant legal framework and the way in which the Agency operates in practice suggest that steering and oversight of its international cooperation is ensured in particular by the Commission and the Member States. Although Frontex's former Regulation only provided for the Commission's *prior* opinion as regards the Agency's working arrangements with third countries, this research revealed that the internal procedures of the Agency required the same role of the Commission also with regard to the working arrangements with international organisations. Moreover, in practice the Commission had been involved throughout the procedure for the negotiation and conclusion of Frontex's working arrangements and had a much more authoritative role than what was formally provided for in the former Founding Regulation. This relativised to some degree the formal distinction between EASA and Frontex concerning the control over the conclusion of their working arrangements, since the role of the Commission did not seem less influential in practice when it gave a *prior* opinion (Frontex) instead of a *prior* approval (EASA).

The main objective of Europol's cooperation agreements was to enable the exchange of information in the areas of crime covered by its legal framework, which is the core task of the Agency. The agreements concluded by Europol so far have been subjected to strict formal controls by the Council (*a priori* 'list' of the third countries and international organisations with whom agreements could be concluded by the agency, approval of each cooperation agreement). Moreover, the case study research revealed the increasing involvement of the Commission in Europol's international cooperation, and a more prominent role of the European Parliament with regard to Europol's cooperation agreements following the CJEU's judgment in Case C-363/14. This supports the picture of a system of formal and informal conditions and controls which significantly limited Europol's discretion in fulfilling its international cooperation tasks, at least with regard to the negotiating and conclusion of its cooperation agreements.

The new founding regulations of Frontex and Europol display a tendency towards streamlining the international cooperation instruments of these agencies in line with the Common Approach on EU agencies, in a way suggesting increased compliance with the principle of institutional balance and the *Meroni* doctrine. In this regard, both Frontex's and Europol's international cooperation instruments require approval of the management board, whilst additionally, Frontex's working arrangements are formally aligned with those of EASA in that the new Regulation makes them subject to Commission's *prior* approval. What is more, the new founding regulations of Europol and Frontex indicate a tendency towards increasing democratic accountability regarding their international dimension through inserting specific and more strict duties to inform the European Parliament with regard to agencies' formal international cooperation instruments.

While the focus of this study was on the formal international cooperation instruments enacted by EU agencies, the investigation of the international cooperation legal framework and practice of EASA, Frontex and Europol also revealed less formalised and also more specific aspects of these agencies' international dimension. Such are the rather *ad hoc* exchanges of best practices and/or information, including personal data in the case of Europol, which the EU agencies may enable with their international partners sometimes without necessarily relying on a *prior* formal international cooperation instrument. Other examples are the various technical cooperation activities involved in EU agencies' cooperation with third countries and international organisations, through various projects and programmes, including under different EU policy initiatives such as the Mobility Partnerships within the Global Approach to Migration and Mobility, or the Stabilisation and Association Process within the EU Enlargement policy. While such instances of international cooperation by the three EU agencies do not seem *prima facie* to run obviously counter the EU agencies' legal framework for international cooperation or the legal parameters used in this study, a comprehensive mapping exercise is still required in order to elucidate their legal and practical implications.

Yet another finding of our case study research is that none of the three agencies examined displayed sufficient autonomy in pursuing international cooperation so as to acquire its own international legal personality. In spite of some variations, all three agencies are subject to a plethora of formal and informal conditions and controls, which significantly limit their discretion in pursuing international cooperation. Even an 'extreme' case like Europol cannot be said to display a sufficient degree of autonomy so as to acquire its own international legal personality. While this finding cannot be applied automatically to all EU agencies, nevertheless the case study selection offers a significant potential for generalisation, in particular through the choice of Europol as a case study. The fact that even an agency like Europol, with such prominent international cooperation powers and status does not appear to meet the standards for international legal personality arguably increases the potential for the case study findings to be applied to other EU agencies. In turn, the three agencies appear to act rather as governance tools for implementing the external dimension of the relevant EU policies, thereby contributing to the extraterritoriality of EU law[6] as well as to the effectiveness of the EU on the global level, and connecting their respective policy areas to the latest developments on the international plane.

7.3 Problematic aspects

Whilst the case study research suggests that the international cooperation activities and instruments of the three agencies examined are generally in line with the principle of institutional balance and the *Meroni* requirements, some potentially problematic aspects were also identified.

Thus, Europol's operational agreements raise the most sensitive legal issues in terms of compliance with the Union's data protection regime and sometimes this may prove problematic in practice, a prime example of this being the 2002 Supplemental agreement with the USA.[7] EASA's working arrangements also appear to raise a few procedural problems because of the lack of involvement of the management board in the procedure, contrary to what is stipulated in the Common Approach on EU agencies. Moreover, the difficulty of identifying a formal EASA decision concluding the working arrangement might arguably impede legal review. As to Frontex's working arrangements with third countries, their seemingly ambiguous legal nature resulting from the mix of potentially far-reaching clauses such as the 'respect for human rights'

6 See on the phenomenon of extraterritoriality of EU law, Joanne Scott 'Extraterritoriality and Territorial Extension in EU Law' (2014) 62 American Journal of Comparative Law 87.

7 See Dick Heimans, 'The External Relations of Europol – Political, Legal and Operational Considerations' in Berndt Martenczuk and Servaas van Thiel (eds), *Justice, Liberty and Security: New Challenges for EU External Relations* (VUBPRESS 2008) 387.

clause or, more recently, the provisions enabling personal data exchanges, and the standard final clause regarding their legal effects might render legal review and individual protection difficult. With regard to the later aspect, Europol's cooperation agreements, generally providing for individual's enforceable rights to have his personal information checked, corrected or deleted, and to obtain compensation, differ significantly from the working arrangements of EASA and Frontex, which do not refer explicitly to such issues. Yet also in the case of Europol, it remains to be seen how individual protection will be ensured under the new legal framework for international cooperation.

Additional areas of concern are the 'shadow' international operational instruments concluded by these EU agencies, and which seem to evade the constraints imposed by their legal frameworks. Examples of such 'shadow' agreements are the MOUs concluded by EASA, in addition to its 'regular' working arrangements. The evidence obtained suggests that EASA's MOUs are a less intensive form of cooperation than the working arrangements, which amount to no more than a declaration of intentions. However, it appears that, in practice, such instruments may cover more than purely technical cooperation, which in turn raises the suspicion that these instruments might transgress EASA's mandate. In any case, for such aspects, authorisation or approval by the Commission seems necessary since the Commission is in charge of the policy aspects regarding the external dimension of aviation policy. Moreover, in light of the CJEU judgment in Case C-660/13, it is not unreasonable to assume that EASA's MOUs might also affect Council's policy-making role in EU external relations under Article 16 TEU. Also, important elements of the cooperation between Europol and its partners are the subject of separate agreements which implement the mother cooperation agreement, but which no longer required the Councils' approval and are not public. Additionally, while Europol exchanged personal data with third countries in the absence or before having a cooperation agreement in place, and may continue to do so under the new Europol Regulation, questions may be raised about the appropriate supervisory mechanisms and legal safeguards ensuring that such cooperation does not infringe fundamental rights or the EU data protection regime. Frontex resembles Europol to some extent, in that its working arrangements sometimes provide for separate agreements in order to strengthen cooperation on certain issues within its scope, without a further indication as to the procedure to be followed. These observations prompt the general question whether the current system of supervision and controls over EU agencies' international activities should be further complemented by increased transparency and (parliamentary) oversight to enhance the (democratic) accountability of these bodies.[8]

The new founding regulations of Frontex and Europol address a number of issues raised under the former legal framework and previous international cooperation practice of the two agencies, but at the same time they also give rise to new legal concerns. Whilst in our view, in the case of Europol, the current EU constitutional framework did not necessarily impose abolishing the Agency's power to conclude cooperation agreements, the new Europol Regulation brings a whole set of questions regarding the way in which the Agency's international cooperation framework will

8 See in this regard Juan S Vara, 'The External Activities of AFSJ Agencies: The Weakness of Democratic and Judicial Controls' (2015) 20 EFAR 115, 129–33.

operate. What is more, the new legal framework raises arguably concerns about the sufficiency of supervisory and controlling mechanisms regarding Europol's working and administrative arrangements. Also, the new Frontex Regulation shows allegedly some degree of inconsistency as some of the legal safeguards and supervisory mechanisms applicable to the Agency's cooperation with third countries do not seem to cover also the cooperation with international organisations.

A different issue concerns the interplay in international cooperation matters between the main EU external action actors as well as the Member States, on the one hand, and the three EU agencies, on the other hand. As pointed out before, the EU agencies' international cooperation actions and those undertaken by the Union on a policy-political level are not always fully aligned, arguably because of insufficient coordination with the EU external relations players (ie Commission, the Council, the EEAS and the EU delegations). With regard to the possibility of the Member States to influence the international cooperation priorities and actions of the EU agencies it is necessary to gain a deeper understanding of the extent to which the Member States may or should influence EU agencies' international cooperation and of the way in which coordination and consistency with Union's priorities in external relations is or should be ensured. Another aspect concerns the instances where the EU agencies pursue international cooperation on behalf of the Member States. Whilst the power of the EU agency to act is grounded in EU legislation, and, moreover, agency's actions must comply with EU law, on the international plane, this situation translates into a potentially complex agency relationship, creating additional difficulties for the purpose of attribution and international responsibility, and further blurring the legal status of EU agencies as global actors.

In view of the findings regarding the (lack of) of international legal personality of the three agencies, as an immediate consequence, the actions of EASA, Frontex and Europol on the international plane are performed ultimately on behalf of the EU. As a result, the technical-administrative agreements concluded by these bodies would ultimately bind the Union under international law. In this regard, para 25 of the Common Approach stating that EU agencies cannot commit the Union to binding obligations is not accurate, as it ignores the international law perspective which may lead to a different outcome. Additionally, from the perspective of international law, it is quite likely that EU agencies' actions will bind the Union, even when they would breach procedural and substantive provisions of the EU legal framework.[9]

9 See art 46 of the 1969 and of the 1982 Vienna Conventions; see also Case C-327/91 *France v Commission* EU:C:1994:305, para 25.

Conclusion

In order to answer the research questions posed in this book, a four-layered approach has been adopted. First, the general legal profile of the EU agencies was examined with a view to determining the status of these bodies within the EU institutional system and to identify relevant legal parameters that shape their powers and actions. The working assumption behind this endeavour was that the general features and applicable parameters of EU agencies' legal status and powers also have relevance for their international dimension. Secondly, by looking into the international cooperation practice and legal framework of the EU agencies, a more 'down-to-earth' picture of some of the most relevant aspects and related legal issues pertaining to the international dimension of these bodies has been provided (Chapter 1). Thirdly, a tailored framework for assessing the EU agencies' legal status and instruments on the international plane has been developed (Chapter 2). This framework includes the EU legal standards which are deemed relevant for shaping international cooperation by EU agencies, focusing on the EU external action area. Furthermore, the concepts of 'international agreement' and international 'legal personality' were included within this framework with the purpose of completing the analysis by adding the inherent international law perspective. Fourthly, the general legal-analytical framework concerning the EU agencies' international dimension has been applied to EASA, Frontex and Europol (Chapters 3, 4, 5 and 6). The three case studies offered a comprehensive analysis of the relevant legal framework as well as meaningful empirical insights into the international cooperation practice of these agencies. The common case study format adopted in this study enabled a comparative assessment of the international dimension of the selected EU agencies in light of the general legal parameters devised in Chapter 2. The case studies also allowed understanding the practical relevance of the international cooperation carried out by these bodies and to identify new issues and areas of concern, which help fine-tuning the overall legal-analytical framework and advancing research on the matter (Chapter 7).

It should be emphasised that the main purpose of this study is to present for the first time extensively the state of art regarding the EU agencies as global actors. As such, the study represents pioneer work geared to map out a field surrounded by legal ambiguity and neglect. In this regard, suffice it to say that the main EU institutions appear to have become aware of the extent and legal implications of the EU agencies' international cooperation only recently and began to show more consideration for this issue, as illustrated by the founding acts of some of these bodies and by various EU policy documents such as the Common Approach on EU agencies. Against this background, this study can at best be seen as a milestone which paves the way for more in-depth research, which may very well lead to adjusting and complementing the initial approach applied to this topic. In what follows, the main findings of this study are presented. As a final step, a list of recommendations is advanced, complemented by an inventory of directions for further research.

1 Main findings

The general examination of the main features of the EU agencies provides support for characterising them as some sort of 'satellite' bodies within the EU institutional system, revolving around the main EU institutions and the Member States, and fulfilling a limited role of a rather technical-administrative nature. The legal design of the EU agencies and their interactions with the main EU actors suggest a complex principal(s)-agent relationship in which these bodies, while enjoying a degree of formal autonomy, are nevertheless subject to supervision and control in particular by the Commission, the Council and the Member States, and increasingly by the European Parliament.

Whilst EU agencies' creation and overall design need to observe the general principles of conferral, subsidiarity and proportionality, as regards specifically the powers entrusted to the EU agencies, the relevant legal standards applicable are those provided by the principle of institutional balance and the *Meroni* doctrine. In the absence of an explicit derogation to that effect,[1] the author takes the view that these legal standards are appropriate parameters as regards the EU agencies' powers in general, regardless of whether they are of an internal or an external nature.

It is maintained, therefore, that the relevant legal standards for judging the international dimension of the EU agencies within the EU are the principle of institutional balance along with the *Meroni* requirements. The *Meroni* doctrine can be seen as a more general test ensuring, *inter alia*, that EU agencies do not abuse their powers, whereas the principle of institutional balance essentially entails that EU agencies' powers should not encroach upon the prerogatives of the EU institutions according to the Founding Treaties. Whilst *Meroni* and the principle of institutional balance are conceptually different, they are tightly connected for the purpose of assessing EU agencies' powers. Therefore, for the purpose of this study, the requirements flowing from these two legal parameters have been integrated, within one single set of conditions. Accordingly, the *Meroni* requirements and the principle of institutional balance, as interpreted by CJEU in the *ESMA* case, essentially entail that the international cooperation powers and instruments of EU agencies: (1) are of executive nature; (2) remain within the limits of the agency's legal framework; (3) there are criteria and conditions limiting the agency's discretion; and (4) do not encroach upon the powers conferred on the EU institutions by the Founding Treaties, in particular in the Union's external action area. The application of these conditions suggests a restricted role for the EU agencies as global actors. More precisely, the international dimension of the EU agencies seems to be restricted to technical-administrative cooperation, which is instrumental to their core mandate.

1 In the *ESMA* case, the CJEU confirmed the validity of *Meroni* as regards EU agencies' powers, without stating any limitation in this respect, Case C-270/12 *United Kingdom v Parliament and Council* EU:C:2014:18.

As regards the institutional balance in the Union's external action area this includes in particular the division of powers regarding the Union's treaty making, but also the powers of the Council and the Commission concerning the overall management of the Union's external relations and EU external representation. The analysis of the institutional balance in EU external relations reveals that it does not prohibit *per se* entrusting certain international cooperation tasks to EU agencies. Although the Founding Treaties do not assign expressly a role to EU agencies in external relations, this does not mean that these bodies are barred *a priori* from any involvement in international cooperation. The development of the EU agencies in the shadow of the Founding Treaties, validated by the Court and finally formalised by the Lisbon Treaty, indicates that these bodies are legally acceptable, under certain conditions, as implementing tools of the various EU policies and legal frameworks. Truly, EU agencies can be seen as '(. . .) a fact of functional life within the EU (. . .)' in that their creation was necessary in response to pressing problems resulting from the interplay and need for coordination between political and administrative actors situated in national and supranational legal orders.[2] This applies *mutatis mutandis* as far as international cooperation by EU agencies pertaining to the external dimension of various EU policy areas is concerned. What is more, in Case C-363/14, the Court reviewed Europol's international dimension and it seemed to accept it as long as it was ancillary and necessary for the performance of Agency's core tasks, and provided that it took place within the framework defined by the EU legislature.[3] Whilst the context of the case was specific, the judgment can be seen, nevertheless, as a first-time confirmation by the CJEU of EU agencies' international dimension.

The overview of the international cooperation legal framework and practice of the EU agencies reveals some diversity among these bodies. Thus, the international dimension of the EU agencies is reflected differently in the EU agencies' legal framework. In some cases, more detailed provisions are included in the founding acts than in others. Overall, the founding acts of the EU agencies reflect the instrumental nature of their international cooperation activities. The founding acts of some EU agencies do not specify the international cooperation instruments these bodies may use, but, even in the cases in which these instruments are mentioned, their legal nature is not clarified, except for EBA, ESMA, EIOPA and SRB, whose founding regulations suggest that they are non-binding instruments. The founding acts often fall short of providing explicitly for supervision and controlling mechanisms concerning the international cooperation powers of the EU agencies, though a careful analysis of the agencies' legal design may reveal general controls covering also their international dimension. Moreover, apparent mismatches between the EU agencies' international cooperation practice and their legal framework have been observed. In particular, it was found that the development of international cooperation practices and instruments are not always paralleled by provisions in their legal framework. This raises the question whether the EU agencies may develop an international dimension solely on the basis

2 Michelle Everson, 'European Agencies: Barely Legal?' in Michelle Everson, Cosimo Monda and Ellen Vos (eds), *European Agencies in between Institutions and Member States* (Kluwer Law International 2014) 53.

3 Case C-363/14 *Parliament v Council* EU:C:2015:579, paras 49–50.

of general provisions on international cooperation, or even in the absence of explicit provisions to that effect in their founding acts.

Whereas for the sake of legal certainty, the founding acts of the EU agencies should include explicit and detailed provisions on the international cooperation tasks and instruments of these bodies, it is maintained that the absence of such provisions does not necessarily preclude EU agencies from pursuing international cooperation activities. On the one hand, international cooperation tasks may be entrusted to EU agencies explicitly by instruments of secondary legislation other than their founding acts and also by international agreements concluded by the EU with third countries and international organisations. On the other hand, in line with the more legal-realistic perspective taken in this study,[4] we maintain that it is possible to adopt a functional approach to the EU agencies' international dimension enabling these bodies to pursue international cooperation, which is instrumental to achieving their core tasks. This entails that the EU agencies can act on the basis of an implied international cooperation mandate that is derived from their core mandate. Such a scenario has been endorsed recently in the Common Approach on EU agencies and in the Commission's Vademecum on EU External Action. In the view of the author, in the absence of an explicit prohibition in the founding act, EU agencies' international cooperation activities and instruments are legally valid as long as they remain within the boundaries of their core mandate, and are in compliance with the general requirements concerning the powers of the EU agencies as well as with the constitutional framework governing Union's external action.

This requires in particular that the international cooperation carried out by the EU agencies remains on a technical/administrative level, subject to supervision and controls limiting the discretion of the agency, and that the institutional balance in external relations is not affected. It remains to be seen, however, whether the CJEU would accept such a functional logic as regards the EU agencies' international cooperation powers. On the one hand, in Case C-327/1991, the Court denied, as a matter of principle, the parallel between internal and external powers when faced with the Commission's claim for a general power to conclude international binding agreements based solely on its core tasks. On the other hand, in *ESMA*, the Court made use of the functional logic, allegedly degrading *Meroni* to a rather flexible test, in order to support ESMA's wide ranging executive powers. One may also wonder whether from the Court's findings in Case C-363/14 with regard to the ancillary and necessary nature of Europol's international cooperation, broader implications can be drawn with regard to the overall international dimension of the EU agencies.

An important aspect concerning the international cooperation mandate of the EU agencies is to clarify the legal nature and effects of the international cooperation instruments and activities of these bodies, and whether they are acceptable under EU law. This entailed examining whether and under which conditions EU agencies may enact non-binding and binding instruments in pursuit of international cooperation. In this regard, the following conclusions are advanced.

First, non-binding international cooperation instruments and activities should not be legally problematic, as long as they remain within the core mandate of the agency and do not affect the powers of the EU institutions, especially in the EU external action area. In our view, the *Meroni* requirements and the principle of institutional

4 See also Everson (n 2).

balance are relevant also for EU agencies' powers to enter into international cooperation that does not result in legally binding instruments. Otherwise, the applicability of *Meroni* and of the principle of institutional balance would be too limited, since the rationale that EU agencies do not act *ultra vires* or uncontrolled holds for their overall powers, not only when they exercise powers resulting in legally binding acts. As regards specifically the institutional balance in EU external relations, the CJEU's judgment in Case C-660/13 has already revealed that this is a valid standard for reviewing also the Union's non-binding international agreements.[5] We see no legal impediment for this finding to apply *mutatis mutandis* to non-binding international agreements concluded by the EU agencies. Since in external relations even non-binding acts can nevertheless give rise to important political and legal consequences, it is also important that the EU agencies are subject to monitoring and control mechanisms, such as informing the relevant EU delegations in advance, acting in coordination with the EEAS or being supervised by the Commission.

Secondly, the scenario under which the EU agencies' international cooperation would result in legally binding instruments seems to raise *prima facie* significant legal problems. More precisely, both CJEU's relevant case law and the current Treaty provisions appear to bar the EU agencies from concluding binding international agreements. Put simply, beside the 'ordinary' Treaty procedure under Article 218 TFEU and the derogations explicitly provided for by the Treaties, there are arguably no other scenarios in which to conclude binding international agreements under the EU legal framework. The author submits, however, that such a view should be relativised, both on the basis of legal and practical considerations. First, in the author's view, Article 218 TFEU does not *per se* preclude limited treaty-making powers being entrusted to other EU institutions and actors, provided that the prerogatives of the main EU institutions under that provision are preserved (ie the involvement of the Commission in the negotiations, *prior* authorisation and final approval by the Council, and consent or opinion of the European Parliament depending on the type of agreement). Secondly, EU institutions and bodies such as the Commission, the ECB and EIB appear to have derived limited treaty-making powers based on specific Treaty provisions regarding their role in international cooperation. This is in spite of the fact that such Treaty provisions do not specify explicitly that the above-mentioned institutions and bodies may conclude binding international agreements. The most obvious examples are the agreements concluded by the Commission with international organisations in carrying out its role under Article 220 TFEU or, even more interestingly, the participation of EIB to the multilateral international agreement establishing the EBRD. Thirdly, the EU legislator has delegated limited treaty-making powers to other EU institutions and bodies. The most obvious example is the General EU Financial Regulation, which entrusts the Commission with the power to conclude financing agreements with third countries and international organisations. Interestingly, the General EU Financial Regulation does not seem to ensure the involvement of the Council and the European Parliament in the procedure in line with their prerogatives under Article 218 TFEU.

Maintaining the view that using Article 218 TFEU as a legal basis is the only possibility for the conclusion of international agreements on behalf of the EU or that, in

5 Case C-660/13 *Council v Commission* EU:C:2016:616, para 39.

the alternative, delegation is only possible if the prerogatives of the Commission, the Council and the European Parliament under that provision are strictly preserved, leads inevitably to the conclusion that the international cooperation instruments mentioned above are obviously in breach of the principle of institutional balance. Following this line of thought, as a rule, 'Article 218 TFEU' agreements should be concluded in all of these cases, instead of the agreements which have in fact been adopted until now by the Commission, EIB, ECB and EU agencies. Such 'Article 218 TFEU' agreements could eventually envisage the involvement of the Commission and other EU institutions and bodies with a view to ensuring their implementation through specific instruments.

This option, however, features two important disadvantages. First, from a practical point of view, it does not seem feasible to use the procedure under Article 218 TFEU for all the international agreements the EU might need to conclude, in particular for those of a very limited and technical scope. For many such agreements, the procedure of the contracting party may not even involve the highest authorities, but rather may involve a ministry or a state agency instead, which would make the use of the 'Article 218 TFEU' procedure inappropriate. Moreover, the time and resources required to follow the ordinary treaty procedure under Article 218 TFEU are likely to affect seriously the effectiveness of the Union as a global actor, by limiting its capacity to enter swiftly into the legal undertakings required by the current needs of international operational and technical cooperation. Secondly, enabling the Commission and other EU institutions and bodies to adopt bilateral international cooperation instruments solely within the framework of 'Article 218 TFEU' agreements would not necessarily remove the legal concerns mentioned above. Thus, the fact that such cooperation instruments are concluded within the framework of an 'Article 218 TFEU' agreement does not mean that they do not entail legal effects, as shown in the case of EASA's international cooperation instruments which implement bilateral aviation safety agreements concluded by the EU with third countries. Provided that such instruments may very well entail legally binding effects, and that the procedure for the negotiation and conclusion of these instruments does not duly observe the prerogatives of the EU institutions under Article 218 TFEU, they could still be suspected of breaching the principle of institutional balance.

An alternative option would be to consider the international cooperation instruments concluded by the Commission and other EU institutions and bodies as non-binding. As indicated by the Court in Case C-233/02, this would remove the burden of maintaining the institutional balance under Article 218 TFEU when assessing the legality of these instruments from an EU law perspective. However, our analysis suggests that the international cooperation instruments concluded by the Commission and other EU institutions and bodies often involve substantive cooperation, laying down concrete rights and obligations for the parties to the agreements, and sometimes also for third parties. In practice, the negotiation and conclusion of these instruments often requires investing significant time and resources, which may be seen as an indicator of the willingness of the parties to enter into more than mere non-binding cooperation.[6] Accordingly, qualifying all international agreements concluded

6 According to Klabbers, 'the idea that statesmen meet, negotiate for some period of time, devote resources to establish something during the negotiation stage, and in the end that they claim that

by the Commission and other EU institutions and bodies as non-binding would simply force the reality to fit into the 'Procrustean bed' resulting from the 'single treaty-making procedure' scenario under Article 218 TFEU. In other words, the EU actors concerned would have to pretend that the agreements concluded with non-EU partners are non-binding, while the present-day conditions of international cooperation require otherwise.

The previous points could also be seen as symptomatic of the incapacity of the current EU constitutional framework to accommodate appropriately the present-day realities of international cooperation. In this respect, the Founding Treaties could ideally include more specific and clearly articulated provisions regarding the conditions and instruments for international cooperation by various EU institutions and bodies outside Article 218 TFEU. Such provisions could mirror, for instance, the provisions of Article 101 of the Euratom Treaty enabling the Commission to conclude, under certain conditions, its own international agreements. For the time being, accommodating the functional realities of international cooperation within the EU constitutional framework requires a creative interpretation of the Founding Treaties.

Hence, a solution is proposed aimed at accommodating within the existing EU legal framework the current practice of international technical-administrative cooperation entered into by various EU institutions and bodies, which will inevitably continue and expand in the context of the ever-growing globalisation. In doing so, we proceed from the assumption that the delegation of treaty-making powers to other actors or the conclusion of international agreements according to different scenarios, outside the scope of Article 218 TFEU, do not automatically upset the institutional balance in the EU external action area.

In this context, it is proposed that the category of 'technical-administrative' agreements be finally acknowledged within the EU along with the category of 'politically significant' agreements, which are concluded by the main EU institutions on the basis of Article 218 TFEU. Such a distinction, reflecting to a certain extent the interplay between legislative and executive-administrative action in the field of foreign affairs, is accepted in one way or another within states and international organizations; notably, this distinction is enshrined also within Euratom on the basis of Article 101 of the Euratom Treaty. As a result, the current international practice actually compels the EU to use such instruments in establishing cooperation on a technical-administrative level. The administrative agreements, as used currently in the EU international practice, are concluded with a view to implementing existing agreements under Article 218 TFEU or to enable external administrative action implementing existing EU legislation. Such agreements may be concluded on the basis of explicit provisions to that effect in the relevant EU legal framework and, arguably, also where the attainment of the core mandate of a certain institution or agency requires instrumental external action.

Such (binding) international cooperation instruments, as a form of external administrative action, must be in line with 'Article 218' agreements and with the Union's secondary legislation. Moreover, they must not affect the balance of powers laid down in Article 218 TFEU and, more generally, in the management of the EU external action area. As far as the latter aspect is concerned, in particular the Council's external relations

they were only involved in a practical joke, is not conceivable': Jan Klabbers, *The Concept of Treaty in International Law* (Kluwer 1996) 256.

prerogatives under Articles 16 and 21 TEU, and the Commission's powers according to Articles 17 and 21 TEU, as well as under Article 220 TFEU must be observed. In this respect, formal and informal limitations and conditions must ensure that these standards are met. This is normally ensured through provisions in the relevant legal framework limiting the scope of international cooperation instruments, and providing for formal authorisations and approvals by the Council or the Commission, duties of information, consultation and reporting, etc.

It should be noted, however, that, in view of the fact that the (binding) administrative agreements are outside the scope of Article 218 TFEU, the control exercised by the main EU institutions does not have to replicate their prerogatives under that provision. Instead, the legislator has discretion to provide for detailed arrangements ensuring that the principle of institutional balance is observed. Such arrangements should ensure that the administrative agreements concluded remain within the subject-matter mandate of the competent institution or organ, and that they are compliant and consistent with the Union's external action, including the relevant agreements concluded according to Article 218 TFEU. This entails coordination with and oversight by the main EU external action actors, in particular the Council, the Commission, the High Representative and the EEAS, as well as the EU delegations. The principle of legality also requires legal safeguards, including the possibility for judicial review of such administrative agreements.

When administrative agreements are concluded by the Commission in ensuring the Union's external representation and in implementing the external dimension of EU policies, coordination with the Council and the Member States seems essential. As for the European agencies, their powers to conclude technical-administrative agreements need to meet the present-day *Meroni* requirements and comply with the principle of institutional balance. This entails more specifically that the EU agencies' international cooperation instruments are '(. . .) coherent with their mandate, the institutional division of tasks in international relations, EU policies and priorities, and Commission's actions'.[7] In this respect, the inclusion of the Commission and the Member States in the design of the EU agencies, together with the formal and informal relationships between these bodies and the Council, as well as the Commission, should guarantee that their administrative agreements remain within the scope of their regulatory framework, and that their discretion is sufficiently limited. Moreover, a channel of communication between the agencies and the EEAS, as well as the EU delegations could provide an additional safeguard for ensuring coordination and consistency between the EU agencies' international cooperation and the Union's overall external action.

In sum, the approach proposed would alleviate the alleged incompatibility between the potentially binding administrative agreements concluded by the EU agencies with non-EU actors and the CJEU's stance in the *France v Commission* case law as well as the current Treaty provisions on the Union's international agreements. Accommodating these practical developments within the existing EU legal framework is important since the enactment of such international cooperation instruments has become a must in the present-day world of ever-increasing regulatory and technical

7 See Roadmap on the follow-up to the Common Approach on EU decentralised agencies (19 December 2012) 8 ‹http://europa.eu/about-eu/agencies/overhaul/index_en.htm›.

cooperation. In this context, functionality also entails a more flexible reading of *Meroni* and of the principle of institutional balance, similarly to the compromise reached by the Court in the *ESMA* case.

Determining the binding or non-binding nature of the international cooperation instruments concluded by the EU agencies requires the application of international law criteria. We take the view that the treaty-like instruments concluded by the EU agencies with non-EU partners are international cooperation instruments, in view of their features, purpose and scope, and not some type of instrument that is governed exclusively by domestic law. The fact that the cooperation entered into by the contracting parties often entails the application/observance of their domestic rules does not change this qualification. The specific nature of the technical-administrative agreements concluded by the EU agencies requires that the contracting parties implement or observe their relevant legal framework, but this does not affect the commitments undertaken by the parties on the international plane. Accordingly, such instruments are governed by international law and their legal nature needs to be determined in line with the requirements applied for international agreements or treaties.[8] According to the definition of the concept of 'treaty' or 'international agreement' in the 1969 and 1982 Vienna Conventions, it follows that the decisive criterion for assessing the legally binding character of international instruments is the genuine intention of the parties to create binding effects governed by international law. As shown in Chapter 2, in order to determine whether this is the case or not, the factors most commonly accepted include the wording and substance of the instrument, as well as the particular circumstances (context) surrounding the negotiation and conclusion of the instrument.

A case-by-case analysis of each instrument and category of international cooperation instruments used by the EU agencies is necessary to determine their legal nature. In this context, the analysis could be two-fold. First, the legal nature of the instruments used by the EU agencies could be anticipated by taking as a starting point the relevant legal framework pertaining to the external dimension of these bodies, including the relevant provisions regarding the procedure for negotiating and concluding international cooperation instruments. Secondly, a more detailed assessment of the international cooperation instruments entered into by each EU agency would result in specific findings as to the legal nature of that instrument, namely whether it is legally binding or not.

In order to examine the legal status of the EU agencies as global actors has been used of the concept of 'international legal personality', as it facilitated a determination of whether the international cooperation carried out by the EU agencies is attributable solely to the agencies themselves or ultimately to the EU. In the view of the author, post-Lisbon, the situation did not change fundamentally as far as the '(in)divisibility' of Union's international legal personality is concerned. The main relevance of Article 47 TEU is that it ends the pre-Lisbon ambiguity and complexities caused by the existence of the Community and the EU in parallel on the international plane. Accordingly,

8 In his opinion in Case C-660/13, Advocate General Sharpston underlined that '[u]nder both international law and EU law, the binding effect of an agreement depends in particular on the parties' intention to be bound as a matter of international law': Advocate General Opinion in Case C-660/13 *Council v Commission* EU:C:2015:787, para 66.

post-Lisbon, the possibility for certain elements of the Union's institutional framework to acquire a functionally limited international personality should not be excluded, although it is not uncontroversial either.

Unlike the Commission, which is a main EU institution in principle always acting on behalf of the Union, the EU agencies are not part of the main EU institutional framework and are entrusted with their own legal personality, as well as with a variable degree of autonomy. While this does not automatically mean that the EU agencies have international legal personality, they may nevertheless acquire such a status if they feature: (1) organisational distinctiveness; (2) separate will so as to act independently from their creators; and (3) international capacity. In view of the specific features of the EU agencies, it is particularly important that: (1) they are entrusted with powers that can be exercised on the international plane (the exercise of certain treaty-making powers would be an important indicator in this respect, although not necessarily a *sine qua non* condition); and (2) they have sufficient organisational and decision-making autonomy so that they can be perceived as an entity acting in detachment from the EU. Accordingly, the EU agencies' international personality and capacity depend essentially on the degree of autonomy and on the tasks and powers they can exercise on the international plane. These conditions must be assessed on a case-by-case basis for each EU agency. At this point, it is important to consider linking the standards that the EU agencies need to meet in order to acquire international legal personality with the need to ensure that their international cooperation powers and activities are in line with the *Meroni* requirements. This permits the assumption that the more intensive the supervisory and controlling mechanisms limiting EU agencies' discretion are, the less likely it is for these bodies to claim their own status on the international plane.

Should the case-by-case analysis carried out conclude that the relevant EU agency has a functionally limited international legal personality, then in principle its international actions should be attributed to the agency itself, with all the legal consequences flowing from this. Conversely, if it turns out that the respective EU agency does not fulfil the criteria for international legal personality, its international actions should be attributed ultimately to the EU, on whose behalf the agency is acting. Contrary to the position expressed in the Common Approach on EU agencies, this entails that the international binding agreements the EU agencies may conclude would ultimately bind the Union. Whereas in the view of the author, the EU Treaty framework does not preclude *per se* the EU agencies from concluding international technical-administrative agreements, utmost care should be taken that these bodies do not go beyond the boundaries of their mandate and that consistency with the Union's external action and legislation is ensured. Should this not be the case, then the EU agency's international agreement has been adopted *ultra vires*, which in turn raises the problem of its legal validity. From the perspective of international law,[9] and considering the CJEU's stance on this issue in Case C-327/91, it seems likely that, in general, the international agreements concluded by the EU agencies in breach of EU law would nevertheless bind the Union on the international plane, since in practice it will be difficult to prove that the breach of EU law was of fundamental importance.

9 See art 46 of the 1969 and of the 1982 Vienna Conventions.

The case studies carried out on EASA, Frontex and Europol revealed that the international dimension of the three agencies is generally in line with *Meroni* and the principle of institutional balance, though the analysis of the relevant legal framework and practice of these agencies also spotted some legally problematic aspects of their international cooperation. In all instances, EU agencies' international dimension seems to be indeed ancillary and instrumental to their core objectives and tasks. Additionally, various formal and informal controls are in place, thereby limiting the discretion of the three EU agencies as well as ensuring consistency between agencies' international cooperation actions and the Union's external relations. The new founding regulations of Frontex and Europol take further steps in this direction by enhancing supervision by the Commission and parliamentary scrutiny over important aspects of the international dimension of these agencies. The relationship between the three agencies and the Member States, in particular when an EU agency needs to rely on the support of the national competent authorities for various aspects of its international cooperation activities, appears to bring about an additional constraint on their international dimension.

As regards the formal international cooperation instruments concluded by the three agencies, the analysis of the agencies' international cooperation legal framework and practice revealed some diversity regarding the labels used (eg working arrangements and cooperation agreements), the procedure for their negotiation and conclusion, the specific types of instruments used by each agency. It also revealed complex developments in practice, which do not seem to match exactly the wording of the relevant provisions in agencies' founding acts, such as the 'shadow' international cooperation instruments concluded by the three EU agencies according to simplified procedures and generally away from the public eye. In any case, the analysis of the content and procedure of the main international cooperation instruments concluded so far by EASA, Frontex and Europol revealed that they can be qualified as binding instruments or, at least, as including limited substantive and procedural obligations. Whilst in all cases they feature a treaty-like structure, wording and clauses, there are nuances among the categories of international cooperation instruments enacted by the three agencies.

In this respect, Europol's operational agreements represent the most obvious case of binding international agreements concluded by an EU agency, the analysis of EASA's working arrangements supports the conclusion that they may qualify as binding agreements or at least they may entail some procedural and substantive obligations, whilst Frontex's working arrangements with the competent authorities of third countries are the most 'foggy', as they seem still to envisage legal effects in spite of the clause indicating that they should not be regarded as binding international agreements. Additionally, in all three cases, the formal procedures for the negotiation and conclusion of international cooperation instruments, as well as the complexity and duration of the whole process can be taken as an indicator that these are regarded as more than mere non-binding instruments.

Remaining overall within the core mandate of the agency and entailing limited technical and operational cooperation, the (binding) international cooperation instruments of EASA, Frontex and Europol are to be included in the category of international agreements of a technical-administrative nature. The case study analysis suggests that the formal (binding) international cooperation instruments enacted by the three agencies comply overall with the institutional balance in EU external relations and also with the *Meroni* doctrine. The new regulations of Europol and Frontex arguably took steps towards streamlining the international cooperation instruments of these agencies in line with the Common Approach on EU agencies. Hence, Europol will only conclude working arrangements and administrative arrangements with non-EU partners in the future, Frontex's working arrangements will require Commission's *prior* approval, for both Europol's and Frontex's international cooperation instruments the management board has the final say, and stricter parliamentary scrutiny over the formal international cooperation of the two agencies seems to be enabled. Whilst these changes suggest increased compliance of the international cooperation instruments of the two agencies with the principle of institutional balance and *Meroni*, new questions also arise regarding the sufficiency, consistency and appropriateness of the legal safeguards and supervisory mechanisms designed by the new regulations.

Last but not least, the case study research concluded that EASA, Frontex and Europol do not meet the criteria advanced in this study for acquiring their own (derived) international legal personality. Whilst having their own distinctive organizational structure and 'domestic' legal personality within the EU, as well as certain international cooperation tasks and powers, none of the three agencies displayed a sufficient degree of autonomy to be seen as acting in detachment from the European Union on the international plane. All three agencies were found to be subject to various formal and informal conditions and controls, which appear to limit significantly their discretion in international cooperation matters. Whilst these findings cannot be generalised automatically to all EU agencies, the application of *Meroni* together with the trend to streamline EU agencies' international dimension in line with the Common Approach are likely to lead to similar conclusions also with regard to other bodies from this category. The lack of the international legal personality of EASA, Frontex and Europol entails that their international actions are to be regarded as being performed ultimately on behalf of the European Union. This conclusion from an international law perspective clashes with para 25 of the Common Approach, stating that EU agencies cannot commit the Union to binding obligations. Additionally, one may also wonder, in those instances where the three EU agencies pursue international cooperation in support of or on behalf of the Member States, whether their actions can also be attributed as a matter of international law to the Member States.

2 Recommendations and directions for further research

In what follows several recommendations are advanced in order to address some of the problematic aspects revealed with regard to the international dimension of the EU agencies. Since this study is only a stepping stone towards a more in-depth exploration of the EU agencies as global actors, a number of directions for further research are proposed.

2.1 Recommendations

First, concepts such as 'EU external administrative action' and '(technical-)administrative agreement' would allow accommodating the existing international cooperation practice by various EU institutions and bodies within the Union's constitutional-legal framework. The category of 'administrative agreements' as a specific form of EU external administrative action is to be distinguished from the Union's legally-politically significant agreements covered by Article 218 TFEU. Technical-administrative agreements could be binding or non-binding and cover the formal cooperation instruments concluded by EU agencies, but also by other EU institutions and bodies involved in external administrative cooperation, such as the Commission, the ECB or the EIB. It is maintained that this concept reflects the current practice and need for more flexible forms of international cooperation in a growing globalised world featuring unprecedented transboundary activities. In this context, increased and multifarious international cooperation on a technical-operational-administrative level is necessary, and Article 218 TFEU cannot be easily employed for every low-level agreement with a state agency.

The administrative agreements, as forms of EU external administrative action, should comply with the 'Article 218 TFEU' agreements and with the EU secondary legislation, and ensure their implementation. They must remain within the scope of the core mandate of the relevant EU institution or agency and, although in practice at times the dividing line might be difficult to draw, they must be limited to technical-administrative issues or, in other words, to 'cooperation between administrations'.[10] This requires in exchange supervision and coordination by the main actors involved in the management of EU external policies to ensure consistency with the Union's overall position and strategic direction in the external action area. For the EU agencies specifically, this translates into observance of the *Meroni* requirements and of the institutional balance in EU external relations, and it entails monitoring and supervision by the Commission, eventually the Council, and preferably also by the European Parliament, as well as coordination with the EEAS and the EU delegations.

Secondly, the author proposes an extension to what appears to be the current trend within the Union with regard to the use of binding international agreements. It should be recalled that currently the default approach appears to consist of concluding binding international agreements only under Article 218 TFEU, and to allow other EU institutions and bodies, including EU agencies, to adopt formal cooperation instruments, often with an unclear legal nature, in the implementation of such agreements.[11] In the absence of an 'Article 218' agreement, it appears that bodies like EU agencies could conclude only non-binding instruments with non-EU partners.[12] In the author's view, the concept of 'technical-administrative agreement' developed previously could allow bodies like EU agencies to conclude legally binding instruments both within the framework and in the absence of an 'Article 218 TFEU' agreement. Often, considering the very limited scope of cooperation intended by the parties, it is not necessary to have recourse to Article 218 TFEU, whilst in practice binding technical-administrative agreements of a limited scope often pave the way towards more enhanced cooperation (ie the conclusion of an 'Article 218 TFEU' agreement). In all instances, it is essential that these instruments remain within the scope of administrative action, and that all other conditions and requirements are fulfilled.

Thirdly, whilst the functionalist approach taken in this study allowed not excluding *a priori* the possibility for EU agencies with a vague or no formal mandate for international cooperation to enact international cooperation instruments, for the sake of

10 See Barbara Dutzler, 'Representation of the EU and the Member States in International Organisations – General Aspects' in Stefan Griller and Birgit Weidel (eds), *External Economic Relations and Foreign Policy in the European Union* (Springer 2002) 158–59.

11 One obvious illustration of this approach, specifically with regard to EU agencies, is the new Europol Regulation.

12 Examples in this regard are the founding regulations of ESMA, EBA, EIOPA and SRB.

legal certainty, it is recommendable that the founding acts of these bodies include explicit and clear provisions regarding the respective agency's international co-operation tasks, instruments, conditions and requirements. This would help alleviating legal controversy regarding the legal basis, the scope and limits of EU agencies' international cooperation, and would facilitate a positive assessment in light of *Meroni* and of the principle of institutional balance.

Fourthly, although to date the EU agencies' formal cooperation instruments have not been reviewed by the CJEU, under the current EU constitutional framework such a possibility should not be excluded. It should be noted that the founding acts of the EU agencies do not include commonly specific provisions regarding judicial review of the agencies' acts, let alone their international cooperation instruments. This entails that the general system of judicial remedies under the Founding Treaties is fully applicable to EU agencies' acts. In this respect, Article 263 TFEU expressly ensures judicial review of the acts of EU agencies 'intended to produce legal effects vis-à-vis third parties'. One may wonder whether EU agencies' international cooperation instruments of a conventional nature and sometimes with an unclear legal status could easily be included within this category.

Yet, in Case C-327/91 the Court made it clear that the powers delegated to EU institutions in international matters cannot escape judicial review of the legality of acts adopted. In that particular case, the act through which the Commission sought to conclude an international binding agreement was annulled by the Court. Moreover, in Case C-233/02, the Court went even further by showing its readiness to review the legality of non-binding agreements, such as the 'guidelines' between the Commission and the US government. This trend has been confirmed recently in Case C-660/13, where the Court reviewed a Commission decision to sign a non-binding international agreement on behalf of the Union, and annulled that decision for breaching the principle of institutional balance.

Nowadays, such a solution should be applicable *mutatis mutandis* to the technical-administrative agreements concluded by the EU agencies, in particular when they prove to be legally binding. Thus, similarly to the agreement examined in Case C-327/91, the binding administrative agreements concluded by the EU agencies can arguably be qualified as 'acts intended to produce legal effects vis-à-vis third parties', most obviously when they could affect natural and legal persons. Accordingly, such agreements, and in particular the decisions adopted in order to conclude them should be open to judicial review on the basis of Article 263 TFEU.

In light of the Court's approach regarding the exercise of international cooperation powers, in particular in Case C-660/13, one may wonder whether also the non-binding agreements concluded by the EU agencies could be subject to judicial review.[13] This issue is relevant since such non-binding instruments could also encompass issues which go beyond mere technical cooperation, thereby affecting the prerogatives conferred by the Treaties on the EU institutions regarding Union's external representation. What is more, EU agencies' non-binding international cooperation instruments may

13 With regard specifically to AFSJ agencies, Vara maintains that CJEU could review the validity of the agreements concluded by Europol and Eurojust because these are binding international agreements, but not of the working arrangements concluded by Frontex, Cepol, EASO as these do not constitute international agreements: Juan S Vara, 'The External Activities of AFSJ Agencies: The Weakness of Democratic and Judicial Controls' (2015) 20 EFAR 115, 134–35.

still be capable to affect the consistency of Union's actions and the attainment of its objectives in external relations.[14] The Court would probably not hesitate to review such instruments, as they could still breach the balance of powers between the institutions in external relations, and contravene the priorities and objectives of the Union's external action. In addition, as pointed out by Advocate General Sharpston in his Opinion in Case C-660/13, not only should a distinction be made between the effects of an agreement under international law and the effects under EU law of the act adopted to conclude it, but also one should keep in mind that even a non-binding agreement may have certain legal effects under international law.[15] In view of these considerations, we are inclined to take the view that judicial review of EU agencies' agreements, be they binding or not, is possible under Article 263 TFEU. In any case, it is recommendable that the procedures for concluding formal cooperation instruments by EU agencies include the adoption of a formal decision either by the executive director or preferably by the management board in order to ease legal review. The latter option would also enable the Commission to make use of the 'Alert system' mentioned in the Common Approach on EU agencies.[16]

In addition to the direct annulment action under Article 263 TFEU, it is possible in our view to consider alternative means of judicial review of EU agencies' international cooperation instruments. Thus, to the extent that the implementation of EU agencies' agreements with third countries and international organisations requires action by the Member States, one may imagine the possibility to start proceedings before a national court, with the national court referring to the CJEU questions on the interpretation or validity of the underlying EU agency's agreement under Article 267 TFEU. Given the generous interpretation of the expression 'acts of institutions, bodies, offices or agencies of the Union' adopted by the CJEU, it seems likely that both binding and non-binding international cooperation instruments enacted by EU agencies can be reviewed under the 'preliminary ruling' procedure.[17] Yet another judicial review scenario entails the possibility to use the plea of illegality under Article 277 TFEU in proceedings before the EU courts, provided that EU agencies' international cooperation instruments qualify as acts of 'general application'.

From an individual protection perspective, a direct annulment action against an agreement between an EU agency and a third country authority or international organisation seems to have little chances of success because of the strict admissibility requirements imposed by Article 263 TFEU on non-privileged applicants. It seems more likely that the individual would be able to challenge EU agencies' international cooperation instruments *via* the preliminary ruling procedure or by using the plea of illegality, for instance, when asking the annulment of an EU agency measure based on such an instrument, and which is directly and individually addressed to him/her. As regards the possibility for the individual to obtain compensation for the damages caused in the application of EU agencies' international cooperation instruments, the general conditions for Union's non-contractual liability seem to be applicable as the founding acts of EU agencies usually do no more than reproducing the wording

14 See Case C-660/13 *Council v Commission* (n 5) para 39.

15 Advocate General Opinion in Case C-660/13 *Council v Commission* (n 8) paras 69–71.

16 Para 59.

17 See, for instance, Case C-322/88 *Grimaldi v Fonds des maladies professionnelles* EU:C:1989:646.

of Article 340 TFEU. However, Europol is a notable exception as, not only provide its international cooperation agreements for special liability clauses, but also Article 50 of Regulation 2016/794 includes some specific liability provisions in case of incorrect data processing. In such cases, which cover also personal data processing under Agency's international cooperation instruments, the Europol Regulation establishes the joint and several responsibility of the Europol and the Member States, enabling the individual to obtain at his/her own choice full compensation either from the Agency or from the Member States in which the event causing the damage occurred. Similar provisions could be included in the founding acts of other EU agencies, having in mind their specific tasks and powers, the characteristics of their policy area, the interplay with other actors, and, last but not least, the features of their international cooperation instruments.

Fifthly, the transparency regarding the international cooperation instruments of the EU agencies should be improved. The limited access to some of the main cooperation instruments concluded by EU agencies (eg the working arrangements between Frontex and international organisations) and in particular to the various agreements and arrangements implementing the main cooperation instruments makes it difficult to assess their legal nature and effects. The limited information available with regard to these instruments also makes it difficult to assess how oversight by the main EU institutions in charge of EU external relations is ensured. Moreover, information about the implementation of agencies' international cooperation strategy and formal cooperation instruments, as well as over their overall international cooperation activities is usually scarce. In this respect, more detailed relevant information and assessments concerning EU agencies' international cooperation in their annual reports as well as on their websites (timely and regularly updated) would probably enhance not only public scrutiny and accountability of these bodies, but also the perceptions regarding their added value as actors on the global level.

Sixthly, whilst the case study research on EASA, Frontex and Europol suggests that the controls exercised mainly by the Commission and/or the Council seemed capable of ensuring that the selected EU agencies remain within the boundaries of their legal framework, increasing the democratic accountability of EU agencies including through more effective parliamentary oversight over their international cooperation activities should be considered. Steps in this direction have already been taken by the new founding regulations of Frontex and Europol which have formally strengthened parliamentary oversight through enhanced information duties, in particular as regards the formal cooperation instruments of these agencies, and reporting to the European Parliament as well as the JPSG (in the case of Europol).

2.2 Directions for further research

This study has addressed some of the critical legal issues concerning the EU agencies' international cooperation. While contributing to the advancement of the scholarly debate on this relatively underexplored topic, it provides neither exhaustive nor definite answers to the problems tackled. Moreover, the research revealed new issues that require closer examination, but could not be dealt with comprehensively in this study. Therefore, in what follows, we propose several directions for further research regarding the international dimension of the EU agencies.

The case study research revealed that the three agencies examined do not meet the requirements for international legal personality and, as a result, they are to be considered as 'agents' of the European Union on the international plane. However, the situation is further complicated by the composite nature of the EU, as well as by the apparent mismatches between the 'domestic' EU legal framework, on the one hand, and international law and practice, on the other hand. In this regard, the EU agencies' founding acts and practice revealed possibilities to assist the Member States in international cooperation matters within the scope of the agencies' mandate. Frontex, for instance, can be assigned implementing tasks through international agreements concluded between a Member State and a third country, whereas the international cooperation instruments concluded by EASA, Frontex and Europol often mention that these agencies act on behalf of or in support of the Member States in certain matters. The case of EASA is particularly interesting as EASA fulfils certain tasks within the ICAO, an international organisation in which only the Member States participate as full members. This reveals the potential for the EU agencies to become part of a complex agency relationship. Such a relationship entails that the agencies, as EU bodies and on the basis of their mandate conferred by the EU legislation, may also act as 'agents' of the Member States on the international plane.[18] This may raise significant problems, not only in theory but also in practice, concerning the division and balance of powers within the EU institutional framework as well as between the Union and its Member States, and with regard to attribution and responsibility under international law. Hence, clarifying and solving this conundrum requires further in-depth analysis combining EU and international law perspectives.[19]

Another relevant aspect concerning the status of the EU agencies as global actors pertains to the way in which these bodies are perceived by their partners. In other words, the question is whether third countries and international organisations with which the EU agencies establish cooperation regard the agencies as EU bodies, as entities acting on behalf of the Member States, or as subjects in their own right. Whereas empirical insights from the case studies suggest that the three EU agencies examined are seen rather as technical agents of the EU, more in-depth research is needed on this point. Empirical evidence to the contrary could offer support for the view that some EU agencies may have acquired a limited functional international legal personality.

The unclear legal status or mandate of some of the EU agencies' partners are a matter that deserves a closer examination. Whereas the preambles to the international cooperation instruments concluded by the EU agencies usually refer to the source of the competence of the agency's counterpart to conclude that instrument, the situation is not always entirely clear as to the status of that entity. In particular, the status of some of the 'international organisations' such as DCAF, ICMPD and UNODC is not easy to elucidate. Moreover, questions can be raised regarding the capacity of such international organisations and also of various authorities of third countries to conclude international agreements. In the author's view, the issue of the competence of an international organisation or third country to establish international cooperation is a

18 See on this issue with regard specifically to EASA, Mikołaj Ratajczyk, *Regional Aviation Safety Organisations. Enhancing Air Safety through Regional Cooperation* (Kluwer Law International 2015) 139–44.

19 See more generally on the possibility for the Member States to 'borrow' the EU institutions for the purpose of implementing international agreements concluded outside the EU legal framework, Bruno de Witte and Tom Beukers, 'The Court of Justice Approves the Creation of the European Stability Mechanism outside the EU Legal Order: Pringle' (2013) 50 CML Rev 805, 843–47.

matter of 'internal' law of the respective organisation or state, which only exceptionally could lead to the annulment of an agreement according to international law. Moreover, the current international practice appears to accept various organisations with an ambiguous legal status as subjects of international law. Accordingly, it appears that the specific features of the parties to technical-administrative agreements, such as those concluded by the EU agencies with international organisations and competent authorities from third countries, have relevance primarily with regard to whom the instrument can be attributed under international law, not necessarily with regard to its legal nature and effects.

Yet another direction for further research concerns the issue of coordination between the EU agencies' international cooperation with the Union's overall external policy. Although our case study research suggests that the oversight and coordination of the international cooperation priorities and actions of the three agencies examined are satisfactory overall, preliminary empirical evidence hints at the fact that this issue also poses significant challenges in practice. In this regard, it appears that the relationship between technical sectoral actors, such as the EU agencies and the actors involved in the Union's external policies (ie the Commission, the Council, the High Representative and the EEAS as well as the EU delegations) requires further improvements. Arguably, the multitude of actors involved in shaping the Union's external policies, the lack of adequate coordination and communication between different Commission DGs, as well as between the relevant Commission's DGs and the EU agencies creates difficulties for the required consistency between the agencies' international cooperation and the Union's external relations. It appears that often the EU agencies are not apprised on time with regard to the relevant developments occurring at policy-political level, whilst, on the other hand, the EU agencies sometimes attempt to pursue cooperation with a certain third country without informing the Commission or the relevant EU delegation in a timely manner. These issues may also raise questions from the perspective of the principle of institutional balance and *Meroni*. To this, one may add that EU agencies may depend, for the effectiveness of their international cooperation actions, on support from the Member States (eg Europol), which may in turn attempt to influence agencies' international cooperation strategy and actions. These issues require in-depth research to map out the existing legal problems and consequences, and to devise appropriate solutions.

Further inquiry is also needed with regard to several particular issues concerning EU agencies' international cooperation mandate and practice. First, the EU agencies with vague or no provisions on international cooperation in their founding acts should be examined more closely. By taking a legal-realist perspective, it has been maintained tentatively that, even in such circumstances, EU agencies could pursue international cooperation based on a functional-instrumental approach. It has been observed that the EU institutions have already acknowledged such a scenario. Here the assessment even went one step further by advancing the assumption that these EU agencies could conclude formal international cooperation instruments provided that the *Meroni* requirements and the principle of institutional balance are complied with. However, it needs to be examined in further detail whether the technical-administrative agreements, in particular those of a legally binding nature, concluded by such agencies in the absence of an explicit mandate, would actually meet the above-mentioned legal parameters.

Secondly, with regard to the EU agencies featuring detailed provisions concerning international specifically cooperation, it is worth looking more closely for international cooperation instruments concluded in the shadow of their legal framework. The international practice of all three EU agencies examined revealed the existence of instruments which are not mentioned as such by their founding acts. These forms of international cooperation have been tackled only marginally in this study, partly because of the specific focus of this research and partly because of practical reasons, such as accessibility. The case study research suggested that usually such instruments might be of a soft law nature and enable cooperation at a preliminary stage or that they are concluded in order to implement the 'mother' agreements between an EU agency and its partner. Such instruments do not normally abide by the same procedural conditions as in the case of the 'mother agreement', which raises the question whether there are sufficient criteria and conditions limiting the discretion of the respective agency. Moreover, the possibility should not be excluded for some EU agencies to use such instruments precisely in order to avoid some of the constraints imposed by their legal framework with respect to the main formal international cooperation instruments.

Thirdly, in this study, criteria for binding international agreements have been used in order to determine the legal nature of the international cooperation instruments concluded by EU agencies. While this approach made it possible to make a distinction between binding and non-binding instruments of the EU agencies examined, in practice complex situations were also encountered in which reaching a 'black or white' conclusion was difficult. In this context, the use of alternative approaches and concepts, such as 'soft law' theories could be explored for assessing EU agencies' international cooperation instruments.[20] Provided that it benefits from a fully-developed theoretical underpinning, 'soft law' could arguably contribute to explaining some of the peculiar international cooperation instruments concluded by the EU agencies, which seem to be somewhere in between binding and non-binding.

Fourthly, it is worth looking more closely into the EU agencies' informal and legally non-binding international cooperation activities to assess their legal and practical consequences, as well as whether they raise particular problems which would require tailored legal solutions. Whilst focusing on formal legal aspects concerning EU agencies' international dimension, this research also spotted more or less *ad hoc* international cooperation activities by these bodies running in parallel or complementing formal international cooperation instruments. These may entail, *inter alia*, participation of EU agencies in various more or less opaque global regulatory networks, involvement in diverse ways in wider EU policy initiatives, carrying out specific technical assistance and support activities and projects, or exchanging liaison officers with third countries and international organisations in order to enhance technical-operational cooperation. Arguably, such less formalised international cooperation activities represent the bulk of EU agencies' international dimension, and they raise legal and good governance questions in terms of delegation of powers and institutional balance, legal certainty, transparency, accountability and legitimacy, just to name a few.

The previous remarks also denote that there are limits to the use of traditional legal concepts and parameters to assess EU agencies as global actors. This is illustrated by the difficulties to determine with precision the legal nature of certain international cooperation instruments enacted by some EU agencies, to establish the legal status of

20 See, for instance, Fabien Terpan, 'Soft Law in the European Union. The Changing Nature of EU Law' (2015) 21 *European Law Journal* 68.

certain international partners of EU agencies, or to explain the complex relationships and interactions featured by global regulatory cooperation involving EU agencies. The use of alternative approaches and perspectives should be considered with a view to close the gap in researching EU agencies' international dimension. Beside soft law theories relevant in particular for explaining the legal relevance of acts and instruments which do not easily qualify as 'hard law', global administrative law (GAL) aiming to provide a comprehensive legal framework to the growing complex global administrative space could also be useful. Considering that GAL attempts to encompass the intricate intermingling between domestic and international regulatory processes as well as the complex and diverse binding and non-binding forms of global regulatory cooperation, it makes sense to look at EU agencies' international dimension also through the lenses of the conceptual framework, legal principles and mechanisms of this emerging discipline.[21] One potential added value of GAL could consist of offering appropriate concepts and standards for charting and for ensuring the legal review of EU agencies' international actions, as well as their accountability as global actors.

Finally, but yet importantly, the issue of 'constitutionalisation' of EU agencies' international dimension could be further explored. As could be seen, the phenomenon of 'agencification' started and developed well before being formally enshrined in the Founding Treaties. This reality has furthermore been endorsed by the CJEU in the landmark *ESMA* case. All this suggests that the possibility for EU agencies to pursue international cooperation does not require inserting special provisions to that effect in the Founding Treaties. Whilst this research has shown that so far EU agencies engaged in international cooperation based on secondary legislation in combination with a logic of flexibility and functionality, one may wonder whether a certain degree of 'constitutionalisation' of EU agencies' international dimension could still be desirable.

This research has revealed that certain aspects of the EU agencies' international dimension (eg the possibility to enact binding agreements, their legal status as global actors, the interplay and coordination with other EU actors, including the Member States) raise complex problems and may require a creative *ESMA*-like reading of 'the formal constellation of the balance of powers'[22] in the Founding Treaties. Therefore, the 'constitutionalisation' of certain horizontal aspects of EU agencies' international cooperation could perhaps bring same clarity as regards their role as global actors, and also attenuate some of the intra-EU law tensions and EU law–international law clashes that the international dimension of these bodies may cause. If such a scenario is contemplated, it remains to be seen what elements of the EU agencies' international dimension should be 'constitutionalised' and how (eg including explicit provisions on administrative agreements enacted by EU institutions, bodies and agencies, on the scope and limits of EU agencies' international cooperation, and/or on coordination between EU agencies' international actions and the Union's external action).

21 On the concept of global administrative law, see Benedict Kingsbury, Nico Krisch and Richard B Stewart, 'The Emergence of Global Administrative Law' (2005) 68 Law & Contemporary Problems 15; Nico Krisch and Benedict Kingsbury, 'Introduction: Global Administrative Law and Global Market Regulation in the International Legal Order' (2006) 17 European Journal of International Law 1.

22 See Everson (n 2) 69.

References

Scholarly literature

Andoura S and Timmerman P, 'Governance of the EU: The Reform Debate on European Agencies Reignited' (2008) 19 *EPIN Working Paper* 1–37

Aust A, 'Alternatives to Treaty-making: MOUs as Political Commitments' in Hollis DB (ed), *The Oxford Guide to Treaties* (OUP 2012) 46–72

Aust A, *Modern Treaty Law and Practice* (3rd edn, CUP 2013)

Baker E and Harding C, 'From Past Imperfect to Future Perfect? A Longitudinal Study of the Third Pillar' (2009) 34(1) *European Law Review* 25–54

Bermann GA, 'Regulatory Cooperation with Counterpart Agencies Abroad: The FAA's Aircraft Certification Experience' (1992/1993) 24(3) *Law and Policy in International Business* 669–781

Bermann GA, 'Executive Power in the New European Constitution' (2005) 3(2–3) *I CON* 440–47

Boyle AE, 'Some Reflections on the Relationship of Treaties and Soft Law' (1999) 48(4) *International and Comparative Law Quarterly* 901–13

Brownlie I, *Principles of Public International Law* (7th edn, OUP 2008)

Burdeau G, 'Les Accords Conclus entre Autorités Administratives ou Organismes Publics de Pays Différents' in Reuter P (ed), *Mélanges Offerts à Paul Reuter. Le Droit International: Unité et Diversité* (Pedone 1981) 103–26

Busuioc M, 'Accountability, Control and Independence: The Case of European Agencies' (2009) 15(5) *European Law Journal* 599 – 615

Busuioc M, Curtin DM and Groenleer M, 'Agency Growth between Autonomy and Accountability: the European Police Office as a 'Living Institution' (2011) 18(6) *Journal of European Public Policy* 848–67

Busuioc M, Groenleer M and Trondal J (eds), *The Agency Phenomenon in the European Union: Emergence, Institutionalisation and Everyday Decision-making* (Manchester University Press 2012)

Busuioc M and Groenleer M, 'Beyond Design: the Evolution of Europol and Eurojust' (2013) 14(3) *Perspectives on European Politics and Society* 285–304

Byrd jr. EM, *Treaties and Executive Agreements in the United States. Their Separate Roles and Limitations* (Martinus Nijhoff 1960)

Carrera S, 'The EU border Management Strategy. Frontex and the Challenges of Irregular Migration in the Canary Islands' (2007) 261 *CEPS Working Document* 1–33

Carrera S and Guild E, 'Does the Stockholm Programme Matter? The Struggles over Ownership of AFSJ Multiannual Programming' (2012) 51 *CEPS* 1–38

Carrera S and Guild E, 'The European Council's Guidelines for the Area of Freedom, Security and Justice 2020. Subverting the "Lisbonisation" of Justice and Home Affairs?' (2014) 13 *CEPS* 1–55

Cavelier G, 'National Treaty Law and Practice: Colombia' in Hollis DB, Blakeslee MR and Ederington LB (eds), *National Treaty Law and Practice* (Martinus Nijhoff Publishers 2005) 193–226

Chalmers D and Tomkins A, *European Union Public Law* (CUP 2007)

Chamon M, 'EU Agencies between Meroni and Romano or the Devil and the Deep Blue Sea' (2011) 48(4) *Common Market Law Review* 1055–75

Chamon M, 'The Empowerment of Agencies under the *Meroni* Doctrine and Article 114 TFEU: Comment on *United Kingdom v Parliament and Council* (Short-selling) and the Proposed Single Resolution Mechanism' (2014) 39(3) *European Law Review* 381–403

Chamon M, *EU Agencies: Legal and Political Limits to the Transformation of the EU Administration* (OUP 2016)

Chiti E, 'The Emergence of a Community Administration: the Case of European Agencies' (2000) 37(2) *Common Market Law Review* 309–43

Chiti E, 'Decentralisation and Integration into the Community Administrations: a New Perspective on European Agencies' (2004) 10(4) *European Law Journal* 402–38

Chiti E, 'An Important Part of the EU's Institutional Machinery: Features, Problems and Perspectives of European Agencies' (2009) 46(5) *Common Market Law Review* 1395–1442

Chiti E and Wessel RA, 'The Emergence of International Agencies in the Global Administrative Space. Autonomous Actors or State Servants?' in Collins R and White ND (eds), *International Organisations and the Idea of Autonomy. Institutional Independence in the International Legal Order* (Oxon 2011) 142–59

Chiti E, 'European Agencies' Rulemaking Powers, Procedures and Assessment' (2013) 19(1) *European Law Journal* 93–110

Cohen FS, 'Transcendental Nonsense and the Functional Approach' (1935) 35(6) *Columbia Law Review* 809–49

Coman-Kund F, 'Assessing the Role of EU Agencies in the Enlargement Process: the Case of the European Aviation Safety Agency' (2012) 8 *Croatian Yearbook of European Law and Policy* 335–67

Coman-Kund F, 'EU Agencies as Global Actors: A Legal Assessment of Europol's International Dimension' (2014) 6 *Maastricht Faculty of Law Working Paper*

Coman-Kund F, Ratajczyk M and Schmidt E, 'Shared Enforcement and Accountability in the EU Aviation Safety Area. The Case of the European Aviation Safety Agency' in Scholten M and Luchtman M (eds), *Law Enforcement by EU authorities. Political and Judicial Accountability in Shared Enforcement* (Eduard Elgar Publishing 2017) 115–40

Coman-Kund F, 'The International Dimension of the EU Agencies: Framing a Growing Legal–Institutional Phenomenon' (2018) 23(1) *European Foreign Affairs Review* 97–118

Coman-Kund F, 'Europol's International Cooperation between "Past Present" and "Present Future": Reshaping the External Dimension of EU Police Cooperation' (2018) 1(1) *Europe and the World* (forthcoming)

Corten O and Klein P (eds), *The Vienna Conventions of the Law of Treaties. A Commentary* (vol I, OUP 2011)

Craig P, 'European Governance: Executive and Administrative Powers under the New Constitutional Settlement' (2005) 3(2–3) *I CON* 407–39

Craig P, 'EU Administrative Law' in De Búrca G, de Witte B and Francioni F (eds), *The Collected Courses of the Academy of European Law* (Volume XVI/1, OUP 2006)

Craig P, *The Lisbon Treaty: Law, Politics and Treaty Reform* (OUP 2010)

Cremona M, 'The Draft Constitutional Treaty: External Relations and External Action' (2003) 40(6) *Common Market Law Review* 1347–66

Cremona M, 'Defining Competence in EU External Relations: Lessons from the Treaty Reform Process' in Dashwood A and Maresceau M (eds), *Law and Practice of EU external Relations: Salient Features of a Changing Landscape* (CUP 2008) 34–69

Curtin DM, 'Holding (Quasi-)autonomous EU Administrative Actors to Public Account' (2007) 13(4) *European Law Journal* 523–41

Curtin DM, *Executive Power of the European Union. Law, Practices, and the Living Constitution* (OUP 2009)

Dehousse R, 'Regulation by Networks in the European Community: The Role of European Agencies' (1997) 4(2) *Journal of European Public Policy* 246–61

Dehousse R, 'Misfits: EU Law and the Transformation of European Governance' (2002) 2/02 *Jean Monnet Working Paper* (NYU School of Law) 1–18

Detter TIH, 'The Organs of International Organizations Exercising their Treaty-making Power' (1962) 38 *British Yearbook of International Law* 421–44

Diaz LM, 'National Treaty Law and Practice: Mexico' in Hollis DB, Blakeslee MR and Ederington LB (eds), *National Treaty Law and Practice* (Martinus Nijhoff Publishers 2005) 439–82

Dunnett DRR, 'The European Investment Bank: Autonomous Instrument or Common Policy?' (1994) 31(4) *Common Market Law Review* 721–63

Dutzler B, 'Representation of the EU and the Member States in International Organisations – General Aspects' in Griller S and Weidel B (eds), *External Economic Relations and Foreign Policy in the European Union* (Springer 2002) 151–89

Eeckhout P, *External Relations of the European Union. Legal and Constitutional Foundations* (OUP 2004)

Eeckhout P, *EU External Relations Law* (2nd edn, OUP 2011)

Egeberg MM and Trondal M, 'Building Executive Power at the European Level. On the Role of EU-level Agencies' (2009) 10 *ARENA Working Paper* 1–25

Eisemann PM and Rivier R, 'National Treaty Law and Practice: France' in Hollis DB, Blakeslee ML and Ederington LB (eds), *National Treaty Law and Practice* (Martinus Nijhoff Publishers 2005) 253–316

Elias O, 'Who can Make Treaties? International Organisations' in Hollis DB (ed), *The Oxford Guide to Treaties* (OUP 2012) 73–92

van Elsuwege P, *From Soviet Republics to EU Member States* (Martinus Nijhoff 2008)

Everson M, 'Independent Agencies: Hierarchy Beaters?' (1995) 1(2) *European Law Journal* 180–204

Everson M, 'European Agencies: Barely Legal?' in Everson M, Monda C and Vos E (eds), *European Agencies in between Institutions and Member States* (Kluwer Law International 2014) 49–69

Fink M, 'Frontex Working Arrangements: Legitimacy and Human Rights Concerns regarding Technical Relationships' (2012) 28 *Utrecht Journal for International and European Law* 20–35

Frid R, *The Relations Between the EC and International Organizations: Legal Theory and Practice* (Kluwer Law International 1995)

Gautier P, 'Article 1' in Corten O and Klein P (eds), *The Vienna Conventions of the Law of Treaties. A Commentary* (vol I, OUP 2011) 21–32

Gautier P, 'Article 2' in Corten O and Klein P (eds), *The Vienna Conventions of the Law of Treaties. A Commentary* (vol I, OUP 2011) 33–57

Geradin D and Petit N, 'The Development of Agencies at EU and National Levels: Conceptual Analysis and Proposals for Reform' (2004) *1/04 Jean Monnet Working Paper* (NYU School of Law) 1–61

Grant T, 'Who can Make Treaties? Other Subjects of International Law' in Hollis DB (ed), *The Oxford Guide to Treaties* (OUP 2012) 125–49

Griller S and Orator A, 'Everything under Control? The "Way Forward" for European Agencies in the Footsteps of the Meroni Doctrine' (2010) 35(1) *European Law Review* 3–35

Groenleer M, 'The European Commission and Agencies' in Spence D and Edwards G (eds), *The European Commission* (John Harper Publishing 2006) 156–72

Groenleer M, *The Autonomy of European Union Agencies: A Comparative Study of Institutional Development* (PhD dissertation, Leiden University 2009)

Groenleer M, Kaeding M and Versluis E, 'Regulatory Governance through Agencies of the European Union? The Role of the European Agencies for Maritime and Aviation Safety in the Implementation of European Transport Legislation' (2010) 17(8) *Journal of European Public Policy* 1212–30

Groenleer M, 'Linking up Levels of Governance: Agencies of the European Union and their Interaction with International Organisations' in Oriol C and Jørgensen KE (eds), *The Influence of International Institutions on the European Union* (Palgrave Macmillan 2012) 135–54

Groenleer M and Gabbi, S, 'Regulatory Agencies of the European Union as International Actors. Legal Framework, Development over Time and Strategic Motives in the Case of the European Food Safety Authority' (2013) 4(4) *European Journal of Risk Regulation* 479–92

Guild E, Carrera S, den Hertog L and Parkin J, 'Implementation of the EU Charter of Fundamental Rights and its Impact on EU Home Affairs Agencies. Frontex, Europol and the European Asylum Support Office', Study for the European Parliament. *Committee on Civil Liberties, Justice and Home Affairs* (2011) 453. 196 PE

Hartley TC, *The Foundations of European Union Law* (7th edn, OUP 2010)

Heimans D, 'The External Relations of Europol – Political, Legal and Operational Considerations' in Martenczuk B and van Thiel S (eds), *Justice, Liberty and Security: New Challenges for EU External Relations* (VUB Press 2008) 367–89

Hillion C, 'ERTA, ECHR and Open Skies: Laying the Grounds of the EU System of External Relations' in Poiares M, Maduro M and Azoulai L (eds), *The Past and Future of EU Law* (Hart Publishing 2010) 224–33

Hofmann HCH and Türk A, 'The Development of Integrated Administration in the EU and its Consequences' (2007) 13(2) *European Law Journal* 253–71

Hofmann HCH and Morini, 'Constitutional Aspects of the Pluralisation of the EU Executive through "Agencification"' (2012) 37(4) *European Law Review* 419–43

Hollis DB, Blakeslee MR and Ederington LB (eds), *National Treaty Law and Practice* (Martinus Nijhoff Publishers 2005)

Hollis DB, 'A Comparative Approach to Treaty Law and Practice' in Hollis DB, Blakeslee MR and Ederington LB (eds), *National Treaty Law and Practice* (Martinus Nijhoff Publishers 2005) 1–53

Hollis DB (ed), *The Oxford Guide to Treaties* (OUP 2012)

Hollis DB, 'Defining Treaties' in Hollis DB (ed), *The Oxford Guide to Treaties* (OUP 2012) 11–45

Hundag Chiu SJD, *The Capacity of International Organizations to Conclude Treaties, and the Special Legal Aspects of the Treaties so Concluded* (Martinus Nijhoff 1966)

Ibáñez GAJ, *The Administrative Supervision and Enforcement of EC Law: Powers, Procedures and Limits* (Hart Publishing 1999)

Jacqué JP, 'The Principle of Institutional Balance' (2004) 41(2) *Common Market Law Review* 383–91

Keukeleire S and MacNaughtan J, *The Foreign Policy of the European Union* (Palgrave Macmillan 2008)

Kingston J, 'External Relations of the European Community: External Capacity versus Internal Competence' (1995) 44(3) *The International and Comparative Law Quarterly* 659–70

Klabbers J, *The Concept of Treaty in International Law* (Kluwer 1996)

Koutrakos P, *EU International Relations Law* (Hart Publishing 2006)

Kreher A, 'Agencies in the European Community – A Step towards Administrative Integration in the European Union' (1997) 4(2) *Journal of European Public Policy* 225–45

Kingsbury B, Krisch N and Stewart RB, 'The Emergence of Global Administrative Law' (2005) 68(3–4) *Law & Contemporary Problems* 15–61

Krisch N and Kingsbury B, 'Introduction: Global Administrative Law and Global Market Regulation in the International Legal Order' (2006) 17(1) *European Journal of International Law* 1–14

Kuchenbecker DJ, 'Agency-Level Executive Agreements: A New Era in U.S. Treaty Practice' (1979/1980) 18 *Columbia Journal of Transnational Law* 1–77

le Bouthillier Y and Bonin JF, 'Article 3' in Corten O and Klein P (eds), *The Vienna Conventions of the Law of Treaties. A Commentary* (vol I, OUP 2011) 66–78

Lenaerts K, 'Some Reflections on the Separation of Powers in the European Community' (1991) 28(1) *Common Market Law Review* 11–35

Lenaerts K, 'Regulating the Regulatory Process: "Delegation of Powers" in the European Community' (1993) 18(1) *European Law Review* 23–49

Lenaerts K and Van Nuffel P, *Constitutional Law of the European Union* (Sweet & Maxwell 1999)

Macleod I, Henry ID and Hyett S, *The External Relation of the European Communities* (OUP 1996)

Majone G, 'The New European Agencies: Regulation by Information' (1997) 4(2) *Journal of European Public Policy* 262–75

Majone G, 'Delegation of Regulatory Powers in a Mixed Polity' (2002) 8(3) *European Law Journal* 319–39

Majone G, *Dilemmas of European Integration. The Ambiguities and Pitfalls of Integration by Stealth* (OUP 2005)

Manin Ph, *Droit Constitutionnel de l'Union Européenne* (Pedone 2004)

Missiroli A, 'Implementing the Lisbon Treaty: The External Policy Dimension' (2010) 14 *Bruges Political Research Papers* 1–28

Mitsilegas V, Carrera S and Eisele K, 'The End of the Transitional Period for Police and Criminal Justice Measures Adopted before the Lisbon Treaty. Who Monitors Trust in the European Justice Area?' Study for the LIBE Committee, *European Parliament, Committee on Civil Liberties, Justice and Home Affairs* (2014) 509.998 (PE)

Monar J, 'The External Dimension of the EU's Area of Freedom, Security and Justice. Progress, Potential and Limitations after the Treaty of Lisbon' (2012) 1 *Sieps* 11–74

Monar J, 'The EU's Growing External Role in the AFSJ Domain: Factors, Framework and Forms of Action' (2014) 27(1) *Cambridge Review of International Affairs* 147–66

de Moor A and Vermeulen G, 'The Europol Council Decision: Transforming Europol into an Agency of the European Union' (2010) 47(4) *Common Market Law Review* 1089–1121

Moreno-Lax V, 'Frontex as a Global Actor: External Relations with Third Countries and International Organisations' in Dony M (ed), *La Dimension Externe de l'Espace de Liberté, Sécurité et de Justice au lendemain de Lisbonne et de Stockholm: un Bilan à mi-parcours* (Éditions de l'Université de Bruxelles 2012) 163–84

Morrison FL, 'Executive Agreements', *Max Planck Encyclopedia of Public International Law* (Oxford Public International Law, May 2007) 1052–55 online publication

Mounier G, 'Europol: A New Player in the EU External Policy Field?' (2009) 10(4) *Perspectives on European Politics and Society* 582–602

van Ooik R, 'The Growing Importance of Agencies in the EU: Shifting Governance and the Institutional Balance' in Curtin DM and Wessel RA (eds), *Good Governance and the European Union. Reflections on Concepts, Institutions and Substance* (Intersentia 2005) 125–52

Ott A, 'EU Regulatory Agencies in EU External Relations: Trapped in a Legal Minefield between European and International Law' (2008) 13(4) *European Foreign Affairs Review* 515–40

Ott A and Wessel RA, 'The EU's External Relations Regime: Multilevel Complexity in an Expanding Union' in Blockmans S and Lazowski A (eds), *The European Union and Its Neighbours* (TMC Asser Instituut 2006) 19–59

Ott A, Vos E and Coman-Kund F, 'EU Agencies on the Global Scene: EU and International Law Perspectives' in Everson M, Monda C and Vos E (eds), *European Agencies in between Institutions and Member States* (Kluwer Law International 2014) 87–122

Parkin J, 'EU Home Affairs Agencies and the Construction of EU Internal Security' (2012) 53 *CEPS* 1–43

Passivirta E, 'The European Union: from an Aggregate of States to a Legal Person?' (1997) 2 *Hofstra Law & Policy Symposium* 37–59

Peers S, 'Governance and the Third Pillar: The Accountability of Europol' in Curtin DM and Wessel RA (eds), *Good Governance and the European Union. Reflections on Concepts, Institutions and Substance* (Intersentia 2005) 253–75

Peers S, *EU Justice and Home Affairs Law* (3rd edn, OUP 2011)

Peters A, 'Treaty Making Power', *Max Planck Encyclopedia of Public International Law* (Oxford Public International Law, March 2009) online publication

Peterson J, 'The College of Commissioners' in Peterson J and Shackleton M (eds), *The Institutions of the European Union* (2nd edn, OUP 2006) 81–103

Piris JC, *The Lisbon Treaty. A Legal and Political Analysis* (CUP 2010)

Plouffe JP, 'Les Arrangements Internationaux des Agences et Ministerès du Canada' (1983) *XXI Annuaire Canadien de Droit International* 176–216

Portmann R, *Legal Personality in International Law* (CUP 2010)

Prechal S, 'Institutional Balance: A Fragile Principle with Uncertain Contents' in Heukel T, Blokker N, and Brus M (eds), *The European Union after Amsterdam. A Legal Analysis* (Kluwer Law International 1998) 273–94

Ratajczyk M, *Regional Aviation Safety Organisations. Enhancing Air Safety through Regional Cooperation* (Kluwer Law International 2015)

Rauchs G and Koenig DJ, 'Europol' in Koenig DJ and Das DK (eds), *International Police Cooperation. A World Perspective* (Lexington Books 2001) 43–62

Raustiala K, 'Form and Substance in International Agreements' (2005) 99(3) *American Journal of International Law* 581–614

Rijken C, 'Legal and Technical Aspects of Co-operation between Europol, Third States, and Interpol' in Kronenberger V (ed), *The European Union and the International Legal Order: Discord or Harmony?* (TMC Asser Press 2001) 577–603

Rijpma JJ, *Building Borders: The Regulatory Framework for the Management of the External Borders of the European Union* (PhD dissertation European University Institute 2009)

Rijpma JJ, 'Hybrid Agencification in the Area of Freedom, Security and Justice and its Inherent Tensions: The case of Frontex' in Busuioc M, Groenleer M and Trondal J (eds), *The Agency Phenomenon in the European Union: Emergence, Institutionalisation and Everyday Decision-making* (Manchester University Press 2012) 84–102

Rovine AW, 'Separation of Powers and International Executive Agreements' (1976–1977) 52(2) *Indiana Law Journal* 397–431

Schachter O, 'The Twilight Existence of Non-binding International Agreements' (1977) 71(2) *American Journal of International Law* 296–304

Schermers HG and Blokker NM, *International Institutional Law. Unity within Diversity.* (Revised 5th edn, Martinus Nijhoff Publishers 2011)

Schmalenbach K, 'Article 2. Use of Terms' in Dörr O and Schmalenbach K (eds), *Vienna Convention on the Law of Treaties. A Commentary* (Springer 2012) 27–48

Schneider JW, *Treaty-making Power of International Organizations* (Librairie E. Droz 1959)

Scholten M, *The Political Accountability of EU Agencies: Learning from the US Experience* (PhD dissertation, Universitaire Pers Maastricht 2014)

Scholten M and van Rijsbergen M, 'The ESMA-Short Selling Case: Erecting a New Delegation Doctrine in the EU upon the Meroni-Romano Remnants' (2014) 41(4) *Legal Issues of Economic Integration* 389–405

Schout A, 'Inspecting Aviation Safety in the EU: EASA as an Administrative Innovation?' in Vos E (ed), *European Risk Governance. Its Science, its Inclusiveness and its Effectiveness* (Connex Report Series No. 6/2008) 257–94

Schusterschitz G, 'European Agencies as Subjects of International Law' (2004) 1(1) *International Organisations Law Review* 163–88

Schütze R, *Foreign Affairs and the EU Constitution. Selected Essays* (CUP 2014)

Schwarze J, *European Administrative Law* (Revised 1st edn, Sweet and Maxwell 2006)

Scott J, 'Extraterritoriality and Territorial Extension in EU Law' (2014) 62(1) *The American Journal of Comparative Law* 87–125

Senden LJ, *Soft Law in European Community Law. Its Relationship to Legislation* (Hart Publishing 2003)

Shapiro M, 'The Problems of Independent Agencies in the United States and the European Union' (1997) 4(2) *Journal of European Public Policy* 276–92

Snyder F, 'The Effectiveness of European Community Law: Institutions, Processes, Tools and Techniques' (1993) 56(1) *The Modern Law Review* 19–54

Surano L, 'L'Action Extérieure d'Eurojust' in Dony M (ed), *La Dimension Externe de l'Espace de Liberté, Sécurité et de Justice au lendemain de Lisbonne et de Stockholm: un Bilan à mi-parcours* (Éditions de l'Université de Bruxelles 2012) 211–19

Terpan F, 'Soft Law in the European Union. The Changing Nature of EU Law' (2015) 21(1) *European Law Journal* 68–96

Thym D, 'Parliamentary Involvement in European International Relations' in Cremona B and de Witte B (eds), *EU Foreign Relations Law. Constitutional Fundamentals* (Hart Publishing 2008) 201–32

Torrent R, 'Whom is the European Central Bank the Central Bank of?: Reaction to Zilioli and Selmayr' (1999) 36(6) *Common Market Law Review* 1229–41

Vara JS, 'The External Dimension of the Area of Freedom Security and Justice in the Lisbon Treaty' (2008) 10(4) *European Journal of Law Reform* 577–97

Vara JS, 'The External Activities of AFSJ Agencies: The Weakness of Democratic and Judicial Controls' (2015) 20(1) *European Foreign Affairs Review* 115–36

Vos E, *Institutional Frameworks of Community Health and Safety Legislation. Committees, Agencies and Private Bodies* (Hart Publishing 1999)

Vos E, 'Reforming the European Commission: What Role to Play for EU Agencies?' (2000) 37(5) *Common Market Law Review* 1113–34

Vos E, 'Agencies and the European Union' in Verhey L and Zwart T (eds), *Agencies in European and Comparative Perspective* (Intersentia 2003) 113–47

Vos E, 'Independence, Accountability and Transparency of European Regulatory Agencies' in Geradin D, Muñoz R and Petit N (eds), *Regulation through Agencies: A New Paradigm of European Governance* (Edward Elgar 2005) 1–20
Vos E, 'European Agencies and the Composite EU Executive' in Everson M, Monda C and Vos E (eds), *European Agencies in between Institutions and Member States* (Kluwer Law International 2014) 11–47
Wessel RA, 'The Inside Looking Out: Consistency and Delimitation in EU External Relations' (2000) 37(5) *Common Market Law Review* 1135–71
Wessel RA, 'Revisiting the International Legal Status of the EU' (2000) 5(4) *European Foreign Affairs Review* 507–37
Wessel RA, 'The EU as a Party to International Agreements: Shared Competences, Mixed Responsibilities' in Dashwood A and Maresceau M (eds), *Law and Practice of EU External Relations: Salient Features of a Changing Landscape* (CUP 2008) 152–87
White ND, *The Law of International Organisations* (Manchester University Press 2005)
de Witte B, 'Too Much Constitutional Law in the European Union's Foreign Relations?' in Cremona M and de Witte B (eds), *EU Foreign Relations Law. Constitutional Fundamentals* (Hart Publishing 2008) 3–15
de Witte B and Beukers T, 'The Court of Justice Approves the Creation of the European Stability Mechanism outside the EU Legal Order: Pringle' (2013) 50(3) *Common Market Law Review* 805–48
Wouters J, Coppens D and de Meester B, 'The European Union's External Relations after the Lisbon Treaty' in Griller S and Ziller J (eds), *The Lisbon Treaty. EU Constitutionalism without a Constitutional Treaty* (Springer Verlag 2008) 143–203
Yataganas X, 'Delegation of Regulatory Authority in the European Union: the Relevance of the American Model of Independent Agencies' (2001) 3/01 *Jean Monnet Working Paper* (NYU School of Law) 1–67
Yin RK, *Case Study Research. Design and Methods* (3rd edn, Sage Publications 2003)
Zilioli C and Selmayr M, 'The External Relations of the Euro Area: Legal Aspects' (1999) 36(2) *Common Market Law Review* 273–349
Zinzani M, *Market Integration through Network Governance: The Role of European Agencies and Networks of Regulators* (PhD dissertation, Intersentia 2012)

Case law

EU case law

Case 9/56 *Meroni & Co, Industrie Metallurgiche, SpA v High Authority of the European Coal and Steel Community* EU:C:1958:7
Case 10/56 *Meroni & Co., Industrie Metallurgiche, società in accomandita semplice v High Authority of the European Coal and Steel Community* EU:C:1958:8
Case 6/64 *Flaminio Costa v ENEL* EU:C:1964:66
Case 22/70 *Commission v Council. European Agreement on Road Transport (ERTA)* EU:C:1971:32
Case 25/70 *Einfuhr- und Vorratsstelle für Getreide und Futtermittel v Köster and Berodt & Co EU:C:1970:115*
Opinion 1/75, of 11 November 1975 EU:C:1975:145
Case 98/80 *Giuseppe Romano v Institut national d'assurance maladie-invalidité* EU:C:1981:104
Case 138/79 *SA Roquette Frères v Council (Isoglucose)* EU:C:1980:249
Case 139/79 *Maizena GmbH v Council (Isoglucose)* EU:C:1980:250

Case 85/86 *Commission v Board of Governors of the European Investment Bank* EU:C:1988:110
Case C-322/88 *Grimaldi v Fonds des maladies professionnelles* EU:C:1989:646
Case C-70/88 *Parliament v Council. Radioactive contamination of foodstuffs (Chernobyl)* EU:C:1991:373
Case C-327/91 *France v Commission* EU:C:1994:305
Opinion 1/94, of 15 November 1994 *(WTO)* EU:C:1994:384
Opinion 2/94, of 28 March 1996 *(Accession to ECHR)* EU:C:1996:140
Case C-466/98 *Commission v United Kingdom (Open Skies)* EU:C:2002:624
Case C-467/98 *Commission v Denmark (Open Skies)* EU:C:2002:625
Case C-468/98 *Commission v Sweden (Open Skies)* EU:C:2002:626
Case C-469/98 *Commission v Finland (Open Skies)* EU:C:2002:627
Case C-471/98 *Commission v Belgium (Open Skies)* EU:C:2002:628
Case C-472/98 *Commission v Luxembourg (Open Skies)* EU:C:2002:629
Case C-475/98 *Commission v Austria (Open Skies)* EU:C:2002:630
Case C-476/98 *Commission v Germany (Open Skies)* EU:C:2002:631
Case C-11/00 *Commission v European Central Bank (ECB)* EU:C:2003:395
Case C-257/01 *Commission v Council* EU:C:2005:25
Case C-233/02 *France v Commission* EU:C:2004:173
Case C-217/04 *United Kingdom v Parliament and Council (ENISA)* EU:C:2006:279
Case C-77/05 *United Kingdom v Council (Establishment of Frontex)* EU:C:2007:803
Case T-187/06 *Schräder v Community Plant Variety Office (CPVO)* EU:T:2008:511
Case C-38/09P *Schräder v Community Plant Variety Office (CPVO)* EU:C:2010:196
Case C-270/2012 *United Kingdom v Parliament and Council (ESMA)* EU:C:2014:1
Case C-363/14 *Parliament v Council* EU:C:2015:579
Case C-73/14 *Council v Commission (ITLOS)* EU:C:2015:663
Case C-660/13 *Council v Commission* EU:C:2016:616

Case law of the International Court of Justice

Reparation for injuries suffered in the service of the United Nations (Advisory Opinion) [1949] ICJ Rep 174
Aegean Sea Continental Shelf (Judgment) [1978] ICJ Rep 3
Maritime Delimitation and Territorial Questions between Qatar and Bahrain, Jurisdiction and admissibility (Judgment) [1994] ICJ Rep 112
Land and Maritime Boundary between Cameroon and Nigeria (Cameroun v Nigeria: Equatorial Guinea intervening) (Judgment) [2002] ICJ Rep 303

(Frequently Used) International Agreements, EU Secondary Legal Instruments, Other Official Documents and Reports

International agreements

Vienna Convention on the Law of Treaties (the 1969 Vienna Convention)
Vienna Convention on the Law of Treaties between States and International Organisations or between International Organisations (the 1986 Vienna Convention)
Convention based on Article K.3 of the Treaty on the European Union, on the establishment of a European Police Office (Europol Convention) [1995] OJ C316/1

Financial Administrative Framework Agreement between the European Community, represented by the Commission of the European Communities and the United Nations (2003)

Agreement on civil aviation safety between the European Community and Canada [2009] OJ L153/11

Memorandum of Cooperation between the European Union and the International Civil Aviation Organization providing a framework for enhanced cooperation [2011] OJ L 232/2

Agreement between the United States of America and the European Community on cooperation in the regulation of civil aviation safety [2011] OJ L291/3

Agreement between the European Union and the Government of the Federative Republic of Brazil on civil aviation safety [2011] OJ L273/3

EU secondary legislation

Regulation (EC) 1592/2002 on Common rules in the field of civil aviation and establishing a European Aviation Safety Agency [2002] OJ L240/1

Council Regulation (EC) 2007/2004 of 26 October 2004 establishing a European Agency for the Management of Operational Cooperation at the External Borders of the Member States of the European Union [2004] OJ L349/1

Decision of the Management Board of Frontex 11/2006 of 01 September 2006 laying down the procedures for negotiating and concluding working arrangements with third countries and international organisations

Regulation (EC) 863/2007 of the European Parliament and of the Council of 11 July 2007 establishing a mechanism for the creation of Rapid Border Intervention Teams and amending Council Regulation (EC) No 2007/2004 as regards that mechanism and regulating the tasks and powers of guest officers [2007] OJ L 199/30

Regulation (EC) 216/2008 on common rules in the field of civil aviation and establishing a European Aviation Safety Agency, and repealing Council Directive 91/670/EEC, Regulation (EC) No 1592/2002 and Directive 2004/36/EC [2008] OJ L79/1

Council Decision 2009/371/JHA of 6 April 2009 establishing the European Police Office (Europol) [2009] OJ L131/37

Council Decision 2009/934/JHA of 30 November 2009 adopting the implementing rules governing Europol's relations with partners, including the exchange of personal data and classified information [2009] OJ L325/6

Council Decision 2009/935/JHA of 30 November 2009 determining the list of third States and organisations with which Europol shall conclude agreements [2009] OJ L325/12

Regulation (EU, Euratom) 966/2012 of the European Parliament and of the Council of 25 October 2012 on the financial rules applicable to the general budget of the Union and repealing Council Regulation (EC, Euratom) No. 1605/2002 [2012] OJ L 298/1

Regulation (EU) 1052/2013 of the European Parliament and of the Council of 22 October 2013 establishing the European Border Surveillance System (Eurosur) [2013] OJ L 295/11

Council Implementing Decision of 6 May 2014 amending Decision 2009/935/JHA as regards the list of third States and organisations with which Europol shall conclude agreements, [2014] OJ L138/104

Council Regulation (EU) 2015/323 of 2 March 2015 on the financial regulation applicable to the 11th European Development Fund [2015] OJ L 58/17

Regulation (EU) 2016/794 of the European Parliament and of the Council of 11 May 2016 on the European Union Agency for Law Enforcement Cooperation (Europol) and replacing and repealing Council Decisions 2009/371/JHA, 2009/934/JHA, 2009/935/JHA, 2009/936/JHA and 2009/968/JHA [2016] OJ L135/53

Regulation (EU) 2016/1624 of the European Parliament and of the Council of 14 September 2016 on the European Border and Coast Guard and amending Regulation (EU) 2016/399 of the European Parliament and of the Council and repealing Regulation (EC) No 863/2007 of the European Parliament and of the Council, Council Regulation (EC) No 2007/2004 and Council Decision 2005/267/EC [2016] OJ L251/1

Decision of the Management Board of Frontex 11/2017 of 30 March 2017 adopting the Rules of Procedures of the Management Board

Other official documents and reports

International Law Commission (1966), Draft Articles on the Law of Treaties with Commentaries, Yearbook of the International Law Commission (YILC), 1966

International Law Commission (1982), Draft Articles on the Law of Treaties between States and International Organizations or between International Organizations with Commentaries, Yearbook of the International Law Commission (YILC), 1982

European Council (1999), Presidency Conclusions of the Tampere European Council, Brussels 15–16 October 1999 (SN 200.99)

Commission (2001), 'European Governance. A White Paper' COM (2001) 428 final

Commission (2002), 'The operating framework for the European Regulatory Agencies' (Communication) COM (2002) 718 final

Commission (2003), Budget Directorate General – Evaluation Unit 'Meta-Evaluation on the Community Agency System' Final Report, 15 September 2003

Commission (2005), 'Draft Interinstitutional Agreement on the operating framework for the European regulatory agencies' COM (2005) 59 final

Commission (2005), 'Developing the agenda for the Community's external aviation policy' (Communication) COM (2005) 79 final

Commission (2005), 'A Strategy on the External Dimension of the Area of Freedom, Security and Justice' (Communication) COM (2005) 491 final

Council (2005), 'The Hague Programme: Strengthening Freedom, Security and Justice in the European Union' [2005] OJ C53/1

Council (2005), 'A Strategy for the External Dimension of JHA: Global Freedom, Security and Justice', 6 December 2005 (15446/05)

Report of the High-level group for the Future European Aviation regulatory Framework (2007), 'European Aviation: A Framework for driving performance improvement'

Commission (2008), 'European agencies – The way forward' (Communication) COM (2008) 135 final

European Court of Auditors (2008), Special Report No 5/2008 'The European Union's Agencies: Getting Results'

COWI (2009), 'External Evaluation of the European Agency for the Management of Operational Cooperation at the External Borders of the Member States of the European Union', Final Report (January 2009)

Rambøll-Euréval Matrix (2009), Evaluation of the EU De-centralised Agencies in 2009, Final Report, Volume I, 'Synthesis and prospects' (December 2009)

Commission (2010), 'Impact Assessment accompanying the Proposal for a Regulation of the European Parliament and of the Council amending Council Regulation (EC) No. 2007/2004 establishing a European Agency for the Management of Operational

Cooperation at the External Borders of the Member States of the European Union (FRONTEX)' Impact Assessment of Regulation No. 1168/2011, SEC (2010) 149
European Council (2010), 'The Stockholm Programme – An Open and Secure Europe Serving and Protecting Citizens' [2010] OJ C 115/01
Europol External Strategy 2010–2014, (2010) EDOC # 434663
Commission (2011), 'Vademecum on the External Action of the European Union', SEC (2011) 881/3
Joint Statement of the European Parliament, the Council of the EU and the European Commission on decentralised agencies of 19 July 2012 (Common Approach on EU agencies)
Emma Disley, Barrie Irving, William Hughes, Bhanu Patruni (2012), 'Evaluation of the implementation of the Europol Council Decision and of Europol's activities' (Technical report), RAND Europe
European Council (2014), Conclusions, 26/27 June 2014, Brussels, 27 June 2014 (EUCO 79/14)
Proposal for a regulation of the European Parliament and of the Council on common rules in the field of civil aviation and establishing a European Aviation Safety Agency, and repealing Regulation (EC) No 216/2008 of the European Parliament and of the Council, COM (2015) 613 final
Europol External Strategy 2017–2020, (2016) EDOC#865852v3

Annexes

Annex 1: EU agencies' international dimension – founding acts and international cooperation practice

EU Agency	*Formal legal framework (founding acts)*						*EU agencies international practice (formal international cooperation instruments)*	
	No provision for international cooperation in the founding act[1]	*Provision for international cooperation in the founding act*					*Established*[2]	*Scarce/Not documented*
		Instruments for international cooperation NOT mentioned	*Instruments for international cooperation mentioned (label of the instrument)*					
			Agreement	*Administrative Arrangement*	*Working Arrangement*	*Other*		
ACER				X[3]				X
BEREC	X							X
CdT	X							X
Cedefop		X						X
Cepol			X[4]		x[5]		X	
CPVO	X						X	
EASA					X[6]		X	
EASO					X[7]			X
EBA				X[8]			X	
ECDC		X					X	
ECHA		X					X	
EEA		X					X	
EFCA					X[9]		X	
EFSA		X					X	
EIGE		X				X[10]		X
EIOPA				X[11]			X	
EMA		X					X	
EMCDDA					X[12]		X	
EMSA		X					X	
ENISA		X						X
ERA				X[13]			X	

ESMA				X[14]			X	
ETF			X[15]		X[16]		X	
EU-LISA	X							X
EU-OSHA		X						X
Eurofund		X					X	
Eurojust			X[17]				X	
Europol			X[18]	X[19]	X[20]		X	
FRA				X[21]		X[22]	X	
Frontex					X[23]		X	
GSA	X							X
OHIM		X					X	
SRB						X[24]		X

1 Provisions regarding the participation of third countries in the work of EU agencies are not considered.
2 According to activity reports, work programmes and information available on EU agencies' official websites.
3 Art 19 of Regulation 1227/2011.
4 Art 8 of former Cepol Council Decision 2005.
5 Art 34 of Cepol Regulation 2015.
6 Art 27 of EASA Regulation.
7 Arts 49–50 and 52 of EASO Regulation.
8 Art 33 of EBA Regulation.
9 Art 4 of EFCA Regulation.
10 Contractual relations, in particular subcontracting arrangements, Art 8 of EIGE Founding Act.
11 Art 33 of EIOPA Regulation.
12 Art 20 of EMCDDA Regulation.
13 Art 44 of ERA Regulation.
14 Art 33 of ESMA Regulation.
15 Co-operation agreements (same as working arrangements), Art 3 of ETF Founding Act.
16 Working arrangements (same as co-operation agreements), Art 3 of ETF Founding Act.
17 Art 26a of Eurojust Council Decision 2002.
18 Art 23 of former Europol Council Decision 2009.
19 Art 25 of Europol Regulation 2016.
20 Art 23 of Europol Regulation 2016.
21 Art 8 of FRA Regulation.
22 Contractual relations, in particular subcontracting arrangements; FRA may also award grants, Art 6 of FRA Founding Act.
23 Arts 13–14 of former Frontex Regulation 2004; Arts 52 and 54 of Frontex Regulation 2016.
24 Cooperation arrangements, Art 32 of SRB Founding Act.

Annex 2: Substantive and procedural limitations on EU agencies' international cooperation mandate according to their founding acts[1]

EU Agency	*Substantive limitations set on EU agencies' international cooperation*						*Procedural limitations on EU agencies' international cooperation*				
	Not provided for	*International cooperation circumscribed to the core mandate of the agency*	*Legal limits set on the scope and nature of the EU agencies' international cooperation instruments*				*Not provided for*	*Prior request*	*Other*	*EU agencies' international cooperation instruments*	
			Compliance with EU law	*No prejudice to EU institutions/ Member States' powers*	*No legal obligation for EU/ Member States*	*Other*				*Prior approval*	*Prior opinion/ consultation*
ACER[2]		X		X	X		X				
BEREC**	X						X				
CdT**	X						X				
Cedefop*		X					X				
Cepol[3]		X			X						X (Commission)
CPVO**	X						X				
EASA		X	X							X (Commission)	
EASO		X	X						X[4]		
EBA		X		X	X		X				
ECDC*		X					X				
ECHA*		X						X[5] (Commission)			
EEA*		X					X				
EFCA		X	X[6]					X[7] (Commission)			
EFSA*		X						X[8] (Commission)			
EIGE*		X	X[9]				X				
EIOPA		X		X	X		X				
EMA*		X						X[10] (Commission)			
EMCDDA[11]		X		X							X (Commission opinion)
EMSA*		X						X[12] (Commission)			
ENISA*		X					X				

ERA[13]		X		X	X				X (discussion with Commission)
ESMA		X		X	X		X		
ETF[14]		X	X						X (Commission opinion)
EU-OSHA*		X					X		
EU-LISA**	X						X		
Eurofund*	X						X		
Eurojust[15]		X						X (Council)	X (consultation Joint Supervisory Board)
Europol (ECD 2009)[16]		X	X[17]					X (Council)	X (opinion Joint Supervisory Board)
Europol (Regulation 2016)[18]		X			X[19]	X[20]	X		
FRA		X	X						X (Commission opinion)
Frontex (Regulation 2004)		X	X						X[21] (Commission opinion)
Frontex (Regulation 2016)[22]		X	X					X (Commission)	

(continued)

Annex 2: Substantive and procedural limitations on EU agencies' international cooperation mandate according to their founding acts *(continued)*

EU Agency	*Substantive limitations set on EU agencies' international cooperation*						*Procedural limitations on EU agencies' international cooperation*				
	Not provided for	*International cooperation circumscribed to the core mandate of the agency*	*Legal limits set on the scope and nature of the EU agencies' international cooperation instruments*				*Not provided for*	*Prior request*	*Other*	*EU agencies' international cooperation instruments*	
			Compliance with EU law	*No prejudice to EU institutions/ Member States' powers*	*No legal obligation for EU/ Member States*	*Other*				*Prior approval*	*Prior opinion/ consultation*
GSA**	X						X				
OHIM (EUIPO)*[23]		X					X				
SRB[24]		X	X		X[25]		X				

* The founding act does not provide for specific international cooperation instruments.
** The founding act does not provide for international cooperation by the agency.

1 Provisions regarding the participation of third countries in the work of EU agencies is not considered.
2 Art 19 of Regulation 1227/2011.
3 Art 34 of Cepol Regulation 2015.
4 In agreement with the Commission as regards cooperation with third countries, Art 49 of EASO Regulation.
5 Art 77 of ECHA Regulation.
6 Only for working arrangements concluded with competent authorities of third countries 'in the framework of agreements concluded between the EU and such countries', Art 4 of EFCA Regulation.
7 Art 4 of EFCA Regulation.
8 Scientific and technical assistance with a view to improving cooperation between the EU, applicant countries, international organisations and third countries, in the fields within its mission, Art 23 of EFSA Regulation.
9 Within the framework of international agreements concluded by the EU according to Article 218 TFEU as necessary, Art 8 of the EIGE Regulation.
10 Arts 28d and 57 of EMA Regulation.
11 Art 20 of EMCDDA Regulation.
12 Technical assistance to States applying for accession to the Union, to European Neighbourhood partner countries and to countries taking part in the Paris MoU, Art 2(5) of the EMSA Regulation.
13 Art 44 of ERA Regulation.
14 Art 3 of ETF Regulation.
15 Art 26a of Eurojust Council Decision 2002.
16 Art 23 of Europol Council Decision 2009.
17 For Europol, this type of limitation is phrased in very specific language, in that the agency can conclude agreements only with the entities put on the list by the Council (decision), Article 23(2) of Europol Council Decision 2009.
18 Arts 23 and 25 of Europol Regulation 2016.
19 Only with regard to working arrangements, Art 23 of Europol Regulation 2016.
20 Working arrangements shall not allow the exchange of personal data, Art 23 of Europol Regulation 2016.
21 Only working arrangement with third countries, Art 14 of former Frontex Regulation 2004.
22 Arts 52 and 54 of Frontex Regulation 2016.
23 Art 123b(2) and Title XIII 'International Registration of Marks' of OHIM Regulation.
24 Art 32 of the SRB Regulation.
25 Art 32 of the SRB Regulation juncto Art 97(2) of Directive 2014/59/EU.

A. Working arrangements

1. Europe

Counterpart	*Terminology*	*Type*	*Parties 'agree'*	*Scope*	*'will/ shall' language*	*Commitments between the parties*	*Third party rights/ obligations*	*Entry into force/ amendment/ termination*	*Suspension of application*	*Dispute settlement*	*Provisions on legal nature/ effects*
Serbia (NAA)	Working arrangement (2015)	New generation Type 1 PANEP	Yes	Regulation of civil aviation safety and environmental protection of products, parts, appliances, personnel, organisations, aerodromes and related equipment and ATM/ANS and related systems and constituents subject to Regulation (EC) No. 216/2008 and its Implementing Rules (mutual acceptance of certificates and technical findings)	Yes	Yes	–	Entry into force on date of signature/in writing by mutual consent/ sixty days following written notification	–	Consultations	Does not affect/limit the rights obligations stemming from ECAA agreement and international agreements Repeals and replaces the previous JAA-EASA transition working arrangement

(continued)

(continued)

Counterpart	*Terminology*	*Type*	*Parties 'agree'*	*Scope*	*'will/shall' language*	*Commitments between the parties*	*Third party rights/ obligations*	*Entry into force/ amendment/ termination*	*Suspension of application*	*Dispute settlement*	*Provisions on legal nature/ effects*
	Working arrangement (2014)	SAFA	Yes	Harmonized rules and procedures for ramp inspections/ collection and exchange of information on the safety of aircraft	Yes	Yes	–	Entry into force on date of signature/in writing by mutual consent/ sixty days following written notification	In case of persistent failure to comply with the clauses thereof	Consultations followed by suspension by EASA of the full membership status to SAFA of the NAA Serbia	Repeals previous SAFA working arrangement
Interstate Aviation Committee (IAC), established by the Minsk Agreement, signed on 30 December 1991	Working arrangement (2004)	Cooperation with an intergovernmental organisation	Yes	Mutual acceptance of design approval, environmental approval, finding of compliance and airworthiness certification of civil aeronautical products Exchange of information on safety and environmental standards and certification systems	Yes	Yes	–	Entry into force on date of signature/by mutual agreement/six months following written notification	–	In case of conflicting interpretation, the interpretation of the Contracting Party whose law/ regulation/standard is interpreted shall prevail	Stipulates the adoption of technical procedures to implement the working arrangement Progress toward a formal bilateral agreement envisaged (something like a BASA)
	Implementation procedure for design approval of aircraft, engine and propeller from CIS (2004)	Instrument implementing the 'mother' working arrangement	–	Validation by EASA of products from CIS	Yes	Yes	Yes (type-certificate holder/ applicant)	–	–	–	–

2. Worldwide

Counterpart	*Terminology*	*Type*	*Parties 'agree'*	*Scope*	*'will/shall' language*	*Commitments between the parties*	*Third party rights/ obligations*	*Entry into force/ amendment/ termination*	*Suspension of application*	*Dispute settlement*	*Provisions on legal nature/ effects*
New Zeeland (NAA)	Working arrangement (2007)		Yes	Mutual acceptance of certificates and technical findings regarding design approval and airworthiness certification	Yes	Yes	Yes (in the Implementation procedures for the approval of products, parts and appliances imported from New Zeeland (annexed to the working arrangement)	Entry into force on date of signature/ amendment by agreement of the parties/three months following written notification	–	By common accord in the following order: 1) the persons in charge of the implementation of the working arrangement; 2) the executive agents who signed the working arrangement In case of conflicting interpretation of regulations/ standards, the interpretation of the Party whose regulation/ standard is being interpreted shall apply	Foresees the conclusion of an agreement between the EU and New Zeeland in the field of civil aviation, beyond airworthiness certification Provides for technical procedures implementing the working arrangement (attached to the working arrangement)
Canada (NAA)	Working arrangement (2013)	SAFA	Yes	Harmonized rules and procedures for ramp inspections/ collection and exchange of information on the safety of aircraft	Yes	Yes	–	Entry into force on date of signature/ in writing by mutual consent/ sixty days following written notification	In case of persistent failure to comply with the clauses thereof	Consultations followed by suspension by EASA of the full membership status to SAFA of the NAA Canada	–

(continued)

(continued)

Counterpart	*Terminology*	*Type*	*Parties 'agree'*	*Scope*	*'will/shall' language*	*Commitments between the parties*	*Third party rights/ obligations*	*Entry into force/ amendment/ termination*	*Suspension of application*	*Dispute settlement*	*Provisions on legal nature/ effects*
Israel (NAA)	Working arrangement (2004)	Implements the Agreement between Israel and Italy concerning the airworthiness certification, approval or acceptance of imported civil aeronautical products and the acceptance of maintenance services	–	Mutual acceptance of certificates and technical findings regarding design approval and airworthiness certification	Yes	Yes	Yes (in the implementation procedures defined in the appendices to the working arrangement)	Entry into force on date of signature/ amendment by agreement of the parties/twelve months following written notification	–	By common accord in the following order: 1) the persons in charge of the implementation of the working arrangement; 2) the executive agents who signed the working arrangement In case of conflicting interpretation of regulations/ standards, the interpretation of the Party whose regulation/ standard is being interpreted shall apply	The content of the working arrangement does not affect the other provisions of the Agreement between Italy and Israel, the latter being implemented in as much as they are not contrary to the working arrangement
Japan (NAA – integrated within the Ministry of Transport)	Working arrangement (2011)		Have confirmed	Procedures for the validation by one Authority of the certificates on civil aviation products, parts and appliance issued by the other Authority	Yes	Yes (more detailed in the Implemen-tation procedures annexed to the working arrangement)	Yes (in the Implementation procedures annexed to the working arrangement: type-certificate/type approval holder; type-certificate applicant)	Entry into force on date of signature/ amendment by mutual consent/ termination after sixty days following written notice	–	Coordination meetings to solve disagreements	Repeals previous working arrangement between EASA and the NAA Japan

											The termination of the working arrangement does not affect the validity of any certificate and other approval granted by the Authorities under its terms
ICAO	Working arrangement (2014)		Parties make the following arrange-ment	Coordination of the ICAO USOAP and EU standardisation inspection activities	Yes	Yes	Yes (EU Member States and the States participating in EASA)	Effective from date of signature/ amendment by mutual consent/ termination after three months following written notice	–	Consultations, followed by referral to the Joint Committee established under MOC EU-ICAO	The working arrangement is without prejudice to activities which are the responsibility of the Commission Nothing in the working arrangement is deemed as a waiver of any privilege or immunity of the parties The working arrangement supersedes the 2006 MOC between EASA and ICAO

B. BASA implementing instruments

Counterpart	*Terminology*	*Type*	*Parties 'agree'*	*Scope*	*'will/shall' language*	*Commitments between the parties*	*Third party rights/ obligations*	*Entry into force/ amendment / termination*	*Suspension of application*	*Dispute settlement*	*Provisions on legal nature / effects*
USA (NAA)	Technical Implementation Procedures for airworthiness and environmental certification (TIP) – 2011	Implementing instrument of the BASA USA-EU (Annex I)	Yes	Certification and validation requirements and working procedure between the authorities for the import, export and continuous support of civil aeronautical products	Yes	Yes	Yes (the applicant)	Entry into force on date of signature/ amendment based on decision by the Certification Oversight Board by signature of the representatives of the Authorities/ termination after sixty days following written notice	–	Consultation and other mutually-agreed means taking several steps in the following order: working level/ management level/ Certification Oversight Board/ Bilateral Oversight Board Conflicting interpretation: the interpretation of the Technical agent whose regulations and standards are being interpreted shall prevail	Termination shall not affect the validity of activities conducted prior to termination Provision for the possibility to conclude further working arrangements for situations which are not addressed by the TIP, but are within the scope of the BASA

Maintenance Annex Guidance (MAG) – 2011	Implementing instrument of the BASA USA-EU (Annex II)	Yes	Detailed working procedures and activities between the authorities to facilitate the reciprocal acceptance of findings in the field of aircraft maintenance	Yes	Yes	Yes (the applicant, except for Part A)	Amendment by the Joint Maintenance Coordination Board (JMCB)	–	Consultation and other mutually-agreed means taking several steps in the following order: working level/ management level/Joint Maintenance Coordination Board (JMCB)/ Bilateral Oversight Board	–
Working arrangement (2014)	BASA implementing tool	Yes	Cooperation regarding the oversight and support to the Airbus A320 Aircraft Family Final assembly line and delivery centre in Mobile, Alabama, United States (technical assistance; production oversight, issuing of export certificates)	Yes	Yes	Yes (Airbus)	Entry into force on date of signature/ amendment by mutual consent /termination after three months following written notice	–	Procedures of EASA-FAA TIP 2011 applicable	The working arrangement organizes cooperation taking into account the parties' obligations under the BASA and other applicable regulations

Annex 4: Examples of Frontex's working arrangements

1. *Third countries (Type 1)*

Counterpart	*Terminology*	*Parties 'agree'*	*Scope*	*'will/shall' language*	*Commitments between the parties*	*Third party rights/ obligations*	*Entry into force/ amendment / termination*	*Suspension of application*	*Dispute settlement*	*Provisions on legal nature /effects*
Azerbaijan (State Border Service)	Working arrangement (2013)	Yes	Operational and technical cooperation covering: exchanges of information (including classified information and intelligence) in the risk analysis area; training; research and development; development of border procedures; coordination of joint operational measures	Yes (in combination with 'may' clauses)	Yes	–	Entry into force on the day following signature/ amendment by mutual consent/ termination ninety days following written notification	–	In case of conflicting interpretation, prevalence of the English version of the document	In the implementation of the working arrangement participants afford full respect for human rights, related international law and principles Not considered as an international treaty Implementation of the working arrangement cannot be regarded as fulfilment of international obligations by the EU and its institutions and Azerbaijan Participation of third country authorities in Frontex coordinated activities financed by Frontex based on separate financing agreement

Canada (Border Services Agency)	Working arrangement (2010)	Have reached the following understanding	Operational and technical cooperation covering: sharing of best practices on integrated border security/management; exchanges of information in the risk analysis area; training; assignment of liaison officers; research and development; participation in joint operations; cooperation on capacity building with third countries	Yes (in combination with 'may' clauses)	Yes	–	Entry into force on the day following signature/amendment by mutual written consent/termination ninety days following written notification	–	–	Exchange of classified information/intelligence on basis of separate security agreement No binding obligations under international law Not intended to confer any right, privilege, benefit to any person or party Implementation carried out according to the applicable framework of the Participants Participants not prevented from cooperating/granting assistance in accordance with their applicable legal framework Participants bear their own costs unless decided otherwise on a case-by-case basis Assignment of LOs subject to a specific liaison officer arrangement

(continued)

(continued)

Counterpart	*Terminology*	*Parties 'agree'*	*Scope*	*'will/shall' language*	*Commitments between the parties*	*Third party rights/ obligations*	*Entry into force/ amendment / termination*	*Suspension of application*	*Dispute settlement*	*Provisions on legal nature /effects*
Kosovo (Ministry of Internal Affairs)	Working arrangement (2016)	Yes	Operational and technical cooperation covering: exchanges of information (including classified information and intelligence) in the risk analysis area; training; research and development; joint projects; coordination of joint return operations	Yes (in combination with 'may' clauses)	Yes	–	Entry into force on the day following signature/ amendment by mutual consent/ termination ninety days following written notification	–	In case of conflicting interpretation, negotiations between the parties (in the meanwhile implementation of provisions subject to disagreement will be suspended)	In the implementation of the working arrangement participants afford full respect for human rights enshrined in international laws and principles, and shall ensure that the rights of persons in need of international protection and other vulnerable groups are respected during all joint activities Not considered as an international treaty Implementation of the working arrangement cannot be regarded as fulfilment of international obligations by the EU and its institutions and Kosovo

Participation of third country authorities in Frontex coordinated activities may be financed by Frontex

Exchange of personal data on basis of separate arrangement/agreement

Exchange of classified information or intelligence, is object of a separate security arrangement/agreement

Frontex and the Ministry of Internal Affairs shall take all necessary measures to ensure adequate confidentiality of the information received under the working arrangement and commit to use this information only for the exercise of their responsibilities related to border management

(continued)

(continued)

Counterpart	*Terminology*	*Parties 'agree'*	*Scope*	*'will/shall' language*	*Commitments between the parties*	*Third party rights/ obligations*	*Entry into force/ amendment / termination*	*Suspension of application*	*Dispute settlement*	*Provisions on legal nature /effects*
Turkey (Ministry of Foreign Affairs)	Memorandum of understanding (2012)	Yes	Operational and technical cooperation in the field of border control covering: exchange of best practices; exchange of strategic information and analytical products; training; research and development; participation in Frontex coordinated joint return operations; secondment of border police officers to Frontex Focal Point Offices	Yes (in combination with 'may' clauses)	Yes	–	Entry into force on the day following signature/ amendment by mutual consent/ termination ninety days following written notification	–	Negotiations, followed by non-application of the disagreed provisions	In the implementation of the working arrangement participants afford full respect for human rights Not considered as a document having effect under international law Implementation of the working arrangement cannot be regarded as fulfilment of international obligations by the EU and its institutions and Nigeria Participation of third country authorities in Frontex coordinated activities financed by Frontex based on separate framework agreement

2. *International organisations (Type 2)*

Counterpart	*Terminology*	*Parties 'agree'*	*Scope*	*'will/shall' language*	*Commitments between the parties*	*Third party rights/ obligations*	*Entry into force/ amendment / termination*	*Suspension of application*	*Dispute settlement*	*Provisions on legal nature /effects*
Interpol	Working arrangement (2009)	Yes	Exchange of information (including confidential information) Training Research and development Mutual assistance joint operations, joint products, pilot projects Exchanges of personnel on a temporary basis Reciprocal representation in meetings	Yes	Yes (in particular as regards information exchange and processing: eg prior consent before disclosing information to third parties)	–	60 days at the latest after being signed by the representatives of the parties (subject to approval by Interpol's General Assembly/ amendment by mutual written consent/ termination six months following notification	–	–	Use of word 'party' to designate the partner organisations Participants bear their own costs unless agreed otherwise on a case-by-case basis Special arrangements agreed on the safeguarding of the security, confidentiality and processing conditions of information exchanged (including table of equivalence regarding confidentiality and security standards) Special arrangements for organising exchange of personnel
United Nations Office on Drugs and Crime (UNODC)	Working arrangement (2012)	Yes	Exchange of information Technical cooperation Reciprocal representation at appropriate meetings	Yes	Yes	–	Entry into force upon signature /amendment by mutual written consent/ termination three months following notification	Right to suspend obligations in case of dispute/any other case where one party is of the opinion that the other party has breached its obligations	Disputes referred to the Executive Directors of the two organisations	Joint technical cooperation activities mutually agreed on a case-by-case basis Working arrangement does not create/imply obligations of a financial nature for the parties. Parties bear their own costs unless otherwise agreed

(continued)

(continued)

Counterpart	*Terminology*	*Parties 'agree'*	*Scope*	*'will/shall' language*	*Commitments between the parties*	*Third party rights/ obligations*	*Entry into force/ amendment / termination*	*Suspension of application*	*Dispute settlement*	*Provisions on legal nature /effects*
										Right to suspend obligations under the working arrangements/ breach by the other party of its obligations No waiver, change or modification is valid or binding unless agreed to in writing and signed by the parties The working arrangement does not affect the privileges and immunities of either organisation Specific activities/ obligations within the framework of the working arrangement require separate agreement

Annex 5: Examples of Europol's cooperation agreements

1. Strategic agreements

A. Third countries

Counterpart	*Terminology*	*Parties 'agree'*	*Scope*	*'will/shall' language*	*Commitments between the parties*	*Third party rights/ obligations*	*Entry into force/ amendment/ termination*	*Suspension of application*	*Dispute settlement*	*Provisions on legal nature /effects*
China (Ministry of Public Security)	Agreement on strategic co-operation (concluded 2017)	Yes	Cooperation as regards organised crime, terrorism and other forms of international crime through exchange of strategic and technical information (exchange of personal data excluded) Exchange of expertise Liaison officers	Yes	Yes	Yes (right to compensation)	Entry into force on the date on which Europol notifies through diplomatic channels the Ministry of Public Security of China that it has received and accepted the notification of the Ministry of Public Security that it has completed its internal procedures / Amendment of the agreement by mutual consent; Article 3(3) and Annexes amended through exchange of notes between the parties/ Termination three months following written notice	–	Consultations and negotiations between the parties; Possibility to suspend the application of the Agreement temporarily pending negotiations	Provision for the conclusion of subsequent MOUs on confidentiality and information assurance and on a secure communication line Provisions on liability in case damage is caused to one party or to an individual as a result of unauthorised or incorrect information processing by the other party The agreement does not affect mutual legal assistance treaties, working law enforcement relationship, any other agreement or arrangement for the exchange of information between China and any EU Member State In case of termination of the agreement, the contracting parties shall reach agreement on the continued use and storage/ destruction or return of the information that has been communicated between them

B. International organisations

Counterpart	*Terminology*	*Parties 'agree'*	*Scope*	*'will/ shall' language*	*Commitments between the parties*	*Third party rights/ obligations*	*Entry into force/ amendment/ termination*	*Suspension of application*	*Dispute settlement*	*Provisions on legal nature /effects*
United Nations Office on Drugs and Crime (UNODC)	Co-operation agreement (concluded 2004)	Yes	Cooperation in combating serious forms of crime within their field of competence through: mutual consultation; exchange of information (personal data and confidential information excluded); technical cooperation; reciprocal representation	Yes	Yes	–	Entry into force upon signature/ Amendment by mutual consent (after approval by the Council)/ Termination three months following written notice	Right of a party to suspend its obligations pending a dispute or when that party is of the opinion that the obligations incumbent on the other party have been breached	Disputes referred to the Executive Director of UNODC and the Director of Europol	Right to suspend obligations Technical cooperation through individual projects to be mutually agreed on a case-by-case basis

2. Operational agreements

A. Third countries

Counterpart	*Terminology*	*Parties 'agree'*	*Scope*	*'will/shall' language*	*Commitments between the parties*	*Third party rights/ obligations*	*Entry into force/ amendment/ termination*	*Suspension of application*	*Dispute settlement*	*Provisions on legal nature /effects*
Liechtenstein (Deputy Prime Minister, Minister for Home Affairs, Justice and Economic Affairs)	Agreement on operational and strategic co-operation (concluded 2013)	Yes	Cooperation in preventing and combatting organised crime, terrorism and forms of international crime through exchange of information (including personal data) Exchange of expertise Training Advice and support in individual criminal investigations Liaison officers	Yes	Yes	Yes (right of individuals to access information related to them and to have information checked, corrected or deleted; right to compensation)	Entry into force on the date Europol notifies Liechtenstein that it has received and accepted the notification that the internal ratification process in Liechtenstein has been completed/ Amendment by mutual consent (after approval by the Council); Annexes amended through exchange of notes between the parties (without Council's approval)/ Termination three months following written notice	Right of a party to suspend its obligations pending a dispute (obligations inherent upon the parties under the agreement remain in force)	Consultations and negotiations between the parties	The agreement does not affect mutual legal assistance treaties, any other agreement or arrangement, or working law enforcement relationship for the exchange of information between Liechtenstein and any EU Member State Exchanges of information take place on the basis of the agreement and in accordance with the legal framework of the contracting parties Provisions on liability in case damage is caused to one party (also in respect of the management of the secure communication line) or to an individual as a result of legal or factual errors in information exchanged (according to the legal framework of the contracting parties) Provision for privileges and immunities of LOs of the contracting parties Annex III of the agreement lays down LOs tasks, rights and obligations, costs, etc.

(continued)

(continued)

Counterpart	*Terminology*	*Parties 'agree'*	*Scope*	*'will/shall' language*	*Commitments between the parties*	*Third party rights/ obligations*	*Entry into force/ amendment/ termination*	*Suspension of application*	*Dispute settlement*	*Provisions on legal nature /effects*
										Implementing association agreement to enable participation of experts from Liechtenstein to Europol analysis groups Provision for a MOU on the assessment of specified types of information and specified sources MOU on confidentiality and information assurance MOU on secure communication line In case of termination of the agreement, the contracting parties shall reach agreement on the continued use and storage / destruction or return of the information that has been communicated between them
USA	Supplemental agreement (2002)	Yes	Cooperation in detection, prevention, suppression and investigation of criminal offences through exchange of information (including personal data)	Yes	Yes	–	Amendment by mutual consent (after completion of internal procedures by both parties)/ Termination three months following written notice	–	Consultations between the parties	Preamble mentions conclusion of the agreement through exchange of letters

Other forms of cooperation Liaison officers	The agreement does not affect mutual legal assistance treaties, working law enforcement relationship, any other agreement or arrangement for the exchange of information between USA and any Member States or EU institution The agreement does not give rise to a right on the part of any private person to obtain, suppress, or exclude any evidence, or to impede the execution of a request, nor shall it derogate from any pre-existing right of a private party to do so Exchanges of information take place on the basis of the agreement and in accordance with the legal framework of the contracting parties Provision on expenses of an extraordinary nature which arise out of the execution of the agreement

B. International organisations

Counterpart	*Terminology*	*Parties 'agree'*	*Scope*	*'will/shall' language*	*Commitments between the parties*	*Third party rights/ obligations*	*Entry into force/ amendment/ termination*	*Suspension of application*	*Dispute settlement*	*Provisions on legal nature / effects*
Interpol	Agreement (concluded 2001)	Yes	Cooperation in combating serious forms of organised international crime within their field of competence through: exchange of operational, strategic and technical information (including personal and confidential data); coordination of activities; secondment of liaison officers; reciprocal representation	Yes	Yes	Yes (right of individuals to access information related to them and to have information checked, corrected or deleted)	Entry into force on the 30th day after receipt of second notification regarding the approval of the agreement in conformity with the internal constitutional procedures of the parties/Amendment by mutual consent in accordance with the statutory requirements of the parties/ Termination three months following written notice	–	Disputes settled amicably between the Secretary General of Interpol and the Director of Europol Disputes not settled amicably referred to an *ad hoc* committee (the advice of the committee submitted back to the Secretary General of Interpol and the Director of Europol)	Provisions on liability for damage caused as a result of unauthorised or incorrect data processing Provisions on privileges and immunities of LOs and for a MOU (between the Secretary General of Interpol and the Director of Europol) laying down LOs tasks, rights and obligations, stationing, etc. Provision for a MOU on the assessment of specified types of information and specified sources (concluded between the Secretary General of Interpol and the Director of Europol) MOU on confidentiality and security standards for the processing of information (concluded between the Secretary General of Interpol and the Director of Europol)

Index